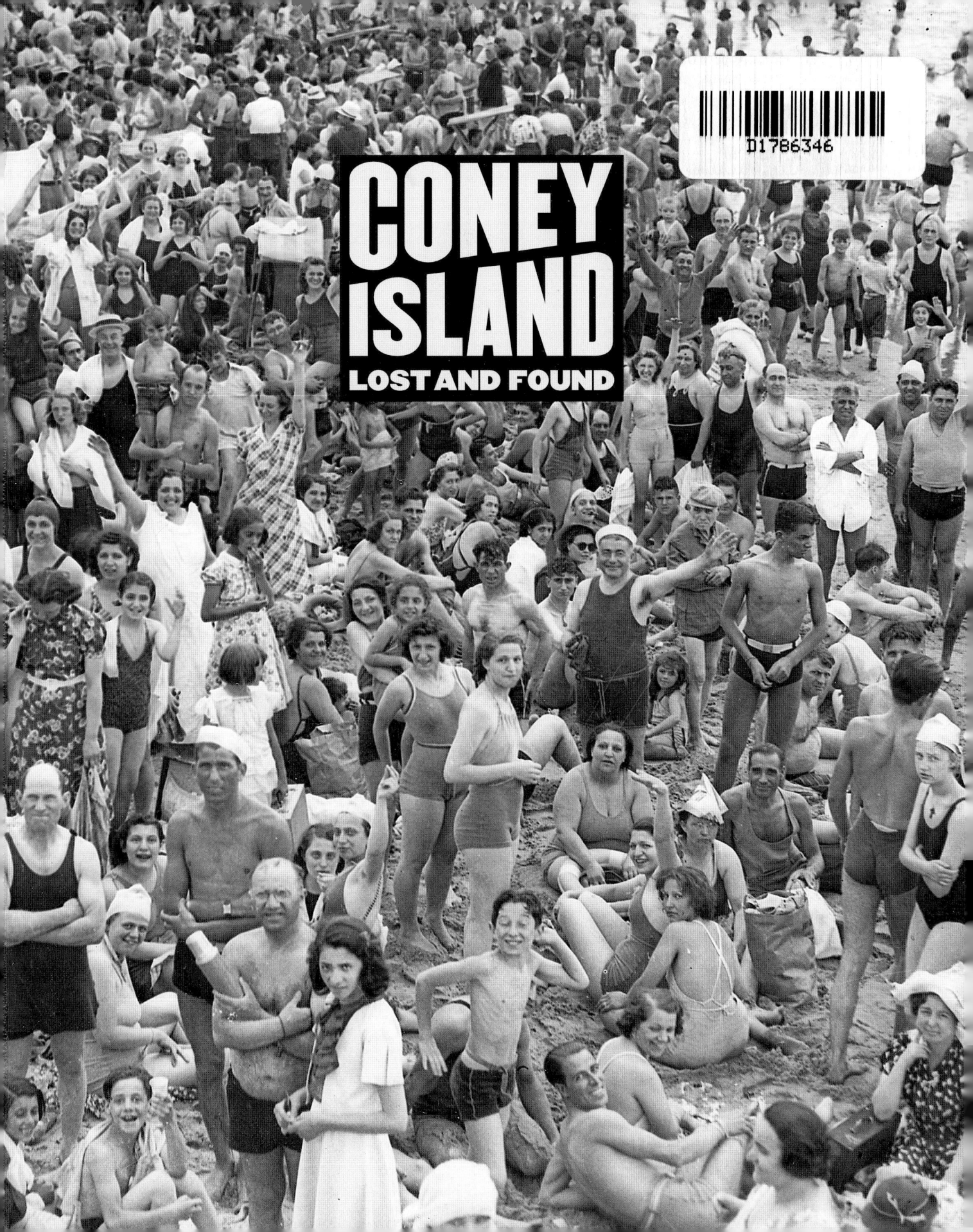

# CONEY ISLAND
## LOST AND FOUND

# CONEY ISLAND
## LOST AND FOUND

• 

**CHARLES DENSON**

Ten Speed Press
Berkeley

Copyright © 2002 by Charles Denson

All rights reserved.
Published in the United States by Ten Speed Press,
an imprint of the Crown Publishing Group,
a division of Random House, Inc., New York.
www.crownpublishing.com
www.tenspeed.com

Ten Speed Press and the Ten Speed Press colophon
are registered trademarks of Random House, Inc.

Library of Congress Cataloging-in-Publication Data on file with publisher

ISBN: 978-1-58008-455-0

Printed in Korea

Cover and text design by Charles Denson
Maps by Charles Denson: pages 4, 27, 34, 36, 38, 170–71, 265

13 12 11 10 9 8 7 6 5

First Edition

PHOTO PERMISSIONS

For author photo credits see page 294. The following individuals and organizations generously gave permission for the use of photographs and artwork. The location of each photograph is noted by the following abbreviations after the page number: t=top, c=center, b=bottom, l=left, r=right.

Florence Adler: 62-tl, 71-t, 71-br, 74-b; Astroland Park: 141-tl; Richard C. Auletta: 259-t, 259-b; Battaglia Inc.: 211, 212, 213-b, 215, 219; Jerry Bianco: 193-c, 193-b; Brooklyn College Library Archives and Special Collections Division: 6-t, 6-c, 8, 20, 26-t, 34-b, 49-t; Brooklyn Historical Society: 14-t, 25-t, 48, 60; Brooklyn Public Library–Brooklyn Collection: 10-b; CIUSA (Coney Island USA): 225-b, 229, 230, 234-b; CIUSA/photo by Cynthia Friedman: 201-b, 225-t; CIUSA/photo by Sam Henriques: 226-b; CIUSA/photo by Costa Mantis: 231-b; CIUSA/photo by Justine Woolner: 222, 224-t, 228-l, 228-r; Coney Island Chamber of Commerce: 57; Corbis: 36-b; Steve Crespi: 209-b; Richard Eagan: 227-b; Stanley Fox: 245-t; Cheryl Giordano: 232-tl; Valerie Haller: 223, 232-tr, 232-cl, 232-cr, 232-bl, 232-br, 233-t; photo ©2002 Hazel Hankin: 227-t; Sam Horwitz: 202, 203-b, 203-tr; Murray Kaufman: 182-bl, 205; Seth Kaufman: 35-br, 62-b, 89-tl; Library of Congress: i, vi, x, 30-t, 33-br, 39-t, 44–45-t, 73-b, 247-t; Philomena Marano: 224-b, 226-t; Nancy McCullough: 136-t, 136-b, 251-br; Gerald Menditto: 148-tr; Chuck Morgenstern: 74-t, 258-t, 258-b; Municipal Archives, Department of Records and Information Services, City of New York: 253-t; Pacific Rim Books, publisher of James J. Onorato's photographic account of the Steeplechase Park demolition: 139-tl, 139-tr, 139-b; Pfizer Inc.: ii, 34-cr, 99-t, 99-b, 132, 137; Dan Pisark: 84-bl, 145-b; photo by Hy Pisark, courtesy Dan Pisark: 75; Lou Powsner: 155-t; Jim Prince: 203-tl, 256-tl, 256-tr, 256-b; Rose Resk: 147; Marie Roberts: 66-t, 236-b, 237-l, 237-r, 238-t, 238-b; Leonard Steen: 68, 69-t, 69-b, 70-l, 70-r, 71-bl, 134, 135; Charlie Tesoro: 81, 133, 257-t; John Tessoriero: 181-b, 254-t, 254-b, 260; Mae Timpano: 216-tl, 216-tr, 216-b, 217; U.S. Geological Survey: 19-b; Gwynne Wolin: 79, 86-bl, 86-bc, 86-br, 91, 98, 108.

*To my wife, Judith,
whose love
made it all possible.*

# Contents

Introduction ... viii

## Part 1 – Coney Island 1645-1955

1. The Settlement Years ... 2
2. John McKane: Coney's "Teflon" Boss ... 9
3. Building a New Industry ... 26
4. The New Coney Island ... 40
5. The Nickel Empire ... 64

## Part 2 – Coming of Age in Coney Island

6. The Coney Island Kid ... 78
7. Coney Island Houses: Before the Fall ... 82
8. A Mysterious Father ... 91
9. Down to the Sea in Ships ... 95
10. The Steeplechase Cathedral ... 98
11. Civil Defense ... 101
12. Coney Island: Lost and Found ... 105
13. Steeplechase 1966: The Final Season ... 109
14. A Day in the Life ... 113
15. Parachute ... 123
16. Solving a Family Mystery ... 127

## Part 3 – Decline and Comeback

17. The Death of Steeplechase Park ... 132
18. The 1970s: A Decade of Revolution ... 147
19. Images of the 1970s ... 167
20. The Trials of Norman Kaufman ... 205
21. The Steeplechase Battleground ... 211
22. Artists' Renaissance of the 1980s ... 223
23. The 1990s: Survivors ... 240
24. Jones Walk ... 260
25. Coney 2000 ... 267

Amusement Milestones ... 286
Selected Bibliography ... 288
Index ... 290
Acknowledgments ... 294

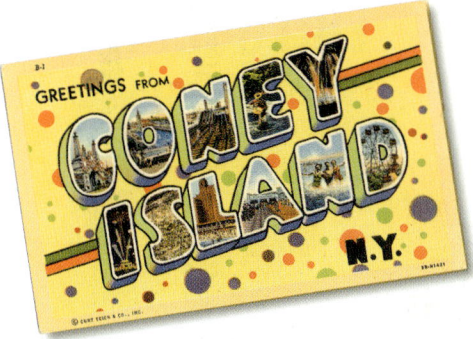

Luna Park, 1903

# Introduction

AS A KID, when I told people that I lived in Coney Island, they'd invariably say, "How can you live in an amusement Park?" I had to explain that Coney Island is a neighborhood, not an amusement park. I grew up in that neighborhood and lived there for twenty years during a period of cataclysmic change. Coney Island is perceived much differently when it's your home and daily reality instead of a weekend destination or a nostalgic notion. I've had family living in Coney Island since the early 1920s, when my great-uncle owned a bungalow in the Brighton Beach section and built a makeshift bathhouse in his backyard for the use of visiting family members. Although I no longer live in Coney Island, I still consider it home.

Lawrence Ferlinghetti used the phrase "A Coney Island of the Mind" as the title for a book of his poetry, and that's where Coney Island exists for most people: in their imagination. For many visitors, Coney Island is a difficult place to comprehend and define precisely, because their memories are shaped and distorted by their overpowering visceral experience of the noise, thrills, food, and other sensual pleasures. A dip in Coney's waters was a baptism, an initiation that lasted a lifetime and created a yearning to return to the Coney of one's imagination.

Today's Coney Island, however, is confined to the mechanical attractions that occupy several square blocks. The media hooks of the late twentieth century—crime and nostalgia—were no more accurate than the purple prose of the late nineteenth century in defining Coney Island. Even in the 1890s, visitors were nostalgic for the good old days of the 1860s. The essence of Coney Island is its ocean and beach, and the loss of that unspoiled environment was what the locals were often lamenting.

In *Coney Island: Lost and Found*, I've attempted to strip away the enticements and illusions of the amusements and concentrate on the complex history of land use. I wanted to answer a common question: how was a remote sandbar transformed into the most famous resort in the world, then allowed to deteriorate into one of New York City's worst neighborhoods?

A predominant theme in the book is urban planning gone awry. I lived in Coney Island from 1956 to 1976 and documented the changes that eroded its reputation. The best symbol of that transformation is Steeplechase Park, Coney's great Victorian amusement park that opened in 1897 and closed in 1964. The fight over the park and its vacant site highlights the sociological, economic, and political forces that re-shaped Coney.

*Coney Island: Lost and Found* is divided into three parts. Part one covers the island's settlement in the 1600s through the theft of the public lands by political boss John McKane in the 1880s, and ends with the 1940s takeover by Park Commissioner Robert Moses, who declared Coney Island a redevelopment zone.

Part two is a memoir and documentation of the period I lived in Coney Island in the 1950s, 1960s, and 1970s. I describe what it was like to grow up during the turbulent decades of rapid decline following the 1964 closure of Steeplechase Park.

Part three chronicles the search for a new identity for Coney Island after the neighborhood hit a low point during the 1970s. Included are stories of the colorful personalities who tried to bring Coney back from the brink.

When I was a child, I always carried a camera with me to record the day-to-day activities in my surroundings. Two of my photographs, on the opposite page, reflect the changes that have occurred over nearly forty years. Both were taken from the same point of view, the first in 1965, the second in 2001. What transpired in between are the events that I witnessed and that are described in this book.

I remember Woodstock in 1969, when a half-million, half-naked people gathered peacefully in a small space to have a good time. The media made a big deal out of it, but I wasn't impressed. After all, that happened every weekend in Coney Island.

**Last days of Steeplechase**
When I took this photograph in the spring of 1965, Steeplechase Park had not yet been sold and was expected to reopen under new ownership. The following year, it was demolished, instigating a thirty-five-year fight over the site.

**KeySpan Park**
This photograph, taken from the same vantage point as the image above, shows the new baseball park when it opened in June 2001. Construction of KeySpan Park stimulated a Coney Island revival.

# PART 1

# Coney Island 1645–1955

THE HISTORY of Coney Island can be characterized as a succession of landgrabs. Control of the island has been in contention for 350 years. The disputes began with disagreements between English and Dutch settlers over the earliest colonial patents in the mid-1600s and continued through the autocratic regimes of political boss John McKane in the 1800s and New York City Park Commissioner Robert Moses and Mayor Rudolph Giuliani in the 1900s. Behind the island's amusement curtain lies a tangled legacy of clouded titles, foreclosures, condemnations, and outright property thefts.

The thirty-five-year controversy over the site of Steeplechase Park that ended with the opening of the baseball stadium, KeySpan Park, in 2001 was typical of Coney's factious past. Although amusements are the island's dominant industry, real estate has always been the driving force. The inspiration and motivation for Coney's magnificent artifice grew out of a simple formula: how to squeeze the greatest number of dollars out of the smallest plot of sand.

Intense competition between landowners fueled creativity. Coney Island never had a blueprint or anything resembling a master plan. As a result, businesspeople found themselves challenged and transformed in their quest for profit. A cheese maker built a giant Ferris wheel; an electrician and a dentist devised a famous roller coaster; a real estate man named George C. Tilyou founded an amusement dynasty. Coney was fertile ground for the imagination, and the public took notice. The resort began in the early 1800s with humble bathhouses on a remote sandbar nine miles from Manhattan. A century later, a million people a day were visiting Coney Island, the most famous playground on earth.

**Magnificent artifice**
Frank Bostock's wild animal pavilion was one of the attractions at Dreamland, which opened in 1904.

## CHAPTER 1

# The Settlement Years

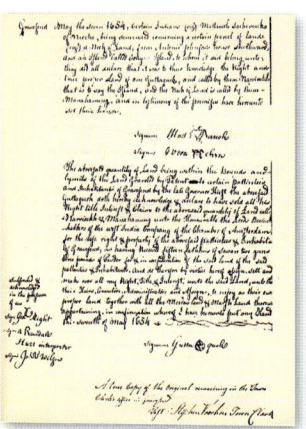

**Bill of sale**
On May 7, 1654, the town of Gravesend purchased a "neck of land" and "an island called Conyne Island" from the local Native Americans. The bill of sale was signed by Guttaquoh, Mattinoh, Iveta Chen, and interpreter Jo W. Wilson. The name "Coney" is believed to have derived from the Dutch word *Konijn*, meaning "rabbit."

THE REAL ESTATE business in Coney Island can be traced to the 1600s, the earliest days of settlement on the island, when it was part of the town of Gravesend. In 1640, Lady Deborah Moody and a small group of persecuted Anabaptists left England, and in 1643, they settled at the extreme southwestern end of Long Island. The tract included Coney Island, a sandbar that lay to the south across a shallow creek. The settlement became the town of Gravesend, the only English town in the Dutch province of New Netherland and the only colony in America founded by a woman.

By 1645, when the town's charter was granted, the area already had a clouded title. Other settlers had patents and farms that predated the founding of Gravesend. Guisbert Op Dyck was granted a patent for Coney Island in 1642; Jansen Van Salee applied for a patent in 1639 (granted in 1643) for land within the boundaries of Gravesend; Anthony Johnson and Robert Pennoyer, local farmers, claimed ownership through earlier patents granted by Governor Willem Kieft. Native Americans, the Canarsee and the Nyack, also had unsettled claims to Coney Island.

Native Americans were the first to challenge the settlers' title to Coney Island. In 1643, they launched an attack on the settlement, forcing Moody and her followers to abandon the town for two years. When New Amsterdam's 1649 offer to repurchase the land from the Natives failed to resolve the issue, Gravesend's settlers sought to clear their title to Coney Island by negotiating a direct purchase of the island. On May 7, 1654, the settlers signed an agreement with Mattinoh, *sachem* (chief) of the *Niockos* (Nyack), for the purchase of the "lands, meadowland and marshland from Antonie Johnson's house southward to an island called Conyne Island." The price was "fifteen fathoms of sewan [wampum], two gunns, three pounds of powder." Coney Island was reunited with the town of Gravesend for the equivalent of $15.

Over the next three hundred years, title to Coney Island would be challenged often. One of the reasons was poor record keeping. Early property transactions in Gravesend were made informally among the original settlers and usually were not recorded until decades, or even centuries, after the death of the owner or the owner's heirs. Another major problem was that Gravesend made the original land divisions among freeholders, enabling those freeholders to take possession and title without deeds. The only record of each transaction was contained in the minutes of a town meeting. Other disputes were jurisdictional. Because Gravesend was founded before Kings County, New York City, or New York State existed, the settlement was governed by the rules and laws of Holland. Colonial grants that included the "lands under water" (Coney Island's beach and shorefront) would be challenged under state laws written two centuries later.

Some of Gravesend's property disputes lingered on for centuries, handled during colonial times by lawyers such as Aaron Burr and settled as late as the 1920s in New York State Supreme Court. Some border disputes with neighboring towns were still not settled when Gravesend was incorporated into the city of Brooklyn in 1894.

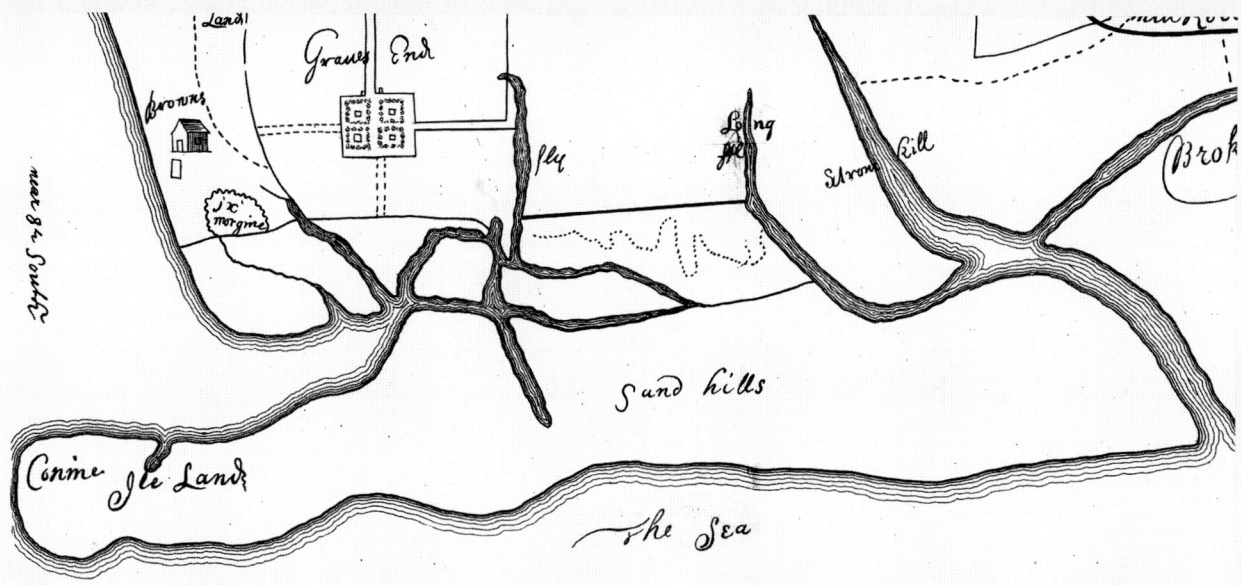

**Coney Island, 1666** James Hubbard's map shows that the island's basic shape has changed little in 350 years.

# Coney Island's Beginnings

GEOLOGICALLY, Coney Island is part of a low glacial outwash plain, the residue of melting glaciers during the last Ice Age. Fifteen thousand years ago, the retreating glaciers of the Wisconsin ice sheet left a rocky moraine that became Long Island. At the smooth outer edge of that moraine lay Coney Island, a barrier island, or sandbar. Coney is considerably different from the other barrier islands along the south shore of Long Island, because it is shaped not only by wave action and the forces of the ocean, but also by the tidal action of New York Bay.

Human habitation of the Coney Island area began roughly twelve thousand years ago after the retreat of the glaciers. At the time of the earliest European exploration during the early 1500s, Coney Island and Gravesend were inhabited by the Canarsee, part of the coastal Algonquian nation that occupied the eastern seaboard from North Carolina to New England. Anthropologist Herman J. Jaffee offers a number of translations of the name Canarsee. One is "a place fenced in," a reference to the waters surrounding western Long Island. Canarsee may have come from the word *konoh,* or "bear," a reference to a specific chief. It also has the broad meaning of "the community," referring to the tribe's major village.

The Canarsee were a matriarchal society that held the land in common and were led by a *sachem,* or clan chief. There were five major Canarsee villages in the Brooklyn area, including one near Coney Island. Massabarkem, a scattered village at the edges of the salt marshes, included a fishing settlement named Narriock located on Sheepshead Bay. The salt marshes were known as *Savanehachee* and were filled with an abundance of migrating waterfowl, shellfish, and small game, including otters and muskrat.

Massabarkem was similar to the other Canarsee villages in its location near a tidal inlet, in this case Coney Island Creek. The Canarsee farmed land around the villages, annually clearing and burning the vegetation and using the ashes as fertilizer. Crops were planted during the spring, and in summer the people of Massabarkem moved to summer camps on Coney Island, where they fished and collected shells for wampum. Fish were dried and saved for the winter months. In late summer, the Natives left Coney Island and returned to their villages to hunt and harvest the corn, beans, and pumpkins planted in the spring. The wampum made on Coney Island was a valuable commodity, used for trade between tribes and later recognized as currency by white settlers.

When the town of Gravesend was founded in 1643, the Canarsee of Massabarkem lost their land to the settlers. Some Canarsee stayed on for a short time and worked small farms in the area; most traveled west to the Illinois region. According to Jaffe, the last Canarsee in the area died around 1800. The native peoples of Massabarkem tread lightly on the land, leaving no trace of their civilization. The only native American artifacts from this late woodland period were discovered in the 1920s in a shell midden just north of Coney Island near the site of Ryder's Pond.

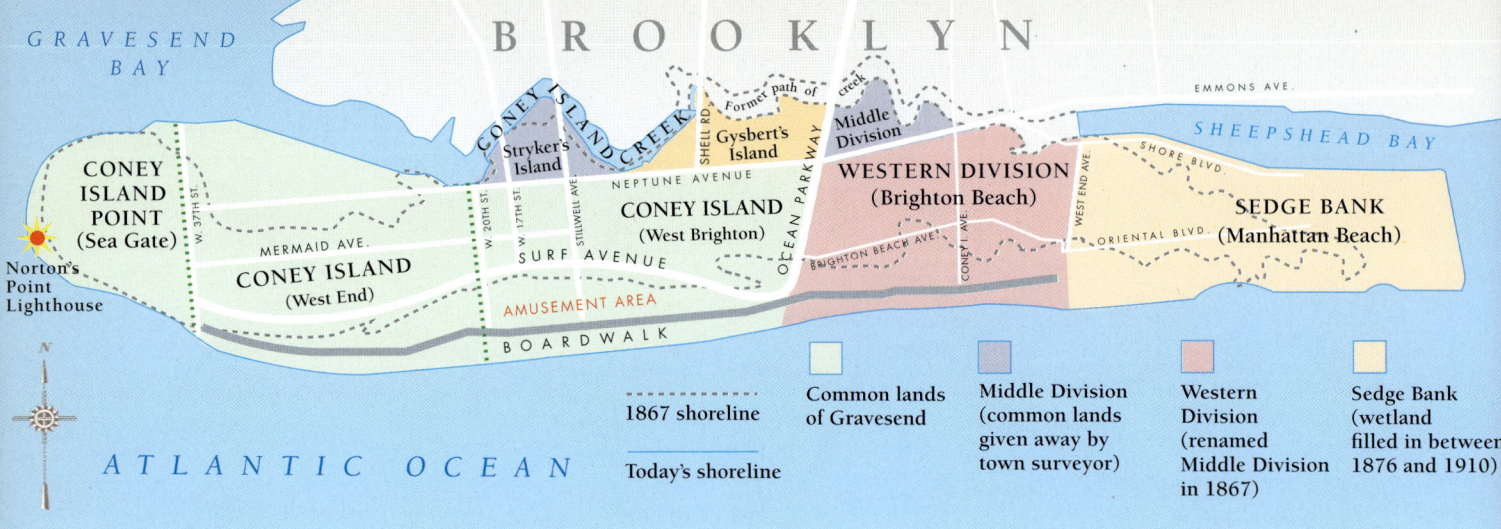

### Divided island

The divisions made by the town of Gravesend determined the future neighborhoods of Coney Island. Separating Coney Island from Brooklyn and Gravesend was a creek that meandered through a 7,000-acre salt marsh. Illegal filling of the creek, a navigable waterway under the jurisdiction of the U.S. War Department, began in 1904 and continued until 1926, when Congress approved plans to widen the creek into a shipping canal. The plans fell through, and in 1931, the creek was declared unnavigable. The former creek bed remained vacant until the state ceded ownership of the lands to the city in 1941. Coney was officially no longer an island.

Gravesend was originally laid out in forty pie-shaped wedges that radiated from a common town center. Each settler received one wedge. Coney Island was not included in this division because it was considered "common land," held in trust by the town for the use of all inhabitants, similar to public city parkland today. The original 1645 patent spelled out the settlers' legal rights regarding use of the common land for cattle grazing: "and asighnes to put what Cattle they shall thinke fitting to feede on grase upon ye afforesd Conyne Island."

Guisbert Op Dyck, the farmer who had been granted a 1642 Dutch patent for Coney Island, believed that Gravesend's 1645 patent was simply an easement that permitted the settlers to pasture their cattle on his island, without granting them actual ownership. Op Dyck farmed the only arable land on the island, a centrally located, eighty-eight-acre plot called Guisbert's (later Gysbert's) Island, which was not literally an island but was a farm surrounded by dunes and marshes. In 1661, Op Dyck offered to sell Coney Island to Gravesend, but the town claimed that it already owned the island, including Op Dyck's farm. Op Dyck eventually gave up, and in October 1661, he sold his farmland to Derick DeWolf, a Dutch businessman.

DeWolf opened a salt works, the first industry on the island, which consisted of a system of levees and gates that trapped and evaporated seawater from Coney Island Creek. The dried salt was then collected and sold. DeWolf informed the townspeople that they could no longer pasture their cattle on the island during the winter. The townspeople became furious, stormed the salt works, and burned it to the ground. The attack on a Dutch business by an English settlement caused an international incident that was smoothed over only after delicate diplomacy. The end result was that Gravesend was granted ownership of Coney Island.

In 1664, when the English took possession of New Netherland and changed the name to New York, the new governor, Richard Nicholls, reconfirmed the patent for the town of Gravesend. Lady Moody had died by then, and the new town patent was granted to her followers: Thomas Delavall, James Hubbard, William Bound Sr., William Goulding, and John Tilton.

### Coney Island Divided

Until 1677, all of Coney Island was considered common land, owned by the town of Gravesend. This arrangement changed on October 19 of that year, when the townspeople voted to divide the arable land of what was by then called Gysbert's Island into thirty-nine fifteen-acre shares owned by the families of the town's original thirty-nine patentees. The farmland, the only part of Coney Island considered valuable, was used communally by the townspeople as garden in the summer and as pasture for cattle in the winter. The plot was fenced, and tobacco and corn were planted.

Shortly after the divisions were made, the first accurate description of Coney Island was recorded by Jaspar Dankewrs and Peter Sluyter, who passed through New York in 1679 while seeking a site for their religious community. They described Coney as "a low sandy island of about three hours' circuit, its westerly point forming with Sandy Hook, on the other side, the entrance from the sea. It is oblong in shape, and is grown over with bushes. Nobody lives upon it, but it is used in winter for keeping cattle, horses, oxen, hogs and others, which are able to obtain there sufficient [food] to eat the whole winter, and to shelter themselves from the cold in the thickets. This island is not so cold as Long Island or the 'Mahatans,' or others, like some other islands on the coast in consequence of their having more sea breeze, and of the saltiness of the sea breaking upon the shoals, rocks and reefs, with which the coast is beset."

By the early 1700s, the sandy wasteland described by Dankewrs and Sluyter was being leased to enterprising townspeople who built fishing huts and mowed salt hay on the mudflats along Gravesend Bay. Leasing of the common lands of Coney Island began in 1702, when the western end of the island was leased to John Griggs and the fees collected were divided among the townspeople. This practice continued for the next hundred years, with leases to Richard Stillwell (1720, 1731); Thomas Stillwell (1727); Captain John Cannon (1733); and Abraham and John Emans, John Van Cleef, and Stephen Voorhies (1789).

By the 1720s, it was commonplace for the Gravesend freeholders to trade or sell the Gysbert's Island lots among themselves. On December 12, 1727, Thomas Stillwell, who owned twenty-seven of the thirty-nine lots, sold to a local farmer, Barent Johnson, who moved to the tract and farmed it. This was one of the earliest recorded land sales on

> On Thursday last, a party, consisting of about 40 people, went from Newark to Coney-Island in a sloop for the purpose of bathing; where unfortunately, two men and a young woman were drowned in the surf, notwithstanding every exertion was made to save them by the rest of the party. One of the men was named DODD or DODGE; the young woman was his daughter; the name of the second man we have not learnt.

Coney Island. From this point on, Gysbert's Island was also known as Johnson's Island. In 1766, the freeholders voted to divide part of the common lands among themselves. The two new divisions, at the eastern end of the island, each apportioned into thirty-nine lots, were known as the Sedge Bank (the future Manhattan Beach) and the Western Division (the future Brighton Beach).

By 1800, the freeholders realized that Coney Island was no longer as isolated as it had been and was attracting outside interest. Boating parties were landing on the beaches at the west end and using the island for picnics. The trespassers cut fences and trees for firewood, and the town elders found it difficult to ignore these new intrusions from the outside world. One of the first references to recreational activity at Coney Island was recorded in 1801 when a boating party from Newark, New Jersey, landed on Coney's beach, and three swimmers drowned in the surf. Incidents such as this forced the town to crack down on trespassers. In April 1807, Gravesend passed edicts that included fines for cutting or destroying timber. The town raised money to appoint a committee to prosecute all trespassers on the common, or undivided, lands of the town.

Increasing interest in the common lands from outsiders forced the freeholders to tighten the town's informal leasing arrangements. At a special town meeting called on March 16, 1811, the townspeople appointed a formal committee with sole jurisdiction over the leasing of the common lands. Until

**Early recreation**
An 1801 *Hartford Courier* contains one of the earliest accounts of recreational bathing in Coney Island. Three of the bathers who came on a sloop from New Jersey drowned in the surf.

**The Coney Island House**
This view of Coney's first hotel was taken in the 1860s, after numerous alterations had been made to the structure. The building, located at what became Neptune Avenue and West Sixth Street, was demolished in 1929.

**The Pavilion**
On May 26, 1845, Alonzo Reed leased Coney Island Point for five years at $25 a year. He built a tent-covered, circular dance platform called the Pavilion. It was considered Coney's first "amusement."

this time, the leases had been approved informally by votes at town meetings. Three Commissioners of the Common Lands would now negotiate all leases. Nicholas Stillwell, Van Brunt Magaw, and John Terhune were appointed as commissioners, and the powers and responsibilities granted to them were formidable.

By 1817, the commissioners became the trustees of all fees collected from leasing the common lands. The fees were no longer divided and distributed to the heirs of the original freeholders as they had been in the past, because the heirs were too numerous and difficult to locate. Instead, the money went directly into the town treasury. In 1815 and 1821, the last two small divisions of the island were made, leaving only one piece as "common lands." This last piece, located between what is now Ocean Parkway and Coney Island Point, became what is known as Coney Island.

The stage was set for the great land rush that would transform the remote dunes and meadows of Coney Island into some of the world's most valuable real estate. Power over the common lands had been transferred from the citizenry of Gravesend to the commissioners, and with that power was the ability to control Coney's destiny.

### The First Hotel

The only way to access Coney Island other than by boat in the early days was to cross what was called the "fording place," a shallow section of creek bed where Coney Island Creek met Sheepshead Bay. The crossing was easy at low tide. The fording place was reached by heading east from the center of Gravesend along Gravesend Neck Road, south to Cowenhouven's Lane, and then southeast along the narrow dirt track that would one day become Sheepshead Bay Road. From Sheepshead Bay, a swampy track led to the farmhouses of Gysbert's Island, the only inhabited portion of Coney Island. It was an arduous trip.

In 1823, the town of Gravesend authorized the formation of the Coney Island Road and Bridge Company to provide better access to Coney Island. By the summer, the company had opened the mile-long Shell Road, paved it with oyster shells, and built a wooden bridge over Coney Island Creek. The new toll road provided a direct southerly route from the town center through the previously impenetrable salt marsh owned by Jacobus Lake to a toll house that stood at what is now Shell Road and the Belt Parkway.

The road proved popular, and carriages began streaming through Gravesend from King's Highway and down Shell Road to the shore. Flimsy wooden shelters began cropping up on the leased common lands along the Coney Island shoreline. So many visitors made the trip that, in 1829, the Coney Island Road and Bridge Company decided to provide better accommodations by building a hotel, Coney Island House, on a portion of Court Van Sicklen's farm at the end of Shell Road. Coney Island had become a resort.

**New-York American.**

MONDAY EVENING, AUGUST 18, 1823.

*Coney Island.*—The road and bridge leading to this delightful island are now complete. It is open to the ocean, with the finest and most regular beach we ever saw, is within 9 miles of Brooklyn ferry, and only a mile or two from the Bath house, where the appetite created by a sea breeze may be abundantly and speedily satisfied.

☞ CONEY ISLAND.—On the hither side of this famous sand hill a Steamboat dock has been constructed, with a good board walk thence to an elevation, whereon a Spacious Tent of Sails has been erected—one of the coolest and airiest resorts we know, with a fine breeze always drawing through and glorious Sea-Bathing just far enough off. The view of the Ocean, with the highlands of Neversink dimly seen on the right, is a superb one, and a couple of hours may be spent here right pleasantly—at least, they *have* been.

The pretty and nimble Steamboat Iolas leaves the South Ferry, Battery, at 7 A. M., 10 A. M., 1 P. M. and 3½ P. M., leaving Coney Island at 8½, 11½, 2½ and 6½, landing at Fort Hamilton each way, and reaching the City on her last trip just after sunset. She is all that could be wished for such a route. The feed on this side of Coney is rather primitive as yet—the variety being Fried Clams and Chowder, with bread and sea-biscuit ; the Agricultural products of the Island being rather limited, and the Culinary department yet in its infancy. The Lemonade is good, however, and the rest is coming on. Fare only 12½ cents.

**Shell Road Toll House, 1860s**
Carriages traveling on the main route to Coney Island stopped at the toll house, located at what is now Shell Road and West Sixth Street.

**Pavilion opens**
On July 22, 1845, the *New-York Daily Tribune* (top left) announced the opening of the new steamboat dock and Coney's first amusement, a "Spacious Tent of Sails," at Coney Island Point.

Other hotels soon opened. John Wyckoff opened the Wyckoff Hotel on the Sand Hills, the dunes just south of Coney Island House. In 1847, Allan Clarke opened the Oceanic Hotel on Coney Island Creek and Shell Road. It burned down that same year, was rebuilt, and burned again eight years later. In 1845, Coney Island Point at the western end of the island was leased to Alonzo Reed, who opened the Pavilion, a dance hall on a raised, canvas-covered platform. The Fort Hamilton and Coney Island Ferry Company was formed, built a pier near the Pavilion, and introduced steamboat service between Manhattan and Coney Island.

A second toll road opened in 1850. The Coney Island Plank Road bypassed the Gravesend town center and crossed Coney Island Creek at the eastern end of Gysbert's Island to connect Coney Island and Flatbush. On July 4, 1862, the Coney Island and Brooklyn Railroad opened a horse car line on Plank Road, the first direct rail line into Coney Island. Coney Island, once remote, was now connected to the world by road, rail, and sea.

As development flourished after the Civil War, the Commissioners of the Common Lands leased out large, cheap waterfront lots along the entire shoreline of the common lands, from the Sand Hills (now West Eighth Street) to Coney Island Point (Sea Gate). The new hotels were, for the most part, ramshackle affairs, large and informal chowder houses, some built of driftwood. Among the earliest pioneers of the 1860s were outsiders Peter Tilyou, Richard Ravenhall, and William Engeman, men who would later make their mark on the island. But the person who would have the biggest impact on Coney Island was a local man from Gravesend, and he was about to make his move.

**Green's Hotel**
Built in the early 1860s, the hotel was located on the old Wyckoff Tract at what is now Trump Village on West Fifth Street. The cottage to the left, Thompson's Hotel, survived until 1960, when it was razed for a Trump Village parking lot.

**John Y. McKane** Rising from carpenter to political boss of Gravesend and Coney Island, McKane simultaneously held many public positions: Gravesend town supervisor and police chief, Commissioner of the Common Lands, and Kings County supervisor. He used his powers to prevent Coney Island from becoming a public park. His many crimes included selling off the common lands of Gravesend.

# CHAPTER 2

# John McKane: Coney's "Teflon" Boss

BEGINNING IN the 1830s, Irish immigrants began to rival the population of Dutch farmers in the town of Gravesend. One of these Irish families, the McKanes, arrived with a one-year-old infant named John. John Y. McKane, born August 10, 1841, in County Antrim, Ireland, was raised in Gravesend. He spent his youth as a clam digger and was apprenticed as a carpenter. McKane dodged the draft during the Civil War by claiming to be an alien. In 1866, the twenty-five-year-old McKane opened a business as a builder in Sheepshead Bay.

While in his twenties, McKane was appointed superintendent of the Sunday school at the Methodist Episcopal Church. He married Fanny Nostrand, daughter of a prominent local citizen. McKane was ambitious and knew how to make friends, and he used his connections to become Coney Island's most successful builder during the "gold rush" years following the Civil War. Realizing that Coney Island was on the cusp of greatness, McKane sought to grab the reigns of power in Gravesend.

McKane saw that the simple farmers of Gravesend were unaware of the real value of the common lands. In the 1860s, leases were still made for paltry sums that brought in just enough money to support the school system. The pious townspeople resented the unruly crowds that were visiting the hotels and bathhouses but felt that they could be controlled. McKane sensed a power vacuum and began working his way into important political positions.

In 1867 McKane was elected as one of

**Building an empire**
In the 1870s, John McKane constructed several structures for Manhattan Beach developer Austin Corbin, including a railway station.

the town's three constables. He used his position to assemble a network of cronies and business contacts. Coney Island's first steam railroad was completed that same year, and other railroads would soon follow. McKane knew that it would be just a matter of time until the big developers arrived and he could cash in on his connections. A naive act on the part of eighth-generation Gravesender William Stillwell pushed McKane to seize power.

The selfish maneuverings of these two men, the artless William H. Stillwell and the scheming John Y. McKane, sealed the fate of Coney Island for the next hundred years. Stillwell allowed big-money interests to acquire nearly two-thirds of Coney Island for a pittance. The remainder of the island, the common lands, became McKane's bailiwick,

**Sea Beach Palace, 1879**
The Sea Beach Railroad terminal was salvaged from the 1876 Philadelphia Centennial Exposition and moved by barge to West Eighth Street and Surf Avenue.

**Chowder house**
George Brainerd's 1874 photograph of Peter Tilyou's bathhouse, which stood at what is now West Fifteenth Street and the Bowery.

tied up and controlled so tightly that it would take nearly fifty years to unravel the chaos he created.

Stillwell, a justice of the peace turned town surveyor, had just completed the official Kings County survey of Coney Island in 1868 when the wealthy and ambitious twenty-eight-year-old William Engeman showed up inquiring about available land. Stillwell, who liked to be called "Judge," knew that two large parcels of salt marsh in private hands were available: the Sedge Bank and the Western Division (once part of the Sedge Bank). The Western Division, the more desirable of the two, was centrally located and owned by heirs of the original thirty-nine Gravesend freeholders, who were scattered all over the world. The Judge became Engeman's front man and agent and began tracing the owners for him.

Through Stillwell, Engeman secretly acquired several hundred acres of prime shorefront, purchasing the land from the landowners for the paltry sum of $20,000. Stillwell, abusing his role of town surveyor, even threw in a small section of the common lands at the easternmost section of Gysbert's Island. In making the sale, he bypassed Gravesend's Commissioners of the Common Lands, setting a dangerous precedent for future land deals.

Stillwell would repeat this feat in 1873 when banker Austin Corbin hired him to help purchase the entire swampy Sedge Bank, or Eastern Division of Coney Island. Corbin paid a total of $15,000 for several hundred acres. Corbin offered Stillwell a share in his company as payment for services rendered, but Stillwell insisted on a salary, passing up an opportunity to make a fortune when Corbin would later develop exclusive Manhattan Beach. Corbin's and Engeman's arrival on Coney Island signaled a change in the scale of development. Big money had arrived.

In the 1860s, the common lands in central Coney Island were still being leased for small sums to people who divided and sublet them for hotels and bathhouses. Being a builder, McKane was aware of these transactions and realized that the ten-year leases would be worth far more if he controlled them. While the rapid development helped McKane's expanding construction business, he wanted more. He felt that he should personally profit from the leases.

In April 1869, John McKane was elected as one of the three Commissioners of the Common Lands. In his first year in office, he doubled the fees for leases, from a total of $728.50 to $1,511.50. At that, they were still undervalued. The townspeople were happy about the increased fees but were unaware that McKane was receiving kickbacks from the lessees, who, in turn, were profiting from sublets. McKane was soon a wealthy man.

The town justices, sensing McKane's ambitions, set up new regulations for controlling the leasing agreements of the common lands. A new 1871 law stated that leases would be made "only at public auction and on the premises or at the town hall" to the highest bidder in parcels with no more than

**William H. Stillwell**
The Gravesend town surveyor, known as the Judge, sold the eastern half of Coney Island for a pittance, essentially giving it away to developers.

# Brighton Beach

AFTER BUYING the Western Division of the Sedge Bank in 1868, William Engeman opened his Ocean Hotel on a desolate stretch of beach, approximately where Brighton Fourth Street now meets Brightwater Court. Then, in 1877, he sold his beachfront property at Coney Island Avenue to the East River and Coney Island Railroad (ER&CIRR) for $160,000. Development of the Western Division took off a year later when ER&CIRR completed a steam railroad to carry passengers and freight from Atlantic Avenue to the ocean. The line became the Brooklyn Flatbush and Coney Island Railroad, today's Brighton Beach subway line.

At the railroad's terminus, the company's directors built a sprawling, 275-room, "stick-style" hotel (later expanded to 600 rooms). The developers needed a name for the resort. One of the directors, Henry C. Murphy, wanted to name it Narrioch Beach, the Indian name for Coney Island, but he was overruled. Instead, the directors named the Hotel Brighton after the British resort of Brighton, England, and the area became known as Brighton Beach.

In 1879, Engeman founded the Brighton Beach Racing Association and opened Coney Island's only racetrack, at Ocean Parkway and Coney Island Avenue. He also built the Brighton Bathing Pavilion and the Ocean Pier in 1881. The track closed in 1907, just before racing was outlawed, then was used for auto racing and briefly as an airfield.

In 1904, Engeman's son, William Jr., seeking to develop the northern portion of his Brighton property into residential lots, began illegally filling in the marshland at Coney Island Creek and Neptune Avenue, the first step to transforming Coney Island into a peninsula.

**Coney's Western Division**
William Engeman (above); the Ocean Hotel (left); 1898 map of Brighton Beach (below).

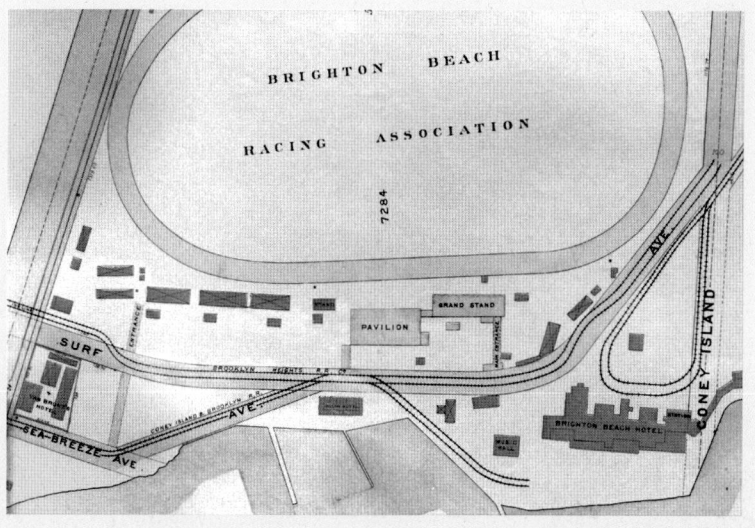

# Culver Plaza

No other tract of land in Coney Island has seen as much change as Culver Plaza. Throughout history, it has been the site of the Iron Pier, Dreamland park, the Iron Tower, the Coney Island Athletic Club, a circus sideshow, and a public park. Today it is the location of the New York Aquarium.

Andrew R. Culver made his money as a lawyer and then began investing in railroads. In 1873–75, he founded the Prospect Park and Coney Island Railroad, which terminated at the ocean between West Eighth and Fifth Streets. His terminal opened onto Culver Plaza, a sprawling, nine-acre park with a bandstand, picnic tables, a camera obscura, and Thomas Cable's hotel. Culver founded the Coney Island Observatory and Signal Company and moved the three-hundred-foot Sawyer Tower from the 1876 Philadelphia Centennial Exposition to his plaza. He renamed the observatory the Iron Tower and opened it to the public on July 4, 1878, charging fifteen cents per ride. A year later, Culver built a rail line to Coney's West End. Service began between his terminal and Norton's Point, Coney's westernmost tip.

When Surf Avenue was laid out in 1880–81, Culver fought against having the street cut through his plaza. He parked a locomotive across the right-of-way and filed a court injunction to keep the street off his property. He eventually lost the fight, and by 1890, the avenue separated his terminal from the ocean.

In 1893, Culver pulled out of Coney Island and sold his rail line to Austin Corbin for $350,000.

**Culver Plaza, 1870s** The Iron Pier and picnic tables (above); Cable's Hotel (below left); the 300-foot-tall Iron Tower (below right).

three hundred feet of ocean frontage. The regulations also required that advertisements for leases be published four weeks prior to a sale in the *Brooklyn Daily Eagle* and *Brooklyn Union* newspapers. McKane ignored the regulations and found ways around them.

McKane knew that it was pointless to oppose the equally ambitious and determined Engeman and Corbin, because they were too powerful. Instead, he was gracious and granted them favors, hoping to obtain lucrative construction contracts from the developers. Gravesend still owned a small parcel of land east of Manhattan Beach called Breezy Point, where a lifesaving station was located. When Corbin sought to purchase this last parcel of the common lands east of his property, the town rebelled and opposed the sale. The farmers knew how valuable the land was, but it was too late. McKane sought to score points with Corbin by telling him that the sale could be authorized by a voice vote at the annual town meeting.

Corbin and McKane packed the meeting with their cronies, and in the midst of the confusion, a resolution was passed authorizing the sale of Breezy Point to Corbin.

Corbin's appraiser, James Armstrong, and the town's appraiser, Stephen Voorhies, were appointed to put a value on the parcel. Corbin had secretly bribed Voorhies shortly before the appraisal. The pair came up with a price of $2,000, which Armstrong claimed was too high. Breezy Point, worth an estimated $100,000, was sold to Corbin's Manhattan Beach Development Company for a mere $1,500. The farmers of Gravesend were outraged and tried to stop the sale, but

**Vanderveers Hotel**
Located at West Fifth Street and Surf Avenue, the hotel was built for William Vanderveer by John McKane in 1875. After Vanderveer's death, his wife, Lucy, ran the hotel and bathhouse.

**Manhattan Beach Hotel, 1877**
This view of Austin Corbin's hotel dates from the year it opened, before Corbin constructed walkways and opulent exotic gardens, a bicycle track, an enclosure for fireworks displays, and a park with wild animals.

### Coney Island Point, 1890s

August Laux captured the beauty of Gravesend Bay and the point, with its brilliant white sand, in his oil on canvas, *View of Brooklyn and Staten Island from Coney Island*. Soon after Laux painted this view, the point was developed into the private community of Sea Gate.

### Early entrepreneur

Charles Feltman came to Coney Island in 1871 and, with a partner, opened this small saloon. He later expanded it into Coney's largest restaurant. It stretched from Surf Avenue to the beach along West Tenth Street.

McKane thwarted the town's attempt to rescind it.

McKane's ability to rig elections enhanced his power. He aligned himself with the powerful Democratic political boss of Brooklyn, Hugh McLaughlin, who became his protector. McKane authorized leases for political friends and allies and, in 1876, was easily elected to Gravesend's top post of town supervisor. The power base had changed, and the town was no longer run by the original farmers. McKane held two of Gravesend's most powerful positions and shifted the town's focus from agriculture to real estate.

Good transportation was the secret to increased real estate values. Back in 1865, the farmers of Gravesend had fought the construction of the first steam railroad into Coney Island and had prevented the line from running through their farms. The West End Line was forced to follow a circuitous route fronting the western shoreline of Gravesend Bay. But just a few years later, with McKane in power, four new railroads went directly through Gravesend's farmland to Coney Island. The state legislature had condemned the land along the right-of-way and allowed the railroad's owners to choose the routes that they felt were most efficient.

Andrew Culver bought out the old Coney Island Road and Bridge Company in 1875 and ran a steam railroad along its route through the very heart of Gravesend, across Gysbert's Island, and into his new beachfront Culver Plaza terminal, located at what is now West Fifth Street. The Sea Beach Railroad followed a similar route in 1879, terminating at the Sea Beach Palace, a spacious steel-and-glass pavilion transported from the Philadelphia Centennial Exposition in 1877 and re-

**Hotel Brighton** Wagons brought guests to the 275-room hotel, opened in July 1878. By 1880, the hotel had 575 rooms. That same year, 1 million visitors came to Brighton Beach by railroad.

assembled just west of Culver's terminal.

Coney Island's rapid development required infrastructure, and McKane quickly solved the practical problems of water and streets. In the late 1870s, a large-capacity well was dug on the Gravesend property of C. D. Stryker at Avenue U, and the water from the well was transported south to Coney via a steam pump and trestle across the marshes to the Sea Beach Palace. Coney Island's main street, Surf Avenue, was laid out and paved in 1880.

The following year, McKane formed his own Coney Island police force and appointed himself chief of police. His power structure complete, McKane began dispensing favors to New York's political bosses. As a favor to New York's William "Boss" Tweed, he leased Coney Island's West End to Robert Furey, a front man for former State Senator Mike "Thunderbolt" Norton and his notorious partner, gambler Mike Murray. McKane allowed the group to open two hotels, the Pavilion and the Point Comfort House, where gambling, prostitution, and prizefighting flourished without interference from the law.

The late 1870s and early 1880s were the boom years for Coney Island development, but Coney's reputation suffered from McKane-sanctioned criminal activity. He fixed elections, used his police department thugs as a private army to assault his opponents, and collected bribes and a percentage of every deal transacted in

**McKane's enforcers** Having appointed himself chief of police, McKane organized his own police force in 1881. It became his private army.

**Norton and Murray's Pavilion** Mike "Thunderbolt" Norton and Mike Murray opened the Pavilion on Coney Island in the 1870s.

**Night bathing**
In the 1880s, Austin Corbin introduced illuminated night bathing at Manhattan Beach. The mile-long beach, considered the island's best, disappeared when the Manhattan Beach Land Company filled it for residential development in the early 1900s.

**Dirty water**
A cartoon from the July 1880 *Puck* magazine illustrated the pollution caused by offshore dumping by New York City garbage scows.

Coney Island. No business operated without his approval. McKane even proclaimed that "houses of prostitution are a necessity on Coney Island." Reputable business interests began referring to central Coney Island as "West Brighton" to avoid confusion with the corrupt activities of the West End. Respectable people avoided the West End entirely during the 1880s. By then, Coney Island had earned the nickname "Sodom by the Sea."

McKane was corrupt and violent, and his greed was boundless, but his biggest crime of all—the one that could never be atoned for—was yet to come. For years, Kings County had been seeking to transform the common lands of Gravesend into a public park. McKane found a way to quash the idea forever and, in the process, grant himself a huge payoff. In 1883, he decided to sell Coney Island to his cronies. The dunes and beaches that made up some of the most valuable land in the world would no longer belong to Gravesend.

In late 1883, McKane presided over a special meeting of the Commissioners of the Common Lands called to authorize the sales of the lots and parcels of Coney Island. A consent of the voters in a town election was required to change the Gravesend charter to permit the sales. The ballots were rigged, premarked with a big "yes." If a voter failed to cross out the "yes," the ballot was counted as a vote in favor of the sales. Thanks to McKane's chicanery, the measure to sell Coney Island passed by a wide margin.

The first sale took place on February 26, 1884, with two more sales following in 1885 and 1889. Most of the bidders were straw men acting for McKane. No one could buy property without his authorization. Although McKane bid only on two small lots, his name soon appeared on property records as owner of the choicest land in Coney Island. The list of buyers included not only McKane's cronies, but also most of Gravesend's public officials—a blatant conflict of interest. Even Town Surveyor William Kowalski decided to grab a parcel for himself. Garret Katen, a corrupt Commissioner of the Common Lands, was also on the list of buyers, as was Justice of the Peace and Election Inspector Jaques Stryker.

A look at the list of bidders turns up some familiar names. Established businessmen such as Charles Feltman, Charles

**Transformed shoreline**
The engraving (above) depicts "Coney-catchers" digging clams in 1881. The trestle in the background is Brooklyn's first elevated line, the Coney Island Railroad, which ran between Hotel Brighton and Culver Terminal. Coney's shoreline began to change in the 1880s after the two Iron Piers were built. The piers caused a large sandbar to form (left), doubling the size of the island's waterfront lots west of Eighth Street.

JOHN McKANE: CONEY'S "TEFLON" BOSS

# Coney's Changing Shape

Coney Island is a sandbar that has been altered over time by natural forces and development but that has maintained the same basic shape since the 1600s. Much has been written about Coney being cobbled together from three or more islands, but the islands were never separate.

The island's true boundaries are difficult to define by traditional means, because sandbars change seasonally. Weather and tides create cycles of accretion and erosion, a state of natural flux. Coney has expanded and contracted often, but over the three centuries between discovery and development, it has always reverted to a semblance of its original form. Of all the westward-drifting barrier islands along the south shore of Long Island, Coney Island was least likely to change, because the flow of water through New York Bay blocked its westward movement.

The main bar of Coney Island was breached on a seasonal basis by tidal inlets cut through by storms. These generally narrow and shallow inlets were easily forded, then closed naturally over a period of time. Between 1660 and 1853, an estimated three hundred storms and hurricanes struck the New York area, and each one changed the island slightly, but Coney always reverted back to a similar shape.

Various names have been attributed to Coney's "component" islands: Common Lands, Broken Lands, Piney Island, Horse Island, Stryker's, Johnson Island, Sedgebank, Gysbert's Island, Konijn Hook, and Schreyer's Hook. Eugene L. Armbruster claimed, in his 1924 monograph, *Coney Island,* that before the great storm of 1839, the "middle island," known as Piney Island, extended south "several miles out to sea." There is no evidence, however, to support his claim.

In fact, the "islands" of Coney Island were not islands at all. Gysbert's Island,

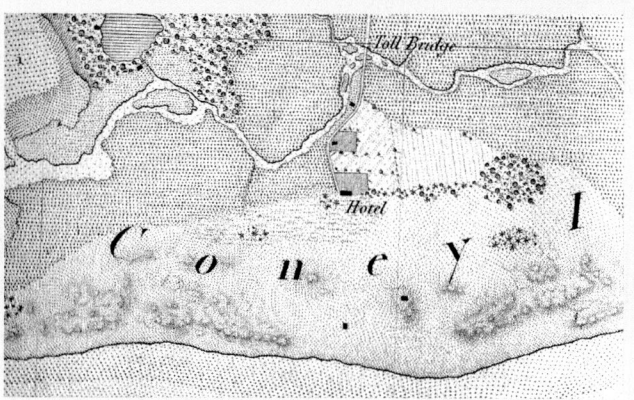

**Accurate maps** The small map shows central Coney Island in 1844; the large map, Coney in the late 1860s. The only buildings in 1844 were the Coney Island House, Wyckoff's Hotel, Van Sicklen's farm, and the Shell Road Toll House.

the central portion of Coney, was an arable salt meadow. Sedge Bank, the "island" to the east, was actually part of the Coney Island salt marsh, a muddy mat of cordgrass riddled with mazes of small inlets, channels, and sloughs, and was often submerged at high tide. Piney Island, the dune- and cedar-covered western third of the island, was usually connected to Gysbert's but was sometimes separated from it by a narrow, meandering seasonal stream known as Pine Inlet.

A review of early nautical charts reveals that Coney Island was approximately the same size in 1900, when the New York City bulkhead lines were established, as it was when the first maps were drawn in the 1600s.

The reported length of Coney Island has always varied widely. Even contemporary accounts are confusing, describing it as being anywhere between two and eight miles long. Coney today is four and a quarter miles long.

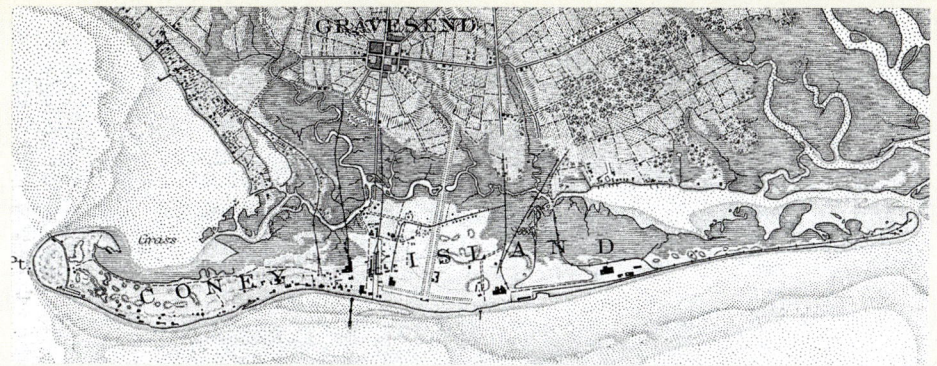

**Birth of a resort** Coney Island in 1879 was a mile longer than it is today. A storm in the early 1870s caused the Pelican Beach sandbar to drift west and attach itself to Coney's eastern end. Just to the north of the island, the farms of Gravesend radiated from the town center. Hubbard's Creek meandered north along Shell Road from Coney Island Creek.

**Coney from the sea** In colonial times, the tall sand dunes of Coney Island were used by mariners as a navigational aid. As a result, the maps of the time were not accurate depictions of the island.

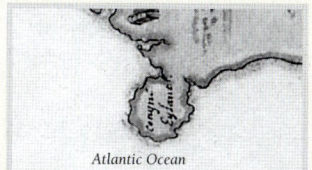

**1639 Manatus Map** The first depiction of Coney Island.

**1730**

**1740**

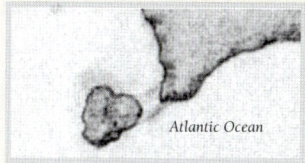

**1776**

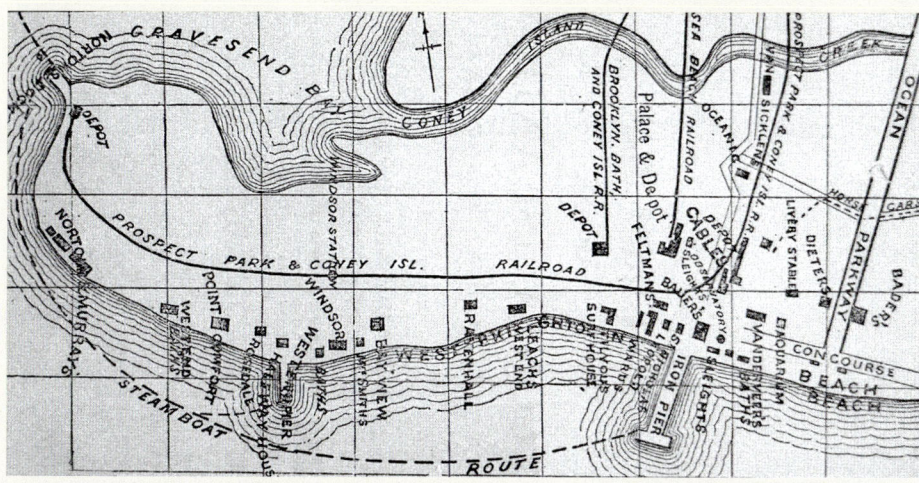

**Early transportation** This 1880 map shows the island's three steamboat piers, three steam railroads, and the Coney Island Avenue horsecar. Surf Avenue had not been laid out yet, and the Prospect Park and Coney Island Railroad provided transportation between the island's center and Norton's Point. Ravenhall, Cable's, Vanderveers, Feltman's, Bauer's, and Tilyou's Surf House were the main hotels in West Brighton. The new Ocean Parkway and Concourse are at right.

**Aerial view of Coney Island, 1992**

**Central Coney Island, circa 1885**
Looking west down Surf Avenue from the Iron Tower, this view shows the Elephant Hotel and, to its right, the Sea Beach Palace. Only one structure from this period has survived: the Grashorn building (circled).

Bader, and Richard Ravenhall—longtime friends of McKane—were able to purchase the land under their establishments for a pittance. Most bidders were fronts for buyers who subdivided the land and sold the properties quickly, reaping windfall profits.

McKane garnered huge kickbacks from the sales. The *Brooklyn Eagle* gave a low estimate of McKane's cut as $500,000. Even worse than the graft was that the sales were rigged to include the "lands under water," the entire beach and shorefront, guaranteeing that the public would never have free access to the ocean. McKane's friends and henchmen were being rewarded with land that should have remained public property.

**Seeing the Elephant**
In 1884, the same year the land sell-off began, James V. Lafferty's Elephant Hotel opened at West Twelfth Street and Surf Avenue. Lafferty, a real estate speculator from New Jersey, had erected similar structures in Atlantic City and Cape May. The hotel, quite different from the ramshackle structures that surrounded it, rose above and stood out from the brothels, saloons, and dance halls that made up West Brighton.

The elephant also carried particular symbolism. Before the phrase "seeing the elephant" became a Victorian euphemism for having sex, it was an expression that had come into vogue during the gold rush of 1849. When a gold seeker returned east from the gold fields, he was said to have "seen the elephant." The phrase represented success over adversity. Gold seekers painted crude images of elephants on the canvas sides of their wagons with charcoal and axle grease, accompanied by the scrawled message, "Have you seen the elephant?" "The universal expression of the gold rush," J. S. Holiday writes in *The World Rushed In,* "'seeing the elephant' symbolized the great adventure of going to California to dig a golden fortune. On the way 'the elephant' revealed himself in the many unexpected difficulties and dangers that beset the goldseekers, and 'to see the elephant' became the expression for suffering a severe ordeal, facing one's worst expectations, overcoming the meanest realities; in a word, knowing the Truth."

The Elephant Hotel became an unintentional monument to the "gold rush" mentality of the McKane years. In the early 1880s, the *Rural Gazette,* a Brooklyn farm journal, claimed that the increase in price of the Coney Island real estate "has no parallel, unless it be the mining regions of California." The "truth" about Coney Island became whatever John McKane said it was.

The irrelevance of truth in Coney Island was proven when McKane was subpoenaed to appear before a special committee of the New York State Legislature established in 1887 to investigate corruption in Gravesend. When McKane testified, he lied and perjured himself, as did all of his friends who were called as witnesses. The only person willing to testify against McKane was Coney Island real estate developer George C. Tilyou, the son of Coney pioneer Peter Tilyou. Tilyou recited a litany of crimes sanctioned by

**Inexhaustible cow**
Located in Culver Plaza, the mechanical cow dispensed milk at five cents a glass. At right is the base of the Iron Tower.

**Surf Avenue, 1880s**
This view was taken at West Tenth Street shortly after the street was opened. Culver Terminal is to the left.

**CONEY'S COLOSSUS**
# THE ELEPHANT HOTEL

**Elephants**
Elephant Hotel, 1885 (opposite); popular elephant ride at Luna Park (inset); cutaway view of the hotel, from *Scientific American*, July 1885 (above); exaggerated view from same article (inset).

**Animal cruelty** Tops the elephant was electrocuted at the former site of the Elephant Hotel in 1903. Paul Boyton had sold the animal to Fred Thompson and Skip Dundy when they leased Sea Lion Park from Boyton in 1902. Tops was used to drag the Trip to the Moon airship attraction down Surf Avenue from Steeplechase to Luna Park. During the move, Tops attacked his handler after being prodded with a pitchfork. The elephant had previously killed a man who fed him a lit cigarette. Thompson and Dundy decided to kill the unfortunate animal by feeding it poisoned carrots. When that failed, they used electrocution.

JOHN McKANE: CONEY'S "TEFLON" BOSS    23

**Culver Plaza attractions**
George C. Tilyou's Ferris wheel (above) was inaccurately advertised as the largest in the world. The Coney Island Athletic Club (below, with red roof) was a 10,000-seat arena where the first indoor world championship heavyweight fight took place on November 3, 1899, between Tom Sharkey and Jim Jeffries.

McKane, including prostitution, gambling, and election fraud. But Tilyou had miscalculated and was forced to leave Coney Island when McKane was kept out of jail by his political connections. Although McKane returned to power, his protector, Democratic Boss Hugh McLaughlin, was becoming increasingly disenchanted with Coney Island's dictator. Instead of keeping a low profile, McKane became even more brazen and continued his reign of terror at the beach. But his fortune would soon run out, and the next trial would be his undoing.

### The End of an Era

The Elephant Hotel, constructed the same year that McKane reached his political apex by selling the public lands, went up in flames in 1896, not long after McKane was sentenced to six years of hard labor at Sing Sing state prison. After his second trial, McKane left the courthouse on February 15, 1894, convicted of eleven felony counts, including assault, oppression, contempt, conspiracy, and violation of election laws. Two months after McKane began his prison sentence, the 250-year-old town of Gravesend ceased to exist altogether when it was annexed to the city of Brooklyn. McKane's legacy was a despoiled Coney Island, left in the hands of private developers.

McKane served his sentence uneventfully and was released from prison on April 30, 1898, just in time to see Brooklyn (and Coney Island) become part of Greater New York. He died a short time later, in September 1899, after falling ill while supervising the rebuilding of some burned buildings he owned in Coney Island. His body lay in state at his home on Emmons Avenue across the street from Sheepshead Bay. He left an estate of only $250,000, a fraction of what he garnered during thirty years of theft and graft.

During the confusion that followed the annexation of Brooklyn, New York City officials began untangling the clouded titles of Coney Island. Just after a fire swept through the amusement area in 1899, the city made its first attempt to reclaim the shorefront land stolen by McKane. New York City Comptroller Byrd Coler launched an investigation into suspect Coney Island property transactions while advocating for a city park on the old Coney Island common lands. The city began tearing down property that illegally extended onto public sidewalks and streets. After carefully scrutinizing the lands owned by McKane, Coler discovered numerous irregularities and found that a McKane parcel on West Fifth Street occupied by Alexander Samuels's Grand Union Hotel was actually owned by the old town of Gravesend and was therefore New York City property.

The city immediately billed Samuels for six years' back rent at $2,500 a year. Investi-

**Culver Plaza, circa 1900**
The beachfront at the eastern end of the plaza was occupied by (left to right) the New Iron Pier, a ride called Shooting the Rapids, and Doyle's Baths. Most of the attractions were removed to make way for Dreamland, which opened in 1904. The New York Aquarium is now on the site.

gators discovered that the property had been transferred through a series of straw owners that included former Commissioner of the Common Lands John Voorhies and McKane's brother James. Coler ordered the city's counsel to take action and reclaim the land. Coler also hinted that other investigations were under way and predicted that the parcels in the fire area would be reclaimed for a park. But the city soon gave up on this expensive and politically delicate task, and the park idea was shelved.

McKane's abrupt departure from the Coney Island scene left a serious power vacuum and no strong leader had emerged to plot the island's development. By 1900, John McKane, Austin Corbin, and William Engeman were dead. Andrew Culver, having given up on Coney Island, sold his interests to Corbin's Manhattan Beach Railroad. The farmland of Gravesend was being sold for residential tracts, and development was rapidly encroaching southward toward Coney Island. In 1904, Corbin's Manhattan Beach Hotel and Land Company went into receivership, and the new owners, headed by attorney George C. Austin, offered to sell Manhattan Beach to the city for a public park. Unfortunately, the deal fell through, and the eastern end of Coney Island, like Sea Gate to the west, was subdivided into building lots and sold off. The city had lost another opportunity to return the "stolen lands" of Coney Island to the public.

**The Razzle Dazzle**
This simple ride in Culver Plaza was owned by George C. Tilyou. He later moved it to Steeplechase Park.

## CHAPTER 3

# Building a New Industry

**Sea Lion Park**
Paul Boyton built the world's first enclosed amusement park in 1895 on filled marshland at Neptune Avenue and West Twelfth Street. Attractions included the Flip-Flap roller coaster (at left), the Shoot-the-Chutes (center), and a circus (at right).

**No parks!**
John McKane's opposition to public parks is lampooned in Homer Davenport's 1890s cartoon from the *Evening Journal*, just before the political boss was sent to Sing Sing state prison.

RETURNING FROM exile after McKane's imprisonment, George C. Tilyou rebuilt his ruined real estate business from scratch. In 1894, he invested heavily in the West End. He and his partners, Albert Buschman and Theodore Kramer, bought three square blocks at West Thirty-second Street, between the ocean and Gravesend Bay, and subdivided the property into lots. Tilyou also entered the amusement business, installing numerous rides, including the Bicycle Railroad and a Ferris wheel, on parcels he owned next to the Iron Tower.

Farther west, on Surf Avenue, Tilyou bought a large beachfront parcel at West Sixteenth Street and subdivided it to sell as lots.

Tilyou concentrated his efforts on his growing real estate empire until a new personality arrived on the scene and redefined Coney Island's fledgling amusement industry.

In 1895, adventurer Paul Boyton leased a parcel of marshland from the Sea Beach Railroad, surrounded it with a ten-foot fence, and opened Sea Lion Park, the world's first enclosed amusement park. Boyton's park was located at West Twelfth Street and Neptune Avenue. Customers paid admission to enter the enclosure and ride the Shoot-the-Chutes and the Flip-Flap roller coaster, watch circus performers, and view trained sea lions in an artificial lagoon.

Tilyou immediately saw the possibilities in Boyton's idea. In 1897, he and his financial backer, Theodore Kramer, fenced his parcel at West Sixteenth Street and turned it into an amusement park. The park's centerpiece was a British mechanical horse race called the Grand National Steeplechase Race Course. Tilyou surrounded the racetrack with elaborate new amusements and whimsical structures, moved his rides from Culver Plaza to the enclosure, and named it Steeplechase Park.

Tilyou was annoyed by the haphazard development that surrounded his new park. The shorefront was in private hands, and landowners were building out over the beach to the surf line and fencing off the shorefront. The beach soon became a patchwork of tiny strips of sand that disappeared altogether at high tide. Tilyou complained that the beach to the east of his property had "been ruined by building decks and pavilions out over the water" and said that "the only real beach on Coney Island is that portion to the west of the end of the Bowery, to Coney Island Point." In March 1897, Tilyou came up with a solution: a permanent Coney Island boardwalk that would compete with the popular four-mile-long Atlantic City Boardwalk, built in 1870.

Tilyou's boardwalk would connect the adjacent properties of Otto Huber, Richard Ravenhall, Conrad Steubenbord, and Paul Weidman with his own. He told the *Brooklyn Eagle* that his $10,000 "Ocean Promenade"

**"Wish you were here"**
Postage for picture postcards dropped to a penny in 1898. Thousands of cards sent from Coney Island helped spread the resort's fame around the world.

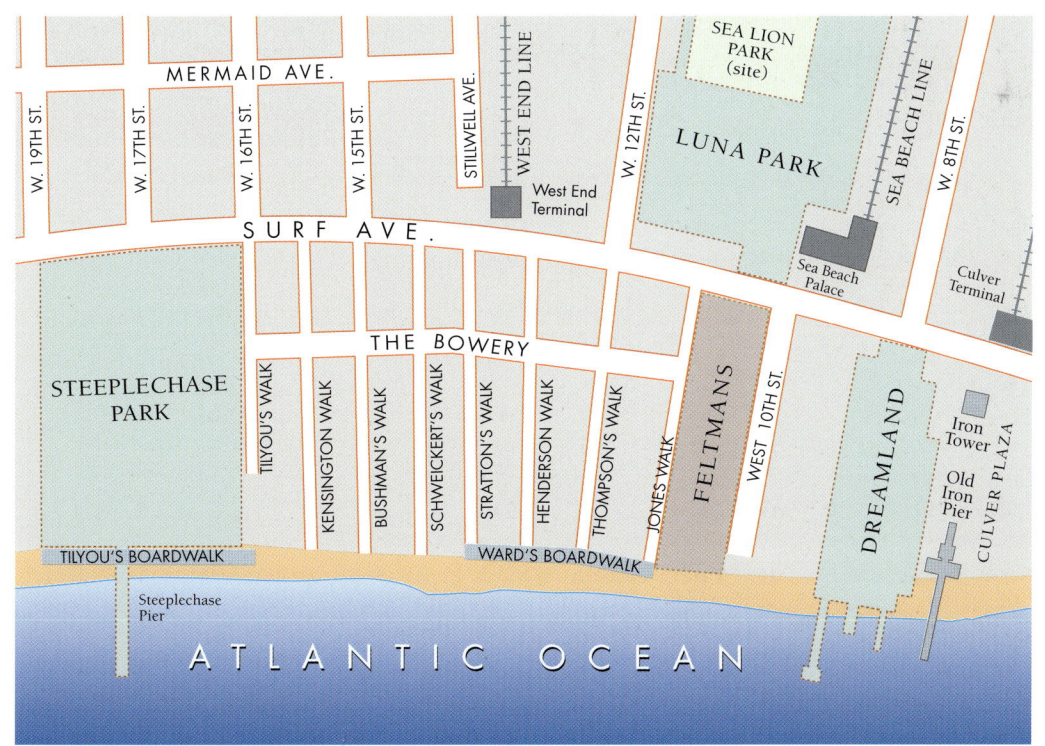

**Private parks**
Private, enclosed amusement parks allowed landowners a measure of control over their patrons, an exteme departure from the McKane era. After Sea Lion Park opened in 1895, Steeplechase Park, Luna Park, and Dreamland followed in rapid succession. Feltmans, with its Ziz roller coaster, Bavarian village theme, and outdoor movie theater, was another form of amusement park.

BUILDING A NEW INDUSTRY  27

would be fifteen hundred feet long and forty feet wide and eventually would extend from his property at Sixteenth Street all the way to Sea Gate, with benches placed along the ocean side and with no structures to block the view of the sea. Tilyou said, "It remains with us whether the entire beach shall be ruined or preserved and my proposition seems to have met with popular favor on every hand." He added that "under the McKane regime, it was useless to attempt to do anything toward improving the condition of Coney Island. A man could not even do as he pleased with his own property, as McKane and his men conducted it for him." Tilyou billed his proposed promenade as "a great attraction for respectable people."

Unfortunately, Tilyou's idea was ahead of its time. The businesspeople of the island, who were trying to squeeze every cent of profit from their beachfront property, did not receive it well. Public improvements had

## Sea Gate

THE PRIVATE, gated community of Sea Gate is located at the western end of Coney Island, known in earlier times as Coney Island Point. The point was first developed in the 1800s, when the town of Gravesend leased the "Western Half Mile" of the point to Alonzo Reed for five years at $25 per year. The lease, dated May 26, 1845, gave Reed "the exclusive right and privilege of erecting such landing place, tents and buildings as to him may seem fit."

Alonzo Reed proceeded to construct on one of the sand dunes a tent-covered wooden platform called the Pavilion, a dance hall that was Coney's first amusement. Reed asked Thomas Bielby, proprietor of the Fort Hamilton and Coney Island Ferry Company, to construct a pier at what is now Bay Fifty-first Street and Bayview Avenue. A steamboat made daily trips from Manhattan to Reed's Pavilion.

By 1859, Coney Island Point had been divided into lots by the town of Gravesend. In March of that year, lot 48, where West Thirty-seventh Street is today, was leased to John B. McPherson, who built a simple frame hotel called the Point Comfort House.

In December 1872, the town leased Coney Island Point to Robert Furey, Francis Swift, and Charles Dodge, who sublet the point to Mike Murray for $12,500. Murray was a front for Mike "Thunderbolt" Norton, who took over the point and built a hotel, also called the Pavilion, known for prizefights and prostitution. In the 1870s, the point became known as Norton's Point.

In 1881, railroad magnate Andrew Culver, whose railroad ran to the point's ferry terminal from Culver Plaza, became interested in developing the area and founded a company that offered to lease Norton's Point from the town of Gravesend for

**Sea Gate, circa 1900** Surf Avenue entrance (above); waterfront mansions (below).

no place in their scheme. Tilyou had to be content with the small boardwalk he built along the beach in front of his racecourse.

After a disastrous season in 1902, Paul Boyton folded his Sea Lion Park and leased the land to showmen Frederick Thompson and Elmer "Skip" Dundy. Thompson and Dundy had operated several amusements at Steeplechase Park, including the Trip to the Moon and the Giant See-Saw, but had left the park after a dispute with Tilyou over rental fees for their attractions. The pair moved Trip to the Moon from Steeplechase to vacant land surrounding the Sea Beach Palace. Backed by financier John W. Gates, they constructed an elaborate amusement park using Boyton's old Shoot-the-Chutes lagoon as its centerpiece. Their phantasmagoric Luna Park opened for business in 1903.

In 1904, Coney's fourth amusement park was developed by ex-Senator William "Billy" Reynolds and his consortium of investors.

$125,000 for two years. Culver drew up plans for a grand hotel in a parklike setting, but he never began construction on what he called West Plaza. Then, in 1885, the town of Gravesend sold the point for $183,000 to financier William Ziegler, owner of the Royal Baking Powder Company.

Ziegler, in turn, sold the land in 1892 to the Norton's Point Land Company, whose president, lawyer Alrick Man, named the tract Sea Gate and divided it into building lots. The point's landmark sand dunes were leveled, sewers were installed, red brick streets and sidewalks were laid, and silver poplars were planted along the streets.

In 1894, the company filed an application with the New York State Public Land Office for a grant to the lands underwater—the beaches—which were then public property. In 1897, the grant was approved by the state, making the beaches the private property of Sea Gate. Bulkheads were built, a fence was erected, and the point became an exclusive private community filled with beautiful mansions and summer homes. In 1898, Norton's Point Land Company created the Sea Gate Association to manage the community.

A 1917 Sea Gate promotional brochure described the community's advantages: "A place within the limits of New York City, easily accessible, cool in summer, warm in winter without the dirt and noise of the city, with a wonderful bathing beach and safe sailing waters with beautiful gardens and comfortable houses, with refined and congenial neighbors. Here is a community with private streets, its own police force, and its own governing board . . . as isolated from disturbing or objectionable influences as if surrounded by a Chinese wall."

At that time, Sea Gate had a commuter ferry that made the trip to Manhattan in about thirty minutes. The brochure also described a "uniformed police force patrolling night and day to keep out peddlers, beggars, picnickers, hurdy-gurdies and other jarring factors."

The Atlantic Yacht Club, built in 1894, was a prime attraction for Sea Gate society. According to an article published in the 1896 *American Yachting Annual*, "[the club] has spacious verandas as cool as the deck of an ocean liner. Perfect for sunsets. Members and their wives may live at the Club House the whole season."

The yacht club also offered "bachelor quarters with a fine view of Gravesend Bay; facilities for first class yachting, rowing, tennis and billiards, and the Pandemonium Dancing Pavilion, a dance club with well-known orchestras." The club, whose members included Manhattan aristocrats such as the Vanderbilts and the Astors, burned in the early 1930s.

**Yacht Club**
Club commodore David Banks (above); 1895 view of one of the club's two buildings on the Gravesend Bay side of Sea Gate (left).

**The Bowery**
The street had a ramshackle, mining-camp look (above) until 1903, when an arson fire destroyed 260 buildings between West Tenth Street and Steeplechase Park (below). The Henderson Theater, at left, and Stauch's Baths, at right, were in ruins.

The thirty-six-year-old real estate speculator was a partner in a company called Realty Associates that invested heavily in south Brooklyn. Reynolds's consortium sought to copy the success of Luna Park, which had opened the previous year.

Reynolds was a slightly shady, larger-than-life character. He had served a two-year stint as a state senator and was a former amateur boxer and horse-racing enthusiast. He had also been involved in a mysterious scandal that had left him "accidentally" shot in the groin by New York Mayor John Mitchell. Reynolds would later develop the Chrysler Building in Manhattan.

The move into Coney Island was a logical one for Reynolds. In 1902, he had made a fortune by filling in and developing Harway Basin, the old millpond on the north side of Coney Island Creek at Cropsey Avenue. He knew the value of Coney Island real estate. In late 1903, Reynolds and his partners had formed a development company called Wonderland Associates and

**New Bowery**
After the 1903 fire, many property owners rebuilt their businesses (left). Louis Stauch (below) opened his restaurant and dance hall (bottom) on the Bowery in 1904.

bought John McKane's old Coney Island Athletic Club and the adjacent Culver railroad property on Surf Avenue at West Eighth Street. They combined the properties into one parcel that included the city-owned bed of West Eighth Street, and they began construction on an amusement park called Wonderland.

By the time it opened in 1904, the park was named Dreamland. Coney now had three major amusement parks and was the mechanical amusement center of the world. No longer just a resort, it was a phenomenon that attracted curious high-brow visitors such as Sigmund Freud and Maxim Gorky. Coney's electric skyline was unlike anything ever seen before. Gorky described it as "shapely towers of miraculous castles, palaces and temples. Golden gossamer threads tremble in the air. They intertwine in transparent, flaming patterns, which flutter and melt away in love with their own beauty mirrored in the waters. Fabulous and beyond conceiving, ineffably beautiful is this fiery scintillation."

Coney's spectacle had become a raucous pleasure dome of sensuality that shattered

Victorian mores. Barr Ferree summed up the new Coney Island in the August 1904 issue of *Architects and Builders Magazine:* "The astonishing idea that any part of Coney Island could be 'good' shocked the island from end to end. And it has never recovered from the blow. . . . Verily this is Dreamland, and one rubs one's eyes and pinches one's arm to see if one be really awake."

BUILDING A NEW INDUSTRY 31

# Steeplechase I

**1897 · 1907**

George C. Tilyou

IN THE 1890s, George C. Tilyou was torn between real estate development and amusements. The former publisher of *Tilyou's Real Estate Telephone* (one issue in 1886) bought half of John Newell's large lot at the end of the Bowery and subdivided it into thirty-five parcels, intending to lease them. But Tilyou changed his mind and created Steeplechase Park instead.

The park's dramatic entrances on Surf Avenue and the Bowery were topped with equine statuary. Horse racing was the park's theme, and the Steeplechase ride, developed by J. W. Cawdrey, enabled ordinary people to experience the thrill of racing by riding mechanical horses along a metal track. The park was landscaped with formal gardens, flower beds, and shaded walks. Tilyou charged a fee to enter his park, enabling him to maintain control and keep out Coney's rougher element. There were no bars, only soda fountains. Steeplechase was a family park, a fantasy land featuring an airship tower, a boat ride along the Grand Canals of Venice, a miniature railroad, a bathhouse, and the largest ballroom in New York State. Tilyou's advertisement for the park called it "the most enchanting and magnetic fun-making resort in the world." His goal was to change Coney's image, and in that he succeeded. He also gained insight into how people wanted to be entertained.

When half the park was destroyed by fire in 1907, Tilyou put up a sign that read: "I have troubles today that I did not have yesterday. I had troubles yesterday that I have not today. On this site will be erected shortly a bigger, better Steeplechase Park. Admission to the Burning Ruins — 10 cents."

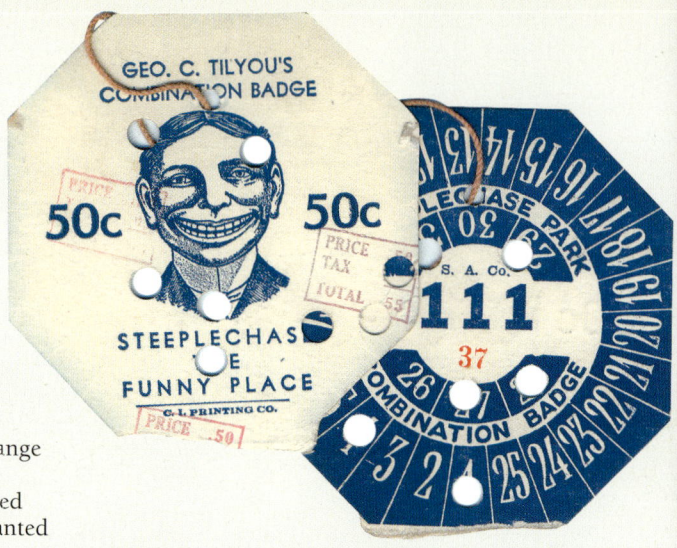

**Grand entrance** An arch topped with charging horses (below) served as the gateway to the park and was flanked by Tilyou's Hotel and a United States Post Office. Steeplechase tickets were punched for each ride (above right). Well-dressed patrons ride a carousel (right).

# GEO. C. TILYOU'S GREAT STEEPLECHASE PARK,

**Steeplechase scenes** A 1903 painting of the park (top) shows the Canals of Venice, the mechanical horse track, and various towers and pavilions. Park visitors could rent clown suits to wear over their street clothing (above). The costumes put them in the mood for fun and protected their clothes while they enjoyed the rides. Performers, also in costume, wandered throughout the park entertaining customers (right).

BUILDING A NEW INDUSTRY    33

# Steeplechase II

**1908–1964**

FOUL WEATHER is the enemy in Coney, and Tilyou designed his new Steeplechase to give him an edge over everyone else. He built a two-acre, enclosed, weatherproof steel-and-glass pavilion as the centerpiece, enabling the park to remain open on rainy days. Tilyou had become an amateur psychologist and knew how to break down inhibitions. Sometimes his attractions bordered on the sadistic.

Entering the park could be an ordeal. Patrons walked through the Barrel of Fun, a rolling barrel that tossed them on top of one another. The mechanical horse race ended at the Blow-Hole Theater, a bizarre ritual that required people to exit on a stage in front of a howling audience, while being hit by a midget with an electric paddle or chased by a clown. A hidden blower lifted women's skirts above their heads.

The park still had staid attractions, such as the sunken gardens, but the most popular rides were the ones that threw people together: the Human Roulette wheel, Whirlpool, Human Pool Table, and Giant Slide. There were also the classics, such as El Dorado, a three-tiered German carousel, and the Bicycle Race, a finely crafted gem built of polished brass and nickel. But the main attraction was always the original one: the mechanical horse race.

**The New Steeplechase**
An advertisement for the "Funny Place" (left). An aerial view of the park, circa 1925, shortly after the Boardwalk opened (below). The famous horse race (right). Map of park, circa 1964.

**Rides** The interior of the Pavilion of Fun, 1941 (top). The Flying Turns, the park's popular Boardwalk roller coaster that burned in 1939 (left). The Blow-Hole Theater (above).

BUILDING A NEW INDUSTRY

# Luna Park

## 1903 – 1946

**Fred Thompson**

In 1902, Fred Thompson and Skip Dundy used elephants to move their attractions from Steeplechase Park to the site of bankrupt Sea Lion Park. The pair had argued with George Tilyou over the percentage they were receiving since moving to his park from the 1901 Pan American Exposition. They took their Trip to the Moon attraction, but left behind the Giant See-Saw, which Tilyou had won from them in a coin toss. The Trip to the Moon ride simulated a moon voyage, complete with landing on a green-cheese lunar landscape peopled by midget moon-men.

A year later, in 1903, they opened Luna Park. The park was a wonder, filled with fantasy architecture: towers, minarets, colonnades, castles, spires, domes, and globes, every inch of them strung with lightbulbs. The structures had no right angles and were elaborately decorated. The park became known as the "Electric Eden" and lived up to its name, especially at night. Luna Park was an instant success, and profitable, too—the pair cleared a $600,000 profit in the first year of operation.

The park's centerpiece was the old Sea Lion Park's Shoot-the-Chutes lagoon, to which was added a magnificent tower. Luna also had a circus, the Helter-Skelter slide, the Monkey Hippodrome, the Dragon's Gorge, and live elephants and camels strolling the park grounds. Theatrical extravaganzas included the Great Naval Spectatorium, which simulated an attack on New York by the navies of the world. Luna Park evolved constantly, but Thompson's personal problems drove the park into bankruptcy in 1911, and the Luna Amusement Company, headed by Barron G. Collier, took over management of the park. Collier expanded Luna in 1920, adding the adjacent Sea Beach Railroad property. The park floundered in the 1930s and burned in a series of fires in the late 1940s. The site is now occupied by high-rises.

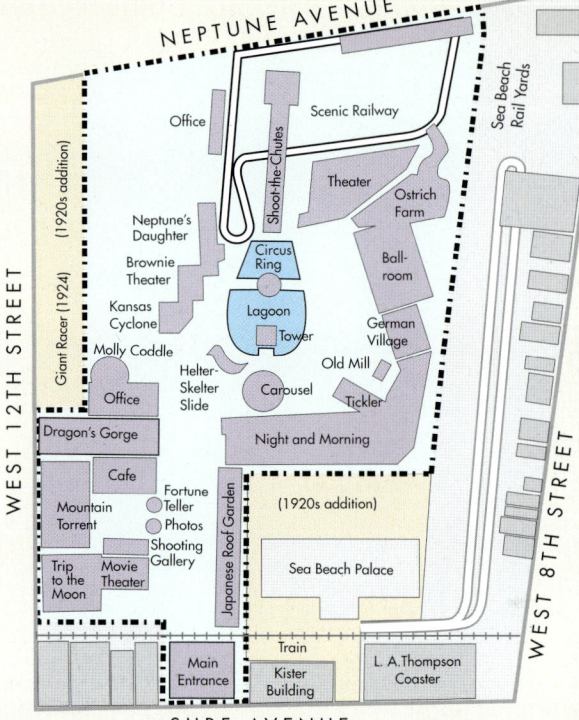

**The Electric City** Aerial view of Luna Park taken in 1921 (below). The park had just expanded and taken over the Sea Beach Palace and the frontage along West Twelfth Street where the Mile Sky Chaser would be erected. The palace would be demolished to make way for a swimming pool. Map of park, circa 1907.

**"Lit up like Luna Park"** Luna's Surf Avenue entrance, shown in 1941, had spinning pinwheels (top). The illuminated towers viewed from atop the Shoot-the-Chutes ride, circa 1904 (left). Luna's entrance burned in 1944 (above).

BUILDING A NEW INDUSTRY

# Dreamland

## 1904 – 1911

**William Reynolds**

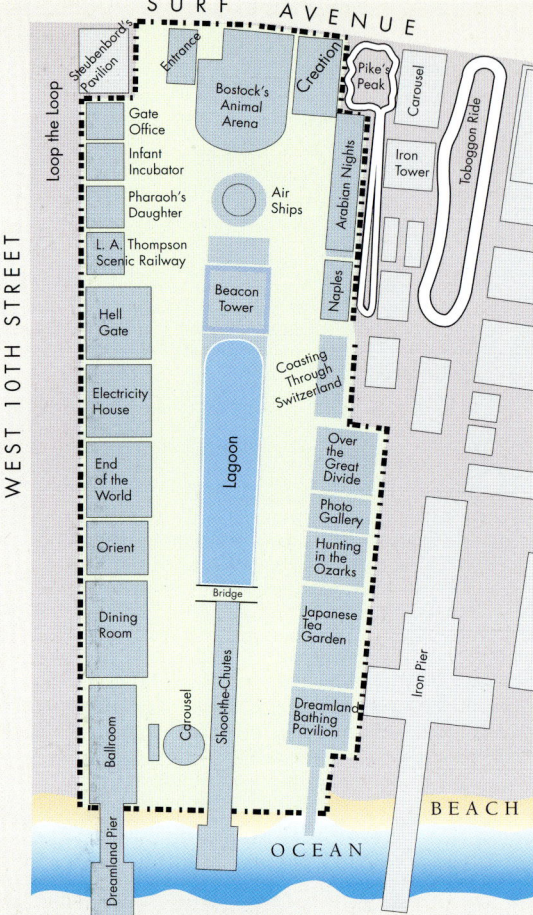

DREAMLAND WAS Coney Island's only corporate amusement park, and it suffered because of it. The park was developed in 1904 by a consortium of politicians and businesspeople led by real estate speculator Senator William Reynolds, who sought to duplicate the success of Luna Park by copying its attractions on a grander scale.

While Luna was colorful and Steeplechase was silly, Dreamland was refined, orderly, and symmetrical with every classical building painted pristine white. The park enclosed a double Shoot-the-Chutes built out over the ocean. Towering over the chute's lagoon stood the park's centerpiece: the magnificent, 375-foot-tall Beacon Tower, Coney's tallest structure. The impressive entrance had an immense statue of a nude angel whose wings shrouded the Creation biblical exhibit.

Dreamland had a lilliputian city populated by three hundred midgets, Dr. Couney's incubators for premature infants, Frank Bostock's wild animal pavilion, five scenic railways, an ocean ballroom on the Iron Pier, a Japanese tea pavilion, and a boat ride called Hell Gate.

Fighting the Flames was a bizarre theatrical production where spectators watched a tenement burn as the tenants were rescued. It was designed to be reassuring to the audience, many of whom lived in such buildings.

The park was never as popular as hoped. It went bankrupt in 1910, was sold at auction to protect the investors, then reorganized. Manager Sam Gumpertz tried to transform the park's image by repainting the buildings in bright colors and changing the Victorian feel, but the move came too late.

On the night of May 27, 1911, a fire that began in the Hell Gate ride leveled the park and adjacent properties. The old Iron Tower buckled and collapsed, and most of the park's wild animals perished. When the park's tower caught fire, the flames could be seen from Manhattan. The park was underinsured and was never rebuilt.

**The midway** The Foolish House (above) was a departure from Dreamland's classical architecture. The entrance to Creation (right). The nudity was tolerated because of the Creation exhibit's biblical theme. Map of park, circa 1907.

**Short-lived park**
Dreamland at dusk as the park's lights came on (above). The Electricity House facade (far left) was designed to resemble a dynamo. The 1911 fire that destroyed the park began in the Hell Gate ride (left).

BUILDING A NEW INDUSTRY

CHAPTER 4

# The New Coney Island

**Residential Coney**
In the early 1900s, large parcels were subdivided into lots, and summer bungalow colonies and apartment houses started to spring up. This advertisement shows an early row house. Buyers were enticed with the prospect of renting out the ground-floor apartment while living in the upstairs unit.

FOR A TEN-YEAR period, between 1900 and 1910, Coney Island was a world-class resort that catered to both the rich and the middle class. The well-to-do summered at the grand hotels of Manhattan Beach and visited the Brighton Beach Race Track. Moneyed vacationers dined at fine restaurants, attended the theater, and watched regattas at the exclusive Atlantic Yacht Club in Sea Gate.

The masses had their own world: a mechanical resort with hundreds of exciting, new innovative rides; dozens of vaudeville houses, music halls, and saloons; and three spectacular amusement parks. As New York City's population swelled with waves of immigrants, Coney played an important cultural role: it became the city's pressure valve, providing relief from stifling tenements and hard labor. The year-round population of Coney Island increased as residential development took hold in the West End. This was truly Coney's Golden Age.

One element, however, was lacking: leadership. After the great Bowery fire of 1903 destroyed the center of Coney Island, wiping out most of the tumbledown development of the McKane era, the area was rebuilt in 1904 and billed as "the New Coney Island." It was an attempt to rehabilitate Coney's "Sodom by the Sea" reputation and make the area more appealing to respectable visitors. Although George C. Tilyou was a leader in the amusement industry, he was unable to dictate overall policy for Coney Island. Instead, power was divided among the real estate interests, a few small-time mobsters, and the new political boss, Kenny "Little Corporal" Sutherland, the onetime McKane crony who had served his jail time and was back on the scene.

It was left to the Germans to keep things running smoothly. This fraternity of German businesspeople belonged to the St. Paul's Lutheran Church on West Fifth Street and Neptune Avenue. The church's pastor, the Reverend J. F. Kitzmeyer, was a reform-minded moralist, and his followers were intent on improving the moral tone of Coney Island. The group included Charles Feltman, Conrad Steubenbord, Chris Feucht, William Mangels, George Kister, Harry Meinch, Louis Stauch, and Philip Schweickert. They were a solid group of property owners and businesspeople with an interest in improving West Brighton's sordid reputation. If rumors that the state would soon outlaw horse racing were true, the exclusive hotels in Manhattan Beach and Brighton would probably close down once the racing crowd moved elsewhere. This possibility fueled fears that carpetbaggers with little

concern for the island's future would overrun Coney Island. The German reformers sought to protect their interests.

In the summer of 1910, the Germans' fears came true. Governor Charles Hughes outlawed betting, forcing the closure of the racetracks. Even more frightening to the Coney Island establishment were the renewed calls by civic groups for a public beach. In response, the business community banded together and formed a powerful organization whose mission was to protect and advance the interests of the amusement resort. It was called the Coney Island Taxpayers Alliance and was composed of the Germans and Coney's moneyed "aristocracy."

The exclusive group let it be known that "only big property owners need apply." These members were the old guard, who considered themselves legitimate businesspeople: Albert Chambers of Chambers Drugstore; Charles Feltman of Feltman's restaurant; S. E. Jackman, owner of Jackman's Thriller roller coaster; William S. Ward of Ward's Baths; William Engeman Jr., owner of the Brighton Beach Race Track; Henry Grashorn of Grashorn's Hardware; Samuel Gumpertz, manager of Dreamland; resort owner Richard Ravenhall; Luna Park's cofounder Frederick Thompson; George C. Tilyou; amusement owner Fred Kister; impresario Fred Henderson of Henderson's Theater; Louis Stauch, dancehall owner; Gilbert Stratton of Stratton's Baths; and John Cook of Cook's Baths.

The alliance was formed not only to promote business interests but, as the members put it, "to raise the moral tone of Coney Island and try to do away with low dives and places where rowdyism prevails." The members promised to fight for better police and fire protection, most of them having lost their establishments to big fires over the years. As a group, they owned more than $15 million worth of property in Coney Island.

Yet another reason for forming the organization was to protect existing property rights. Alliance members feared a move by the city to reclaim the beaches and property between the high and low waterlines along the shore. The landowners wanted to avoid a court ruling on the validity of the land grants that gave them rights to the beaches. But for this, it was already too late. Soon after the group was formed, it met its biggest challenge.

In 1910, the New York City Board of Aldermen, led by Alderman James E. Campbell, came up with a plan to build a public boardwalk. "Under the existing conditions at Coney Island today," Campbell said, "persons are prohibited from walking along the beach except patrons of various owners of the bathhouses or such other

**Bungalow colonies**
In 1912, a sprawling bungalow colony managed by Sam Gumpertz, owner of the Dreamland Circus Sideshow, sprang up on the site of the Ocean Hotel, between Ocean Parkway and Brighton Sixth Street (above and left). At Coney's West End, thirty-seven bungalow colonies were constructed at around the same time, replacing the big frame hotels as a middle-class destination.

THE NEW CONEY ISLAND 41

**Last holdout**
Orphanages and children's summer homes along the shore fought the plan for a boardwalk, fearing it would destroy their beachfronts. Saint John's Home was the only orphanage that remained after boardwalk construction was completed. The organization's summer pavilion, above, on West Twenty-eighth Street, was the future site of the Half Moon Hotel.

businesses as there are along the beachfront." He referred to a state law giving New York City the title to shoreline property located between the high and low waterlines.

The landowners sought to diffuse the issue by offering to finance a boardwalk at their own expense, rather than by having the city build it with property tax revenue or "improvement" assessments on private property. They hired publicists to promote the plan, and newspaper headlines trumpeted the idea of the private boardwalk.

Brooklyn Borough President Alfred E. Steers and Controller Prendergast called a hearing to discuss public versus private boardwalk "improvements" to be constructed along the high waterline from the Concourse at Ocean Parkway to West Thirty-seventh Street. Charles Ward, chief engineer of the Brooklyn Topographical Bureau, was asked to draw up a plan. Ward discovered that the Coney Island Taxpayers Alliance had petitioned to have the private boardwalk built two hundred feet out into the ocean. Ward was critical of the alliance plan, calling it a "landgrab" and claiming that "the businesses had a secret plan to fill in the two-hundred-foot gap and steal public land worth millions of dollars." Ward felt that the "primary and main object of a boardwalk should be to give the public an unobstructed view of ocean." The Engineers Club of New York, backing Ward, recommended construction of a boardwalk, providing it was paid for by property assessment of those who benefited most.

In July 1911, the city's chief engineer, Nelson P. Lewis, harshly criticized the alliance's private boardwalk plan, categorizing it as "selfish." "The idea of private capital building the boardwalk was not in the public interest," he said. "It should be a public improvement with the local property owners assessed accordingly." Lewis, like Ward, saw the owners' proposal as a scheme to increase the value of their property while destroying the look of the oceanfront. In his opinion, the surf would be broken, and the beach would have a "shut-in" appearance if the project went forward. He wanted the beach kept in a natural state.

That same year, a civic group called the West End Improvement League of Coney Island endorsed a popular movement for reclaiming the beach. The league drew up a plan and circulated a petition calling for free access to the beach via legally opened public streets to the ocean. The plan was enthusiastically embraced by a little-known public official named Edward Riegelmann, head of the New York City's Street Opening Bureau.

Riegelmann pushed to combine the new streets with a free boardwalk. Buying back the land for streets, however, would be quite expensive. John McKane had sold the land right down to the waterline. While many officials felt that the sales could be challenged under state law, others felt differently. "Proprietorship of the lands on the ocean bed was interesting and obscure," said one city report. "It appears that some patents from the state include submerged lands and these will have to be taken into consideration."

Another threat to private enterprise emerged in 1911 when the city-run Municipal Bathhouse opened on city property adjacent to the burned Dreamland site. The concrete bathhouse, the first public facility on the island, was inexpensive and fireproof. It proved so popular with the public that plans for expansion were made after only a year of operation. Much to the chagrin of the private bathhouse owners, the city was now competing with private enterprise. The success of the Municipal Bathhouse emboldened city officials to try to reclaim the devastated Dreamland site for a public park.

A committee consisting of Comptroller Prendergast, Board of Aldermen President John P. Mitchell, and Brooklyn Borough President Alfred Steers was appointed to look into the feasibility of the city's purchase of the Dreamland site. Several months later, the committee made its recommendations. At the end of the year, the board approved the committee's grandiose plan for purchasing not just the Dreamland site, but the entire shoreline of Coney Island, from West Fifth Street to Sea Gate and from Surf Avenue to the Atlantic Ocean. The city's proposal seemed preposterous to the landowners: it would require the demolition of every structure and all businesses south of Surf Avenue. A story in the July 27, 1911, issue of *Municipal Life* magazine described the city's plan: "All the shooting galleries, Japanese cane-and-ring stands, merry-go-rounds, pop-corn and candy kitchens, saloons, dance halls, the huge Steeplechase; in short, the entire lot of noisy, glaring, garish, entertaining shacks and places would be swept away by the laying out of a public park. But it would be worthwhile, presuming that the land could be obtained at a reasonable rate."

The board of aldermen's committee proposed a long, bucolic park laid out with bathhouses surrounded by lawns and flower beds, with tents "for the use of women and children" set up at intervals along the beach. The cost of condemning the land was $9.6 million, not including the land underwater. It was an expensive proposition. The cost of condemnation might have been reduced if the easements for the public streets to the ocean still belonged to the city. But it was discovered that McKane had even sold the rights to the street beds.

How had this happened? In 1869, the first land map of Gravesend was drawn, and a commission for planning and building

**Shoreline obstructions**
Private property owners appropriated the beachfront for their own businesses. This view shows Oriole Baths' private boardwalk, the Red Devil roller coaster, and the Kensington Baths before the Thunderbolt coaster was built above it.

**Public bathing**
The Municipal Bathhouse at West Fifth Street and Surf Avenue is shown on opening day in June of 1911. The concrete building survived the fire that had destroyed adjacent Dreamland park. Coney's first city-run bathhouse allowed the public to change, store their belongings, and shower for a set fee.

THE NEW CONEY ISLAND 43

**Dreamland in ruins**
After the Dreamland fire, many businesses reopened before the ashes were cold. Tents and shacks along Surf Avenue served beer and charged admission to view the ruins from wooden walks set up for the purpose.

streets was appointed. Five years later, the official street plan for Coney Island was filed. In the early days of street openings, the town acquired an easement for the streets but not the actual title to the land. The town's easement would lapse if not exercised within six years. Gravesend Supervisor McKane had not exercised the easement, and the town had lost the land. Now the city would have to pay exorbitant prices to buy back its own streets.

Edward Riegelmann's unenviable job was to transform the layout of Coney Island from the sprawling mining-camp jumble of John McKane's days to the modern street grid that still exists today. All obstructions and structures that occupied the beds of the planned streets would have to be removed or demolished and the owners compensated by the city.

By 1911, the street openings had begun, with West Twenty-third Street as the first street opened and extended to the high waterline. The narrow walks and alleys of central Coney that connected Surf Avenue to the beach presented a problem. Unlike the West End, the walks here were heavily developed and owned by businesspeople with the money and incentive to fight court battles. They would be difficult to reclaim as streets.

**Eden Musee**
Sam Gumpertz (above) bought P. T. Barnum's World in Wax and added it to his many attractions at the Dreamland site (right).

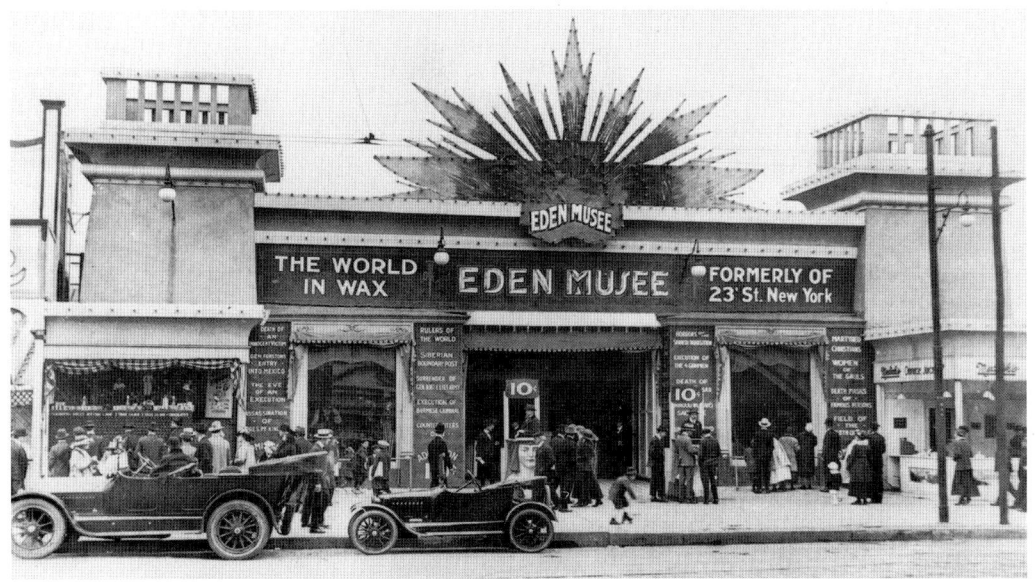

The city saw that acquiring all of the shorefront would be too expensive and decided to concentrate instead on developing the Dreamland site. The boardwalk would have to wait.

On June 3, 1911, the Parks Committee of the New York City Board of Aldermen, led by Alderman Alexander Drescher, inspected the Dreamland site and found it ideal for a park because it could easily be combined with the adjacent Municipal Bathhouse, Seaside Park, and Ocean Parkway Concourse, all of which the city already owned. The plan was presented to the full board, which gave unanimous approval.

Dreamland owner William Reynolds, sensing a business opportunity, started wheeling and dealing with the city, offering the Dreamland site along with the adjacent Balmer's Baths parcel. He initially asked $1.5 million for his parcel, but he remained cagey. "I'm not going to put any price on the property, until someone with authority comes along with an idea of buying," he said. He proposed to broker a deal combining all the adjacent burned lots into a single forty-acre tract for $3 million. "The whole business for three million is a bargain all right," he said. "All this talk about the owners trying to squeeze the city is bosh. We'll sell cheap, I'll say that much."

A syndicate of Coney Island amusement promoters, headed by ride builder William Mangels, offered Reynolds $1 million for the Dreamland site, but he turned it down. He knew how badly the city wanted the site. The city considered condemning the land, but A. R. Schorer, secretary of the Parks and Playgrounds Association, disagreed with that approach. He felt that the Dreamland property alone was not enough for the park and wanted to acquire the entire tract, not disconnected parcels. He knew it would be difficult to deal with individuals and thought the city could buy the entire tract for less by using Reynolds as the broker.

The deal soon became a scandal. Just a year before the Dreamland fire, the park property had been assessed at $375,000,

**Future park**
The 1912 land map (below) showed the compromise division of the Dreamland property: the portion along Surf Avenue would remain in private hands, and the beachfront would become a public park.

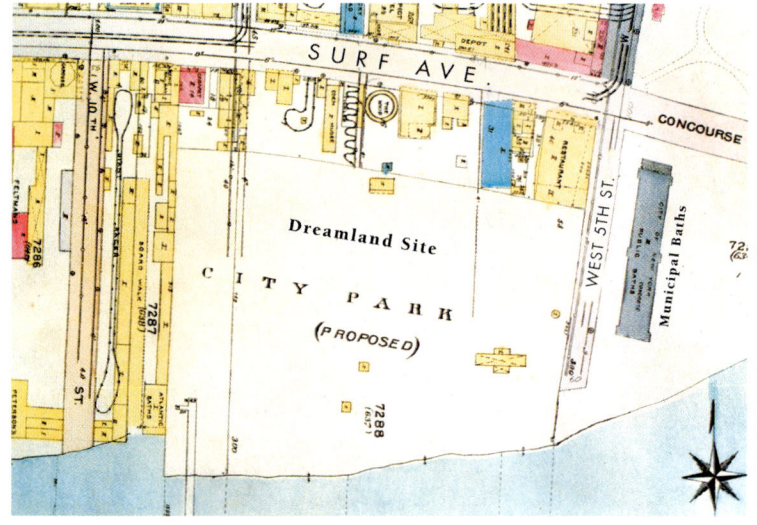

THE NEW CONEY ISLAND 45

**Shorefront development**
Looking west from West Eighth Street circa 1910. Feltman's Bavarian Village is in the foreground; the Steeplechase pier is in the distance. Property owners built out to the surf line, leaving only a sliver of beach that would disapear during high tide. The city sought to reclaim the beaches for the public.

$55,000 less than Reynolds had paid for it in 1903. A new controversy arose when Reynolds was accused of "stealing" West Eighth Street during the construction of Dreamland. When the Wonderland partnership originally planned the park, it purchased lots on either side of West Eighth Street and then built the park right over the street so fast that the city fire hydrants were not removed. No one had tried to stop the construction.

When asked about West Eighth Street, Reynolds told the *Brooklyn Eagle:* "It was never legally opened by either the town of Gravesend or the city of New York. No awards were ever made to the property owners on either side whose land was taken and no assessments were ever levied on them for improvement. The street was never paved or curbed and the old pier which we bought was built right in the center of it. As a matter of fact the street only existed on the city's map and the city possessed only a public easement on it. If the street had been allowed to divide our property, we could have had only two small parks instead of one great big one. It was in everybody's interest to close the street and to improve the property. We agreed to pay the city for any easement rights it had. A commission recommended the closing and the hearings were legal and above board."

Reynolds was also asked about Dreamland's unmetered use of city water from the fire hydrants on West Eighth Street. "Dreamland never used a bit of city water it didn't pay for," he said. "We paid $3,000 a year for water, and the chute's pond and canals were salt water."

Reynolds weathered the scandal, and on October 19, 1911, the city decided to buy the Dreamland property. The New York City

Board of Estimate voted to acquire seven acres with an option on the adjoining properties of seven and a half acres owned by the Prospect Park and Coney Island Railroad and Balmer's Baths. The New York Board of Condemnation Commissioners set a purchase price not to exceed $1 million. If Reynolds did not agree to the price, condemnation proceedings would be initiated to acquire the land. He agreed, and Coney Island was on the verge of building a new park.

**The Morey-Lott Suit**

In early 1912, Reynolds and the city were ready to proceed with the sale, but their plans were halted when a bizarre court case was filed in New York State Supreme Court by ten people who claimed to own not only the Dreamland parcel, but all of Coney Island, from Ocean Parkway to the tip of Sea Gate. The value of the land they filed suit to claim exceeded $100 million. This was the challenge that all the landowners of Coney Island had long dreaded. Whether or not the case had merit, the trial shook the island to its core. The legality of the McKane land sales and the ownership of Coney Island were about to be challenged in the state's high court.

On August 8, 1912, New York State Senator Albert A. Wray, attorney for the plaintiffs, filed the first of several claims at the county clerk's office on behalf of his clients: James E. Morey, Henry Lott, Hattie Keith, Horace and Elizabeth Pine, William Lott, Albert Cameron, Amena Hayes, James A. Brewster, and John Rubin. Wray claimed that this was the first in a series of suits he would file to regain possession of Coney Island for the rightful claimants. What was particularly frightening to the Coney Island Taxpayers Alliance was that the litigants were going after the Coney Island establishment. Wray filed ejection suits against the wealthiest business interests that owned the island's most valuable property and held titles and deeds that seemed beyond reproach. The defendants were the Feltmans;

**Contested property**
Two of the properties sought by the Morey-Lott heirs: Feltman's restaurant (above) and the Dreamland site (left).

Senator Reynolds; Prospect Park and Coney Island Railroad; and hotel owner Catherine Balmer's estate. While some dismissed it as a nuisance suit, others were worried, thinking that the misdeeds of John McKane had returned to ruin them.

On the surface, the Morey-Lott suit seemed shaky. James Morey claimed that his mother, Elizabeth Morey, "had acquired about two-thirds of Coney Island in 1883 from Elizabeth Johnson, whose unrecorded deed to the island dated back to Hendrick Johnson, who claimed he bought the entire island from the Indians in 1645 for 'a blanket, a gun and a tea kettle.'"

The case required examination of all the Gravesend grants, patents, and deeds going back to 1645. The trial would decide if Gravesend actually had title to the land that McKane had sold between 1884 and 1889. The defendants' attorney demanded a jury trial and asserted that the plaintiffs had no legal right to file together as their interests were

- Steeplechase Park
- Ravenhall Baths
- Majestic Baths
- Washington Baths
- Brooklyn Children's Aid Society
- Twenty-second Street
- Charles Woolsey subdivision
- Twenty-third Street
- New York Children's Aid Society

**Before the Boardwalk**
The two parallel lines near the beach show the path of the proposed Boardwalk. The dotted line indicates the extent of the beach after sand was pumped from offshore in 1921.

different. The case went to trial, delaying the sale of Dreamland.

As evidence came to light, the case was further complicated by the fact that New York's mayor, William J. Gaynor, had been the counsel to Gravesend during the 1880s. He was the very man who had helped engineer McKane's crooked land sales; his signature was on all the deeds. Mayor Gaynor had broken with McKane and testified against him at his 1894 trial and was now being drawn into an embarrassing fracas that would damage his reputation. Much to the chagrin of the defendants, in December 1912, the supreme court decided to hear the case. Wray declared that he had won the first round and would soon be ready for the trial.

When the trial began in December 1912, defense counsel Samuel Whitehouse launched a fierce attack against the Morey heirs, emphasizing that the deeds had gone unrecorded for more than ten years. Wray explained that Elizabeth Morey's deeds had "been kept tied up in a purse and hidden in her attic." Whitehouse then asked James Morey why his mother, who had died in 1907, had not questioned McKane's sale of the common lands when it originally took place. Whitehead declared that the plaintiffs were only looking for a payoff to drop the suit and that his clients would not pay a penny.

Wray denied that his clients were after a payoff and added that Elizabeth Morey had done all she could to assert ownership. When asked to explain, Wray said that Morey, who had lived in a bungalow on Coney Island Creek, "drove a cow around the lands she owned, and rode on Coney Island trolleys for five years without paying her fare." This ludicrous statement caused pandemonium as spectators erupted with laughter. When it became obvious that the Morey-Lott case had no merit, Wray tried various tactics to delay the trial. The case was held over until October 6, 1913, when it collapsed entirely. The plaintiffs failed to appear when the case was resumed, and the case was dismissed.

William Reynolds and the other landowners received monetary awards totaling $2 million from the board of condemnation for the Dreamland site and adjacent parcels. The public park could finally be built. Yet there was little rejoicing at the conclusion of the Morey-Lott trial. Something much bigger had come up. Another suit to reclaim Coney Island had been filed, this time by the state of New York—and this suit was legitimate. The state of New York was preparing to take back the beaches.

"State Sues to Win Back<br>
Coney Island Beach for People"<br>
—*Brooklyn Eagle*, October 24, 1912

The state's assertion of ownership came down to a line in the sand: the high waterline as it existed in 1912. Although the state owned the beach up to the high waterline, the beach was radically different in 1912 than it had been when property lines were drawn in the 1800s. Land that formerly had been upland was now submerged. Other parcels had grown in size when sand accumulated along the beaches. The court would need to settle the sticky issues of a property owner's rights versus public access to the beach.

The battle began when the state of New York filed suit against Coney Island property owners George C. Tilyou and the Steeplechase Park Company, Emilie Huber, Elizabeth Burgess Hoge, and Tilyou Realty. The suit was a test case designed to force the defendants to remove all obstructions, fences, and piers from the land between high and low waterlines. The complaint stated "that among the rights of said people [the public] in said beach, they have always had and now have the right to use the same all times for the purposes of bathing, boating and fishing and to pass over the same free from unnecessary and unreasonable obstructions and restrictions." The Steeplechase obstructions were described as "pilings, fence posts, planks, boards, dead trees, barbed wire, and other materials." The complaint demanded removal of these public nuisances. The state's case would decide the ownership of the beach and riparian rights.

When the case went to court, the landowners lost, and they lost big. The boardwalk was finally going to be built. The 1913 New York State Supreme Court ruling stated that the land in question was not private property but belonged to the state. Brooklyn Borough President Steers quickly began proceedings to reclaim twenty-seven submerged acres of waterfront to build a public park.

In 1917, after twenty years of debate, the plan for a boardwalk, a public beach, and a permanent bulkhead was formulated. Passage of a state law called the Green Bill enabled the state to cede Coney Island's underwater lands to the city of New York, provided that the city started construction within three years. The main tasks confronting the boardwalk's builders were to provide recreational use of the beach and shore protection while avoiding any interference with the rights of upland property owners.

The Coney Island Taxpayers Alliance decided to stop fighting the boardwalk. Its most influential members had died off—Charles Feltman in 1910 and George C. Tilyou in 1914. The alliance soon merged with the Coney Island Board of Trade and the Boardwalk Association. In 1924, the

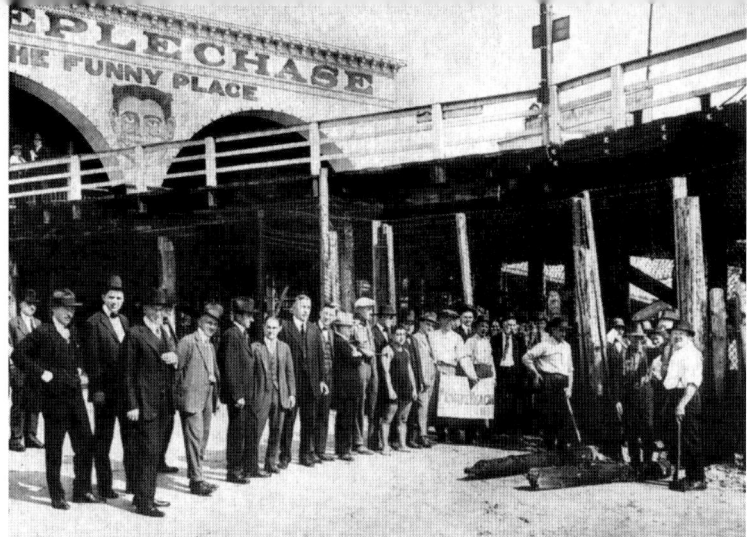

**Steeplechase obstructions**
City workers began removing obstructions at the Steeplechase pier in October 1920. The Tilyous fought to keep their pier and private beach, but lost both.

**The first stake**
Borough President Edward Riegelmann drove the first stake for the new Boardwalk on September 29, 1921.

**Opening day**
On December 24, 1922, just over a year after driving the first stake, Riegelmann, holding the rope, inaugurated the first completed section of the new Boardwalk, between Ocean Parkway and West Sixteenth Street.

group evolved into the populist and influential Coney Island Chamber of Commerce.

## Building the Boardwalk

In 1919, the city began the process of acquiring the property necessary to build the boardwalk and defining the area of assessment for projected improvements costing $4 million. The plan would also define a new high waterline three hundred feet out to sea. The cost of construction would be offset within five years by increased valuation and taxation of the upland properties. It was predicted that the creation of the new beach and boardwalk would double the value of upland properties, estimated at $15 million, in ten years. The estimates were based on the boardwalk improvements of Atlantic City.

In December 1919, the New York City Board of Estimate began hearings on the proposed design. As expected, there was much opposition from local property owners, but the project moved ahead quickly. The boardwalk had gained a staunch new ally: Edward Riegelmann, head of the Street Opening Bureau, had been elected Brooklyn borough president, and he personally began supervising all aspects of the project.

Other complicated issues arose. In June 1920, the Tilyou family petitioned to prevent condemnation of their Steeplechase pier and proposed an alternative layout designed to exclude Steeplechase Park from the city's boardwalk plan. The Tilyou Corporation offered to cede other lands it owned if the city did not take the park's pier and beachfront. In addition, the Brooklyn Chamber of Commerce strongly objected to the 65 percent assessment levied on taxpayers who would not directly benefit from the boardwalk. As expected, most of the wealthy shoreline property owners, who derived their revenues from charging the public for "bathing privileges," opposed the plan. Their rights would have to be taken into consideration. Nevertheless, the board denied the petitions of private bathhouse owners and others to be excluded from the boardwalk plan. Two months later, the Tilyous filed suit in a last-ditch attempt to retain ownership of their pier, but their request was denied. The city now had total control of the beach, and the final plans were approved.

On October 1, 1920, Riegelmann ordered the shoreline cleared of all obstructions, piers, and fences. An army of city workers stormed the beaches, attacked the obstructions, and opened the beach to the public for the first time in fifty years. Shortly thereafter, Riegelmann drove a ceremonial stake into the beach. A $1.8 million contract was awarded to Phoenix Construction Company to build the boardwalk.

Phoenix Construction worked quickly, enabling Riegelmann to open the first completed section of the boardwalk, from Ocean Parkway to West Sixteenth Street, on Christmas Eve, 1922. Riegelmann was rewarded for his heroic efforts on April 17, 1923, when the Coney Island Boardwalk was named for him. One month later, on May 15, 1923, he presided over the formal dedication.

The Coney Island Boardwalk was finished at a cost of $1.9 million. Property acquisitions had cost the city an additional $2 million, but adjacent property values had increased by $5 million. In conjunction with the project, thirteen new streets were constructed from Surf Avenue to provide access to the beach and Boardwalk. The public was thrilled with the changes, and the transformation of Coney Island was instantaneous. The completed Boardwalk was a beautiful promenade. Pedestrian traffic shifted from crowded Surf Avenue to the Boardwalk, which became Coney's new "Main Street." The surrounding streets, however, still looked like a war zone. Facades had been shaved off buildings to permit the widening

**The Concourse**
Built in 1878, the beachfront plaza at Surf Avenue and Ocean Parkway (bottom) created the elegant and respectable atmosphere that the chamber of commerce desired for the rest of Coney Island. In the center of this 1926 view are the monumental archways of the BMT elevated line crossing Ocean Parkway. The Hotel Shelburne, Brighton Beach Theater, and Reisenweber's Casino (left, from top), constructed along the Concourse, catered to the upper-class racing crowd.

**Winter strollers**
The new Boardwalk promenade replaced Surf Avenue as Coney's Main Street. This view, circa 1923, looks east from Stillwell Avenue.

of streets. Some venerable buildings had been moved or demolished. The gap between the old shoreline and the Boardwalk became the most valuable real estate on the island. These plots fronting the Boardwalk, which had once housed ramshackle bathhouses and restaurants, were soon filled with expensive and ornate terra-cotta palaces. It would take another year for the surrounding area to recover from the effects of the demolition and street construction. But recover it did, and a prosperous Coney Island soon rose from the ruins.

### A Building Boom

Once the Boardwalk was finished, the boosterism began. There were some who believed that the days of the small-time concessioner were over. For others in the business community, the goal had always been to turn Coney Island into a year-round resort with Atlantic City as the model. Now that dream was beginning to come true. In 1923, an editorial in the first issue of *Boardwalk Illustrated* made a prediction: "In buying or leasing boardwalk property it is planned to make it as much like Atlantic City as possible. All the cheap concessions, such as Coney Island is now familiar with, will be weeded out as rapidly as possible from a position on the boardwalk and the space rented to national concerns that will maintain permanent exhibits there as along the boardwalk in Atlantic City."

One of the "national concerns" mentioned was Coast Holding Company, a Manhattan corporation with a branch office in Coney Island on West Tenth Street and the

Boardwalk. Coast Holding began managing some of the biggest attractions and bathhouses: Giant Racer roller coaster, Red Devil roller coaster, Giant Racer Baths, Bushman Baths, Red Devil Kensington Baths, Majestic Baths, Hahn Baths, and Roosevelt Baths. Coast Holding also leased out commercial space along the Boardwalk from Tenth Street to Thirty-seventh Street.

It seemed that Coney was going corporate, and small entrepreneurs and the family-run businesses were on the way out. In 1923, Coast Holding offered leases of expensive Boardwalk units with 250 to 25,000 square feet of concession space. Looking ahead, an article in the 1923 *Boardwalk* stated that "various dummy corporations have been formed to buy some of the additional parcels, it is reported, but all are acting for the same group of financiers. Ultimately, it is predicted, these various holding companies would be consolidated into one corporation, and the property will be managed as one enterprise."

Not wanting to erase Coney's past altogether, the new developers discussed plans to preserve some of the "mechanical fun." They wanted to acknowledge Coney's reputation as the home of every mechanical device invented in the amusement industry, from roller coasters to the Wonder Wheel. *Boardwalk* magazine proclaimed: "While the Beach Front will gradually take on a more imposing and business-like atmosphere—the home of theaters, large hotels, auditoriums, and shops—the back streets would still provide mechanical thrills, to provide loud laughter and relaxation from office, shop and factory." The Boardwalk was finished, and times were good. It was in this optimistic atmosphere that the Coney Island Chamber of Commerce was formed.

The chamber of commerce was founded on December 13, 1923, with the stated purpose of "developing Coney Island on a larger and broader scale." The chamber's first meeting took place at the Coast Holding Company offices on the Boardwalk at West Tenth Street. Edward Tilyou, son of Steeplechase Park founder George C. Tilyou, was its first president; William Ward, president of the Coney Island Bank, was vice president; Leslie Stratton, owner of the *Coney Island Times,* was secretary; Alfred Feltman, owner of Feltman's restaurant, was treasurer.

The Coney Island Chamber of Commerce was a powerful new organization with

**Coveted site**
Boardwalk real estate quickly became the most valuable property in Coney Island. The new Ward's Baths building at West Twelfth Street had elegant retail stores. To the right of Ward's is Feltmans and the Giant Racer roller coaster.

**Hot dog kiosk**
The new Feltman's Boardwalk restaurant opened in 1923. Behind it is the Wonder Wheel.

a bright future. The chamber operated out of the Tilyous' Atlantic Amusement Company headquarters in the post office building at Steeplechase Park before moving to an office in William Ward's new Coney Island Bank building on West Twelfth Street.

A month after the chamber's founding, when New York City was chosen to host the 1924 Democratic National Convention, Tilyou promised that Coney Island "will do its part in the way of providing entertainment for the visitors." At a packed public meeting at P.S. 80, Tilyou declared a "Coney Island Day." Convention delegates would be escorted from their Manhattan hotels by various chamber officials and taken to Coney by automobile and ferryboat to enjoy clambakes, dancing, and a beauty contest on the new beach and Boardwalk.

The chamber also launched an expensive publicity campaign. Ads in national magazines and newspapers announced plans for new year-round theaters, a $200,000 makeover of Henderson's Music Hall, and a variety of quality developments along the Boardwalk, including an opulent Child's Restaurant and Stauch's Baths building.

Coney Island became flush with cash in 1924, when 120 property owners finally received their condemnation settlements for parcels taken by the city for the streets and Boardwalk. The total came to $6 million, the largest condemnation settlement in the city's history up to that point. Coincidentally, many recipients of this largesse were members of the new chamber of commerce. Joe Sartori and Joe Balzarini of Ravenhall Baths received $407,000; Theodore Kramer and the Tilyous, $764,000; the Henderson estate, $610,000; Albert Buschman, $110,000; Gilbert Stratton, $355,000; roller coaster owner Stephen Jackman, $146,000; and the Feltmans, $93,000. Old-timers had much to celebrate: all of the awards were given for land that the city would have owned had it not been for John McKane's corruption.

With the new money came exciting new projects. In March 1924, the Coney Island Improvement Company announced the building of a new $1.2 million Chanin Theater at Stillwell and Surf Avenues. The same month, the Tilyous revealed plans for a new twenty-five-hundred-seat RKO Keith vaudeville theater, built of terra-cotta and granite in the Italian renaissance style. William Ward's Coney Island Bank opened a new $300,000 headquarters at West Twelfth Street and Surf Avenue. In 1925, with the support of the Tilyou family, Our Lady of Solace began construction of an imposing new building with a soaring bell tower on Mermaid Avenue.

Also in 1925, a new open-air boxing stadium rose on vacant railroad property behind the Culver Depot, at West Fifth Street. The facility was to be operated year-round, with a swimming pool in summer and an ice-skating rink in winter. The land, leased for twenty-nine years at $500,000 per year, would use the new parking concession being built on the former site of Dreamland. The Feltmans planned to keep their restaurant and carousel open year-round, hoping to take advantage of an influx of winter visitors.

Property owners were soon surprised to learn that the Boardwalk Improvement Company, a subsidiary of the United Cigar Company, had signed a forty-three-year, $6 million lease for the Stauch's Baths property. No one had ever seen leases this high before. They proved that Coney Island was well on the way to competing with Atlantic City. The one missing element was a world-class hotel, but not for long. The Sea Gate Hotel and Baths Corporation announced plans to build a $1 million, twelve-story, three-hundred-room hotel at West Twenty-fifth Street and Surf Avenue, to be completed by April 1925.

**Live from Coney Island**

The inaugural dinner of the Coney Island Chamber of Commerce was planned to take place on Tuesday, February 26, 1924, at the Shelburne Hotel at Ocean Parkway and Seaside Park. The main speaker would be the Boardwalk's builder, Brooklyn Borough President Edward Riegelmann. The subject of his speech was "The Story of Coney Island." What made the event monumental was that the speech would be broadcast live to a national audience over radio station WEAF. Radio was still in its infancy, and the event was a coup. Newspaper stories described the upcoming event. A *New York American* article stated, "As the borough president delivers his address, his voice will not be confined to the guests at the banquet, but his voice will be carried through the air via radio throughout the entire universe."

The dinner and radio show began at 9:45 P.M. with Chamber President Edward Tilyou introducing Charles Craig, city comptroller. Craig was a short, balding, cigar-chomping politician, chosen as the warm-up speaker for Riegelmann. He was an unsophisticated man, and what he blurted into the airwaves gave the audience indigestion. Taking the microphone and speaking

**West End carousel**
The glass-enclosed Weber's Carousel (foreground), owned by Jimmy Landis, was at the Boardwalk at West Twenty-seventh Street. The Boardwalk amusements, including bathhouses, restaurants, nightclubs, swimming pools, and hotels, once stretched from Ocean Parkway to West Thirty-seventh Street.

# Telling the World

**On the air**
On February 26, 1924, Brooklyn Borough President Edward Riegelmann gave a radio address extolling the virtues of Coney Island, calling it "the playground of the world."

in a gravelly voice, Craig told a confused audience of nationwide listeners the story of Coney Island's latest land dispute. He said that Coney Island land titles were clouded and claimed that New York City was going to confiscate the property of taxpaying landowners along Neptune Avenue. Thanks to the boorish Craig, a local land dispute was suddenly transformed into national news.

A flustered Riegelmann jumped up and grabbed the microphone from Craig. Taking issue with Craig's statement, he said that the city would not be taking anyone's land and promised his personal assistance to anyone with a problem. He then launched into a story about the history of Coney and announced new projects, new streets, a new pier, and a Boardwalk extension.

Riegelmann regained his composure and finally began his prepared speech: "We want to make Coney Island what it is known to be: The playground of the World. I think that the new Coney Island presents a picture bright as any spot in the city of New York. I want to congratulate the businessmen of Coney Island for what they have done for Coney Island. . . . I don't mean the fellow who comes down here in his fly-by-night way trying to get the edge on the other fellows and always trying to put over some fake or bunco game. I don't mean the fellow who travels around with the motto in his hat 'Never give a sucker an even break.' I speak of the businessman who has stood by Coney Island, year in, year out and made Coney Island what it is today, a decent clean healthy spot for recreation where a man can bring his wife and children and feel satisfied that they will not see anything out of the way."

## Coney's Roaring Twenties

The borough president's predictions came true. Coney Island grew at an astounding rate, and the 1920s would prove to be a golden decade for the outdoor amusement industry as well as for the fledgling winter resort business. The chamber of commerce boosters were confident that Coney Island would soon eclipse Atlantic City as the premier East Coast resort.

Transportation to the island had improved considerably since 1898, when the first direct Manhattan to Coney Island rail service had opened on the Sea Beach Line. In 1900, the four main rail lines into the island were combined into the Brooklyn Rapid Transit Company, and by 1921, all the lines had been routed into the new Stillwell Avenue terminal.

Opening in 1920, the Wonder Wheel became the first new addition to the skyline, followed by five new roller coasters. First was the Big Dipper, built in 1921 by the L. A.

**Chamber portrait**
The founding members of the chamber of commerce posed for a photograph in 1924. Top row, left to right: A. Garmise, William Mangels, Morris Goldberg, William Meinch, Alexander Von Wagner, John Ryan, Philip Winorsky, Edward Tilyou, Charles Feltman, Louis Cargulia, Charles Schiffman, and William Avitable. Bottom row: left to right: Stephen Barrera, Charles L. Feltman, Joseph Sartori, William Ward, Jennie McMahon, Mary Dillon, Agnes Stephenson, Herman Bergoffen, and Philip Nash.

Thompson Company. In 1924, the Mile Sky Chaser, the world's longest roller coaster, opened in Luna Park, running a hilly course from Surf Avenue up West Twelfth Street, along Neptune Avenue to West Eighth Street, and back again.

In 1924, the Econopoly's Baths site on Stillwell Avenue was purchased by the L. A. Thompson Company's Frank Darling, who later built an extremely narrow coaster called the Bobs, which was renamed the Tornado in 1929. George Moran bought the Kensington Hotel in 1925 and above it built the Thunderbolt roller coaster. Two years later, the Cyclone roller coaster was erected on the site of the Giant Racer by the Rosenthal Brothers. In early 1929, the Rosenthals bought the Big Dipper, with plans to demolish it and build Coney's biggest coaster on the site.

By the late 1920s, Coney Island had been transformed. An imposing row of monumental structures had risen along the north side of Surf Avenue, including the opulent Loews and RKO Tilyou Theaters and the sprawling new, multilevel Stillwell Avenue Subway Terminal. On the south side of Surf Avenue, the claustrophobic alleyways leading to the ocean had been carved into wide streets that ran straight to the beach and Boardwalk. Thompson's Walk became West Twelfth Street, Bushman's Walk became West Fifteenth Street, and Tilyou's Walk became West Sixteenth Street. The biggest change was the widening of Stratton Walk into the broad expanse of Stillwell Avenue, complete with two rows of much-needed parking down the center. The intersection of Stillwell Avenue and Surf Avenue became known as the Times Square of Coney Island.

The construction boom spread to the West End, where dozens of new residential apartment buildings were rising, including four classy elevator buildings, along with several new banks, synagogues, and supermarkets to serve the new residents. Even Manhattan Beach, which had lost the exclusive Oriental and Manhattan Beach Hotels when the racetracks closed, was attracting fun seekers to Joseph Day's new Manhattan Beach Baths and band shell.

The one structure that defined the New Coney Island more than anything else was the Half Moon Hotel. The hotel was the final piece of the puzzle, the key to converting Coney Island into a year-round resort. The Half Moon Hotel was big—the largest building in Coney Island. Described as being

# Coney Island Souvenirs

**T**HE BACKDROPS and the fashions changed, but the sly, knowing smiles were always the same. They said, "We're here to have fun!" Coney had hundreds of portrait studios producing tintypes, framed souvenirs, postcards, cartes de viste, and humorous cutouts. There was even a "shoot-a-photo" gallery (right) that snapped your picture when you hit the target.

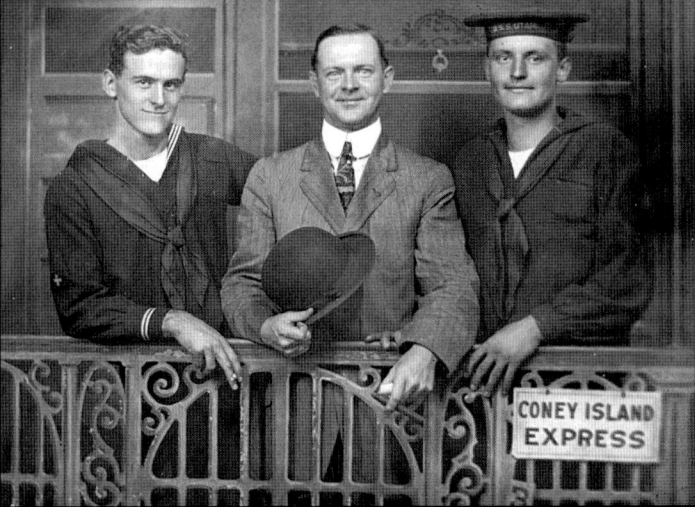

**The new Culver Plaza, circa 1927**

1. Culver depot
2. Boxing stadium
3. Dreamland parking facility
4. Stubbman Carousel
5. Hotel Eleanor
6. Dreamland Circus Sideshow
7. Big Dipper
8. Hotel Sagamore
9. Ben Hur Race
10. Sixtieth Precinct
11. L. A. Thompson Scenic Railway
12. Luna Park
13. Feltmans
14. West Eighth Street elevated station
15. Prospect Hotel

fourteen stories, it was actually 225 feet tall, the equivalent of twenty-two stories. The hotel's tower was topped by a colorful mosaic-sheathed dome with a golden weather vane in the shape of Henry Hudson's ship, the *Half Moon*. The building was designed by George B. Post and Sons and constructed by Cauldwell-Wingate Builders at a cost of $3 million. It was scheduled to open in 1927.

The Half Moon was the first project financed by the Coney Island Chamber of Commerce. Before construction even started, the hotel received publicity from a major politician. New York Governor Alfred "Al" Smith planned to move from his home in Sea Gate to an eleventh-floor suite that would serve as his summer home and the state executive office for the season.

The idea for the hotel had first been proposed at a 1923 chamber meeting by Morris Goldberg, inventor and manufacturer of the Skee Ball game. Two years later, the chamber founded the Coney Island Hotel Corporation, with banker William J. Ward as president.

Ward quickly raised $197,000 in pledges from the local business community to start the hotel. George Post was hired as the architect, and one month later, in April 1925, the corporation began to issue stock to investors. An oceanfront site at West Twenty-ninth Street and the Boardwalk was chosen, and ground was broken for the Half Moon.

In the *Coney Island Times* of April 30, 1927, William Ward made a glowing prediction: "If the picture in my mind's horizon becomes true, Coney Island's Boardwalk will be studded with hotels, similar to the Half Moon, within the next decade. It takes no great vision to paint such a picture. This resort caters to more than 50,000,000 persons annually. It offers visitors attractions not found in the average metropolis. What city in the United States offers its public a playground such as Coney Island? Coney Island's future is roseate. It is a sage investment for capital. Property here is ever rising in value. Buildings of an older day are making way for structures of stone, brick, concrete and steel."

Real estate agent Herman Bergoffen, interviewed in his spacious office in the Loews Theater building, predicted in the *Coney Island Times* that Coney Island was "ripe for rapid developments." "The Half Moon serves as a beacon for builders and investors," he said. "More hotels and apartment houses are certainty of the immediate future."

In truth, the hotel, which opened in 1927, was a house of cards, sited in a poor location and vulnerable to the whims of the economy. If not for the Great Depression, the hotel might have had a chance. The person most responsible for locating the hotel nearly a mile from the center of the Coney Island amusement area was a man who should have known better: developer William "Willie" Avitable.

Avitable was a proponent of the concept of building at the outer fringes of a region to spur development of the area in between. He also had ulterior motives in the choice of the hotel's location. Avitable had developed the West End by building dozens of the ubiquitous three-story buff-brick row houses on Mermaid Avenue and the side streets that became known as "Avitables." He also owned a large parcel on Surf Avenue adjacent to the hotel site on which he would build two large apartment houses as soon as the Half Moon Hotel opened. Some chamber members became angry with him because they had been led to believe the land would be used for a park. Instead, the hotel's patrons looked out at the clotheslines of the apartment tenants.

Coney Island reached an apex in 1928. Summertime resident Governor Al Smith was nominated as the Democratic candidate for president. If Smith were elected president, Coney Island would have a chance to become a center of power, and Sea Gate would become the summer home of the president of the United States.

A year later, it all came to an abrupt end. The stock market crashed, and orders for new amusements were canceled. Smith lost the election, ending the fantasy of a Coney

**Willie Avitable**
In the 1920s, Avitable was the largest residential developer in the West End.

**Coney's Times Square**
Loews Theater and the multilevel subway terminal at Stillwell and Surf Avenues were at the heart of the new Coney Island.

## The Myth of Henry Hudson

THE HALF MOON HOTEL was named for Henry Hudson's ship. Many believe that Hudson landed on Coney Island in 1609. But the surviving log of Hudson's first mate, Robert Juet (Hudson's log was destroyed by the British), suggests that the explorer, who was sailing north, anchored off Sandy Hook, New Jersey, not Coney Island. The recorded longitude and latitude of the anchorage indicate that the ship was at Sandy Hook, and the log's description of the shoreline matches the nearby New Jersey Highlands. Early explorers approached New York by hugging the New Jersey shoreline to avoid the East Bank Shoal near Coney Island. The deep, sheltered waters off Sandy Hook offered the logical first anchorage for Hudson and his crew.

**Fantasy landing**
Hudson's crew checks in.

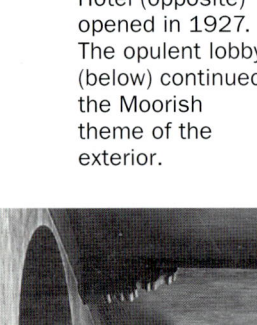

**Luxury hotel**
The Half Moon Hotel (opposite) opened in 1927. The opulent lobby (below) continued the Moorish theme of the exterior.

Island White House. The building boom was over, and the money dried up. Willie Avitable fled to Europe, and his investors lost everything. He became a symbol of broken dreams and empty bank accounts.

The Half Moon was the first and last Boardwalk hotel built in Coney Island. Stranded at the West End, the financially strapped hotel never attracted a Manhattan crowd. Local businesspeople kept suites there, but the dream of a grand resort was over. Outside capital never came back to Coney, and no new rides were built until the 1940s. The big holding companies went bankrupt, and control of the bathhouses returned to the small-timers.

Coney Island's Roaring Twenties had been shaped by three powerful forces: the business community, local politicians, and local gangsters. On the political front, Kenny Sutherland, Coney Island's political boss, lost power after the press floated rumors that he had received kickbacks from developers during construction of the Boardwalk. Sutherland decided to let things cool down and took a patronage job as clerk to the supreme court.

The ten-year reign over rackets and bootlegging in Coney Island by crime boss Francesco "Frankie Yale" Uale ended when the mobster was gunned down on July 21, 1928. Yale had been a fixture, and his murder triggered a bloodbath that left eight local gangsters dead. After the 1933 repeal of the Volstead Act, which had banned the sale of alcohol in 1920, Coney lost its appeal to organized crime. The end of Prohibition stopped the flow of easy money into Coney Island, and Yale's successor, "Little Augie" Carfano, never commanded the respect or influence that Yale had. After the ouster of corrupt New York Mayor Jimmy Walker in 1932, Fiorello La Guardia was elected on a reform ticket. No longer with strong leaders, Coney became easy prey for an ambitious man named Robert Moses.

THE NEW CONEY ISLAND

CHAPTER 5

# The Nickel Empire

**On parade**
Mayor Fiorello La Guardia, riding in a flower-covered float, led the Coney Island Mardi Gras in 1936. Two years later, the mayor ceded control of Coney Island to Parks Commissioner Robert Moses.

**Grab joint**
Nathan Handwerker's famous five-cent frankfurters were popular during the Depression.

**R**OBERT MOSES hated what the tyrannical John McKane had done to Coney Island. The two men had similarities, however: a thirst for absolute power and dictatorial tendencies. The main difference between them was that Moses did not seek personal fortune when he reclaimed the lands of Coney Island. Instead, he sought to control Coney's destiny.

Robert Moses was appointed Commissioner of the New York City Department of Parks in 1934 under Mayor Fiorello La Guardia and wasted no time before setting his sights on Coney Island. La Guardia and Moses immediately disagreed over the fate of a twenty-five-acre tract of landfill on Coney Island Creek. Moses wanted the land for a public park, but the mayor had already promised the site to the board of education to build a junior high school.

The power struggle became public knowledge, and local newspapers played up the rift. When the mayor told the press that the land would be the ideal site for a school, the reporter checked with Moses, who became furious. "I thought this administration wanted playgrounds," Moses said. "Either they do or they don't." Moses effectively attacked his boss through the press, and the embarrassed mayor learned early on not to tangle with him in public.

Moses demanded that La Guardia hand over the Coney Island parcel to the New York City Sinking Fund Commission, the agency that held title to all city-owned land. Deputy Mayor Douglas Matthewson, the fund's legal adviser, told Moses that his demand for the transfer of board of education land to the Parks Department was illegal. Moses attacked Matthewson viciously and personally in the press, forcing him to back down and transfer the parcel.

Moses's tactic of intimidation worked. In March 1935, the Sinking Fund Commission gave the property—a large parcel on Neptune Avenue between West Twenty-fifth Street and West Thirty-first Street—to the

Parks Department. Moses outlined his ambitious plans: a dance pavilion; a roller-skating rink; tennis courts that could be used as a winter ice-skating rink; a wharf for motorboats and canoes; handball courts; children's playgrounds; an athletic field for baseball, football, and soccer; and a wide promenade fronting Gravesend Bay.

Local civic groups were delighted with the plan. The Coney Island Landowners Association felt that the development would improve their property values. The project was named Kaiser Park for Leon Kaiser, former principal of Coney Island's P.S. 188. The park was eventually completed on a much smaller scale than Moses had proposed, and a corner of it was allotted for Mark Twain Junior High School. By then, Moses had moved on to bigger things.

Throughout the Great Depression, Coney Island remained popular with the public. The amusement area boasted sixty bathhouses, thirteen carousels, eleven roller coasters, two hundred restaurants, and more than five hundred small, independent businesses. Perhaps the most symbolic change during the 1930s was the rise of Nathan's Famous and the decline of Feltman's restaurant. Nathan's was a nickel "grab-joint," and Feltman's was a sit-down restaurant with tablecloths. Cheap thrills were replacing the refined entertainment proposals of the 1920s. Sideshows and strip joints became popular forms of entertainment.

*Fortune* magazine analyzed the business of Coney Island in its August 1938 issue and declared it the "Empire of the Nickel." "[Coney Island] retains an intensely jealous civic consciousness and a chamber of commerce all its own," the anonymously written article stated. "The community that the chamber represents, in theory at least, is a city of 100,000 that swells in summer to 200,000 and is divided into two parts by a Main Street known as Surf Avenue. To the north is the year-round Coney Island of the commuters—a section of drab rooming houses and inferior residences, tapering off in a blighted area along the polluted waters of Gravesend Bay and what is left of Coney Island Creek. On both sides of the avenue itself, and in the single long strip of land to the south, that ends at the Boardwalk and the beach, is concentrated the Coney Island that lives only four months out of the year."

Coney Island's amusement area had always been depression-proof and had weathered bad times before. But by the end of the 1930s, business was hurting. The reason was not the economy, but the harassment of the business community by Robert Moses, whose Parks Department had assumed control of the Coney Island beach and Boardwalk.

## The Robert Moses Takeover

In 1937, the New York City Charter was altered to transfer jurisdiction of Coney Island's beach and Boardwalk from the Brooklyn borough president to the city's Parks Department. Park Commissioner Moses then presented to Mayor La Guardia an elaborately illustrated report dated November 30, 1937, with an optimistic-sounding title, *The Improvement of Coney Island, Rockaway and South Beaches*. The commissioner proposed radical changes: "The history of the beach at Coney Island is a sad

**Coney's most destructive fire**
On July 13, 1932, forty-mile-per-hour winds drove a fire that started on the Boardwalk and burned four square blocks from West Twenty-first to West Twenty-fifth Streets. The blaze resulted in $5 million in damages and left more than a thousand people homeless. It was the only fire ever to jump Surf Avenue. The brick Childs Restaurant building served as a firebreak and saved the amusement area to the east.

**Sideshow life**
Performers from the Dreamland Circus Sideshow gathered at Stauch's (right). In his attempts to improve Coney Island, Robert Moses tried to ban loudspeakers from the Boardwalk and wanted to prohibit strip shows and ballyhoo. Many sideshow performers (below) made a good living, but in the 1950s, well-meaning reformers banned shows that featured people with deformities.

**Boston Hotel**
Dave Rosen's sideshow (right) in the Boston Hotel at Surf Avenue and West Twelfth Street.

commentary on the lack of foresight of the citizens. . . . The lands and lands under water originally belonged to the old town of Gravesend, and they were sold off about the year 1878. . . . A review of the acquisition of land by the city, and construction of improvements in Coney Island, indicates that the public authorities were actuated more by a desire to please the large property owners than to provide proper accommodations for the public. The boardwalk was constructed too near the water. . . . There is no use bemoaning the end of the old Coney Island fabled in song and story. The important thing is not to proceed in the mistaken belief that it can be revived. There must be a new and very different resort established in its place. . . . There must be more land in public ownership, less overcrowding, stricter enforcement of ordinances and rules . . . less mechanical noise-making and amusement devices and side shows, and a more orderly growth of year-round residents, and an increasing respect for permanent, as distinguished from temporary values. . . . This will not be accomplished overnight, but only over a period of several years."

Moses assumed control of the Boardwalk and beaches on January 1, 1938, ten years after he had built the Jones Beach resort on Long Island. His desire to develop a similarly sterile resort at Coney Island set the stage for a destructive pattern of development that would cause problems for Coney Island over the next sixty years. His pathological dislike of the Coney Island amusement community was obvious and his intentions blatant. His first acts were harassment: banning new advertising along the Boardwalk, prohibiting the use of loudspeakers near the beach, and putting up large signs that spelled out his rules and regulations.

The next phase of his plan was the realignment of the Boardwalk between Stillwell Avenue and Ocean Parkway. Moses complained that the beach had eroded, but rather than pursue the obvious solution of expanding the beach, he proposed moving the Boardwalk four hundred feet inland and demolishing the beautiful new buildings along that section of the Boardwalk. The budget for his plan, including property condemnation and reconstruction, was a staggering $5.5 million. Beach expansion would have cost a fraction of that figure.

Although the business community protested moving the Boardwalk, Moses got his way. In 1941, it was relocated inland and extended to the border of Manhattan Beach. The change proved detrimental to the amusement area in many ways: Seaside Park was reduced by several acres when Surf Avenue had to be realigned, half of the Municipal Bathhouse was demolished, and the public park on the Dreamland site was reduced to a mere sliver. The Boardwalk property owners, fearful of Moses and strapped for cash, replaced their elegant Boardwalk buildings with lesser structures.

Moses further accelerated Coney Island's process of decay by intimidating property owners. Believing that more condemnations were inevitable, many were reluctant to invest in property that might be taken by the government for urban renewal. Moses proceeded to squeeze the amusement area on its eastern and western flanks. He planned a playground and Parks Department headquarters on the West Twenty-seventh Street site of McLochlin's Baths, a site he obtained through tax liens. At the eastern end, he planned a new public park for the old Dreamland site.

On February 6, 1941, Moses announced plans to move the New York Aquarium from its historic Battery Park home inside Castle Clinton—an 1812 fort that Moses wanted to demolish—to the Bronx Zoo. The Aquarium was popular, logging 2.5 million visitors per year, and Mayor La Guardia thought the Bronx Zoo would be too inaccessible for the general public and vetoed the move. Moses was angered by the mayor's veto and decided to banish the Aquarium to Coney Island's old Dreamland site, a combination of public parkland and private property fronting Surf

**The greatest ride**
Few new rides came to Coney during the Depression. Then, in 1941, the Parachute Jump was moved to Steeplechase Park from the 1939–40 New York World's Fair. The ride was the most exciting ever to hit the island.

**Luna Park site**
When the twenty-acre Luna Park site, vacant since the 1946 fire, was declared a Title I urban renewal zone in the 1950s, Coney's amusement area was reduced by a third.

THE NICKEL EMPIRE

# Chuck Steen and the Parachute Elite

THE OPERATORS of the 250-foot-tall Parachute Jump, the biggest, most exciting ride ever to hit Coney Island, were considered the elite of Coney's ride handlers. They were younger and stronger than the other Steeplechase Park employees, wore jumpsuits with images of parachutes stenciled on the back, and never worked on the park's other rides. "We were snobs," said Leonard "Chuck" Steen, the ride's chief mechanic until 1953. "We didn't bother with anybody else. All the fellas at the jump were young because it was a very strenuous job. I used to lift weights, and the chute was tailor-made for me."

Steen's job involved a lot of climbing and sometimes "riding the hook": clinging to the small mechanism that hauled the parachutes to the top. Steen even met his wife while working there. "There was a blower at the chute and that's when I first saw my wife. She'd just gotten out of high school and didn't know about the ramp blower. When her skirt went up, I said, 'That's a pretty nice pair of legs there.'"

Chuck Steen was sixteen years old in 1941, when the Parachute Jump was installed at Steeplechase Park. He was at the beach and wandered over to watch the steelworkers rig a jib beam to raise the steel. One of the riggers asked him to buy them coffee. "I was just a poor kid, and they gave me some money and told me what they wanted," he said. "They gave me a dollar tip—Jesus, to a sixteen-year-old that dollar was a big thing. So every day I bought them coffee." As the structure began to rise, the workers didn't have time to come down, so Steen climbed up the tower to deliver the coffee. When the tower was topped off, he stayed and became the jump's chief mechanic.

There were changes when the Parachute Jump was moved to the Boardwalk.

**Life at the top** A young Chuck Steen hangs cables 250 feet above the beach and Boardwalk.

The big Lifesaver candy advertisement was ordered removed by Park Commissioner Robert Moses, who didn't want advertisements along the Boardwalk. The parachutes had to be modified to withstand Coney Island's strong ocean breezes. "The wind from the ocean would tip each chute," Steen said, "so we had to stabilize it by adding four cables to hold the ring surrounding it. This kept the chute semi-round so it caught the wind and came down gently. On really windy days we had to shut the jump down, because the damn chutes wouldn't inflate.

"There were twelve chutes but we only operated ten. Everybody wanted to ride the ones up front near the ocean so the people on the Boardwalk could see how brave they were. The fare would increase on weekends, and our top ticket was fifty cents. Jimmy Onorato, the manager of Steeplechase, would come out and look at the crowd, and if it was small he'd say, 'Hmm, thirty-five cents.' Then, if the crowd got really big, he'd come out and say, 'Good crowd. Fifty cents.' We kept raising or dropping the fare depending on the crowd."

Getting stuck or tangled in the cables was one of the biggest fears for parachute riders. "You'd hear all kinds of nonsense from people: 'Oh, I got stuck on the Parachute Jump.' But there were only a few times that it actually got stuck. Once was during the war, when some sailor must have had his girlfriend under the Boardwalk doing whatever sailors do. They took a ride, and in order to get rid of her panties, he threw them, and unfortunately the damned wind wrapped the panties around the cables and jammed the chute.

"That was a job to get them down—let me tell you, it was quite a process. When a chute was stuck, the seat was no longer horizontal, but was at a very extreme angle. What we'd do was loosen the cable's turnbuckle at the very bottom and then go up on top and unfasten a shackle to get some slack in the cable holding the chute, and then a couple of us would pull in a couple of inches of the cable to free it up. There was a box up on top near the flagpole where a six-hundred-foot rope was kept. We'd get the rope, tie it onto the end of the cable, put the rope over a beam, and lower the whole cable down, bringing the chute down with it.

"Another funny thing was that we had to keep spare cushions because women, and sometimes men, would piss in their pants. That's the truth! The women had to take their shoes off, because in those days, all the girls wore penny loafers, and you didn't want to get hit in the head with a loafer after it came off 250 feet up in the air."

Steen and his coworkers came up with an advertising gimmick. "If we weren't doing much business, and two girls came on and they looked like screamers, we would send them up about two hundred feet and turn the motor off. If there were a thousand people in Coney Island, in ten or fifteen minutes we had a thousand people in front of the chute while these girls were screaming their bloody heads off. That's how we generated our business. There were times when we put two girls

**Ready for action**
Parachute operators prepare for the day's influx of riders.

on and turned off the motors, and they'd just sit there. Well, that was no fun, so we'd let them down and wait till two more came in that were screamers.

"If you were a kid you had to ride up with one of the operators. When we first opened up, we didn't realize that. One day we put some little kids on, and it was pretty windy. We had a hell of a job getting the chute back down, because the kids were so light. Eventually the chute came down. But it would come down and then sort of hover around and wouldn't free-fall. So we decided not to let kids ride alone. The reason we didn't let single people ride alone was that we were always afraid of a jumper, a suicide. Even if you were a man, an operator went with you. If you were a girl or one or two

**Parachute crew** The ride handlers were much younger than most Steeplechase Park employees. Manager Jimmy Onorato used them to break up fights in the park's ballroom. George C. Tilyou III, grandson of the park's founder, is at far left.

**Daredevils** Chuck Steen (above), standing on top of the jump, holds the ball-peen hammer he used to check the bolts on the structure. He carried this photo in his wallet for fifty years. A mechanic (left) rides the hook to the top.

light kids, an operator went with you. We never had injuries, and only one guy ever tried to sue us. He allegedly dislocated his shoulder, and naturally we zipped him into Larry the insurance agent, who took all the information. About two weeks later Larry came back out and said, 'You know, the guy's a real faker. He's dislocated his shoulder in every place you can imagine all over New York.'

"The closest we came to an accident was with two sailors. By god, I thought they were dead. We were having trouble maintaining everything during the war, and we had two sailors come on and the damn chute almost came apart. I was standing with Jimmy Onorato and we were talking and I heard this sound—if you can visualize wheels turning too fast, like a *zzzzzz*—and I looked up and here comes the seat with the chute fluttering. When that son of a bitch hit the shock absorbers, I swear to god that those guys went up another ten or fifteen feet in the air and came down like a rubber ball, boom, boom, boom. We all ran over, and I figured I was going to see their heads down in their chest somewhere. But they didn't say a word. They just got up and left. They were just so goddamned scared or in shock.

"After that, Jimmy insisted that we test the seat without a parachute. We rigged the seat so that it was overloaded with sandbags. We wanted to see if it would actually bottom out, so that you'd smash your legs, because don't forget, your legs were dangling down. Well, the shock absorbers held those sandbags. There was a lot of safety built into the Parachute Jump.

"Lightning used to hit the Parachute Jump all the time.

**Greatest ride of all time** A crew poses under a chute (left); an operator hangs from a cable while freeing a stuck parachute (above); wind sometimes forced closure of the ride (right).

We used to sit up in the motor room playing cards and we could hear the tower crackle. It was grounded of course, and we were smart enough not to lean against one of the walls. You knew that lightning hit when you could smell the ozone.

"On bad days, customer wise, we would send all twelve empty chutes up simultaneously, but we couldn't let all twelve hit at the same time, because when all twelve hit, the tower would move. It rocked back and forth, not so much that it would knock you off your feet, but you could feel it. We would stagger the chutes. There were times when we turned all the chutes off and let them hang there to generate a crowd. It was a lovely sight."

THE NICKEL EMPIRE 71

**Robert Moses's Boardwalk move**
The dotted lines indicate the proposed path for the Boardwalk. This aerial view, taken in 1939, shows the following features:

1. Manhattan Beach
2. Brighton Beach
3. The Gut
4. Seaside Park
5. Municipal Bathhouse
6. Culver terminal
7. Stubbman's pavilion
8. Dreamland park site
9. Cyclone roller coaster
10. Feltmans
11. Luna Park
12. Wonder Wheel
13. Ward's Baths
14. Stillwell Avenue Subway Terminal
15. Henderson's Theater
16. Tornado roller coaster
17. Loews Theater
18. Nathan's Famous
19. Stauch's Dance Hall
20. Thunderbolt roller coaster
21. Steeplechase Park pavilion

72   CONEY ISLAND 1645–1955

Avenue. He persuaded the city to spend $1 million in public funds to acquire the private property along Surf Avenue. The cost to the taxpayers for relocating the Aquarium was ultimately $11 million, and the move would take sixteen years.

Moses planned high entrance fees for what was formerly a free attraction. As Robert Caro noted in *The Power Broker:* "The people of the city would actually be paying for Moses' revenge forever. . . . The high admission fees set for it insured that many New Yorkers were going to visit [the Aquarium] infrequently if at all." Caro was right; for nearly a decade after it was built in 1957, the Aquarium was a financial disaster and sparsely attended. It did not even advertise the fact that it was located in Coney Island because of the neighborhood's poor reputation. The condemnation and destruction of several blocks of amusement frontage on Surf Avenue to make room for the Aquarium's parking lot were another serious blow to the area. It took decades for the new facility to catch on and become popular.

## The Robert Moses Attack

To this day, most people don't realize that it was Robert Moses who set up the destruction of Coney Island's West End through urban renewal. Mayor John V. Lindsay usually gets the blame, some of it deserved, but it was Moses who chose the renewal sites sixteen years before Lindsay was elected.

After the Boardwalk was moved, Moses's next attempt to acquire land in Coney Island was thwarted. In June 1947, he asked the New York City Board of Estimate to transfer jurisdiction of shorefront land between West Twenty-ninth Street and West Thirty-second Street to the Parks Department so he could build a five-hundred-car parking lot for beachgoers. Democratic Councilman Edward Vogel supported the plan and tried to sweeten the deal by adding a children's playground to the parking lot proposal. Vogel told the board that "our present play facilities in Coney Island are so jammed as to make them completely inadequate for safe and healthful recreation." But the board of estimate denied Moses and Vogel's request without comment. It would be Moses's first and last defeat in Coney Island.

In 1949, in the midst of the postwar urban housing shortage, the federal government enacted a new law to remedy the problem. The policy was called urban renewal, and the program was known officially as Title I. The program was frightening in its magnitude and concept and dealt a severe blow to the civil liberties of New York City's residents. Author Robert Caro described it best in *The Power Broker:* "For the first time in America, government was given the right to seize an individual's private property not for its own use but for reassignment to another individual for his use and profit."

Most city governments around the country were slow to take advantage of this new federal power, but not Robert Moses. Already serving as the city's park commissioner, construction coordinator, and member of the planning commission, Moses soon gained jurisdiction and control over the city's Title I urban renewal sites. He alone had the power to condemn any New York

**Surf Avenue**
Robert Moses claimed the amusement frontage on Surf Avenue and West Fifth Street for the Aquarium. The Stubbman Carousel Pavilion (above right) was one of the landmarks he demolished. The structure with towers was the old Galveston Flood Building, seen below in 1910. It was a survivor of the 1911 Dreamland fire.

# Life in the Gut

One of the first areas that Robert Moses declared a Title I urban renewal site was the Gut, between Ocean Parkway and West Sixth Street, and the Brighton El and Neptune Avenue. Coney's oldest neighborhood, it was a mixed area made up of everything from beautiful six-story apartments to ramshackle bungalows. It had a shopping district on Neptune Avenue, a theater called the Tuxedo, and an old trolley-car barn. Most of the land wound up being used as parking for the highrises.

Florence Adler and Chuck Morgenstern grew up next door to each other in the Gut on West Second Street and lived there from the 1940s until the 1950s, when their families were evicted and the sprawling co-ops called Trump Village and Warbasse Houses were constructed. Adler's father worked in Coney Island, shucking clams at the Gayway Bar and Grill on Stillwell Avenue. Later he was a ticket taker for the Cyclone roller coaster.

"We grew up poor and didn't know it," Adler said. "Our backyard was the beach and the amusement area, and we always thought that's what everybody had in life. We didn't know that kids in Manhattan were playing under fire hydrants because that's all they had. I never thought the Gut was a slum. I had no comparison.

"We went to the beach every day, saw fireworks on Tuesdays, and in the fall went to Mardi Gras. Every Saturday we went to the Tuxedo Theater, a block away. For twenty-five cents we saw two features and cartoons. It was an all-day thing. If you had the winning color ticket, you got a prize: dishes or a free movie the following week."

Chuck Morgenstern's family rented out bungalows seasonally, and his aunts and uncle ran a backyard bathhouse on West Second Street called Lichtbau Lockers. "Lichtbau's had little teeny lockers, just big enough to change, and a few cottages," Morgenstern said. "It was right in our backyard. I remember the sign out front: 'Lichtbau's Lockers: Day, Week, and Season.' People rode on the subway for hours just to get where we lived. It was paradise. The lockers were like something out of 'Spanky and Our Gang,' as if someone had put them up over night. When we were kids, if a pretty girl was in one of the lockers, we'd drill a hole and peek through to have a look. "My uncle, Morris, had seven sisters, and most of them lived right there, in the several houses around a courtyard. Morris was the oddest person I ever saw, six foot two, 130 pounds, with a long hooked nose. He wore size fourteen triple-A shoes that looked like bananas. He ran the lockers and was a great con artist. My mother hated him. My family was in a railroad apartment in an old frame house. We had a black family living in the basement of the building: Moses and Jessie Mae.

"I didn't grow up spoiled. I was on the P.S. 100 basketball team. We never played home games, because in our gym the basket was right against the wall, and if you drove to the basket, you slammed into the wall. We played teams that had beautiful uniforms, but we wore little green T-shirts with numbers sewn on the back."

Morgenstern worked in Coney Island until he graduated from college. "I worked at Willie's Custard Stand on Stillwell Avenue," he said, "and then, the first year Astroland opened, I worked the water flume with Normie Kaufman. It was fun, because when you worked a ride, you'd ride for free on the other rides.

"In 1961, Trump got permission to tear everything down. I don't know how he did it. My kindergarten teacher, Mrs. Reilly, chained herself to her house and said, 'You're gonna have to pull us out to tear down our house.' Her family had lived there for seventy or eighty years. I was bitter and angry when everything was demolished."

Adler also remembers leaving. "We had to move in 1961. Fred Trump had to give everyone one hundred dollars per room to move. Then he tore everything down. We were offered housing in East New York, but we moved to Luna Park Houses instead. Everything happened so fast. Trump destroyed our neighborhood overnight. I would have stayed in the Gut forever because it was a great place to live."

**Lichtbau's Lockers** Chuck Morgenstern (front row, far left) and Florence Adler (center).

**West Second Street**
The Adler family in front of their home.

City neighborhood he saw fit and was able to transfer ownership of the sites to his private developer friends at a fraction of the property's real value.

The broad scope of Title I left it open to abuse and corruption, and it did more harm than good. It obliterated countless neighborhoods, leaving no recourse for hundreds of thousands of displaced residents. Robert Moses saw Coney Island as a prime target, and with his Title I powers, he could not be stopped. The neighborhood lacked the political clout to fight him, and the developers who garnered the building contracts would be indebted to him for providing shorefront sites. Moses had been unofficially directing the policies of the New York City Housing Authority since 1938, when he had begun restructuring the agency, redirecting it from La Guardia's policy of tenement renovation to a policy of wholesale slum clearance that leveled entire neighborhoods. The real reason for slum clearance, as Moses designed it, was not to create better housing, but to provide increasingly profitable contracts for big developers. Using his political connections, Moses had installed his allies in the housing authority's key posts and was secretly running it. In 1949, he combined his federal Title I powers with his city housing authority connections and launched a large-scale landgrab in Coney Island.

Moses unveiled long-range plans to replace Coney's amusements with housing. In an October 6, 1949, *New York Times* interview, Moses revealed the method he would use to acquire land. Referring to Coney Island, he noted that "by setting up his own staff in the city Corporation Council's office, he had been able to set up some choice sites through foreclosure." He mentioned several lots he had acquired this way, particularly along Surf Avenue: "I wouldn't want to sink Surf Avenue, but just get rid of about a third of it," he said. He also predicted that eventually he would "obtain about two-thirds of Coney Island's Boardwalk lots as well."

Moses's first housing project in Coney Island was the low-rise Gravesend Houses, proposed in 1949 and completed in 1954 on mostly vacant land along Gravesend Bay. Next he reclaimed the three blocks of beachfront properties adjacent to the Half Moon Hotel that had eluded him seven years earlier. In April 1953, Moses revealed plans for his first superblock high-rise housing project: Coney Island Houses. The 528-family development required clearing a three-block site to construct five fourteen-story buildings surrounded by a public playground. The planning commission approved the plan in May 1953, with construction set to begin in 1954.

Several weeks before the housing project was approved, the planning commission had given its rubber-stamp go-ahead for Moses's plan to rezone Coney Island into what the *New York Times* called "an area of predominantly residential character." The article in the May 7, 1953, *Times* quoted Moses as "feeling that time would spell the end of many of Coney Island's amusements and that the entire famous oceanfront region, noted the world over for its garish sights and sounds, would be transformed in a few years into multi-family dwellings." His battle plan was to attack Coney Island from its western flank and work his way east into the amusement area.

Murray Handwerker, CEO of Nathan's Famous, was president of the Coney Island Chamber of Commerce in the 1950s and

**Mardi Gras**
An inflatable locomotive rolled down Surf Avenue at West Twenty-third Street. In the early 1950s, Coney's sense of community was best expressed by the annual Mardi Gras.

THE NICKEL EMPIRE 75

**Beginning of the end**
Robert Moses (above). His first big housing project was called Coney Island Houses. Ten years after it was built, the entire West End was condemned. In 1953, his plan was announced in the *New York Times* (below).

**PLAN BOARD BACKS BIG CONEY PROJECT**

**Housing for 420 Families at Cost of $6,485,000 Will Use 6.91-Acre Site**

Plans for a $6,485,000 housing development to be known as Coney Island Houses were approved yesterday by the City Planning Commission. The multi-building project, to accommodate 420 families near the southernmost tip of Brooklyn's shore, will be put under construction early next year.

Commission action on the housing project followed by only a few weeks that body's approval of a general over-all program, designed by Park Commissioner Robert Moses, for rezoning Coney Island into an area of predominantly residential character.

Mr. Moses was represented as feeling that time would spell the end of many of the Coney Island amusements and that the entire famous oceanfront region, noted the world over for its garish sights and sounds, would be transformed in a few years into multi-family

fought Moses. "I didn't want to see Coney Island lose its entertainment features and amusement zone," Handwerker said. "Moses was trying to get the zoning changed, to take over Coney Island like he did Jones Beach in Long Island. Moses wanted all the private industry out. He wanted to make everything south of Surf Avenue into a public beach. Moses wanted Coney Island for himself. He built the pedestrian overpass on West Eighth Street because he didn't want anyone who was going from the subway to the Aquarium to walk on Surf Avenue. That's why I fought him tooth and nail. He was against private industry, and he didn't want amusements. Little by little he was trying to destroy Coney Island."

In December 1954, the planning commission, manipulated by Moses, quietly adopted a master plan for a residential development and redevelopment zone in Coney Island that included two main sites. The entire West End, from Twenty-second to Thirty-seventh Streets, would be developed by the city's housing authority, and the area known as the Gut, between Sea Side Park and Neptune Avenue, from Ocean Parkway to West Sixth Street, would be taken for a Title I redevelopment site. Rather than eliminate only the small pockets of substandard housing in the area, Moses proposed a scorched-earth policy that would obliterate both neighborhoods.

Once rumors began circulating that these Coney Island neighborhoods might be chosen for urban renewal, landlords were reluctant to make major improvements and repairs to properties that could be condemned. Tenants and landlords alike were kept in a constant state of anxiety over when their properties might be taken. There was no incentive to invest in neighborhoods that were rapidly deteriorating.

The Title I program was rocked by scandal all throughout the 1950s, when it was exposed for what it actually was: a benefit for developers that destroyed the lives of the city's poorest tenants, who were relocated from neighborhood to neighborhood as urban renewal decimated the housing stock. Fred Cook best described the Title I abuses in an article in the summer 1961 issue of *Dissent:* "Throughout most of the nation, municipalities condemned the land, moved off the people and razed the buildings before turning the sites over to build as quickly as possible. But Moses insisted that the system that had worked elsewhere wouldn't work in New York. Instead, he turned entire tenement areas over to private developers at knock-down prices, with buildings still standing, fully populated, producing hundreds of thousands of dollars in rents. The result was inevitable: the temptation to milk the slum dwellers as long as possible before tearing down the tenements and rebuilding proved irresistible."

Moses ran the city's Slum Clearance Committee and awarded developers millions of dollars in tenant relocation contracts. A fraternity of bankers, builders, and politicians received handsome rewards from these projects, yet Moses remained above the fray because he never personally profited. He was buying friends, increasing his power, and setting the scene for developers such as Fred Trump, who used dubious means to reap windfall profits from federal contracts and Title I developments. In 1949, Robert Moses predicted that within ten years "one out of ten in New York will look to the City Housing Authority as his landlord." In Coney Island, his goal was accomplished beyond his wildest dreams.

Moses's 1937 improvement plan for Coney Island had claimed that when McKane sold Coney Island in the 1880s, "an indispensable community asset had been virtually given away" to private interests at a "preposterously low price." Yet in the 1950s, Moses committed the same crime. When it came to Coney Island, Moses was no better than John McKane. By the time Moses lost power in 1968, he had reclaimed the common lands of Coney Island and returned them to the city—but at what price?

**PART 2**

# Coming of Age in Coney Island

**W**HEN MY family moved to Coney Island in the 1950s, it was a community in transition. We lived on the beach in the first high-rise housing project to be built in the West End. From an early age, I had a strong sense of place and an identification with the neighborhood and its structures. This awareness was spurred by my father, a strange and mysterious man, whose secretive nature instilled in me a desire to find answers, to be an explorer.

My parents' divorce and my father's move to Manhattan in 1959 changed me and gave me a mission: to discover everything I could about my surroundings. Exploration was a substitute for learning about a father who refused to be known. My childhood experience of Coney Island was much different than that of most of my friends. I was always trying to connect the past and present. On some level, I identified more with the structures and buildings around me than with people. Coney was an odd place, a hodgepodge of tiny cottages, monumental structures that had seen better days, fantasy architecture, and rambling old wood-frame hotels—all waiting to be investigated. When I reached adolescence, Coney's atmosphere matched my mood. The disintegration of Coney Island paralleled the dissolution of my family. My father and the neighborhood went downhill and died at just about the same time.

**Snow-covered West Sixteenth Street, 1968**
Winter in Coney Island created a sense of isolation that made me feel as if I was living on an island.

### CHAPTER 6

# The Coney Island Kid

**M**Y FASCINATION with the mysteries of Coney Island began during a storm. On March 6, 1962, when I was eight years old, a fierce northeaster rolled in and battered the East Coast for two days and nights. The March Storm, as it was dubbed, coincided with freakish high tides and enormous waves that severely eroded a beach still recovering from Hurricane Donna two years before. As the storm subsided, I stood on the Boardwalk watching mountains of brown foam swirl across a gray shoreline. Waves surged over the leveled beach, under the Boardwalk, and all the way up to Surf Avenue. It was then that I noticed the ruins.

Below the Boardwalk, where the beach had once been, appeared the weathered brick foundation of a building, wrapped in a tangle of rusty pipes surrounded by wooden pilings. With every wave, more artifacts were revealed: wooden steps leading nowhere, broken pottery, old bottles. A few days later, the mysterious ruins were covered up by the shifting sands.

For years I fantasized about a civilization that existed before the beach and the Boardwalk were built, and I had wanted to find out what that world had been like. Until that storm, my main source of local lore had been Al the Ice Cream Man, a grizzled Good Humor vendor who parked his ice-cream wagon near the beach. Al always regaled me with stories about old Coney Island while I ate my ice cream. I thought he'd made up the stories, because they seemed too incredible to be true.

Another piece of the puzzle appeared in the winter of 1964 when I was eleven. The

**Over the fence**
In 1965, the year after Steeplechase Park closed, a friend photographed me looking for a way into the park from the Boardwalk.

**Grabbing the brass ring**
I made one of many tries for the brass ring at Lenny McCullough's carousel at the Stillwell Avenue Subway Terminal in 1963. The ride, known as the Villa Eileen Carousel, had been moved from West Fifteenth Street and operated at the terminal through the 1960s.

*Daily News* ran a full-page reproduction of an old map of Coney Island dating from 1869. It resembled a storybook treasure map and bore no resemblance to the Coney Island where I lived. I tried matching the map to the streets and shoreline that I knew, but it didn't fit. I clipped the map and hung it on my bedroom wall and decided to search for the Coney Island that it depicted. As a starting point, I chose the only landmark that still matched the old map's contours: the curving shoreline of Sea Gate, the gated community at the western tip of the island.

That night I stood at our living room window watching the sun set behind the Coney Island Lighthouse. I asked my mother how old the lighthouse was. "It's very old," she said. "Well, how old do you think Coney Island is?" I asked. "It's so old that there were once pirates on Coney Island," she said. "There's a treasure chest buried on the beach, and it's still there, because sometimes old silver dollars wash up after storms." Now I was hooked.

I walked to the public library on Mermaid Avenue and asked for books on Coney Island. The librarian told me that there was a reference book on the subject and handed me a copy of Edo McCullough's 1957 classic, *Good Old Coney Island*. I sat at a table and read it cover to cover, lost in paradise.

The book became my bible. I learned about the pirates and the mutiny aboard a sailing ship called the *Vineyard* in 1830. According to the book, the treasure was buried on Pelican Beach. But where exactly was Pelican Beach? I'd never heard of it. As I read more, my neighborhood took on new meaning. I had been exploring Coney Island for years. Every building interested me, every block contained secrets that I wanted to solve, and now I was finding the answers to questions that I'd never asked. There was history right below my feet.

What affected me most was learning the history of Steeplechase Park, because there were rumors in 1964 that it might be sold or torn down. Not that I had ever taken the park for granted—I loved the place. It was the heart of Coney Island. As I read more about the park's history, I became distraught and overwhelmed by an impending sense of loss. I could never feel the same about Coney again. Coney was always changing during my childhood. The effects of storms, fires, and urban renewal altered the face of my neighborhood on a daily basis. I wanted something I could hold on to.

I told my father about my Coney Island revelation. "Did you know about any of this?" I asked him, as if he'd been covering up some secret. He looked serious as I expressed my concern that Steeplechase might be torn down, and he said, "Why don't you do something about it?"

So the following year I did. The street address of Steeplechase Park was in the phone book. I wrote a letter to the park's owner, Marie Tilyou, whose name had been in the paper, and begged her not to close the park. Then I spent several anxious weeks awaiting a reply that never came.

I needed to talk to someone who knew about Coney Island, someone who would pay attention to a twelve-year-old. "Why don't you write to the chamber of commerce?" my father said. "The chamber of what?" I said. "It's run by the businesspeople," he said. "They might be able to help you." I sat down and wrote a letter to the Coney Island Chamber of Commerce at 1015 Surf Avenue, expressing my concerns about the future of Coney Island. This time I received a reply.

**The landmark Kister Building**
Walter E. Burgess and the chamber of commerce shared an office that served as Coney Island's de facto headquarters.

It came in a bright yellow envelope with a drawing of a green roller coaster above the return address. I recall my excitement as I tore it open and found a letter inviting me to visit the chamber. It was signed by William Nicholson, Executive Secretary. Over the next few days, I was filled with anticipation. Somehow, the word *chamber* made me think of marble halls or something formal. One afternoon after school, I summoned my courage, dressed in a jacket and tie, and walked to West Tenth Street and Surf Avenue to visit the Coney Island Chamber of Commerce.

There were no marble halls at the old chamber. Far from it. After climbing the narrow, creaking stairway to the second floor of the old Kister Building, I found myself in a noisy room filled with pungent cigar smoke and surrounded by nicotine-stained, yellow pine paneling. Ancient oak desks were piled high with papers. It looked like something out of a Sam Spade movie. The chamber shared the office with Walter E. Burgess Inc., the insurance and real estate company that had a sign on nearly every piece of available property in Coney Island. A large man named Jimmy Tesoriero took a drag on his cigarette, looked me over, and said, "What can I do for you?" "I'm here to see William Nicholson," I said.

A tall, dignified man of about sixty, with dark hair and a warm smile, came over and introduced himself as Bill. He had a patrician bearing and a friendly manner that instantly put me at ease. "What exactly are you looking for?" he asked. "I want to save Steeplechase," I blurted out. "And I want to know about Coney Island." "Right this way," he said, and he ushered me into a small conference room in the back office.

I'd hit a nerve with Nicholson. It must have seemed like comic relief when I showed up. I had no idea of the magnitude of the problems that Nicholson was facing. The Coney Island of 1965 was in desperate straits, and the chamber was frantically trying to broker a deal to save Steeplechase Park. Nicholson went to a file cabinet, pulled out an envelope, and handed it to me. "Here's Coney Island for you," he said. Inside was a file folder filled with photographs, old annual reports, and promotional material. He apologized for not having more to give me and said that the chamber's files had been destroyed in a fire in 1960. Nicholson told me stories and answered my questions. I was grateful that he was treating me with respect, as if I were an adult.

It was getting dark when I left, and a young man sitting at a desk asked me where I lived and how I was getting home. I told him that I lived in the projects and would take the bus. "Oh no you don't, I'll give you a lift." This was how I met Jimmy's son, Charlie Tesoriero, who would later change his name to Tesoro ("cost me twenty-five bucks," he liked to say). He was twenty-three years old at the time and working for his father, the owner of Walter E. Burgess Inc. "I can't believe a kid like you lives in the projects," he said when he dropped me off at Coney Island Houses. "Nothing wrong with the projects," I said.

When I called Nicholson the next day to thank him for his help, he mentioned that a television crew was coming down to film a story on Coney Island over the weekend and maybe I'd like to watch. He said to meet him at Gargiulo's restaurant on West Fifteenth Street. When I arrived, Nicholson introduced me to the chamber's president, Fred Garms, who owned the Wonder Wheel ride, and Louie Gargiulo, owner of Gargiulo's. Nicholson presented me to the film crew as the "Coney Island Kid." I didn't realize it, but he was setting me up. Nicholson sensed that a kid's voice would add something to the interview, especially a kid who knew Coney Island. Soon I was nervously babbling on camera about how "Steeplechase must be saved!"

I wound up tagging along to Gargiulo's for lunch. I'd been living in Coney Island for ten years, and this was the first time I'd been in the famous restaurant. It was a classy place with a huge plaster-of-paris octopus on the ceiling over the main dining room. At the bar, Bill was treated like royalty. Then the stories began.

It turned out that Nicholson had been the one to discover the crumpled body of a gangster named Abe Reles, who was pushed out a window at the Half Moon Hotel. Nicholson was in his office at the hotel, looked out his window, spotted Reles, and called the police. Then I heard a story about a gangster named Frankie Yale, who had gotten his start working in Kister's pool room, where the chamber's office was now located.

Rumors and gossip flowed with the drinks. But I had trouble connecting these older men in suits and ties with their wild Coney Island stories. I couldn't believe they had lived the lives they were describing.

There was something else going on that I was too young to perceive, a sense of urgency bordering on panic in the amusement community. Although the chamber still had 140 members, it was in its final days as a powerful organization, and everyone realized that it could all disappear with the death of Steeplechase Park. I was having lunch with the man who held Coney Island together with his charm and personality, a very important man whose entire life was wrapped around his job as protector and promoter of Coney Island, a job he'd held since 1928. Bill Nicholson was Coney Island's bright guiding light, and very soon that light would be extinguished forever. Within a few years, Bill Nicholson and Steeplechase would both be gone.

**Boys of winter, 1960**
A night out at the Clam Bar (left to right): Johnny Bernard, local tinsmith; Bill Olsen, New York City's ride inspector; Bill Nicholson, executive secretary of the Coney Island Chamber of Commerce; Chris Feucht, former owner of the Cyclone and Drop the Dips roller coasters; and Fred Garms, owner of the Wonder Wheel and Spookarama.

### CHAPTER 7

# Coney Island Houses: Before the Fall

MY FAMILY moved into a New York City housing project called Coney Island Houses on a cold December night in 1956. The buildings were new, the landscaping unfinished; we walked in through a foggy moonscape of smoldering construction debris. I was three years old and I remember standing in our new fifth-floor apartment, staring out of the living room window into an inky void filled with stars and distant pinpoints of flashing light and wondering where we were.

The next morning was sunny and bright, and the frightening void turned out to be the blue expanse of the Atlantic Ocean. The beach was at our doorstep, and the world's greatest playground was our backyard. We were one of a few lucky families given an opportunity to leave the cramped tenements of Manhattan for a life at the beach. For all practical purposes, we lived in a resort—a lower-middle-class beachfront paradise.

In the 1950s, Coney Island's West End was a tough New York City neighborhood in transition. Coney Island Houses was the first high-rise apartment complex built in the neighborhood. The five fourteen-story buildings were utilitarian, faced with red brick and arranged perpendicular to the ocean along a three-block site. They were perfect examples of the plain, modernist "Tower in the Park" architecture, in the style of Le Corbusier, that the New York City Housing Authority had come to prefer: oversized buildings surrounded by minimalist landscaping that was off-limits to the tenants. Proximity to the ocean softened the buildings' institutional look.

By all design standards, this drab, monolithic, "superblock" housing project—the kind that urban critic Jane Jacobs called a "marvel of dullness and regimentation, sealed against buoyancy or vitality of city life"—should have been an instant failure. But it was not. For the next ten years, for reasons that would be hard to repeat today, Coney Island Houses was a wonderful place to live and raise a family.

There were many important differences between this project and later ones. Its construction displaced few residents (only eight), and its size matched the scale of the massive Half Moon Hotel across the street. The narrow, north-south alignment of the buildings in relation to the ocean neither overwhelmed the neighborhood nor blocked

**Coney's first high-rise**
Construction of the first of five apartment buildings was under way in October of 1955.

**The promised land**
A 1954 architectural rendering of the proposed Coney Island Houses offered an idealistic picture of living in a beachfront housing project.

the sunlight. The most important difference was that the diversity of the tenants matched the racial and ethnic balance of the existing neighborhood. Instead of disrupting the fabric of the surrounding community, as did most projects in other parts of the city, Coney Island Houses brought new life and vitality to an aging neighborhood. Soon after the project opened, a new school, a community center, and a supermarket were built nearby, the first new construction since the 1930s.

But Coney Island Houses was successful mainly because of the time in which it was built. Families who populated the project moved out as they moved up economically. Fifty-two percent of the tenants were military veterans with young families, relocated from substandard housing. It was not the welfare dumping ground that later housing projects would become. The tenants were grateful to have a decent place to live.

We were one of the first families chosen to live in the new buildings. Qualifications were strict. To apply for an apartment, a family had to be living in substandard housing, as confirmed through a visit from a housing authority inspector. The family actually had to be in physical danger to be accepted. My family was living in an apartment in Hell's Kitchen on Manhattan's West Side. At night, there were shootings and sirens, and my mother remembers having to walk through puddles of blood to leave the building. She says we had no problem meeting the requirements: "The housing authority fellow came with a list on a big clipboard and had to inspect everything—the heating, the water, the bathrooms—to see if the place was dangerous for little children. It was like they were rescuing you. They were very rigid about applications, and the waiting list was tremendous because there was such an apartment shortage in New York. We moved to Coney Island and our rent doubled. It went from fifty to one hundred dollars. We didn't get to pick the apartment, but we now had clean, new, wonderful facilities for children. Every project didn't have a beach and a boardwalk."

The apartments at Coney Island Houses were small but solidly built. The floors were

**Surf Theater**
This 1956 view from my living room window shows the theater shortly before it became a bowling alley.

**Beach culture**
Beachgoers at Bay 18 at West Twenty-seventh Street in the late 1950s.

**West End skyline, 1969**
The Half Moon Hotel (far right) served as building six of Coney Island Houses.

industrial-grade asphalt tile, and the walls were real plaster painted light green. The hallways were polished yellow cinder block, devoid of ornamentation and illuminated by bare bulbs. Heating pipes were exposed, enabling kids to communicate between floors "prison style" by tapping out messages on the pipes. Every floor had the same layout, with a floor plan that provided for an interesting mix of residents: two-bedroom apartments for young families, all with one or two children of preschool or grade-school age; three-bedroom apartments for families with three or more children, usually teenagers; and "one-bedrooms" for older tenants, generally elderly widows, which ensured that every floor had a resident "grandmother" to bake cookies and watch over us.

A minimum of sixteen children lived on each floor, meaning that a tribe of more than one thousand children grew up together in close quarters. Families mingled, and children drifted in and out of each other's unlocked apartments. The hallways were safe. A milkman, a seltzer man, and even a bagel man delivered fresh goods daily right to the door. The egg man shouted, "Fresh eggs," like a Lower East Side peddler. Tenants could leave their shoes or umbrellas in the hall without fear of theft. But what made our lives really special was beach culture.

The beach was an extension of the projects, and we treated it like our private club. During the 1950s, the beach was a crowded but safe place for children. In all the years we lived in the projects, of the thousands of kids who passed through, I don't remember anyone ever drowning. Lifeguards were on duty all summer long, and in the early days, lines of multicolored, striped barrel floats were tethered out in the deep water.

Sunny summer days were beach days, and everyone left their apartments carrying umbrellas, blankets, coolers, and folding chairs for a daylong encampment on a beach filled with hundreds of splashing, laughing children. Jetties divided the beaches into bays, with each bay numbered. Our beach was called Bay 20. The bays were territorial: some were predominantly Italian or Irish, and others were populated by people from other Brooklyn neighborhoods. Visiting another bay was like visiting another country.

In the late 1950s and into the early 1960s, the turn-of-the-century summer bungalow colonies and bathhouses were still in operation and gave the neighborhood a faded summer-resort feeling. The West End followed the cyclical nature of seasonal

**Looking west**
This 1961 photograph taken from Coney Island Houses looks down Surf Avenue and shows, from lower right, the Surf Bowling Lanes, the Atlantic Hotel, Dalton's Beer Gardens, McCabe's Bar, and Sea Gate.

operation. The rickety wooden buildings were shut down and boarded up in the fall, then painted and reopened in the spring. Within a small radius from Coney Island Houses were Jefferson Baths, Lincoln Baths, Luna Villa, Kalinas Colony, Carlton Court, Ocean Baths, Sea Gate Villa, Fulton Baths, the Catholic Youth Organization summer camp, Villa Nova bungalows, West End Villa, Scoville's, and Bell Buoy Baths.

Mermaid Avenue, our main shopping district, was lined with supermarkets, clothing stores, delicatessens, banks, small department stores, shoe stores, cleaners, restaurants, pet shops, doctor and dentist offices, pharmacies, a Woolworth's, and an A&P supermarket. Big churches and synagogues were located there too.

The Surf Theater (which later became the Surf Lanes bowling alley) was right across the street from us, and the Mermaid, Loews, and Tilyou Theaters were all within walking distance. Within a two-block radius were four corner luncheonettes, each with its own following of dedicated customers, as well as a barbershop, a drugstore, Weepy's Pool Hall, a TV repair shop, a tailor, and Coopey's Corner, the toy and candy store.

Coopey's Corner was a magnet for the children of Coney Island Houses. It was next to the supermarket on West Thirtieth Street and was probably visited several times a day by every child in the projects. Coopey's was run by Mr. Cooper and his wife and was the source of all of our childish pleasures.

The front of the cramped store contained a candy counter, which guaranteed a living for the dentists of Mermaid Avenue, and a wall of comic books, which fueled our superhero fantasies. Coopey's sold plastic models, toys, pink "spaldeens" and stickball bats, tops, yo-yos, baseball cards, cold sodas, and ice cream. The kids from the projects were on the cutting edge of every fad, from Slinkies to hula hoops. Coopey's windows were used as a showplace for plastic scale models made by local kids. The store sold us film and processed our pictures. Mr. Cooper essentially ran an adolescent cultural center.

Our games were traditional New York City street games, brought from the neighborhoods of our parents and played on concrete squares. We filled bottle caps with melted crayons and played skelly on sidewalk courts drawn with chalk. We shot marbles and flew kites with rag tails. We played tag, hide-and-seek, potsy, ring-o-levio, and johnny-on-the-pony. We played stickball and punchball and the dreaded dodgeball. One summer, we spun customized

**A friend to all**
Al the Ice Cream Man at his station in the Big Park.

**Life in the projects**
In 1957, my sister, Diana, and I played in the snow behind our apartment house (right). The four-story apartment house in the distance was the childhood home of writer Joseph Heller. In 1964, tenants were permitted to plant flowers (center), the first change in the strict housing authority rules. My sister dressed up to ride her tricycle (far right) on a sunny day in 1957.

tops. The next summer, we made primitive scooters and skateboards from split roller skates nailed to two-by-fours and shook our teeth loose riding them down the bumpy Boardwalk ramps.

Coney Island Houses had its own customs and language. Every building had a number, and that became one's identity, as in "Charlie from building three" or "Steve from building four." We never used formal addresses. Each building was a separate community within a community. The three parks in the projects also had their own identities. There was a Big Park and two Little Parks. The little parks were paved with asphalt and furnished with the standard concrete structures and steel monkey bars designed to cause severe injury. If you hadn't broken a bone or received multiple stitches by the time you were twelve, you just weren't trying hard enough.

The Big Park, the heart of the projects, was located right against the Boardwalk. The broad expanse of asphalt had cobblestone islands, wood slat benches, and a scattering of scarred plane trees that we climbed like monkeys. Leo, one of the "park men," marched from the park house every morning and raised an American flag, which flew over the park from dawn until dusk. There were six basketball hoops, a handball court, big swings and little swings, a water sprinkler to play in or wash beach sand off, two water fountains, slides, a sandbox, and six concrete chess tables. A useless shuffleboard court was converted into a punchball diamond.

The park was divided in two by a cobblestone sidewalk that ran under the Boardwalk to the beach. This was where Al the Ice Cream Man parked his Good Humor wagon. Al was a park fixture and a friend to everyone. When the Big Park first opened in 1956, it was staffed by the two park men, Jean and Leo, a Mutt-and-Jeff team who presided over a park house stocked with games, toys, basketballs, Chinese checkers, and jump ropes, all of which were city property.

The equipment didn't last long. By 1960, it had disappeared, and the two-acre park was being redesigned by the kids to suit their own needs. First to go were the chain-link fences that surrounded the park and had two gates that were closed at night. Large gaps began to appear, and eventually the fences were no longer replaced.

Two stickball courts were devised. One used the park house as home plate and the other used the granite flagpole base. Games went on all summer long. In another corner of the park were several concrete tables with terrazzo checkerboards used mainly for card games instead of checkers or chess. This is where the men of the projects played poker on weekends. Small-time bookies took bets at the tables for sporting events that were monitored on transistor radios. On rare occasions, the housing police would sweep

**The Big Park**
This view of the park, the center of Coney Island Houses, was taken in fall of 1969. Sam's Knishes can be seen on the Boardwalk in the distance.

into the park to break up the card games and issue summonses.

The surrounding park benches were always filled with ever-changing cliques of adolescent boys and girls who, as they got older, paired off and disappeared into the shadows under the Boardwalk to learn about love. This "underwood hotel" and the buildings' staircases were the teenage hot spots, places to go to avoid spying eyes. Every window in the projects had a view of the Big Park, and the kids' activities were observed by their parents, who called them home for dinner or screamed at them to stop fighting. It was always noisy. My sister, Diana, compared life in the projects to an ant farm: "There were so many things going on at once. It was a mob scene. You could look out the window and decide which activities to join. There were so many choices for socializing, and you were never alone."

The rules in the projects were strict in the early days. Children weren't permitted to play on the grass or on the rooftops or to hang out in hallways. Despite this strict environment, there were ways to have fun. When tenants left unwanted items in a disposal area behind the buildings, my friends and I scoured the area to find material for practical jokes. Once we found a pile of discarded furniture and used it to make a tableau in the building's elevator. We set up a lamp, a table, and chairs and hung pictures. When the elevator door opened, it revealed a complete living room, where we sat at the table playing cards. We ignored the startled looks of the tenants as we offered them a sandwich or a drink. We also liked the old trick of unscrewing all the lightbulbs on a floor and then ringing all the doorbells. We made dummies from old clothing and hung them from the windows of upper floors, as a shill down below let out ghastly screams. It was all innocent fun.

The projects fit nicely into the neighborhood, bracketed by the Half Moon Hotel on the east and two Boardwalk restaurants and a bungalow colony on the west. The Half Moon served as "building six" of the projects' skyline. The hotel had been sold in 1950 and turned into the Hebrew Home for the Aged, but we always called it the Old Age Home. Many of my friends had elderly relatives who lived there.

The Boardwalk restaurants, at West Thirty-second Street, were Sam's Knishes and Larry and Vinny's pizza parlor. Sam's was owned by Orthodox Jews who made the best cherry-cheese and pineapple-cheese knishes on Coney Island, even better than the legendary Mrs. Stahl's. Larry and Vinny's, run by the Ferrovechio family, was famous for its pizzas and Italian ices. The Ferrovechios also operated a little storefront next door to the pizza place called the Fun Fair Arcade that had games and pinball machines and a jukebox that provided a soundtrack for the Boardwalk. Larry and Vinny's mother, Anna, the matriarch of the family, lived above the restaurant and made it seem like home.

On Tuesday firework nights during the summer, the Boardwalk in front of the restaurants was jammed with people. The bungalows were lit up with Chinese lanterns, and music poured from open windows. Groups of teenagers gathered to sing a cappella. A generation of old-timers had rented the bungalows for years, and their children and grandchildren visited to watch fireworks or have barbecues. The summer colony, consisting of Sea Gate Villa and the Lincoln Baths cottages, was crowded with people sitting on folding chairs and playing cards or dominoes. Balmy summer nights became memorable when the smells of food, the ocean, and gunpowder from the fireworks mixed with excited voices to create a festival atmosphere.

The residents of Coney Island Houses were the proletariat, a mixed bag of middle-class families with the same income level. Few of the mothers worked, and the men were mostly veterans employed as police officers, schoolteachers, truck drivers, small-business owners, postal workers, subway motormen, garment workers, union organizers, and house painters. Some were Coney concessioners. Local luminaries such

## Finding the West End Resort

I ALWAYS WONDERED what my neighborhood was like long before Coney Island Houses was built. There were many clues: old trolley tracks along Railroad Avenue; boarded-up bungalows, rambling frame buildings that had been converted into rooming houses, and the ruins I saw exposed on the beach during the storm of 1962. All of these were remnants of a culture that had disappeared.

It took me years to discover more about that world. I found old maps showing Whitney's Resort and Edwards Hotel on a street called Edwards Place that no longer existed. There was the Sparkle Inn, Hahn's Baths, the Seabourn Hotel, the exotic-sounding Celtic Baths, and the formal-sounding Roosevelt Baths.

I also found photographs and postcards, including pictures of the Railroad Avenue trolleys and steam trains. I read descriptions in old guide books of the big hotels that predated the bathhouses: the Halfway House, the Windsor, the Bayview.

The most fascinating discovery was that in the 1890s most of the property around Coney Island Houses belonged to Steeplechase Park owner George C. Tilyou and that a ferry pier had been located at the foot of my street, West Thirty-second Street, in the 1880s. My block had once been an important part of the West End resort.

**The Whitney Hotel** The resort (above) had bathhouses, a restaurant, and galows and took up a full block on West Thirtieth Street between Surf Aven and the ocean.

as Lincoln High School's football coach and dean of boys lived there. Lou Gossett, who later became an actor, lived in my building.

I remember the first time I discovered the concept behind public housing. I told my mother that I'd visited a rich kid on the eleventh floor. She asked me why I thought the family was rich. "Because his father smokes big cigars, and they have gold furniture covered with plastic," I replied. My mother explained that everyone in the projects was equal and had the same income and that tenants would be thrown out if they made too much money.

Coney Island Houses was integrated but reflected the population of the surrounding neighborhood, which was mostly European and Russian Jews, along with blacks and Puerto Ricans. At Christmas and Hanukkah, the windows glowed with menorahs and Christmas lights. My family celebrated Christmas without any religious attachments. My father was half Methodist and half Baptist, and my mother was Catholic and Jewish. Although my family did not subscribe to any organized religion, my sister and I had been baptized Methodist, which caused us to stand out, because the only other Methodists in the projects were blacks. Of the other seven families on our floor, six were Jewish and one was Irish Catholic. I was taught to be tolerant and respectful of other people's religious beliefs, but I considered religion and the Bible to be the same as the classical myths and fables that my mother read to me.

**West End transportation** The Norton's Point Trolley ran through backyards along Railroad Avenue between Surf and Mermaid Avenues until 1948. It was also called the Toonerville Trolley.

**Carlton Court** Located at Surf Avenue and West Thirty-fifth Street, this was one of the West End's first bungalow colonies. It was torn down in 1971.

**Boardwalk storefronts** Edwards Baths (opposite) and Hahn's Baths (left), on West Thirtieth Street, had gone out of business by the time they were replaced by Coney Island Houses.

**The last resort**
Sea Gate Villa on Surf Avenue and West Thirty-third Street, across from Coney Island Houses, was the last operating summer bungalow resort in Coney Island. Every summer until 1978, elderly beach-goers moved in for the season and set up their beach chairs along the street to gossip and play cards.

**View from the beach, 1995**
The five buildings of Coney Island Houses, with the Half Moon Hotel and Parachute Jump in the distance.

Beautiful houses could still be found on the tree-lined side streets of Coney Island in the 1950s and early 1960s. I was envious when I visited my friend Ellen's home on West Thirty-fifth Street. It was a big, rambling, three-story frame house with a winding staircase, a basement, an attic, and a backyard garden. The house had a large front porch with flower-filled planters and a wicker porch swing. There was a sense of freedom, with no housing authority rules to follow. I wanted to live in a house—until a few years later when the neighborhood declined and so many houses burned down.

For more than ten years, Coney Island Houses was the only high-rise in the West End. Then urban renewal came in, and the projects were lost in a sea of buildings. The city didn't know when to stop and destroyed the surrounding neighborhood in the process. Everything was soon out of balance. The early 1960s were the final days of Coney's West End resort. As the neighborhood deteriorated and a criminal element moved in, the residents of Coney Island Houses withdrew from the community and became more like inhabitants of an isolated village. Many fled the projects when the crime wave began, but for a time, on hot summer nights, the park benches and sidewalks were still crowded, and the voices of children filled the air as the lights of Steeplechase Park whirled in the distance on Surf Avenue. For a while, we held the high ground in towers that overlooked the kingdom of Coney Island. It was a time of fun and innocence that came to an end by 1965. The successful experiment could never be repeated.

CHAPTER 8

# A Mysterious Father

WHEN I answered the phone, a deep voice would say, "Let's go to Crazy Ghosts!" It was my father's way of telling me that he was coming to Coney Island for the weekend. Crazy Ghosts was a spook house on Surf Avenue, and my dad got a kick out of saying the name like a barker. He also liked making up word games and nicknames for places in Coney Island, like the small beach on Gravesend Bay near Sea Gate that he called Creepy Beach. From the time I was seven years old, my father and I spent a lot of time at Creepy Beach.

I never knew anyone else who went to this beach, because it was a very creepy place. That's why I liked it. It was a secret spot, just a few blocks from Coney Island Houses, a seaside junkyard surrounded by a few old bungalows and abandoned piers that acted as a catch basin for all of the flotsam and jetsam floating out of New York Harbor.

My father was an expert mechanic and went to Creepy Beach to work on his car without being disturbed. Using only the tools in his trunk, he could disassemble the engine and put it back together right there on the street. He taught me how to replace piston rings and adjust carburetors and install new brake shoes. When he sometimes let me borrow his tools, I would go off and dismantle abandoned cars on the beach just for fun.

The beach was known locally as Bayview, and the derelict piers had once belonged to the Atlantic Yacht Club, which had burned in the 1930s. The sands were a dumping ground scattered with rotted timbers, the skeleton of an old ferryboat, and rusting machinery, an apocalyptic setting where oily bonfires burned night and day. Occasionally the beach was used as the final resting place for corpses, victims of mob hits that were dumped at night or had floated downriver and washed up. The only dead thing I ever found there was the bloated corpse of a big white goat.

I nearly became a corpse myself once when I was ten years old. Some teenagers at Creepy Beach threw a sealed fifty-five-gallon drum of gasoline onto a fire and ran off, leaving me sitting on a log ten feet from the fire,

**Father and son**
My father held me for a photograph in front of a beachfront bungalow in 1955, when I was two years old.

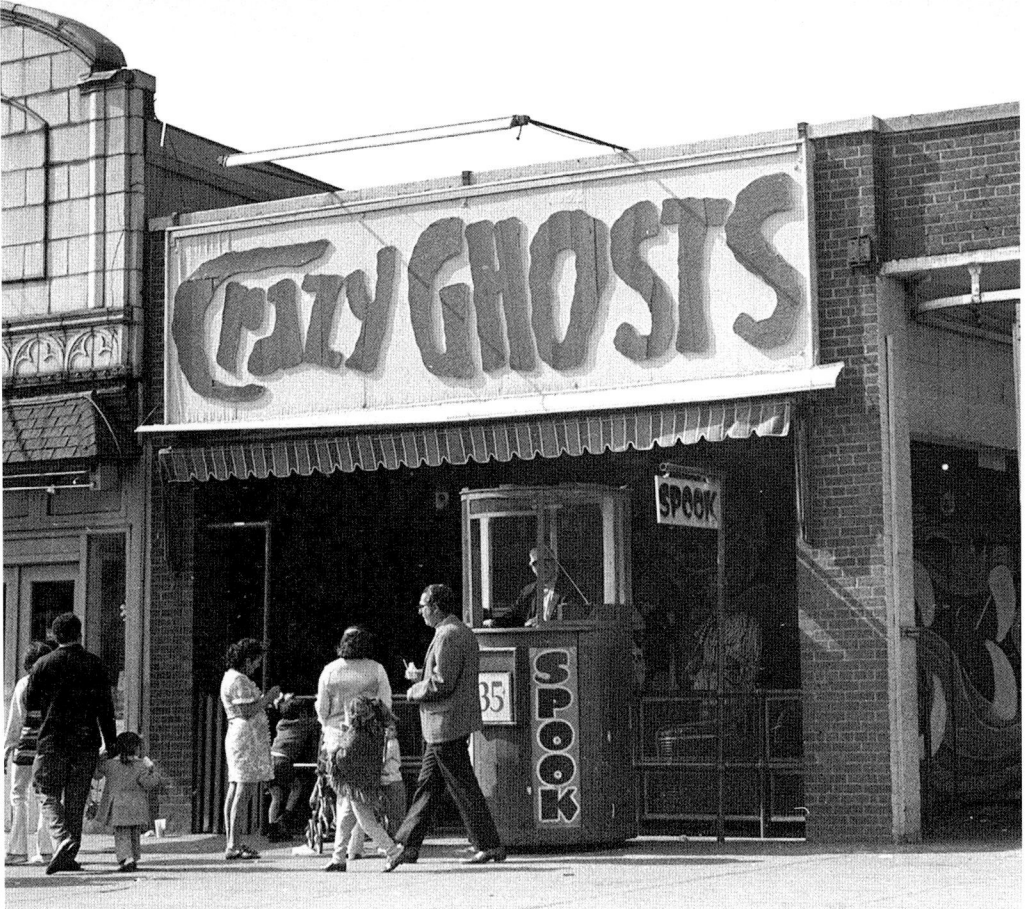

**Haunted terminal**
The Crazy Ghosts spook house was located next to the entrance to the Stillwell Avenue Subway Terminal. The laugh of the mechanical clown echoed throughout the building.

watching the can heat up and expand. I finally got bored and walked back toward my father's car just before the entire beach exploded into a fiery black mushroom cloud. The log I'd been sitting on was vaporized.

Creepy Beach wasn't the only place where my father took me. Other times we'd stay at his place in Manhattan and visit the Museum of Natural History or Central Park or go to Times Square for a movie. It was unpredictable. One week we'd visit Sagamore Hill, the home of his boyhood idol, Theodore Roosevelt; the following week, we would be sitting in the stands at a demolition derby in East Islip.

But most of our time together was spent in secluded spots around Coney Island working on his car. For a while we worked in the Gut, the abandoned neighborhood near West Fifth Street and Neptune Avenue that was being cleared for a housing development; then we parked along ruined stretches of Coney Island Creek, where I explored old coal silos and warehouses. I got to know the ins and outs of Coney Island this way, and I came to like Creepy Beach the best because it was a truly mysterious place, and I loved solving mysteries. I wanted to know why the piers were there, the names of the shipwrecks on the beach, and who had lived in the old houses along Coney Island Creek.

★

The mystery I could never solve was the one surrounding my father. He never talked about himself or his past, and I had stopped asking him questions long ago when he had left us. For a few years, we had lived together as a family in our apartment overlooking the ocean, and my memories of this time are happy ones. I remember the smell of bacon and eggs cooking in the kitchen every morning, the aroma of the wildroot hair tonic that my father smoothed into his hair before leaving for work, and the salty scent of the ocean that hung in the cool morning air.

Each morning, my little sister and I would watch my father from our fifth-floor window as he waited to catch the bus to the Stillwell Avenue Subway Terminal. He always looked sharp in his suit and tie and stood apart from the small crowd at the bus stop on Surf Avenue, lost in thought while reading his paper. When the bus came, it was two-toned, light green, and streamlined and bulbous, just like my father's 1952 Rambler-American station wagon.

On weekends my sister and I would jump into bed with my parents, and my father tickled us and made faces and told jokes, and he held us in the air while we spread our arms to pretend we were flying. I'd ask to see the bullet hole in his leg, and he'd point at two deep, white, spidery scars on his calf and say, "Here's where the bullet went in, and here's where the bullet came out." He never said how the bullet wound up in his leg, and I learned not to ask.

After breakfast, we would all go to the beach. The beach was never crowded in the morning, and we could put our blanket anywhere we wanted. My father would run across the sand, dive headfirst into the breaking waves, and swim out so far that I was afraid he'd never come back. When he did come back, he'd carry my sister and me, screaming and squirming, into the deep green water. We clung to him while he held us tightly to his chest as waves swept over our heads.

Sometimes he would take me for a walk down to Stillwell Avenue to see the tattoo parlors. My father had a large tattoo of a nude woman on his arm that he called his "mistake." He showed me the tattoo parlor where he'd had it done. Although we lived in Coney Island, my dad always seemed to be taking it all in for the first time. As the two of us ambled along the Bowery and Boardwalk, he pointed out new rides or told me stories about the famous old ones. Life in Coney Island was pretty good until one day in June 1958, when my father got a call telling him that his father had died. He silently packed his suitcase and left for the funeral in Opelika, Alabama.

He was never the same after that. He returned from Alabama a different man. My grandfather's death had crushed him. It was as if they both had died. Things had never gone smoothly between my parents, and it all fell apart quickly. My father began to disappear for long periods of time. When he came home and emptied his wallet and change onto the bedroom nightstand, he put a shiny black pistol there, too. When I asked him about the gun, he just said to leave it alone.

During the next year, my parents fought constantly, and my father would storm out in a rage. I'd watch from the window as he walked down Surf Avenue toward the neon sign over McCabe's Bar on Thirty-fifth Street, wondering if he'd ever come back.

**Creepy Beach**
My father striking a humorous pose on one of our many visits to the beach.

In the summer of 1959, around my sixth birthday, my mother announced that we were taking a family trip to Alabama to "get a divorce," and then she explained what a divorce was. She told me that Alabama was where my father had grown up and that we would visit his family while we were there. The four of us piled into our green Nash on a hot August morning and headed south. My father loved road trips, and we stayed in rustic cabin motels and visited roadside attractions, little family-run operations with caged animals, stagecoaches, concrete dinosaurs, and woodsy furniture. We swam in motel pools and ate in diners. My mother took movies of the entire odyssey, the best family trip we ever had.

We reached Alabama and visited my father's family in Opelika. Then we drove to Phoenix City, Alabama, a tiny, wide-open town on the border near Fort Benning, Georgia, where my parents got a "quickie" divorce. Then we drove home.

A few days after we returned to Coney Island, my father packed his bags and moved to an apartment in Manhattan, which came as a shock to my mother, who, for some strange reason, had assumed that he would still live with us.

★

My father's new life in Manhattan was a complete blank. He led the kind of quiet existence that fed my fantasies, and I always believed that he'd come back some day and take us away from the projects to one of those big old houses in Alabama, with porches and green lawns and magnolia trees. Instead he showed up and took me to Creepy Beach.

He still came to Coney Island on weekends, and we still did things together as a family, but he rarely interacted with other people in the projects. He disliked talking to the neighbors, with the exception of one person: Dave Dudley, the father of Randy, Sandy, and Candy, our neighbors down the hall. Dave was a beefy man and a heavy drinker, a wild, one-eyed Irish electrician who liked to pluck out his glass eye when he was drunk. Dave and my father used to go over to McCabe's together to drink.

My father never talked about himself or what he did for a living. But he had a wealth of information about everything else: philosophy, jazz, cars, current events, and world issues. He knew everything about Manhattan: the clubs, restaurants, landmarks, and streets. As far as his personal life, I knew he worked in an office somewhere, but he never talked about it. I once asked him about the deep scars on his face, and he told me that he had cut himself shaving. I pointed to every scar, and he told me the same thing, before saying, "That's enough."

I called him the "fighting philosopher," because he really was a philosopher, with a degree in philosophy from New York University. He'd also been a boxer, and he still worked out at Stillman's Gym in Manhattan. He knew his stuff, how to take care of himself in a brawl. Once he showed up in Coney Island with a bandaged hand and would only say, "I had to hit a fella." Sometimes he seemed frightening. He always carried an undercurrent of violence, a dangerous side that he kept under control.

The thing that I didn't look forward to were the boxing matches he set up between me and my friends. He bought me two pairs of boxing gloves one Christmas, the Christmas before he gave me a rifle. The gloves were kid size, dark blue with soft tan leather insides. Boxing was his thing, not mine, but he insisted on teaching me. The bloody little matches held in the living room of our apartment were something to be endured. "Jab! Jab! Keep your head down. Protect your face!" My friends were into it but felt that I shouldn't have to prove myself to him. I knew he had my best interests in mind. "A fella's got to know how to protect himself," he'd say. But I soon found other ways to protect myself.

I became an explorer and began a solitary search as a young boy. It was during this time that I transferred my curiosity about a father who wasn't there to a place called Coney Island that was. I began searching for answers on an exciting island. Somehow tying the two together, I thought that if I could figure out Coney Island, I would understand my father. My searches were always for father figures, to help gain self-knowledge and find adventure. It was a quest that led me down some strange and confusing paths in one of the strangest places in the world.

CHAPTER 9

# Down to the Sea in Ships

**Running aground**
My friend Gary and I tried to grab any derelict boat that came ashore. Sometimes the police got there first.

During my childhood, I dreamt of going to sea. We lived surrounded by water and the smell of salt air. From my bedroom window, I could see ships and lighthouses and the open ocean. To the west was the Coney Island Lighthouse capped with a flashing red beacon. On clear nights, our living room was washed by a dim warmth that dripped down the walls, sensual and reassuring. On foggy nights, the light pulsed through the mist, beating in rhythm to the foghorns.

Across the distant southern horizon were the silhouettes of three more lighthouses: the Roamer Shoal, Old Orchard Shoal, and West Bank lights. At night, the ocean turned into a mysterious galaxy of twinkling lights, flashing buoys, and sweeping beacons. Brightly lit ships traced slow arcs through the distant channel, while closer to shore, tugboats plowed through the darkness, displaying tall masts lit up like Christmas trees.

A dozen yards off the beach, just past the end of the jetty, was the Coney Island Channel, a busy shortcut for the workhorse tankers and tugs steaming between Rockaway Inlet and Lower New York Bay. The channel came closest to shore right at our beach, and a red bell buoy marked its edge. This "bellboy," as we called it, was my link to the sea, the nearest offshore object that I could reach. It became a rite of passage

to swim out to the rusty, barnacle-encrusted buoy and climb aboard to ring the bell. An appreciative audience always gathered along the shore to enjoy the noisy show, especially when two people climbed aboard and rocked the buoy like a giant pendulum.

The constant clanging of the bell, which could be heard even with the windows closed, became part of my consciousness, calling to me. I never realized how big the buoy was until the first time I swam to it. The swim was the impulsive act of a teenager on a chilly fall afternoon at slack tide. I was sixteen years old, sitting on the rocks at the end of the jetty talking with a local girl named Nannette Brandt, and somehow I sensed that the time was right. Nannette was surprised when I jumped into the water, fully clothed, and began swimming out to sea. But I was focused, and there was no turning back. I had to reach the buoy before coming to my senses. Climbing aboard required extreme coordination, and my first attempt left me choking in a tangled mass of seaweed and barnacles. I succeeded on my second attempt by grabbing the buoy's base as it dipped into a swell and hanging on while it rose and pulled me aboard. I stood on the buoy, shivering and ecstatic, ringing the bell for an invisible audience on an empty beach.

★

Two miles beyond the red buoy, across the broad expanse of East Bank Shoal, was the Ambrose Channel, the forty-foot-deep main shipping channel into New York Harbor. Ambrose was marked by a procession of lighted buoys that stretched north from the Jersey Highlands to the Chapel Hill Channel, just off the tip of Sea Gate. Ships entered the main channel at the Ambrose Lightship. At night, this light was the brightest of all.

From my bedroom window, I watched ocean liners, carriers, tankers, and freighters steaming across the bay. The most dramatic of all was the *Queen Mary*, last of the "three-stack" ocean liners. During summer months, the movement of these ships in and out of the harbor was a major event for people on the

Coney Island beach. The reason for that was "The Big Wave."

The Big Wave was a myth and a local joke, but that didn't stop everyone from waiting for it. The wake from a big ocean liner was said to produce a freak wave so large that it would sweep you out to sea if you were caught in it. Parents on the beach took the myth seriously and called to their small children to "get outta the watta or y'll get drowned!"

To me, the smaller boats and tugs that plied Coney Island Channel were more fun to watch than the liners. They were close enough that we could see figures appearing in hatchways and cigarettes flipped from portholes. Even the voices of deckhands and the hum of the diesels carried ashore. The tugs were muscle boats, groaning along low in the water, hauling long wooden barges filled with sand and gravel.

I never got to ride the boats but was content to pick up pieces of wrecks that washed ashore: a chunk of wood painted with a boat's name and with a brass cleat attached, or a shredded lifejacket. I salvaged the pieces and brought them home, hoping someday to build my own boat. I realized the fantasy when I was ten years old and made my first boat from a stack of wooden pallets. It was a shaky raft, lashed together into a Kon-Tiki sort of craft with an improvised outrigger to stabilize it. I sailed it with some friends in a small lagoon near Coney Island Lighthouse. The raft swamped but didn't sink as we sloshed across the deck. It hung just below the surface, giving the impression that we were walking on water.

There were other boat rides that winter. Anything that came ashore, no matter how damaged or derelict, we patched up and put to sea. My friend Gary and I found a nice rowboat at Plumb Beach and tried to pole it into Sheepshead Bay, but it took on water and sank near shore. We were soaked to the bone, and our pants legs froze during the long bike ride home.

Shortly after that adventure, a sand barge broke loose from its tow and came ashore on the beach at West Thirty-third Street. It was the first shipwreck I'd ever seen. The barge soon became a local attraction, a pirate ship crawling with a crew of neighborhood kids who pumped the bilge pumps, pulled broken hawsers, and explored the small holds below deck. At high tide, the barge was surrounded by water, and the games turned ugly. Many kids wound up in the drink after being forced to "walk the plank." For a few weeks, I moved aboard the barge and spent all my time on it, morning till night, until the Parks Department finally dispatched a crane to dismantle it.

I built my last boat in early 1967, at age thirteen, shortly after Steeplechase Park was demolished. The Steeplechase site had been cleared but not graded, and heavy winter rains completely flooded the grounds from Surf Avenue to the Boardwalk. I was looking over the abandoned site with Gary when we found some wooden pallets in a pile of junk. Gary and I looked at each other and smiled. We were eight years old again. We placed the pallet in the water, hopped on, and pushed off. Huck Finn and Tom Sawyer poled the craft through little ice floes, past the ghost of the Steeplechase pavilion, and toward the ocean.

**Coney yacht**
There was a small boat dock (above) on Coney Island Creek behind the Stillwell Avenue junkyard. The owner told me he could take his boat out only when the tide was low enough to get under the Stillwell bridge. He didn't go out very often.

**Sunset, 1970**
The Half Moon Hotel and Coney Island Houses are distant silhouettes (opposite).

CHAPTER 10

# The Steeplechase Cathedral

IT IS NOT the memory of Steeplechase Park's rides that has stayed with me from childhood, but rather an enhanced sense of place. Although memories of the park have dimmed over time, the park's classical details have stayed with me. I somehow absorbed an experience that people were calling "old-fashioned" in the space-age world of the early 1960s.

The Steeplechase Park I remember was made of space, light, color, and soaring heights. The quality of light within the pavilion is what affected me most. The only comparable experience was the first time I saw the magnificent stained-glass windows of the cathedral at Chartres in France.

The windows at Chartres inspired visions of sunny, late-summer afternoons when the shadowy interior of the Steeplechase pavilion was illuminated by dusty shafts of golden amber light pouring through the glass wall of the pavilion's south side. As the sun traveled west, different attractions were spotlighted for a few blinding moments, before being left in the gloom as the shafts slowly swept across the wooden floor. The north facade of the building produced an entirely different effect. It was a backlit abstract mosaic of muted colors, oranges and umbers, with backward lettering surrounding cutouts of leaping horses and a silhouetted Steeplechase funny face, all painted to be seen from the street, not from the interior. It created a bizarre but memorable impression.

The architecture of Steeplechase was alive and visceral. The echoing interior space between the massive glass facades was spanned by delicately curving steel roof trusses supported by rows of Corinthian columns, each column surrounded at the base by four caryatids, female nudes with outstretched arms holding lamps. The impact was overwhelming. As my eye traveled from ground to roof, I soared. Corinthian colonnades lined West Sixteenth Street, brick archways led to tiny catwalks and staircases, and formal gardens and manicured walkways unfolded to reveal strange visual surprises. The prismatic cut-glass windows of the ballroom threw rainbows on the walls. This was my earliest exposure to classical architecture, and I was not aware of the deep impression it made on me at the time, or that it would stay with me for a lifetime.

**Steeplechase meditation**
On a 1958 visit to the park, I took a moment to sit on the fountain in the sunken gardens.

**Hypnotic park**
The rides were dizzying, but so was the architecture.

**Mosaic of primary colors**
The vibrantly painted south facade was like an immense stained-glass window. Equally colorful was the Silver Streak, which was eventually moved inside the Pavilion of Fun.

The memory I have of Steeplechase is more of a visual delight than of an amusement park. The place was the land of Oz, and the Bowery served as the yellow brick road. Visitors traversed a three-block gauntlet of noise, temptation, and distraction before arriving at the park's imposing entrance. Once they entered, the outside world was forgotten, and they could relax and explore. It took me years to understand and define my childhood feelings about the place. For some reason, I was captivated by the Victorian artifice. The same sense of awe felt by turn-of-the-century visitors to Luna Park and Dreamland, the primitive reaction to music and light, could still be experienced in the 1960s.

I don't know why, but all the Steeplechase rides seemed to move slowly, in a dreamlike state. The attractions I remember best were the simple ones. The Caterpillar was a spinning tunnel of love that began as an open ride and was slowly covered by an unfolding green canopy that permitted lovers to smooch in the dark. The California Red Bats in a cage, in a small tower at the top of a flight of wooden steps, were not small flying mammals but red baseball bats (you fell for that trick only once!). The Ferris wheel was a Victorian relic with slowly moving, brightly painted cars resembling little houses. The ballroom was converted into a television theater filled with black-and-white TV consoles to allow mothers to watch soap operas while their children played in the pavilion's kiddie park. Even the mechanical racehorses circling the park on metal tracks seemed to move in slow motion.

Steeplechase could also be a physical experience that involved sacrifice. Like many children of that era, I wore the "Steeplechase burn," the painful friction abrasions on the forearms caused by trying to slow myself down while riding the giant slide. It didn't matter how many times I was told to fold my arms when going down the slide—once I was moving at a good clip, I'd instinctually put my arms down, leaving skin on the polished wood. There it was: a burn that scabbed over and left a scar that was worn like a badge of honor.

Visual imprints lasted along with physical scars. Visions of shining, whirling silver and gold, stamped tin, whimsical lettering, fluted columns, manicured trees, and elegant statuary are the legacy of Steeplechase. Compared with the rest of Coney, Steeplechase moved slowly. But that only gave me more time to take it in and remember it.

## CHAPTER 11

# Civil Defense

UNTIL THE EARLY 1960s, a large sign hung just inside the Surf Avenue entrance to Stillwell Avenue Subway Terminal, right above Philips candy store. The ominous billboard with red lettering on a yellow background read,

> IN THE EVENT OF AN AIR RAID,
> DO NOT PANIC.
> YOU ARE NOT IN A TARGET AREA.

It was the first thing anyone saw before reaching Surf Avenue, and the tone was not reassuring. I'm not sure if the sign was a holdover from Word War II or if it had been installed during the early 1950s, but it served as a constant reminder of nuclear war.

Not that we needed reminding. At P.S. 188, we practiced duck-and-cover drills, huddled under our desks, faces turned away from the window and heads covered with hands to shield ourselves from flying glass. The drill seemed silly and scary at the same time. The teachers never appreciated the sound effects we made—they were dead serious, and on some level, their adult anxiety penetrated our preadolescent brains. In my preschool days, I believed that the large gray Navy blimps that routinely lumbered across the ocean off Coney Island were free-floating atomic bombs looking for targets. The blimps looked like bigger versions of "fat man" and "little boy," the atomic bombs dropped on Japan during World War II.

The 1950s Coney Island air shows didn't help ease anxieties. The shows were well-attended pageants designed to foster the notion that a nuclear war was inevitable but winnable. The 1962 show was a particularly elaborate assertion of force. The U.S. Air Force brought in an arsenal of ballistic missiles on flatbed trucks and arranged them, in launch position, at the New York Aquarium parking lot and along the entire length of West Tenth Street, from Surf Avenue to the Boardwalk. The array of Atlas and Minuteman missiles created a futuristic amusement park strangely out of place surrounding the Cyclone roller coaster and Wonderland Kiddie Park. The show began on the beach with a simulated nuclear explosion—"a make-believe atomic burst" was the official description—beside the Steeplechase Park pier. A billowing, sooty black mushroom

**Top secret**
This abandoned World War II facility just inside the entrance to Sea Gate was a mystery to me and my friend Daniel Stern, pictured above. Finding a way to sneak into it became my mission.

101

**War relic**
Remains of two gun batteries were left standing on the Sea Gate beach.

cloud filled with flames exploded with a deafening roar and must have fueled more than a few nightmares.

The explosion was quickly followed by a mock invasion of Coney Island by landing craft and soldiers in full battle dress who stormed ashore to take up positions against the swimsuit-clad "enemy." A sonic boom announced formations of fighter jets from Brooklyn's Floyd Bennett Field, which performed acrobatics above the crowds on the Boardwalk. Sky divers dropped from planes and landed on the beach. The air force then orchestrated a slow-speed flyover of light fighter jets and huge prop-driven troop transports that hung at stall speed just over our heads.

The 1962 air show rivaled the massive military displays in Moscow's Red Square. It was the era of the Cuban Missile Crisis and the Berlin Wall, and the show was supposed to be a reassuring diversion for a nervous population in an unstable world. It said, "Don't worry—it's winnable!"

Civil defense was big then. An air raid siren on the light pole in front of Coopey's Corner sounded every day at noon, deafening us as we stood inside the store reading comic books. The siren was also tested regularly at odd times, and we never knew if "this was it." The siren box looked like the head of a robot with a gray funnel hat.

But it wasn't all show. Coney Island was surrounded by target areas such as the Nike missile base a short distance away at Rockaway Point. Sonic booms were a noisy daily occurrence as jets took off from nearby Floyd Bennett Field. Day-Glo yellow fallout-shelter signs began appearing on the buildings of Coney Island Houses just around the time that a civil defense command post was opened in Manhattan Beach at the old U.S. Coast Guard training station.

Coney Island had many mysterious structures, but one in particular captured my imagination. On the ocean, just inside the entrance to Sea Gate, was a small government facility that, I was convinced, was a secret base. The facility consisted of several corrugated metal buildings topped with odd cylindrical ventilators. Next to the buildings was a seventy-foot-tall steel tower and a squat concrete bunker with narrow metal slits facing the ocean. A chain-link fence topped with double rows of barbed wire and signs that read "KEEP OUT—GOVERNMENT PROPERTY" surrounded the enclosure. On the beach in front of the base were two cylindrical concrete pillboxes perched on a ring of wooden pilings. The facility seemed abandoned, but I was convinced it was a secret military command post.

I was told that the compound was a World War II remnant, an old radar station that was part of the submarine defense net that ran from Sea Gate to Staten Island. I was sure it was more than that. I suspected that the government was hiding something both terrible and wonderful right on the beaches of Coney Island: a big surprise for Soviet attackers.

My paranoia came to a head one night in 1962, when I awoke to the sound of diesel engines. A row of unmarked black trucks was lined up on Surf Avenue, and men were carting boxes, metal drums, and what appeared to be machinery into my building. The operation was efficient, taking an hour or less before the empty trucks rumbled off into the night.

My mother thought I had been dreaming, and my friends just thought I was crazy. But my suspicions were confirmed when I mentioned what I had seen to the maintenance man, John. He smiled his gold-toothed smile and said, "Charlie, just hope you never have to find out what's down there." Of course that was the wrong thing to say, because I knew immediately that I would have to find out.

A year later, when a friend told me that the big steel doors to the lower-level incinerator room were not always double-locked and could be opened by using the pointed end of a rat-tail comb, I knew that I'd have to act. My curiosity about the basement had only grown over time, and I finally convinced two friends to accompany me on a secret mission to solve the mystery.

We opened the doors one night and stood nervously at the top of a flight of concrete steps peering at the dim light from the landing below. We were tempted to go back. Maybe this was something that we shouldn't see, and the government would have to kill us if we saw it. Maybe it was something radioactive. But curiosity got the best of us.

When we reached the lower landing, the boxes were visible. We opened the first box and found cans of peanut butter. The second box held cans of water, the next one, tampons. And so it went: toilet paper, first aid kits, the sundry items and everyday supplies needed to survive a nuclear holocaust.

This was not the secret command post that I had envisioned. This was not the stuff of war movies. It was embarrassing and ordinary. It was the banal reality of our national policy of Mutually Assured Destruction. In a Cold War standoff, these cans of food and supplies were as powerful a weapon as nuclear missiles, and none of them would ever be used. We would have to keep our mission a secret.

**Hot property** The command bunker on the Sea Gate beach.

## The Sea Gate Fortress

**W**HEN I was a kid, I couldn't find anyone who knew about the bunkers in Sea Gate, which just made me more curious. In 2000, I finally examined the records of the Sea Gate Association and found the answers.

Just after Pearl Harbor was attacked in 1941, the United States War Department contacted the Sea Gate Association to obtain an easement and construct an army defense battery on the shorefront at Beach Thirty-eighth Street. The battery consisted of antiaircraft gun emplacements, a barracks, a bunker, and a fire control tower to direct the guns. The association was paid $1 for the easement, which was to last for the duration of the war. In 1942, the association sought to dispel rumors that the government had condemned all of Sea Gate and took out advertisements in the *New York Times* announcing that Sea Gate was still in private hands.

In June 1943, the U.S. Army stationed a company of more than one hundred soldiers at the facility and housed them at a barracks on Atlantic Avenue, which has since been turned into a private home. The beachfront was relinquished by the military in 1946, and the bunker was demolished in the 1970s. The circular foundations of the concrete artillery emplacements were never removed—and guard the beach to this day.

CHAPTER 12

# Coney Island: Lost and Found

**Preparing for urban renewal** Bulldozer Bob pulled down the Atlantic Hotel on West Thirty-third Street (above). Terra-cotta medallions of King Neptune were left among the ruins of the Washington Baths Annex (opposite).

ONLY THROUGH war metaphors could what was happening to my neighborhood in 1965 be described. The populace had braced for the invasion. It was not unexpected. Some residents became refugees and fled, others were unable to escape and became prisoners in their own homes, and a small minority tried to fight it out and were crushed. The city was taking their homes. A propaganda campaign attempted to soften up the populace. Billboards appeared on street corners throughout the main area of conflict, announcing "Urban Renewal," followed by a laundry list of names with Mayor Robert Wagner and Governor Nelson Rockefeller at the top. Then the notices arrived from the government, the families packed up, and the doomed buildings were marked with spray paint.

The battleground was populated by residents who had lived in Coney Island for many years. There were men who had built their wood-frame houses with their own hands and women who had given birth to their children in the houses that their husbands had built. Sometimes several generations of one family occupied the same house. Among them were the families of my friends from school, mostly Irish, Italians, and Eastern Europeans. By the time the war ended ten years later, nearly forty city blocks of homes and businesses had been destroyed.

The hardware of war arrived on the back of a flatbed truck. Diesel engines roared to life, and the battle began with the sound of steel treads rattling across pavement like a tank in an old newsreel. The skirmish started on West Thirty-second Street. Condemned houses, marked with an ominous "X" in a crudely painted box, silently awaited their fate. A machine backed across the street and set its sights on a row of wooden bungalows. The bungalows were arranged around a once-picturesque courtyard with a large shade tree in the center. A lattice gazebo and rotted wooden benches surrounded the tree.

The dozer operator wore an old-fashioned leather aviator helmet, with bulging green goggles, and chomped on an unlit cigar. A black cloud of exhaust belched from the machine's rusty stack as it lurched forward and scraped up and over the curb,

105

**Architectural layers**
Demolishing Boardwalk buildings revealed structures that had been hidden for fifty years. The Kensington Hotel beneath the Thunderbolt roller coaster came to light when the Lido Building was torn down in 1979.

shattering the sidewalk. The big steel-toothed bucket dropped down on the roof of the bungalow closest to the street and in an instant ripped it in half, splitting wood and breaking glass. The machine rumbled back and forth across the buildings until nothing but splintered wood, twisted plumbing, tangled wiring, and fields of lath and bricks remained. The sweet smell of wet plaster and cedar rose from the ruins. It was an impressive operation, and by the end of the day, I had gotten to know the operator, a grinning maniac I called Bulldozer Bob. I began to spend a lot of time in the ruins.

Bob was a likable guy who was dedicated to his work. He really loved demolition and he taught me a lot about demolition and deconstruction. In the early days of the war on Coney Island, there were no rules. It was a free-for-all. Buildings were violently crushed or pulled apart without any thought to safety. Sidewalk scaffolding was never erected to protect pedestrians, and the streets were never closed to traffic. Bulldozer Bob had a clear path of destruction. All he had to do was avoid the houses that were still occupied. Sometimes he missed.

Bob became a model of efficiency. He developed a neat trick of threading a one-inch steel cable through the windows and doors of an entire row of houses. He then clipped the cable to the back of the dozer and pulled it as if it were a loose thread on a button. The snapping began, sounding like a series of gunshots. A window shattered, then a porch collapsed, and then, all at once, something gave with a loud crack and all the buildings crashed to the ground. Bob crushed the buildings into a splintery pulp that was easy to scoop and load onto a truck. The big brick buildings were much harder to pull down, however, and the cable trick worked only if the outer walls were weakened.

I could never figure out why the big four-story brick apartment houses were being torn down. It made no sense, even to Bob. But he was just following orders and doing his job. The buildings weren't very old, the plumbing worked, the wiring was still good, and the oak parquet floors were still polished. I had been inside all of the buildings and found beautiful art deco fixtures and stained-glass windows. Salvagers told me that the wooden floor joists were of a quality and length that couldn't be found anymore. Some of the older buildings even had brass plumbing. These apartment houses were a gold mine for scavengers, and as soon as Bob knocked them down, the scavengers pounced on the rubble like hungry jackals. I was pouncing along with them.

I was an eleven-year-old scavenger, working an after-school job that I learned

106  COMING OF AGE IN CONEY ISLAND

**Pink palace**
The ornate terracotta Washington Baths Annex, designed by Michael Marlo and built in 1933, was one of the most beautiful buildings in Coney Island. It was demolished in 1972. Childs Restaurant, to the right, is still standing and may gain landmark status.

from a local guy who drove his old Ford junk wagon over from Cropsey Avenue. I helped him load lengths of cast-iron pipes onto his truck and learned the tricks of the trade, like how to remove copper wires from insulation and get lead out of cast-iron joints.

The trick was fire. We tossed coils of armored wire and broken sections of iron pipe into the big open fires that were always burning on the vast plain of rubble between Surf and Mermaid Avenues. The insulation in the wires and the oakum in the iron joints burned off, leaving tarnished strands of copper and silvery pools of lead. Then I carted everything over to the truck. I was paid by the pound for metal weighed on an old produce scale that hung off the back of the truck. I learned to carry a magnet with me to test painted metal for brass and copper fittings.

I soon went into business for myself, gathering lead to make fishing sinkers to sell to the fishermen on Steeplechase pier. I shattered cast-iron joints for the lead rings, which I folded and carted home to melt on our kitchen stove. My mother supported my endeavor and even gave me a rusty old iron skillet to use for my home foundry. My first batch of sinkers was primitive, cut from lengths of raw metal. I banged the soft lead into strips, cut the strips into sections, and drove a nail through the top to form a hole for fishing line. It was hard to sell the sinkers because they were ugly and the weights were inaccurate. So I saved up and bought a sinker mold at Cy's Tackle Shop on Sixteenth Street. It was a waffle-iron-type contraption that produced perfect teardrop sinkers with molded numbers on the sides.

I soon tired of carrying heavy weights around, and melting lead on the stove became too much trouble. I thought it would be better to stockpile scrap under my bed and sell it all at once for a big payday. But the lead ingots I created were too large to be moved. Eventually my mother asked the building maintenance man to remove the entire stash. "What kind of kid are you raising?" he asked her as he hauled the heavy metal from our apartment. After my anger subsided, I began to wonder the same thing.

I continued to spend my time in the ruins, because the desolation seemed to fit my mood. I began collecting decorative architectural items, the gargoyles and terra-cotta lions and eagles knocked from their high perches. I would have happily spent the rest of the summer in the ruins except that something unexpected happened. I returned home one afternoon to find my mother waving a letter from my school. My heart sank as she opened it, but I wasn't in trouble this time. The letter said that I'd won a scholarship to attend summer art classes at the Brooklyn Museum of Art. Art was my favorite subject in school, mostly because of the influence of Mrs. Pomerantz, my art teacher at P.S. 288. Early in the spring, I'd won a school prize for two of my drawings, which were later exhibited in the annual Lever House art show in Manhattan. We'd even taken a class trip to see the show. The scholarship was my prize.

I had to take a bus and two trains to get to my classes at the museum. My teacher was Mr. Reynolds, a talented, middle-aged black man. He took us on field trips to Prospect Park and the Brooklyn Botanical Gardens for life drawing and to the museum galleries to draw objects from the African art collection. It was during one of Mr. Reynolds's field trips that I discovered the museum's sculpture garden.

The garden was a fenced-in, weed-covered lot behind the museum next to the parking lot and was not open to the public. It was littered with bits and pieces of demolished buildings from all over New York City. There were ornate street lamps and manhole covers, gargoyles and friezes, sandstone cornerstones and limestone animals. It was filled with the same stuff that I had at home, the things I had saved from the ruins of Coney Island. I realized that what I had at home was an art collection, and that these objects were appreciated. Mr. Reynolds said that the museum was planning to display the items. He told us about the demolition of Penn Station in Manhattan and the crimes committed by greedy developers.

The sculpture garden reminded me of a lost-and-found department, a refuge for all the beautiful items the city was losing, a place where such objects could be kept safely until reclaimed. I imagined that someday the objects I was saving in Coney Island would wind up at the museum to be appreciated, instead of being destroyed. That is exactly what happened.

Today, visitors to the carefully landscaped sculpture garden can take a walk down the central path to a small glass building. There they find a terra-cotta King Neptune, with green flowing hair and a golden crown and trident. For years, King Neptune had gazed out to sea from atop the Washington Baths Annex building on Coney Island's Boardwalk. When the building was destroyed in 1972, I rescued King Neptune from a pile of rubble. After spending many years with me, Neptune was the first piece I donated to the Brooklyn Museum. There are now other lost pieces of Coney Island in the garden. They may someday be reclaimed and returned to their former glory.

**King Neptune**
I salvaged a medallion from Washington Baths and donated it to the Brooklyn Museum in 1981.

CHAPTER 13

# Steeplechase 1966: The Final Season

**Great expectations**
I took this photograph in 1965, the year after the park closed. The following year, my friends and I found our way back into the park.

NINETEEN SIXTY-SIX would be our last summer of freedom, the last year before my friends and I got summer jobs. A brutally hot July had followed Coney Island's first race riots the previous May, leaving a certain edginess to the neighborhood. The island was changing fast, but so were we.

We were wild thirteen-year-olds that summer, and our attention was elsewhere, mostly on girls. But unexpectedly, we found a way to hang on to our childhood just a little longer. Ever since Steeplechase Park had closed two years before, we had probed the perimeter, searching for a way to sneak in. Then we finally found it. This would be the summer of our last season at Steeplechase Park. Now that we had discovered the secret entrance, the park was all ours.

What we'd found was not an actual entrance, but a way to sneak in without being seen. Halfway up West Nineteenth Street was a row of tall plane trees standing along the twenty-foot, corrugated-tin fence surrounding the Steeplechase roller coaster. By placing our backs against the fence and our feet against the trees, we could walk horizontally up the tree, one step at a time, grab a tree branch, and swing over the barbed wire and onto the roller-coaster platform. The trees camouflaged us as we climbed, and once inside, we were hidden by the enclosed coaster shed. The coaster, swimming pool, and bathhouse were fenced in on both sides, creating an enclosure cut off from the watchman and his dogs. We had season passes to our own amusement park, and the August 1966 season was officially open for business.

The first time we went in, we didn't go too far. We just sat in the coaster's cars waiting to see if we'd be discovered. Our initial visits were secretive, and we played it safe by whispering and tiptoeing around, not knowing if we could be detected. Once we felt secure, the first order of business became exploration, to see how far we could penetrate into the park. From the coaster shed, we walked along the tracks to the first dip, where we found the powerhouse shed, a small sheet-metal building containing tools, oil cans, and the main motor and belts. We transformed the shed into a clubhouse and cleaned it by spreading pails of sawdust and

sand onto the greasy floor. Then we made seats out of empty oil cans. This became our center of operation.

During our first tentative foray into the southern end of the enclosure, I made an interesting discovery: the remains of the base of the old Giant See-Saw, a ride I had seen only in old postcards, an immense steel structure with a cantilevered arm supporting Ferris wheels at either end. The ride, part of the original Steeplechase Park of 1897, had been dismantled years ago, but the base had survived, and the roller coaster had been built around it.

On the northern side of our clubhouse was the smokestack of the old power plant, another holdover from the original park. The coaster tracks circled the chimney and dipped down beside the empty swimming pool. It didn't take long to find our way to the Steeplechase tower overlooking the pool. The

**Probing the perimeter**
A cat prowled the lawn at the closed park (above). In winter, the Boardwalk entrance was fenced (right). In summer, the circular sign was topped with a multicolored canvas tent.

unlocked door at the tower's base opened onto a ladder. Three of us scrambled up the steel ladder to a balcony on the roof just below the flagpole. A dusty American flag was still sitting on a shelf, carefully folded.

There was a small room at the top of the tower, crossed by a thick beam and a pulley for lifting materials. Larry, the stuntman of our group, immediately grabbed the beam and swung out over the abyss. "What are you gonna do if that beam breaks?" I asked him. "Grab the ladder," he said. "You'd be on the ground with that beam through your skull before you could ever let go," I said. He knew I was right. We had stumbled onto something special, and I didn't want anyone to spoil it by getting killed.

The tower hideout was our big discovery. It was a secret perch, the perfect place from which to observe the park and keep an eye on the watchman. I discovered that we could move the watchman around the park like a puppet by unscrewing lightbulbs and tossing them to the ground in different directions. The dogs would run toward the sound, and the watchman would follow. He never thought to look up. We became more brazen and started going into Steeplechase at night to watch the fireworks from the tower. By then we'd formed the Steep Club and made up rules of conduct. One of the rules required us to wear all-black clothing when sneaking in at night. We had taken in a few new members, and when one of them showed up wearing white Keds sneakers, we sent him home.

Firework nights were the best times of all, because we could watch them from atop the tower, the best seat in Coney Island. But the fireworks also exposed us when some people outside the fence noticed us during a bright explosion. We heard voices from the street: "Hey, look at that, there's a bunch of kids up there!" By the next flash, we had dissolved into the shadows and could no longer be seen.

By September, I had become so brazen that I decided to put my own lock on one of

**Watching the watchman** The guard patrolled the central court of the closed park (above). My friends and I tried to monitor his movements while on our reconnaissance forays. The Bowery entrance (below) had zinc lions perched at either side of the vaulted arch. The lions were later donated to the Brooklyn Museum.

STEEPLECHASE 1966: THE FINAL SEASON   111

**Clubhouse**
This section of the park was our private domain. The guard dogs did not patrol it, and sneaking in was easy. The tower served as our lookout, and we would watch fireworks from the top balcony on Tuesday nights. The building behind the tower, a remnant of the 1897 park, had survived the 1907 fire.

the coaster's exit gates so that we wouldn't have to climb in. Next to the big smokestack on Surf Avenue was a fire exit that had a sliding bolt that was easily opened. I brought the lock and chain from my bicycle and slipped the chain through a hole in the fence and through the gate. The padlock hung outside and could be opened with a key. For the next couple of weeks, I felt like the park's owner as I walked around Coney Island with the key to Steeplechase Park hanging around my neck.

The plan worked beautifully until we arrived one morning to find that the lock and chain had been cut and the door bolted shut. It was an eerie feeling. Only years later did I figure out what had happened. We didn't know it at the time, but Jimmy Onorato, the former manager of Steeplechase, still had an office above the marquee of the Tilyou Theater across the street. He must have seen us from his window and tipped off the watchman. We knew that they were onto us.

We were soon careless again, and that's how we were eventually caught. Having grown bored with our enclosed roller-coaster compound, we decided to take a chance and sneak over to the main pavilion. Larry, Howie, and I were tiptoeing across the handball courts when the dogs spotted us and gave chase, with the watchman following close behind. We ran at full speed toward our only escape: the parking lot entrance on Nineteenth Street. We were so terrified that we failed to see a low chain-link fence blocking our escape. We hit the fence at full speed, bouncing backward as if slung from a slingshot. I jumped to my feet and scurried under the fence, while Larry climbed over it, tearing his hands. Howie lay there, stunned and choking, until he disappeared from view as the dogs were upon him.

Larry and I were shaken but laughing as we trotted toward Surf Avenue. What were we going to do? We had once found a dead cat in the maze of lockers in the old Steeplechase bathhouse. The cat had been trapped and killed by the dogs. Its bloody paw prints on the wall were a horrifying reminder of how vicious the dogs could be. And now the dogs had Howie!

Larry and I had turned onto Surf Avenue to look through the fence when we spotted Howie being dragged to the Seventeenth Street entrance by the watchman. Howie was crying as the dogs followed him in a pack, snarling at this heels. "Down Nellie, down Girl," the watchman yelled as he tried to break up the dogs. Nellie was the pack's leader, a vicious yellow beast that wanted a piece of Howie. Her fangs tore his pants leg as he was shoved onto the street. "Stay out of here if you know what's good for you," the watchman sneered as he locked the gate. "Or next time you're going to jail."

Larry and I were in stitches and couldn't catch a breath. It was just too hilarious. "Whoa, Nellie!" we screamed. "Dooooown, Nellie Girl!" "Nellie, Nellie, Nellie!" we howled over and over as we walked home. It became our slogan, and Howie would never forgive us.

CHAPTER 14

# A Day in the Life

GARY HEIDEN was my best friend and was almost as much of a loner as I was. Being friends with Gary was as close to being alone as one could get while still having a friend. We met when we were three years old and spent our childhood years exploring the neighborhood together. Gary's family used an odd expression, "going down below," to describe a visit to Coney Island's amusement area. It was a euphemism that conjured subterranean images: a trapdoor, a ship's engine room, deafening, greasy, and stifling, with pistons pounding. Or it could have meant hellfire and brimstone. "Where are you two going?" Gary's mother would ask. "We're going down below, Ma," Gary would reply, as we took off on one of our adventures.

"Going down below!" And off we went.

Coney Island never seemed to be divided between the amusements and the apartments and other buildings. The transition from grocery store to spook house was gradual. It was possible to walk from my front door to any ride in Coney Island without crossing a street. We only had to climb onto the Boardwalk in front of our apartment building, and it was a straight shot to any ticket booth on the island. The rides and amusements, privately owned and located on city streets, seemed more like storefronts, only louder and more colorful.

Gary and I always had scams. After the big Ravenhall fire burned half a block of Boardwalk businesses in 1963, we took a wagon down to the site and loaded it up with crates of orange soda that we found in the

**No crowds**
Early summer morning, before visitors arrived, was my favorite time of day. I prowled the Bowery to find odd jobs.

ruins. We sold the soda for five cents per bottle in the projects, but people weren't happy with the taste, and we had to give out a few refunds before skipping out. Another summer we collected Yoo-Hoo bottle caps from every soft drink machine on the island. Yoo-Hoo had a promotion where three caps got you on most rides for free. We never bought a bottle of the stuff—we just emptied the caps from soda machines or grabbed them as people opened a bottle. Our pockets were bulging with caps, and we rode for free all summer.

Gary and I had a regular route through Coney Island that began with the peepholes in the windows of Silvers Baths, where we peered in at the naked ladies, and ended late in the day outside Steeplechase Park, where we asked departing patrons for their tickets. Then we told the ticket takers that our parents were inside and asked to be let back in. Sometimes it worked, but more often it didn't.

In the winter, we fed the feral cats that lived under the Boardwalk ramps. We weren't allowed to keep dogs and cats in the projects, but Gary and I were always tending the strays of Coney Island. We adopted stray dogs and kept them around the grounds of the projects until housing management called the pound to take them away. It was impossible to hide them. Cats were easier. I brought home any pregnant cat that I saw around the neighborhood. My mother didn't mind, because she felt sorry for the cats, especially in winter. We kept the kittens for a while and tried to find them homes. But it was always risky, because the management could evict tenants for keeping cats or dogs.

Gary and I had all kinds of small pets: turtles, lizards, fish, and the rabbits that we stole from the hutches behind the Sea Gate Garage. When anyone asked where we got the rabbits, we said that we had found them on the beach. Gary told his friend Virginio about the rabbits, and Virginio asked him for one. Soon afterward, we saw Virginio and his brother Poppo carrying a bag of rabbits down Surf Avenue. I told him he was being a little greedy and asked him how many pets he needed. Virginio said he was selling them to people on Thirtieth Street. "They're good to eat, man, delicious." Soon the rabbit hutches disappeared from behind the garage.

There wasn't much in the way of wildlife around the projects. The area seemed sterile. Sometimes a bat or a hapless squirrel would appear and cause big excitement. The one phenomenon that drew in everyone was the migration of monarch butterflies. It was a sad ritual. When the spring migration made landfall at Coney Island, the kids went crazy. "The moniks are here! I see a monik!" All the

**Lost landmarks**
I took these photos in 1965: Tilyou Theater (left) and Sixtieth Precinct on West Eighth Street (right), a former courthouse built by John McKane.

little brats would run to Coopey's Corner to buy butterfly nets and catch the creatures. Soon jars full of struggling monarchs were displayed proudly by their captors. By the end of the day, the sidewalks of the projects were littered with broken glass and shredded luminescent wings.

★

The ocean provided us with food and recreation. Gary and I caught flounders, porgies, stripers, and sometimes bluefish from the rocks and jetties along the beach. On winter nights when the tides were right, big schools of Boston mackerel ran close to shore. I'd bundle up, pull on big rubber boots, and ride my bike to the Steeplechase pier to fish all night. Gary and I used jigs of white surgical tubing pulled over long hooks and set up a rig of up to five hooks. Sometimes we hooked five fish at once and could barely reel them in. It was so cold one night that the mackerel were quick-frozen right on the pier. I took a basket of them home and put them in the kitchen sink to clean. My mother came in just as the big pile of frozen fish began to thaw and go into spasms, twitching and sliding around on the floor. She hated fish with the heads on, and they nearly scared her to death.

★

A big problem with Gary and most of my other friends was that they slept late. I was a morning person, always up at daybreak and out beachcombing before anyone else woke up. It was a good way to find interesting things and make money, but I had to get an early start. On winter days, the wind scoured the beach, leaving coins perched on tiny pyramids of sand ready to be harvested. Silver coins were tarnished black and had to

**Magic Carpet**
At the end of this walk-through ride, a couch dropped riders onto a canvas conveyor belt that dumped them out the front exit to the cheers of onlookers.

A DAY IN THE LIFE 115

**Madhouse**
This dark ride on Stillwell Avenue was underneath the Tornado roller coaster in a space formerly used by the Central Baths. It was originally called the Devil's Pit.

be cleaned before spending; the pennies were crusted with a green corrosion that was harder to remove. The most exciting finds were Indian head pennies.

In the summer, I used a sand sifter made from a wooden soda crate. I attached driftwood handles and nailed chicken wire to the bottom and a narrow strip of tin to the front. The contraption was pulled through the sand by the handles and tilted from side to side so sand could be shaken out and valuables revealed. The best spot was under the Boardwalk, where people dropped copious amounts of change through the cracks. But it was also a place that yielded syringes and glue tubes left by junkies and glue sniffers. I had to watch my back while working alone in the gloomy shadows, but it was better than arguing over the split.

I usually combed the beach down to West Tenth Street and then hit the Bowery looking for odd jobs, anything that a kid could do for a fast buck. Early on Saturday mornings, I could be found painting concession stands, unloading "plush prizes" from the back of a concessioner's station wagon, washing rubber floor mats with a hose, or carrying trash from private stalls and dumping it illegally into city trash cans. My big ambition was to turn fifteen and get working papers to operate the rides. But sand sifting was still the best way to make money, because it seemed like magic. Money from heaven.

I also collected interesting things that I found on the beach and kept a "Coney Island cabinet of wonders" filled with strange objects and artifacts, including odd pieces of driftwood amusement signs, homemade fishing lures and floats, old bottles, and an array of plastic toys and doll heads. I organized expeditions with various friends and journeyed to the far corners of Coney Island to find specimens.

Daniel Stern and I chiseled away at Dead Man's Rock in Sea Gate and carried home boxes of "fossils." John Van Alst helped me bring home old offset printing plates found outside the office of the *Brooklyn Daily* on West Twenty-fifth Street. The centerpiece of my living room was a life-sized papier-mâché sculpture of Cleopatra that I scavenged from a promotional display outside the Tilyou Theater after a showing of the movie *Cleopatra*. My family's apartment was different than the others. It was cluttered, filled floor to ceiling with books and strange artwork in a building where most people had spotless floors and protected their furniture with plastic slipcovers. Kids liked to visit because my mother wasn't a fussy housekeeper.

Every day was an adventure in Coney Island. There was always a spectacle going on, natural or man-made, from the crackling ice floes that danced in the surf during the winter to the air shows and fireworks of summer. The line between natural and unnatural sometimes blurred. For instance, we had two sunsets. The first occurred when the sun set in the west, and the second came shortly afterward. As the last glow of daylight faded, a small flotilla of barges was towed out to sea. When the procession reached a point directly south of Coney Island, it slowed and erupted into a conflagration that burned brightly for several hours, then faded, leaving a thin red line on the dark horizon. It was the nightly ritual of New York's garbage scows being towed out to sea and burned. Hours later, if the wind was right, a silvery shower of ash would reach the shore, falling on us like snowflakes as the barges were towed back into the harbor. This strange practice continued until the early 1960s.

Another phenomenon that we took for granted was the sticky tar that coated the beach. As a child, I thought that the big globs of tar were natural, something produced by the ocean, like seaweed or barnacles. After leaving the beach, my sister and I always carried seashells to scrape the bottoms of our feet before going home. We didn't know that the tar was heavy bunker oil released from ship bilges as they entered New York Harbor. We didn't question these things—we accepted them as part of life.

Everyone had a favorite part of Coney Island. What I liked best were the mechanical figures that populated the dark rides. One was a laughing clown that sat on a box at the Crazy Ghosts spook house located at the bus stop outside the Stillwell Avenue Subway Terminal. The clown was memorable because I couldn't escape his laugh while waiting for the bus. Wearing a polka-dot jumpsuit and a conical hat, he moved in clacking spasms, rocking rhythmically to an annoying laugh-loop. Repeated over and over, the laugh was mocking, as if he could detect your anxiety over missing the bus. The laugh track echoed so loudly that it made the entire terminal seem like Coney's biggest dark ride.

The mechanical figures that really fascinated me populated the Torture Chamber on West Twelfth Street. The chamber was a grisly exhibit with an entrance flanked by a mechanical elephant crushing a man's head. The big gray foot moved up and down as recorded shrieks played on a scratchy

**Street scene**
In 1968, I stood next to a friend's car on Surf Avenue in front of Coney Island Houses.

A DAY IN THE LIFE   117

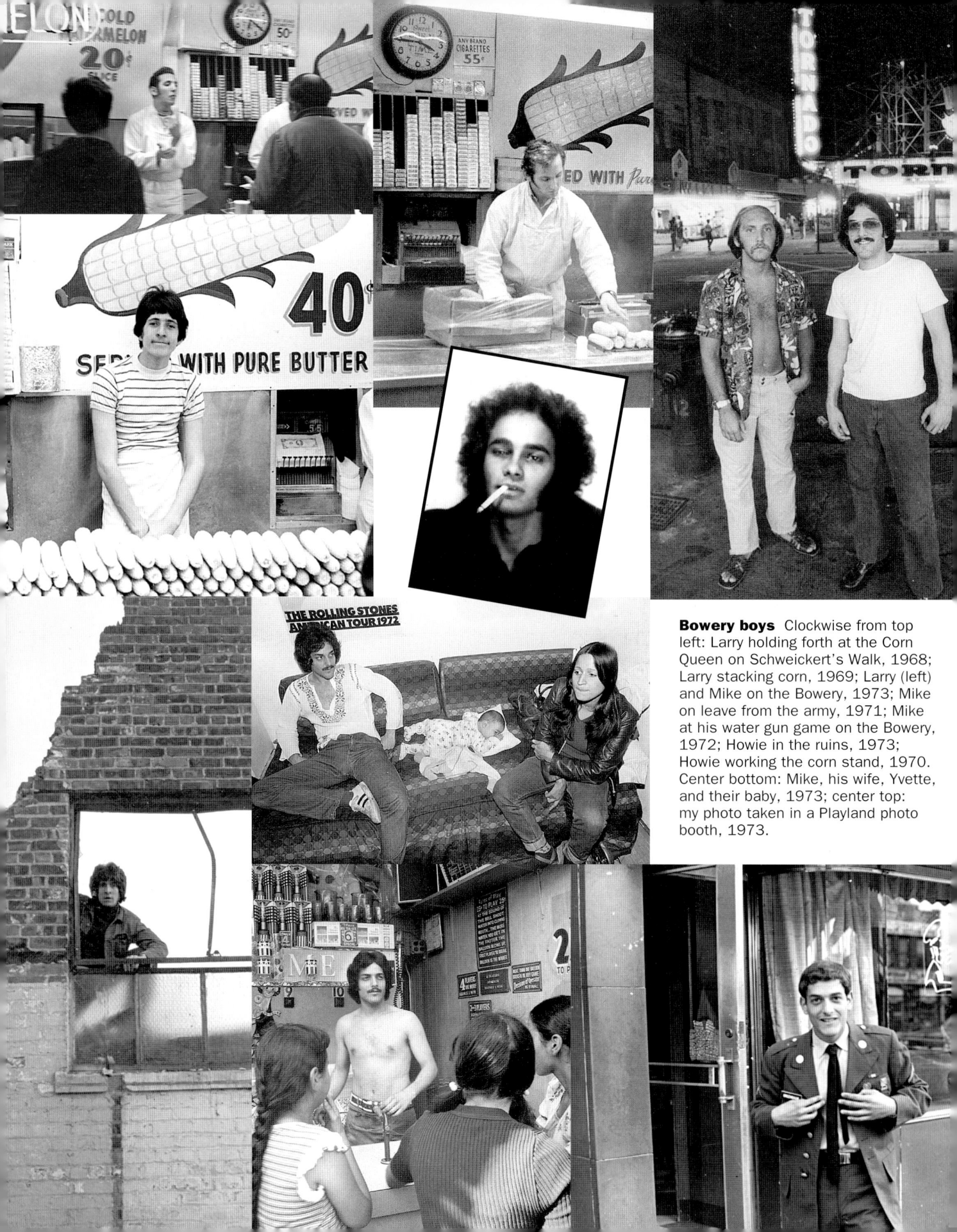

**Bowery boys** Clockwise from top left: Larry holding forth at the Corn Queen on Schweickert's Walk, 1968; Larry stacking corn, 1969; Larry (left) and Mike on the Bowery, 1973; Mike on leave from the army, 1971; Mike at his water gun game on the Bowery, 1972; Howie in the ruins, 1973; Howie working the corn stand, 1970. Center bottom: Mike, his wife, Yvette, and their baby, 1973; center top: my photo taken in a Playland photo booth, 1973.

record. I asked my father to take me there, but he thought it wasn't good for a ten-year-old. So I went by myself one day and paid a dime to get in. It was dark, and I was the only customer. I wandered around the dank exhibit hall looking at each diorama: an unfortunate man with hot molten lead being poured into his iron boots, a poor soul tied to a cross and being stung to death by bees, and a victim being drawn and quartered.

A hand gripped my shoulder, and I turned to find a beautiful woman telling me that I was too young to be in the chamber. I was startled: she looked as if she had just stepped from an exhibit, perhaps one of the jilted women seeking revenge. She didn't seem real, and I didn't know what to say. I was embarrassed but excited by the strangeness of the experience and turned to look at the exhibit. When I turned back, she was gone. It left me with an eerie feeling.

I had a crush on an attractive mechanical woman installed at the entrance to a Bowery dark ride. She moved in three directions: she turned right, then turned left, and then looked straight ahead and down. I liked to stand in front of her so that when she turned to look down she was looking straight at me. I enjoyed the eye contact. She was curvaceous, with dark black hair and the most realistic blue eyes. I visited her nearly every day until the season ended and the ride was shuttered. When the season opened the following year, I went to visit her and was shocked to find that she had been painted a bilious green, clothed in rags, and turned into a goblin. I was heartbroken.

★

When you grow up in Coney Island, the novelty of the rides wears off very fast, and you have to create your own adventure. That's why my friends and I formed the

**Just my type**
I was always drawn to attractive sideshow workers. This talker at a typical traveling show on West Twelfth Street was trying to lure the crowd inside to see a gorilla transform into a shapely woman.

**Bowery girl**
A hot summer evening on the Bowery, 1972.

Jackass Club. We were every ride owner's nightmare. Joining the club was easy: we had to go on every major ride in Coney Island at least once. The higher levels of "Jackass" were more difficult to attain because they required us to perform certain stunts, beginning with "no hands" in the front car of all the roller coasters. We started with a simple coaster such as the Wild Mouse and worked our way through the Tornado, the Thunderbolt, and the Bobsled, until we reached the Cyclone. That was level one.

The next level involved standing up on a ride while braced against the safety bar, not a dangerous stunt but one that gave the club its name. Reaching the level of "ultimate Jackass" was the hardest. For that, we had to go on a ride the first day it was allowed to reopen after a serious accident or injury, preferably in the same car where the incident occurred. After a summer of stupidity, the Jackass Club became boring, and we soon became interested in girls and used the rides for a different purpose.

Sex was everywhere in Coney Island, and it wasn't hidden. There was always a free "live sex show" under the Boardwalk. It was hard to avoid stumbling across amorous couples who were so distracted or drunk that they didn't care what they were doing or who was watching. As we got older, we found it easy to meet girls who came down to Coney Island for a little fun. The relationships never got serious, because as soon as the girls' parents found out we lived in Coney Island, they assumed the worst. We never got a second date. We had to stick with the local girls.

The real reason for working in Coney was the women. When my friends and I began getting jobs on the Bowery, we had it made. It was easy to pick up girls or get phone numbers. Even if one of us had a steady girlfriend, there were always plenty more on the side. All of my buddies from the 1966 Steep Club worked the concessions. Larry worked the corn stand in the alley across from Nathan's. Howie at first worked the corn stand, too, but he left to become the "Mad Guesser" of people's ages and weights, and then wound up selling souvenirs at the Gold Mine on Jones Walk. Both had good spiels, but Mike's was the best.

Mike was a true carny: a talker, a hustler, and a comedian. It was in his blood. He could seduce anyone into playing his game. We called him "Mike the Mouth" because he had the best rap on the Bowery for attracting women. Everyone had a gimmick, and Mike's was his shy but sincere act that always attracted the girls, who wanted to mother him. The microphone meant power to Mike, the power to seduce. He worked balloon races, greyhound races, the dime pitch, the basket toss, anything and everything that put him in the spotlight before an audience of girls.

Working the corn stand even entailed routines that attracted attention. The corn wasn't just buttered. It was buttered while being twirled and tossed in the air. The watermelons and pineapples were sliced with a big machete, with the fingers kept as close to the blade as possible to amuse and terrify the customers. During winter, the counter's corn boilers were kept uncovered to create the mysterious illusion of invisibility. The customers couldn't see the operator as the corn was handed through a curtain of steam. A face would poke out of the cloud and then disappear.

Mike was the one who always went first.

He was the first to work the Bowery, the first to get laid, the first to join the army, the first to get married, the first to have a child. And the first to die. After leaving the army, where he had made a lot of money running poker games, Mike seemed lost and needed work, so his brother got him a job on Wall Street. When I went to visit him there, I found him sitting in the mail room wearing plaid pants and an oversized tie, smoking a big cigar, with his feet up on the desk as he told jokes to his coworkers. He looked like a clown. The job didn't last more than a few weeks, and he went right back to Coney Island. It was his life.

Mike sometimes made midnight calls from the Bowery. "Charlie," he'd say, "you can't believe this girl I met, and she's got a car. Can you watch the stand for me?" "It's late, Mike. Why don't you just close up?" But he'd plead, "Charlie, it's just for an hour. She's got a car and lives in Bensonhurst." I once took over the stand for Mike just before his boss showed up to ask what the hell I was doing there. Mike didn't mind. Women came first, and there would always be other jobs.

The rest of us went on to other things, but Mike stayed. He did the Coney carny routine for more than twenty-five years, working long summer hours and collecting unemployment all winter. I lost touch with him over the years. Larry worked for the New York Transit Authority at the Stillwell Avenue Subway Terminal. He saw Mike occasionally, and they remained friends. "Even after he got sick," Larry said, "Mike could still beat me at basketball. He never slowed down."

Howie lost touch with Mike but ran into him one winter afternoon while cashing a check at the bank on Twelfth Street. It was about a year before Mike died, and he was alone, walking through the snow toward the Boardwalk carrying a can of cat food and a can opener. He told Howie that he came down to Coney every other day to feed a cat that he had befriended over the summer. The two hadn't seen each other for a while, and it was an awkward encounter.

Mike worked at Coney Island as long as he could. Only toward the very end did he tell people he was dying. I found out too late and didn't make it to his funeral, but I was glad to know that he had continued doing what he loved. Mike stayed in Coney Island after the rest of us moved on. He was a true carny to the end.

**True believer**
The last time I photographed Mike was the summer of 1974, when he was working at Pete's Water Race on the Bowery.

CHAPTER 15

# Parachute

THE MOST FAMOUS landmark in Coney Island, the Parachute Jump was known as the "Eiffel Tower of Brooklyn." The yellow-and-red steel tower rose from a six-sided art deco base and gradually tapered to a narrow stem topped with twelve cantilevered steel arms, spreading out like petals on a flower, each arm lifting one parachute. It resembled the Eiffel Tower wearing a lattice sombrero. Originally operated as a thrill ride at the 1939–40 New York World's Fair, the tower was dismantled and moved to Coney Island when the fair closed.

The Parachute Jump was developed for the military in the 1930s as a training simulator for airborne troops. Each furled parachute with its rider seated in a harness was carried aloft by a lift rope and guided by six steel cables. When the parachutes reached the top, a release mechanism was tripped, and the parachutes and riders went into free fall for several seconds until the chutes opened and slid down the cables. Their fall was broken by shock absorbers mounted on tall poles. When the parachute frame caught the springs, the riders swung wildly through the air until the ground crew was able to secure the chute and let them off.

The Parachute Jump was very temperamental and rarely made money. It could not operate when it was windy and needed a large ground crew. The parachutes sometimes got tangled in the cables, requiring dangerous rescues. Most people were just too afraid to ride it.

But riding it was my childhood fantasy, and the billowing, orange-and-white silk chutes were always in my dreams. My attempt to ride it became a yearly ritual. At the beginning of every summer, as far back as I can remember, my father and I would take a walk on the Boardwalk and stand beneath the freshly painted tower, and he'd say to me, "Want to take a ride?" We'd approach the ticket booth, and I'd stand on tiptoe next to a ruler painted on the side of the booth. And every year I was rejected for being too small.

My father was a brooding and mysterious man, a muscular man with a wry sense of humor that was offset by his dark side: his drinking. He was my hero, and I treasured each moment spent with him. The disappointment of being unable to ride the Parachute Jump with him was magnified by the fact that he made the offer only once a year, and each time I came up short.

In 1962, all of that changed. I was almost nine and had grown up—I was finally tall enough to ride. I had come of age. From the moment he bought our tickets, everything moved in slow motion. We were ushered

**Coney monument**
The cables hanging from the tower whipped in the wind (opposite). I took the photo at left from the top of the motor room, looking straight up. The tower forms a perfect six-sided star.

123

through a portal to the parachutes. My father then helped me onto the worn canvas seat. A tangle of wires and cables and buckles attached us to the lines of the chute above. A safety strap, really no more than a rope with a brass latch, secured us to the seat. The strap was at my chin, and I could have easily slipped out. The ground crew stepped back, a switch was thrown, and we jerkily began our ascent.

That moment is fixed forever in my mind. I was finally reunited with the father who had abandoned me. Now it was just the two of us, rising into the heavens, fulfilling a fantasy I had had for years. As the cable lifted us, the sounds and music from the beach and Boardwalk seemed to get louder and then began to fade, muffled by the whirring cables and rustling silk above our heads. It was sunny and warm, and my father smiled at me. He looked strong and serene, and he draped his big tattooed arm across my shoulder to keep me securely in the seat. A soft whooshing sound came from above as another chute sailed past us toward the ground.

Gradually, the view opened up. Just in front of us was the monolithic housing project where I lived. Spread out along the sweeping curve of Surf Avenue were rows of multicolored bungalows and bathhouses dotted with ailanthus trees and the crowns of big oaks and the shimmering ocean beyond. In the distance rose the great mosaic turrets of the Half Moon Hotel. A kaleidoscope of colorful rides and crowds of people spun below us. Higher and higher we rose. Compressed into those sunny moments were all of my childhood yearnings, finally answered. Then, without warning, we reached the top.

The chute hit and exploded. We were falling. A thought flashed through my mind: "No, please don't let it end so soon." But all thoughts soon faded as the wind rushed past my ears as we sailed to the ground. Years of listening to the screams of parachute riders had not prepared me for the dizzying sensa-

**Going up**
In 1973, I climbed partway up the tower and took this photo.

**Parachutists**
More than anything else, I wanted to ride the Parachute Jump. I knew that someday It would be my turn.

tion of the fall. We slid down the cables with the billowing shroud rippling above us, the ground rising rapidly. I could see upturned faces watching us.

The chute caught the springs, and we bounced like marionettes until little wooden stairs were brought over and we shakily stepped to the ground. I could barely get the words out: "We did it, Daddy, we really did it." And in my childish exuberance, I imagined that something had changed, that somehow I'd proven myself, and maybe my father would move back with us and then we could ride the Parachute Jump all summer long. Anything seemed possible.

We walked across the Boardwalk to the railing overlooking the beach. My father pulled his curved silver hip flask from his pocket and took a long swig, wiped his mouth, and put the flask back in his pocket. Then we walked home, my mind reeling with the wonder of it all.

★

Three years later, on June 9, 1965, I stood mesmerized, watching a bare-chested man clinging to the aircraft warning mast high atop the Parachute Jump. A crowd of onlookers taunted him from the Boardwalk, three hundred feet below. He unscrewed the warning lights from the top of the mast, cursed, and hurled them to the ground. Shattering glass sent the crowd running for cover. The man hooked his legs around the top rung of the mast's ladder and rose his fists, arched backward, and howled at the sky.

A twin-engine plane approached from the west. The silver plane had bold lettering on the side: "*New York Daily News:* New York's Picture Newspaper." A photographer hung from an open door and took pictures. The man on the mast clawed at the air, a miniature King Kong, frantically swinging at the airplane, challenging his tormenters. The plane circled twice and headed south over the ocean.

The man scurried up and down the ladder like an insect. He shook his fist at the men in blue uniforms climbing toward him across the spindly steel framework of the Parachute Jump. Spiderlike, they moved

(NEWS foto by Nick Sorrentino)
Cop keeps an eye on crowd watching precarious rescue attempts atop parachute jump.

**Looking up**
On June 9, 1965, I watched a dramatic rescue attempt. The next day, I saw myself (circled) in the *Daily News*.

across the web of steel, trailing silky tethers as they slowly encircled him. But the man on the mast had no tethers. He was free: a tiny speck silhouetted against a brilliant blue sky, raging at the world.

An hour later, the man was brought down safely. The gawkers on the Boardwalk had grown bored and dispersed, feeling cheated out of a dramatic jump or fall. I was still waiting, hoping to catch a glimpse of the climber. Finally, a door at the base of the tower swung open, and a handcuffed man holding a cigarette emerged, surrounded by a ring of policemen. He was a thin Puerto Rican with a narrow face and a slight mustache, wearing black slacks and no shirt. I pressed my face against the chain-link fence and stared at him. As he passed, he paused and looked right at me. For an instant, our eyes met, and I turned away in embarrassment.

The next morning, the whole episode was given big play in the *Daily News*. The man was identified as Carlos Ortiz, thirty-eight, a laborer who had gotten into a fight with his wife, gotten drunk, missed work, and, in a fit of despair, decided to climb the abandoned Parachute Jump. In the centerfold spread was a photograph of the onlookers on the Boardwalk. At the right was a policeman holding a nightstick. The caption read, "Cop keeps an eye on crowd watching precarious rescue attempts atop parachute jump." At the extreme left side of the picture was a twelve-year-old boy, wearing a short-sleeve shirt, arms folded, staring intently into the sky.

**Top of the world**
I stood on the roof of the motor room just before starting my 1973 climb up the tower.

126   COMING OF AGE IN CONEY ISLAND

CHAPTER 16

# Solving a Family Mystery

SOMETIMES IT seemed as if my family had been banished to an island and was living in exile. Assorted relatives visited us, but I felt disconnected from them as they drifted in and out of our lives. Just when I got to know them, they were gone. We were on our own.

I never knew my Sicilian grandfather well until he got married for the third time to an Italian mail-order bride and, at the age of sixty-nine, had a child with her. He brought his new wife and baby to visit us in Coney Island Houses. Paul Calabro, my grandfather, was an artist, an eccentric, and a talented painter and jeweler. He had old-world manners and a superstitious mind. He was a reclusive man who believed in the evil eye. Paul owned property in Long Island and had built a large house with his own hands. My mother didn't know him very well, either, because her parents had separated when she was a child. Shortly after Paul started his third family, he cut us off, and I never saw him again.

My grandmother, Ruth Gilbert, Paul's first wife, was a true bohemian. She was a large woman, foul-mouthed, sarcastic, witty, and flirtatious, and she could eviscerate you with her vicious sense of humor. She smoked marijuana before it was popular and spoke Chinese and a little Arabic. Ruth was the entertainment editor for the *New York Herald Tribune* and fancied herself a celebrity. Grandma Ruth, as I called her, would sweep into our apartment on a cloud of French perfume, swoop me up, and take me away to the opera or ballet. One moment I was hanging around with my felonious friends in Coney Island, and the next I'd be at the Bolshoi ballet or eating in a fancy Manhattan restaurant with Ruth's friends, all of them artists and writers, most of them gay. Ruth had multiple lovers of every nationality and was married many times. Her last two husbands were Norwegian, one an architect, the other a scallop fisherman, and both alcoholics. Ruth was fun but dangerous, and we wound up being close friends.

My father's side of the family was completely different. His family lived in the Deep South, in Opelika, Alabama, and my father never talked about them. When I visited Opelika, I found it impossible to connect my relatives to the man who was my father, but I never let on. His people were prosperous, outgoing, and friendly. They were Methodists and Baptists, decent people who served as pillars of the community. My grandfather was a respected attorney, the son of an Alabama supreme court justice, and my grandmother was a saintly woman who loved my father and always told me that he was the smart one, the "deep thinker" of the family. I thought my father was the opposite,

**Three generations**
My great-grandfather, Joseph Gilbert; my mother; my grandmother, Ruth Gilbert; and my great-grandmother, Anne (left to right) stroll down the Boardwalk in 1938. The Municipal Baths building is at left.

**Family life**
My parents and me at home in Greenwich Village, 1953.

secretive and estranged, and I could never figure out why.

★

My mother was an intelligent but naive young woman, unsure about how family life was supposed to function. She had been abandoned by her parents, Paul and Ruth, at the age of three and had grown up with different relatives and in boarding schools. She met my father in 1951 when she was a teenager and they were both living in Greenwich Village. He was a decade older, and she told me that he wore an ascot, smoked a pipe, and was as handsome as a movie star. The relationship was never meant to be.

A year after my father moved out in 1959, my mother needed a job, so she took the civil service typing examination and was listed in the newspaper as the fastest typist in New York. She was soon hired as a medical transcriptionist at Coney Island Hospital. My mother worked six days a week, and when the pressure became unbearable, she played hooky and spent the day at Faber's Fascination, a Coney Island arcade. Sometimes I watched her sitting for hours among a row of people perched on stools and rolling rubber balls across a table into pockets to win prizes. She said it relaxed her.

My mother liked children and organized activities for the kids in our building. She played the accordion and put together a children's rhythm band, with cymbals, triangles, recorders, rhythm sticks, and an assortment of instruments that were easy to play. Even when she was broke, she managed to buy season passes to Washington Baths for my sister and me, and she once took the kids from our building on a ferry ride around Coney Island. Mostly she liked to read books: fantasy and science fiction, myths and fables, all the classics. Reading was her escape.

We didn't have much money, but my mother always had dimes for ice cream or pizza. To earn extra money, my mother cared for my Great-Uncle Harold's parrot, Lulu. The little green bird lived in a big cage in my bedroom, and in return my uncle paid my mother $16 a month. On weekends, Uncle Harold liked to come to Coney Island to eat, and he'd take my sister and me with him to Nathan's and Shatzkins and buy us anything we wanted. Then he'd drive us around in his big Lincoln Continental before taking us home.

We always felt like outsiders within the family, mostly because of my father. I had learned not to question him about his life, and by the time I was seventeen years old, he was still a distant mystery. His health was declining, and he became depressed. I sensed that time was running out but was unable to break through to him. My mother and sister and I were growing and moving on, but my dad seemed stuck. In 1970, I was accepted to the City College School of Architecture, my sister received a scholarship to go to school in France, and my mother learned to drive, bought a car, and was attending Brooklyn College at night. But my father was going in a direction I couldn't follow. He had quit his job and was talking about going south, maybe to open a gas station in Charleston, South Carolina.

When my father visited Coney Island for the last time, during Christmas 1970, we went for a walk on the Boardwalk. It was a windy, frigid day, and the once-powerful

**Mystery man**
My father in 1961.

man seemed cold and frail but kept up the facade that everything was okay. He didn't want to talk about his condition. Months before, we'd had a falling out and argued over the war in Vietnam. I would soon have to register for the draft, and he felt that I should go to Vietnam if called up. I didn't agree. "Don't ruin your life," he said. Arguing with him seemed pointless.

I had started a part-time job at *New York* magazine, and he asked me if I'd ever met Jimmy Breslin, one of his favorite writers. I told him that I had, and he seemed impressed. We talked about everything but the obvious, his health and his future, and then I took a photo of him on the Boardwalk that would be the last. When he left that night, I walked him to his car, which he'd parked in front of McCabe's Bar, across the street from our apartment, and we said good-bye.

After he went home, I found a note that he'd left for me. The note was written in his beautiful script, on the back of a torn white envelope. It read: "Charlie: 'The integrated person can without dismay entertain notions which, if translated into action, would land him in prison or a mental hospital.' Or as the philosopher Santayana said: 'Every sane man keeps within him a lunatic on a leash.'" Over the years, he had given me similar quotes and sayings in his letters and notes, something that had always angered me. I knew that my father communicated by using other people's words so he would not have to reveal his own feelings. A month later, I heard shouts and breaking glass and looked out our kitchen window as McCabe's went up in flames.

On April 7, 1971, not long after the fire, my mother found my father dead on the floor of his apartment. My sister and I accompanied him home to Opelika, Alabama, where he was buried next to his father.

★

The last photograph I took of him on the Boardwalk turned out to be double-exposed, and I was crushed. But when I examined it carefully, I discovered something unusual.

**Final images**
McCabe's Bar (above), my father's favorite, had been closed for several years when it went up in flames in 1971, shortly before my father died. The last photograph I took of my father (left), an accidental double-exposure.

My father appeared to be covered with ice and was superimposed on the Steeplechase pier. Surrounding him were two ghostly images: an old man diving into an icy ocean and a young boy with his head lowered on the snowy beach. My father was staring straight out of the frame, his image breaking up like

**Demise of McCabe's** This series, taken in 1971 from my kitchen window in O'Dwyer Gardens, documents the razing of McCabe's.

ice in the spring. He was forever combined with the Coney Island images I had shot shortly before our walk.

Years later, while sorting out my father's belongings, I discovered something that he'd never told me: that he'd visited Coney Island as a boy. I found out by reading his childhood diary. He had been fourteen years old and traveling with his brother to Europe in 1937 for the international Boy Scout Jamboree. The brothers had taken a train from Alabama to New York to sail on the ocean liner *Normandie* to France. While in New York, he had gone to Coney Island twice.

His diary described going on rides and meeting Coney Island characters: "We saw a crazy or drunk fellow who looked like Popeye, who would try to guide us and would sing crazy songs." My father had ridden the Tornado roller coaster, rented lockers at Central Baths and gone swimming, ridden the Virginia Reel, and eaten in Coney Island restaurants. I found his ride tickets pasted into the diary. He had been young and starry-eyed, and the sights of New York had made a powerful and lasting impression. Once on the *Normandie,* Dad had won the ship's raffle, and his prize had been to dance with Marlene Dietrich, who was also sailing on the liner. He must have thought that life would always be magical.

I began to understand him after reading the diary. I saw why he had left Alabama. He was star-struck and loved New York City. He became a jazz fan and haunted the clubs of Fifty-second Street. He attended New York University, became a philosopher, and lived in Greenwich Village. He had big dreams that never came true. In the end, all that remained from his childhood experiences was Coney Island. And it was too late to ask him about it. I started to comprehend what it had been like for him to walk though this hallowed place he'd visited as a young boy, and it saddened me. By the time I discovered what I'd been searching for in Coney Island, it was already gone.

130    COMING OF AGE IN CONEY ISLAND

**PART 3**

# Decline and Comeback

**C**ONEY ISLAND hit rock-bottom around 1975. New York City was broke, the Boardwalk was crumbling, landowners were abandoning their property, pollution closed sections of the beach, and successive fires destroyed historic buildings. The rows of new housing projects were referred to as Coney Island's "tombstones." The West End, my neighborhood, became institutional, as drug treatment centers, welfare offices, public clinics, and nursing homes replaced stores and private residences.

Many cynics wrote Coney off at the time, predicting that the island was finished as a resort. But the true believers still flocked to the beach and Boardwalk, visionaries made plans for revival, and, against all odds, Coney Island survived.

As with many down-and-out sections of New York, Coney began to attract artists in the 1980s. Making successful efforts to revive the area's traditional art forms and popular culture, the artists kept Coney in the public eye and helped reverse its negative image. During the next two decades, preservationists gained landmark status for the Parachute Jump, the Wonder Wheel, and the Cyclone, and the city began cleaning up the blighted housing projects with the eventual goal of privatization. Then came the new ballpark and, with it, national attention. By the end of the century, the future began to look bright.

**Closed for the season** Freddie Moran's Lido building, 1973.

CHAPTER 17

# The Death of Steeplechase Park

**M**ARIE TILYOU, the president of Steeplechase Amusement Company, was a small, nervous woman. She was born in 1897, the same year that her father's world-famous park opened to the public. Until she was fifty-seven years old, Marie shared a penthouse apartment with her aging mother, Mary, widow of Steeplechase founder George C. Tilyou, who died in 1914. Marie liked to paint and aspired to be an artist but felt restrained by the duties of caring for her mother. Toward the end of her life, the two men most important to her were Jimmy Onorato and Bill Nicholson. In 1964, she made a decision that destroyed the lives of both.

Jimmy Onorato was born and raised in Coney Island just a few blocks from Steeplechase Park, where he was later to serve the Tilyou family for more than fifty years. He began his career as the Steeplechase office boy in 1918 at the age of ten. By the time he was twenty, he had become general manager of the world's most famous amusement park, the only job he would ever hold. Onorato also served as president of the Steeplechase Amusement Company from 1932 to 1958, the only person outside the Tilyou family to hold that position.

But he did much more than his title indicated. Jimmy of Steeplechase, as he was known to the rest of Coney Island, lived and breathed Steeplechase Park and was the person responsible for every aspect of the park's operation. He described his duties from 1928 to 1964 in a 1966 résumé: "supervised the installation, repair and seasonal dismantling of every ride in the park; purchased all supplies for the park; hired and managed all of the park's personnel (consisting of 290 employees); and was responsible for the decoration, painting, operation, and management of the Park." The Tilyou name may have been on the pavilion, but in reality, it was Jimmy's Park.

Jimmy's reputation was well known in the amusement business. Over the years, he was recruited by many other amusement park owners, including Walt Disney, whom Onorato escorted around the park in 1953, two years before Disneyland opened. He

**Last days**
The annual Pfizer outing was held at the Steeplechase Pavilion one day before the park closed.

**Saviors**
Bill Nicholson, Jimmy Tesoriero, Thomas Tesoriero, and a Luna Park employee (left to right) stand outside the Luna Park administration building in the late 1930s. Thirty years later, Nicholson and Jimmy Tesoriero would try to save Steeplechase Park.

turned them all down. He could never leave Coney.

Jimmy's most important role was not on his résumé. What he did best was serve as a "baby-sitter" for the dysfunctional Tilyou family. After the death of founder George C. Tilyou's widow in 1954, Onorato wound up being a go-between for the squabbling, self-absorbed heirs to the Tilyou fame and fortune. Toward the end of his career, Onorato became Marie Tilyou's closest friend, confidante, and business manager. In the end, she treated him shabbily.

Coney Island came under attack on several different fronts in the early 1960s. In 1961, William "Bill" Nicholson, executive secretary of the Coney Island Chamber of Commerce, knew that Coney Island was in serious trouble, and he knew this better than anyone else. Every year since the 1930s, Nicholson had written a personal message for the chamber's annual report. His message was always an upbeat review of the organization's latest accomplishments and proposals for the future. His letter of 1961 was uncharacteristic: it was a dire warning to the business community about Coney Island's prospects. It was a prophesy that went unheeded.

Nicholson warned that television had changed the nocturnal habits of the public. Coney Island was also facing new competition from other amusement parks, including Rockaway Playland, Freedomland, and Palisades Amusement Park, which could afford expensive advertising and promotional campaigns that kept their names before the fun-loving public. He ended his letter with a challenge: "Stated in stark simplicity, our

THE DEATH OF STEEPLECHASE PARK 133

**Jimmy of Steeplechase**
Jimmy Onorato, the general manager and soul of Steeplechase Park, makes his rounds in 1942.

potential for greatness in the outdoor amusement field is equal to our willingness to invest and to work together to create greatness. Cooperation and willingness to invest in the future of Coney Island by the so-called old-timers were the ingredients that made Coney Island the Playground of the World. It's time for a little soul searching. It might be later than you think."

Nicholson served as Coney's ambassador to the outside world. He was a tireless promoter, a charismatic leader, and a truly gifted negotiator who held the many factions of Coney Island together. He was respected by large property owners such as the Tilyous and the Handwerkers of Nathan's Famous, as well as by the clannish Italian, Irish, Greek, and Jewish concessioners and small-business owners. He hobnobbed with politicians at all levels of government and served as liaison between business interests and city departments such as police, sanitation, health, and licensing, which considered Coney Island a headache and a liability. Everybody liked Nicholson. John Tesoriero, who shared an office with Nicholson for many years, described him as "a role model, a consummate gentleman . . . suave, conservative, polite, and a good businessman with finely tuned peacemaking abilities that always smoothed things over and calmed people down."

Coney had run into hard times during the 1950s as many of the old-timers had begun to die off and their properties had been transferred to absentee owners with no long-term interest in Coney's future. In the early 1960s, Coney Island was being torn apart. Private developers wanted beachfront land for high-rise housing, the government wanted land for urban renewal projects, and racial unrest was creating an image problem. Tilyou family members, the biggest landowners in Coney Island, were consumed with internecine squabbles. By 1964, Coney's future seemed even bleaker than Nicholson had predicted three years earlier.

What made it painful for Bill Nicholson was that the biggest threat was coming from one of his oldest and dearest friends: Marie Tilyou. The two had been friends since childhood, and neither had ever married. Both were Irish, but they came from very different backgrounds. Tilyou was a millionaire, raised in Eileen Villa, the family's Victorian on Surf Avenue at Fifteenth Street. Nicholson came from the other side of the tracks, born to a poor family on West Sixth Street in a neighborhood known as the Gut.

Nicholson and Tilyou had attended school together and as adults had similar tastes. They liked to reminisce about old times in Coney Island. They liked the track and were heavy drinkers who enjoyed spending long afternoons together at the Clam Bar, an elegant Surf Avenue restaurant run by Thomas Bevilacqua. Most importantly, their entire lives revolved around Coney Island, and they shared a desire to preserve the Coney Island of their youth.

A friend of Nicholson's recalls their peculiar relationship: "Marie was crazy about Bill Nicholson. They'd go out to the track all the time. They'd go to Monmouth Park with crazy Freddie Garms. By eleven in the morning, she'd already had two or three martinis, smoked about twelve cigarettes, and she'd send Fluffy, her chauffeur, over to pick Bill up at the chamber office. She really had the hots for Bill Nicholson. I'd tell him, 'Hey, Bill, this is a real hot-shot over here, you should marry this broad,' and he'd give me a dirty look. I don't know how Bill felt about her."

In 1964, Steeplechase was having family problems. Ownership of the park was divided among four warring factions of Tilyou siblings: Marie Tilyou, sixty-seven years old; Eileen McAllister, sixty-three; Frank S. Tilyou, fifty-six; and the family of George Tilyou Jr., who had died in 1958. Another brother, Edward, had died without heirs in 1944. Frank was president of the family's parent company, Tilyou Realty, and Marie was president of Steeplechase Park, having assumed the position after the death of her brother, George Jr.

Frank Tilyou, the dominant male sibling, was able to keep the factions in line. He believed in modernizing Steeplechase Park. The others had varying interests: The McAllisters were mostly concerned with the Tilyou family's Atlantic City holdings, and George Jr.'s heirs were heavily in debt to the company and wanted to pay off the loans. Marie, the wealthiest heir, who held the controlling interest in the park, had formed a separate alliance with Park Manager Jimmy Onorato. The two held similar views on the park's operation and its future. Although the park was still viable and profitable at the beginning of the 1964 season, the enthusiasm necessary for its operation was gone. The Tilyou children lacked their father's inventiveness and drive, and the park had become stodgy, with few new rides. Frank had suggested ways to update the park, among them by purchasing amusements from the 1962 Seattle World's Fair, but was voted down by his nervous siblings.

Five days after Steeplechase opened for the season on May 8, 1964, Frank S. Tilyou died of cancer at his home in Arizona. The next day, Jimmy Onorato sent a curious letter to his son Michael, hinting at an impending sale: "Top Secret—The Park may be sold for an apartment project. It's in the talking stage and looks mighty close. . . . Frank's death had nothing to do with the possible sale as it [has] been in the works for about 2 months."

After Frank's death, Marie assumed control of all of the family interests. She depended heavily on Jimmy Onorato for the park's operation, but he was getting older, and she could not imagine anyone replacing him. Marie had to make a difficult decision, and she knew that Onorato would defend her decision no matter what it was. He was as protective of her as he was of the park.

The family had been examining their options in early 1964, but Frank Tilyou's death essentially doomed the park. Jimmy Onorato and Marie Tilyou feared that after they were gone, Steeplechase Park would not be operated in the manner that they would like it to be run, and they made an unofficial decision to close it.

Changes in Coney Island also affected Marie Tilyou's decision. With urban renewal projects encroaching on Steeplechase, attendance was down. The surrounding neighborhood was in decline, and the racial unrest elsewhere in the city affected Coney as well. Civil rights demonstrations had marred the April 25 opening of the New York World's Fair, and Onorato feared similar demonstrations over Steeplechase's unofficial policy of segregation at the park's pool. Rather than integrate the pool, he had closed it down for the 1964 season. Marie Tilyou revealed her feelings in a letter to Jimmy's son Michael on October 20, 1964: "Naturally I feel very sad to even think of George C. Tilyou's Steeplechase Park closing but one night walking along Surf Avenue after dining at the Clam Bar & milling with the horrible types one sees in the summer now I decided that Steeplechase, with all its splendor, drama and real beauty, stood out like a gorgeous rosebush in a garbage can."

**Third generation**
George C. Tilyou III (at left) wanted to save the park by changing the way tickets were sold. He was voted down by the rest of the Tilyou family.

In the end, the Tilyou family did not see a bright future for Coney Island.

Steeplechase Park closed at the end of the season on September 20, 1964. Marie Tilyou, Bill Nicholson, and Jimmy Onorato were together at the traditional closing as the park's bells were slowly tolled once for every year of operation. The park's sound system played "There's No Business Like Show Business" and then "Auld Lang Syne." Thousands of lights were switched off slowly, row after row, on each toll of the bell. As it turned out, the park went dark for the last time. Bill Nicholson left the closing ceremony with Tilyou and her friends and walked to the Clam Bar for drinks.

### Selling of the Park

The official vote to sell Steeplechase Park was made less than a week later at a shareholder meeting on September 25, 1964. Jimmy Onorato wrote in his diary that the family "voted to sell the park for building purposes." The decision was not made public, because the family was sure that a quick sale to a developer was in the works. Secrecy was important, because if the park sat empty, the insurance carriers would cancel all coverage and create a financial liability for the owners. But keeping the pending sale secret also prevented the chamber of commerce from finding a qualified buyer who might keep the park open.

The Tilyous had expected a quick sale, but negotiations with an "unnamed builder" dragged on through October. Still no official announcement was forthcoming, but rumors were flying. At the end of the month, the Tilyous were forced to notify their tenants, the concessioners, that they would have to remove their property or be obligated to renew their leases for the 1965 season. Boardwalk tenants were permitted to stay, because an empty facility could not be insured.

On November 7, 1964, when the Tilyous sold their block-long West Eighth Street property to the New York Aquarium, it be-

# The McCullough Carousel Family

**McCullough dynasty**
James McCullough (left) in the ticket booth of the Mangels carousel (below) that he operated for the Tilyous.

ONE OF the concessioners who removed his property from Steeplechase Park was James McCullough, who operated the park's Boardwalk carousel with his son Jimmy. The McCulloughs were related to the Tilyous and to the Stubbmans, who owned the Stubbman Carousel Pavilion on West Fifth Street. The family had deep roots in Coney Island. Leonard McCullough, a cousin, owned the Eileen Villa Carousel on Surf Avenue, and another cousin, Edo McCullough, was author of the 1957 classic *Good Old Coney Island*, the book that sparked my childhood interest in Coney's past.

The McCullough and Tilyou families were partners in various Coney Island properties. McCullough's kiddie park was on a Tilyou parcel on West Eighth Street. When the Mangels carousel at Steeplechase Park burned in the 1950s, James McCullough Sr. moved the Stubbman carousel to the site and operated it until shortly before the park was sold. The McCulloughs combined the Stubbman carousel with Feltman's carousel and installed it at the 1964–65 New York World's Fair.

Jimmy McCullough is the owner of Coney's last big carousel, the B&B, located on Surf Avenue. He also owns a kiddie park and three major rides on West Twelfth Street. He operates the park with the help of his daughters, Carol and Nancy.

**The last roundup**
Every year, the Pfizer pharmaceutical company held its annual picnic at Steeplechase Park. Employees dressed up for the occasion and rode the Steeplechase racecourse.

came apparent that the family was pulling out of Coney Island altogether. Still no official announcement about Steeplechase was made. In January 1965, the park's summer workers were paid a severance that they considered inadequate, and the disgruntled workers began telling reporters that the park was closing.

On February 5, 1965, the story finally broke in the national press, creating an impression that Coney Island itself had closed and sending shock waves through the local amusement community. Onorato refused comment. Eleven insurance companies began canceling the park's policies, and the owners now had a serious liability problem.

Onorato and Marie Tilyou knew that the park's closure would cause irreparable damage to Coney Island and leave Tilyou open to criticism. Onorato sought to diffuse the issue by writing a memorandum to the business community. Titled "The Right to Sell Park Property," the memo defended the owners' right to destroy the park in the name of progress. Onorato sounded as if he were trying to convince himself that the right decision had been made: "Steeplechase feels that for any property owner or for the chamber of commerce to oppose any change in zoning would be considered an unfair act. . . . We can't stand by and have some property owner say what's good for us. We have been through the mill for sixty-nine years and we believe we should know what is the best thing to do with our property and we intend to do it."

Bill Nicholson and the chamber of commerce scrambled to find a buyer who would maintain the park. Astroland owner Dewey Albert and a consortium of Coney landowners that included Murray Handwerker of Nathan's Famous made an offer but were turned down. Marie Tilyou and Jimmy Onorato were trying hard to sell the park to a developer. Nevertheless, they maintained the charade that the park might be reopened under new ownership.

Potential buyers, aware that the Tilyou family was worried, submitted low offers in an attempt to knock down the asking price

THE DEATH OF STEEPLECHASE PARK 137

**Last hope**
The Tilyous ignored all offers that would have kept the park open under new ownership. The *World Telegram and Sun* of February, 6, 1965, leaked news of Astroland's bid.

**Death sentence**
On July 1, 1965, Marie Tilyou sold Steeplechase Park to Fred Trump.

of $3 million. The panicked Tilyous briefly considered selling stock in Steeplechase to local businesspeople with the goal of keeping the park open, but the idea was deemed too expensive. George C. Tilyou III suddenly took an interest and suggested reopening the park for the 1965 season with an open-gate policy that would cut down expenses by allowing patrons to purchase tickets for individual rides rather than requiring them to buy multiple-ride tickets. His plan was rejected as well.

At a March 31 meeting, the family examined five offers, including one from developer Fred Trump. High-rise developers made offers with a provision that the Tilyous apply for a zoning change for the property to permit the construction of twenty-five-story apartment houses. At the time, Steeplechase was zoned only for commercial use and low-rise housing. The Tilyous refused, because the application process would take more than three months. Negotiations came to a standstill.

Jimmy Tesoriero was a Coney Island native with a vested interest in trying to preserve the park. To Tesoriero and Nicholson, who shared an office, finding a buyer to keep Steeplechase going was a life-and-death proposition. Tesoriero, owner of Walter E. Burgess Inc., was the biggest real estate broker in Coney Island. If he found a buyer who could save Steeplechase, he would be considered a hero. Ever since the earliest rumors of a sale, he had been trying to find a qualified buyer. One finally appeared. Irving Rosenthal, owner of Palisades Amusement Park, contacted Tesoriero with an offer to buy Steeplechase.

Rosenthal seemed the perfect buyer. He had started his amusement career as a child, selling souvenir pails and shovels at Steeplechase Park. He and his brother had built the Cyclone roller coaster in 1927 and operated it until they sold it to George Kister in 1937. Palisades Amusement Park, located in New Jersey, was having problems, and it appeared that Rosenthal wanted to get back into Coney Island. Tesoriero scheduled a secret meeting between Rosenthal and his lawyer, Marie Tilyou, and Jimmy Onorato, for 3 P.M. on April 20, 1965, at the Steeplechase offices on Surf Avenue. Everyone considered Rosenthal to be a known entity in Coney Island, someone who might be acceptable to the skittish Marie Tilyou.

On the day of the meeting, news of Rosenthal's interest in Steeplechase was plastered all over the morning papers. The headline in the *World Telegram and Sun* screamed, "Master Showman to Buy Steeplechase Park." Rosenthal's publicity agent, Sol Abrams, had broken the story to the press, a move that proved disastrous.

Rosenthal arrived at Tesoriero's office decked out in his "master showman" costume: a colorful tie, a gray vest, and a black homburg. He and Tesoriero then rode in Rosenthal's chauffeur-driven Cadillac to Steeplechase Park's Seventeenth Street entrance, only to find a locked gate. Jimmy Onorato came to the gate and refused to let them in, claiming that Marie Tilyou wasn't there. When Tesoriero pointed to her car parked just inside the gate, Onorato claimed that the car was John Tilyou's and said that the meeting was off. Rosenthal had his driver park the limo at the corner and waited, radio telephone in hand, for Marie Tilyou to call and explain the situation. The call never came. When the party later convened at Tesoriero's office, it became clear that Tilyou was furious about the advance publicity. If anything had come of the deal, she wanted to be the one to announce it. Many were

**Terrible view**
Jimmy Onorato took pictures of the demolition of his beloved Steeplechase Park (left) from his office above the marquee of the Tilyou Theater (above).

**Desecration**
Holes remained in the facade of the Pavilion of Fun after guests at Fred Trump's demolition party hurled bricks through the glass.

convinced that Rosenthal set up the whole thing as a publicity stunt. Rosenthal was apologetic, but his agent's indiscretion had hurt Jimmy Tesoriero's reputation and killed any chance for a sale.

Onorato later told his son Michael that the Rosenthal affair "made us look like bumpkins on a log." Tesoriero's son Charlie remembers the incident clearly: "Dad set up the deal, and it was supposed to be a secret, but Irving Rosenthal called the papers. My father was very embarrassed that he couldn't get Rosenthal inside the gate. Jim Onorato called and said, 'Don't bring him over. She'd rather see the park destroyed than see this guy buy it.'" The whole incident set the stage for a sale to Fred Trump.

The family was now desperate for a sale. On April 20, 1965, a man named Paul Futterman made an offer, and the Tilyous accepted his deposit. Jimmy Onorato suspected that Futterman was fronting for Trump, but he deposited the $200,000 check. His suspicions were right. Fred Trump was hoping to get a better deal by hiding his identity. The closing took place on July 1, 1965, with a selling price of $2.2 million.

Jimmy Onorato had always assumed that he would be rewarded for his years of loyalty to the Tilyous. He expected to receive a percentage of the sale. Instead, they gave him a small severance package consisting of two years' salary, a pittance for a lifetime of work. But he remained a faithful servant to the end, agreeing to stay on and sell off the park's rides. After Trump took over the park, Jimmy and his brother Rocco, who had also spent a lifetime at the park, rented a small office in the Tilyou Theater just above the marquee. Although he finally resigned his job as the park's manager, Jimmy consented to handle Marie Tilyou's financial affairs after her lawyer died.

### Demolition of the Park

When Steeplechase sold and failed to reopen for the 1965 season, the resulting publicity created a worldwide impression that the whole of Coney Island had closed. It fell on the shoulders of Bill Nicholson and the Coney Island Chamber of Commerce to try to change that perception. It was during this period that, as a twelve-year-old, I first visited the chamber and met Bill Nicholson. I had no idea what he was going through and how precarious the situation really was.

Crushed by the sale of Steeplechase, Nicholson felt betrayed by the secrecy of his friend Marie. But as Jimmy Onorato found out, the Tilyous considered money more important than loyalty. Nicholson tried

### 6 Bikinied Beauties Attend Demolishing Of Coney Landmark

The huge barn of a building, that once housed many of the rides in Coney Island's Steeplechase began to crumble under a wrecker's bulldozer yesterday. But, in spite of the rain, it crumbled with Coney Island class—there were food, drink and six—count 'em—six bikinied beauties.

Fred C. Trump, the real estate developer who bought the 12.5-acre, 67-year-old site from the Tilyou family over a year ago for $2.5-million, took his turn in the bulldozer. The girls pulled down tiny pieces of the structure that had previously been attached to ropes. They also stood in the bulldozer scoop and drank champagne toasts to the glory that was Steeplechase.

The Trump Organization office views the acreage as a potential site "for a modern, Miami Beach-type high-rise apartment development." An official said yesterday, "We

**A classless act**
The *New York Times* covered Fred Trump's bizarre celebration of the park's demolition.

everything he could to keep Fred Trump from obtaining the zoning change that would allow him to demolish Steeplechase. He called in a lifetime of favors and contacted every politician he knew. He wired Stewart Udall of the U.S. Department of the Interior and personally called New York Mayor Robert Wagner, Governor Nelson Rockefeller, and every member of the New York City Planning Commission. Having worked around the clock, he finally succeeded. It was the last big win of the chamber of commerce. But it was bittersweet, because Coney lost the park anyway.

When the city refused to change the zoning, Trump tried a different tactic: he submitted a redevelopment proposal that would cover the entire amusement area with an indoor park, designed by Alan Lapidus, alongside Trump's housing project on the Steeplechase site. When that idea failed, he sought revenge. Trump, known as a ruthless businessman, realized that there was a chance Steeplechase might be landmarked, so he decided to demolish the park. With the park gone, the city would be more receptive to a zoning change.

Trump mailed out engraved invitations to a party on September 21, 1966, celebrating the demolition of Steeplechase. He offered bricks to guests to throw through the funny face painted on the windows, and many of the invited obliged. Jimmy Onorato turned down Trump's invitation and watched in horror from his office across the street as bikini-clad models posed in a bulldozer's shovel for publicity photos. Most guests remember the event as a disgusting display. Demolition began the following day, and by January 1967, Steeplechase Park was just a memory. But even after the demolition, Trump would never get his zoning change.

I remember riding the bus past the site on the day that the demolition began and seeing the Steeplechase tower lying on its side in the empty swimming pool. The wreckers had cut the base and pulled it over in one piece. It was an image that was so troubling that I avoided the site for as long as I could. I finally walked over one Saturday morning and saw two kids about my age riding bicycles out the front gate. The watchman closed the gate behind them. They were carrying little targets from the shooting gallery, and I asked them how they had gotten in. They told me their father "owned the company that was tearing the place down." I'll never forget the sense of injustice I felt at that moment. Their father was destroying a landmark, and his kids were being rewarded with souvenirs.

### Riots Raging

Coney was in for a bumpy ride after Steeplechase was torn down. Since the closing of the park, Coney's big stories were about crime or eccentrics such as Murray Zaret, a Coney Island character who ran the Animal Nursery petting zoo on Surf Avenue. Zaret made news when he opened a discotheque and sidewalk café in the old Clam Bar, which had closed shortly after Steeplechase. The Clam Bar had once been the classiest restaurant in Coney Island, a hangout for Mayors Jimmy Walker and Fiorello La Guardia. During Prohibition, rumrunners and bootleggers had mingled with politicians at the dark mahogany bar, which was decorated in the style of a Norwegian hunting lodge.

Zaret called his new disco the Mad Hatter and hired dancing waitresses and a bouncer. He announced that his establishment "would cater to couples only, men with dates," and put a sign out front that said: "Don't dance? We will show you how. Frug, Monkey, Swim, Watusi. Couples only: 1 male 1 female." Trump had let Zaret operate his animal show inside Steeplechase for a two-month period in the spring of 1966, but it had failed. Zaret had become the media darling of Coney Island. It was a sad commentary.

The one bright spot during the 1960s was the 1963 opening of Astroland Park, a space-age theme park created by Dewey

# Astroland Park: Journey to the Twenty-First Century

**Space city** The Astroland Mercury Capsule Skyride.

ASTROLAND PARK occupies the former site of Feltman's restaurant on West Tenth Street and Surf Avenue. Dewey Albert, Herman Rapps, and Nathan Handwerker of Nathan's Famous bought the property in 1955. Murray Handwerker later told me that his father acquired the property to keep it out of the hands of New York Park Commissioner Robert Moses and to ensure that it would be zoned for amusement use. Dewey Albert was in the construction business, building apartments in New Jersey, but had grown up in Coney Island, lived in Sea Gate, and was a partner in the Fascination Game, with outlets all over the East Coast. Albert's syndicate leased the Boardwalk portion of the property to the Garto brothers for a kiddie park called Wonderland. The park evolved slowly at first, leaving most of the Feltman's building and the restaurant's famous carousel intact. The Alberts leased space to ride owners who bore the brunt of bad business.

Beginning in 1963, the Alberts began piecing together an outer-space-themed amusement park with the installation of a Cape Canaveral Satellite Jet ride. Jerry Albert, Dewey' son, teamed up with Bill Campbell of Arrow Development, a ride builder for Disney, and put in the Water Flume ride, the first such ride on the East Coast and still a popular ride today. Fred Pickard, also a ride builder for Disney, added the Mercury Capsule Skyride.

In 1964, the Alberts sold what they called the "old-fashioned carousel" and installed the 270-foot-tall Astrotower as the park's centerpiece. The ride became known as the "bagel in the sky" for its rotating glass-enclosed car that rises to the top of the tower.

In the 1970s, the Alberts began taking a more active role in the park. After the last Feltman's building burned in a suspicious fire in 1976, they stopped leasing space and began installing only their own rides. The park survived Coney's darkest period and is still thriving today.

**Futurists** Dewey Albert (left) and his son Jerome (right) proved that an amusement park could be a viable business in Coney Island when they transformed the Feltman's property into a space-age theme park named Astroland.

**Out with the old** The Alberts sold the historic Feltman's carousel and demolished the century-old building that housed it. Known as the greatest of all American carousels, the seventy-two-horse ride was carved in 1903 by Marcus Illions in his Coney Island shop and was originally called the Superba.

**Transformation**
The block-long Feltman's property was cleared in 1963 for the construction of Astroland Park. A section of the old restaurant on Surf Avenue was preserved and turned into the Astroland Restaurant.

Albert and Herman Rapps on the site of the old Feltman's restaurant. Although the park would struggle for a few years, its eventual success proved that an amusement park could still be viable in Coney Island. But it was not enough to lift up Coney Island. Crime was still the main issue covered in the press.

Another new venture was the ice-skating rink and convention hall. The $2.3 million pork-barrel project was located on the site of Ravenhall, a bathhouse that had burned in 1963. The rink turned out to be one of the ugliest buildings ever erected in Coney Island. Designed in the "brutalist" style by Daniel Chiat, it had five reinforced concrete Y-shaped supports facing a big parking lot. It was appropriately named the Abe Stark Rink, after the Brooklyn borough president who had pushed the project through. Stark had billed the rink as a "first step toward revitalization of Coney Island." But the rink was on an uninviting site surrounded by vacant lots formerly occupied by Steeplechase Park and the Washington Baths resort. The project was a failure from the start, and no convention would ever be held there.

★

Bill Nicholson had his hands full in 1968. Schaefer Beer, the company that had sponsored Coney Island fireworks displays since 1949, pulled out, and the fireworks were canceled. Nicholson had to do something dramatic. He decided to reach into the past and resurrect the Coney of his childhood.

In early April of 1968, the chamber of commerce announced big plans to transform the image of Coney Island. The plan, for a summer "Gold Rush Season," seemed quaint and naive. The chamber was counting on nostalgia to bring people back to Coney. The entire season would be full of free events: a national twins convention; a pig-tail contest; an Easter parade; a "toss-the-girl-in-the-blanket" contest; a beauty contest to choose the "Coney Island girl who's the easiest to watch"; and weekly fishing competitions at the Steeplechase pier. The chamber even found a new sponsor for Tuesday night fireworks.

The biggest event would be a resurrection of the Coney Island Mardi Gras, which had not been held since the 1950s. The new Mardi Gras would take place on Labor Day, and all vendors were invited to participate by decorating their businesses. Contests would hold their finals that same weekend. Nicholson was drawing on the innocence and pleasures of another era to prove that Coney Island was still safe and fun.

Just two weeks later, Coney Island experienced the worst riot in its history. Sunday,

April 14, was hot and crowded, and an estimated 600,000 people jammed the streets and Boardwalk. It was only ten days after Martin Luther King Jr. had been assassinated. The crowds were younger and angrier than usual. Concessioners sent word among themselves to shut down before dark. When the rides began to close, the crowds became enraged.

The riot began at about 8:30 P.M. when teenagers started stealing money from the booth of the A&H Skooter ride on the Bowery. The group then taunted the ride's patrons by screaming, "Kill the white man." Police moved in and herded the crowds from the Bowery to Surf Avenue, where they merged with a larger group congregating in front of Nathan's at Surf and Stillwell Avenues. A vat of mustard was hurled at the police and bystanders. Then a police officer was hit in the head with a bottle, and the mob went on a rampage, swarming down Mermaid Avenue as far as West Twentieth Street, breaking windows, looting stores, throwing rocks and bottles, and attacking bystanders.

Busloads of reinforcements from the Police Tactical Patrol Force arrived and sealed off Coney Island by closing Brighton Beach Avenue, Neptune Avenue, Stillwell Avenue, and the local exits of the Belt Parkway. After an hour of violence, the police were still unable to contain the crowd of about three thousand and began moving the people toward the Stillwell Avenue Subway Terminal. It would prove to be a tactical error.

The rioters streamed onto the terminal's platforms and attacked dozens of people waiting for trains. They pulled emergency cords and smashed windows. Conductors refused to move their trains without police protection and abandoned them. Passengers trying to escape from Coney Island were stranded and harassed during the confusion. Six vandalized trains had to be taken out of service, and trains that managed to pull out of the station were packed with rioters who continued their attacks throughout Brooklyn and into Manhattan, robbing and beating passengers at every stop. Thirty rioters were arrested at Whitehall Street, and the riot finally ended at Times Square, where injured passengers were removed from the station and taken to Polyclinic Hospital. Forty-seven people were arrested, and twenty-one were hospitalized. Coney Island's riot made national news.

It was not the publicity the chamber had hoped for. The days of innocence were over, and all of the chamber's publicity events were canceled. There would be no Mardi Gras that summer. The unfortunate and bizarre event destroyed Coney's reputation. The rest of the summer was peaceful, and the regulars still came, but it would take a long time for the general public to forget the images of 1968.

There were other repercussions after the riot. The New York City Transit Authority installed rolling steel emergency gates across all the entrances to the Stillwell subway terminal. The barriers, resembling prison gates, were designed to roll shut at the first sign of trouble. The gates had an immediate negative psychological effect. Those of us living in Coney Island realized

**Bad press**
Coverage of Coney's crime wave and the closure of Steeplechase Park in the *Daily News* (above) and other newspapers caused a public relations problem that was impossible to overcome.

**Tilyou Theater**
Jimmy Onorato stayed on in the empty theater building (top), even after the front entrance was boarded up to keep vandals out. The theater was demolished in 1973 (above).

that we were being shut off from the outside world.

The day of the riot, I had been on the Bowery but had gone home when things started to get ugly. My friends and I could hear sirens, and there were rumors of a mob heading west down Mermaid Avenue toward Coney Island Houses. We felt trapped: there was no way out of the West End except through the amusement area, nothing between us and the rioters. Everyone was down in the Big Park joking about "defending Coney Island Houses." But for a lot of people, it wasn't a joke. They thought Coney Island would only get worse and decided to move out.

★

After the riots, Bill Nicholson was never the same. Steeplechase had closed on his watch, killed off by one of his best friends, and the chamber's valiant attempt to restore Coney's image had failed. The riots had ended his career, and he began drinking heavily, so much so that his friends began to worry about him. Two months after the riots, Nicholson was diagnosed with cancer. He died before the summer's end.

Jimmy Onorato was offered Nicholson's job but turned it down, citing the problem of "too many factions, nothing to gain but headaches." His real reason was that he had never been a mixer, and some people in the business community had never forgiven him for his secrecy during the Steeplechase sale. Onorato remained in his little office in the Tilyou Theater building. When the movie theater closed in 1969, Jimmy and his brother Rocco stayed on as the theater's only tenants while they tried to sell the building for the Tilyous.

Jimmy Onorato's office window faced the vacant Steeplechase Park site, and it's hard to imagine what must have been going through his mind. The theater building slowly deteriorated and suffered a string of break-ins by vandals who destroyed Onorato's office and his files. By the time he was forced to move out, the once-proud man was using a portable oil heater and had to bring his own water in buckets to flush the toilets because vandals had stolen the plumbing.

Onorato's health began to fail after he left Coney Island in August 1971. He died of a heart attack eight months later, in April 1972. Marie Tilyou lingered on in poor health and followed her two closest friends five years later.

# The Demise of Resort Culture

Dan Pisark's grandparents moved to Coney Island in the 1920s and bought a house on West Twenty-seventh Street near Neptune Avenue. He grew up in the family home, and after he married and left Coney in the early 1970s, his parents stayed on in the changing neighborhood.

"I always tell people that I was raised on the Boardwalk," Pisark said. "Even in the winter, we were up there on sunny weekends. Behind our house, we had a bungalow for boarders. Our bungalow had guys who came right until the early 1960s. These guys all lived on Lower East Side. My mother called them 'the bachelors.' They were single guys who rented the bungalow year after year from my grandmother, who was the original owner. They went to the beach all day and came back at night to play pinochle under a bare twenty-five-watt bulb. They were there until the summer of '62; then they were gone, and I don't know what happened. I remember big changes in my last year of school in 1963, rumblings that there were problems in the western end of Coney Island. Some of our long-cherished friends were leaving.

"My parents decided, in their great wisdom, that they were going to stay behind. Their whole world and culture left overnight. Why my parents didn't follow I don't know. It was a very uncivil time in Coney Island. Suddenly, it was considered dangerous to go out at night. Then, in 1975, they sold the house and moved to the O'Dwyer Gardens housing project on West Thirty-third Street. They didn't want to own a house again. Dad had minimal means, and mother wanted to stay in Coney. She was a dedicated beachgoer and spent weekends, twelve hours a day, on the beach. She couldn't fathom leaving. She even talked all winter about the beach: 'I can't wait. Remember that beach party last Labor Day, when we had sandwiches and played music?' My parents still went down to Twenty-seventh Street, to their old beach, to be with the last people they knew."

The Ferrovechio family rented out summer bungalows and rooms above their pizza parlor on the Boardwalk during the 1950s and 1960s. Larry Ferrovechio now lives in New Jersey and remembers the family's resort business:

"Our Boardwalk strip had the Jefferson Baths, Bell Buoy Baths, and Ocean Tide Baths with its big swimming pool. In 1954, we bought the building at 3212 Boardwalk. It was strictly summer rentals when we first took it over. People came to Coney Island for the season, and we rented them one-room apartments with bathrooms in the hallway and showers downstairs. The house was three stories with four rooms on a floor. My father named it Villa Ferro, shortened from Ferrovechio. Most of the people we rented to were older single people, but we also rented to families. If they had kids, they'd rent a whole bungalow next door. The father would come at night or on weekends, and the mother would stay all week. They came from Brooklyn or the Bronx, local people. My father used to move the people from the Bronx because they didn't have cars. At the time, we'd charge fifteen dollars to move them. One truckload, and that was it for the summer, because we provided the furniture. They just brought clothes and junk. We used to get two or three hundred dollars for a season that lasted from Memorial Day to Labor Day.

"The summer bungalow people were a mixture of all nationalities, Italian, Irish, but mostly Jewish, and predominantly older women. Irish families used to come down, and we'd sell them barrels of beer. Everybody got along, because they were there to have a good time, and there was no trouble. People used to sleep on the beach. We'd go out drinking, to McCabe's, get loaded, and sleep on the beach all night. Nobody would bother us. Sometimes we walked on the Boardwalk all night and then went straight to work."

The family's business came to an end in the 1960s. "As soon as they knocked down the private homes and put up the projects, people stopped renting. There was no more property tax revenue, so the rest of us had to pay higher taxes. That's how it worked. We had to let our rental property go for back taxes."

**Villa Ferro** Anna Ferrovechio in the window of the rooming house above the family's Boardwalk pizzeria, 1970.

**Raised on the beach**
The Pisark and Jacobs families on the beach in 1959.

THE DEATH OF STEEPLECHASE PARK

CHAPTER 18

# The 1970s: A Decade of Revolution

DURING THE 1970s, I began a day-by-day photo documentation of my neighborhood. Coney Island was changing so rapidly that it was sometimes difficult for me to keep up. Living in the neighborhood had become a wild ride. The decade was a period of transition, the biggest transformation since the gold rush mentality of the previous century. The changes were unsettling at times, and it seemed as if the city government had abandoned the island, just cut it loose, hoping that it would float away. But Coney Island was my home. Even after moving to Manhattan to attend college, I returned twice to live there. Coney Island was an addicting experience.

During the decade, Coney Island was deconstructed piece by piece. Neglect and indifference on the part of landowners and the city created a climate of decay. By mid-decade, the city had gone broke and the federal government had cut off funding to the area, leaving a wasteland of unfinished projects. The unfulfilled promises of Mayor John V. Lindsay's administration merged into the bankrupt administration of Mayor Abraham Beame. By the end of the 1970s, Mayor Ed Koch presided over the false hope that casino gambling would revitalize Coney Island. It would take a long time for the area to recover.

Coney Island during the 1970s is best symbolized by the battle over the Cyclone roller coaster. The Cyclone is located between the New York Aquarium and Astroland Park and across the street from the highrise towers of Luna Park Houses. In 1975, the coaster came under attack from all three of its neighbors: the tenants of Luna Park, the director of the Aquarium, and the owner of Astroland Park all wanted it torn down.

The city of New York had purchased the coaster property in 1971 for $1 million from owner Sylvio Pinto to allow for future expansion of the Aquarium. Pinto leased the coaster back from the city and operated it for $25,000 a year on a season-to-season basis. The Aquarium had always had an uneasy relationship with Coney Island and, in 1975, began lobbying to have the roller coaster demolished.

The New York Zoological Society's general director, William Conway, summed up the city's attitude toward Coney Island when he told the *New York Times* on May 27, 1975, that the coaster's demolition was a "clear choice between honky-tonk and culture." "The Cyclone looms over the Aquarium," Conway said, "and the noise and the shrieking and the visual pollution are pretty grim.

**Sign of the times**
The 1923 Lido Building (opposite) was a casualty of the 1970s.

**Cyclone battle**
Sylvio Pinto (with glasses) acquired the ride in 1954 for $450,000. In 1971, the city purchased the coaster for $1 million and then leased it back to him. When he lost the lease to Astroland in 1975, Pinto left Coney Island for good.

147

**Landmark**
Coaster enthusiasts fought successfully to save the Cyclone.

**The landmark Cyclone**
Gerry Menditto (right), a former Astroland park electrician, became operations manager of the Cyclone in 1975 after the park acquired the lease. Ralph Paluso, who had built and repaired Coney's rides for decades, taught Menditto the tricks of the coaster business.

You're going around looking at some seal or octopus and this thing is coming around a curve screaming and yelling at you. It's not conducive to the kind of message we are trying to get across."

When the city canceled Pinto's lease, the plan was to turn the Cyclone over to the Aquarium and have the organization operate it to raise funds for the expansion. Conway then claimed that the ride needed $127,000 in repairs and was too expensive to fix. The Coney Island Chamber of Commerce accused the Aquarium of exaggerating the repair costs because it wanted the coaster demolished immediately. Conway attacked the chamber, telling the *Times* that the Aquarium was "trying to do something for the City, while all that Coney businessmen want to do is make a buck." Astroland owner Dewey Albert, siding with the Aquarium, called for demolition of the Cyclone. He feared that an abandoned roller coaster would hurt business at his amusement park, but he also may have had concerns about competition from a city-owned coaster.

The most bizarre attack against the Cyclone came from Murray Raphael, president of the board of directors of Luna Park Houses. Raphael told the *Times* that the

tenants had "complained of the rumbling of cars along the roller coaster tracks and the screams of the customers." Raphael wanted the coaster gone. The delicate souls at Luna Park had somehow failed to notice over the years that they were living across the street from an amusement park. Suddenly, they were complaining about noise.

The chamber of commerce did not want to see Coney's amusement zone reduced and a famous ride demolished, and it pushed for a way to save the Cyclone. The issue was finally resolved in 1975 when the city put the coaster up for bid, and Dewey Albert, in partnership with Herman "Hy" Singer and Harold Glance, was able to wrangle the city lease away from former owner Sylvio Pinto, who also bid for it. The partnership signed a ten-month lease on the ride for $54,000. Albert eventually bought out his partners, obtained a long-term lease, and incorporated the Cyclone into his Astroland Park. The eastern end of the amusement area was saved, but the rest of Coney Island was not so lucky.

**New York Aquarium, 1970**
In the 1970s, the Aquarium was engaged in a feud with Coney Island's amusement community. The city wanted to condemn the Cyclone roller coaster and adjacent properties to expand the Aquarium. Residents of nearby high-rises were known to complain about the mating calls of the Aquarium's walruses.

During the 1970s, most of the Boardwalk businesses west of Stillwell Avenue closed or burned. The last of the family-oriented saltwater swimming pools, Washington Baths, had failed to open for the 1969 season. The city had given owner Fred Warmers a six-month deadline to install filters for the pool, but the $300,000 cost was too much. The three remaining bathhouses—Bushmans, Cook's, and Stauch's, all operated by Ruby Jacobs—remained popular and still drew the old-timers. But many of the amusement properties were let go for back taxes, and the city refused to help with tax relief.

Coney became known throughout Brooklyn for prostitution. Most nights the four-block strip of Surf Avenue west of Fifteenth Street was lined with cars picking up prostitutes, desperate women who were mostly drug addicts. At night, the parking lot of the Abe Stark Rink was filled with hookers and their johns. The rink, planned when Steeplechase Park was still operating, opened in 1970; a decade later, it resembled a fenced-off prison surrounded by vacant lots. The city did little to promote it and never opened the rink's Boardwalk restaurant, which might have attracted customers to the area.

The most tragic loss of the decade occurred on Stillwell Avenue. The intersection of Stillwell and Surf Avenues was always considered the crossroads of Coney Island, the amusement area's Times Square. Located there were Nathan's Famous, the venerable hot dog "grab-joint" that remained Coney's biggest draw; Loews Theater; the Stillwell Avenue Subway Terminal; and the old Henderson's Theater. By the 1970s, the majestic Loews had become an X-rated porno house renamed the Shore, and the terminal that had served 15 million passengers a year during the 1920s was just a dark cave, its ridership having dropped to 3 million per year. Henderson's, a one-time vaudeville showcase, housed the Melody Bar, the World in Wax, and the Surf Hotel, a fleabag.

Nathan's remained in the hands of the original owners, the Handwerker family, but

**The Tornado**
During the 1970s, the Tornado's slurred tape loop repeated over and over: "Ride the Tornado, seventy-five miles an hour. Oh boy, oh boy, what a ride." Originally known as the Bobs, the coaster had a succession of operators.

the rest of Stillwell Avenue was in transition. Carlton Klink, a proper Bostonian and absentee landlord, had inherited the Henderson estate, which included the Tornado roller coaster, the Surf Hotel, and the old Atlantis Nightclub on the Boardwalk. Klink wanted out of Coney Island because it offended his sensibilities. The landmark Stauch's Baths property across the street from Henderson's belonged to Joe Bonsignore, a Coney old-timer who also owned the Bobsled ride. Nobody imagined he would ever sell, but the right offer soon came along.

In the mid-1970s, Klink and Bonsignore sold their properties to Hy Singer, owner of the Himalaya ride on West Twelfth Street, who also had hotel interests in the Catskill Mountains. After the Stillwell purchases, Singer became Coney's largest property owner and, for a short time, operated the two coasters with his brother-in-law, Arthur Lessack, and ride handler Andy Badalamenti.

Singer's properties were plagued by misfortune. The Tornado was destroyed by three mysterious fires, the Bobsled fell into disrepair and was demolished, and Stauch's beautiful terra-cotta palace burned so often that it was sometimes described as Coney's "largest outdoor barbecue." At one point, Singer rented the venerable building to a Hollywood film crew who sprayed the Boardwalk facade with graffiti for a scene in the gang movie *The Warriors* and then left a defaced facade to greet visitors for a decade.

Ownership of the Shore Theater, once the amusement area's tallest and proudest building, also changed hands during the decade. The building was sold to Horace Bullard, owner of a fried chicken franchise. Bullard opened one of his Kansas Fried Chicken restaurants in the ground-floor space formerly occupied by the Gayway Bar. The Shore also had a ten-story office tower that deteriorated after the city opened a welfare office in the building. The remaining tenants fled the onslaught of crime and vandalism caused by some of the city's clients. After being stripped of its art deco fixtures, the building stood vacant except for Bullard's restaurant.

Some ride operators were their own worst enemies. The competition became cut-

**Triple-X intersection**
When I was growing up, the Loews Theater was a classy place that had first-run movies as well as theatrical events and live performances by comedians such as Jerry Lewis. In the 1970s, the theater became an X-rated movie house. Next door was Murray Zaret's Animal Nursery.

throat, especially for newcomers. Arson was the most common form of revenge, but vandalism worked, too. When a Kentucky Fried Chicken restaurant opened on the Boardwalk, its power lines were cut just before the Fourth of July so that all the food spoiled on the biggest business day of the year. The son of a well-known Boardwalk food-stand owner was caught destroying the fixtures of a restaurant that had folded on West Twelfth Street because he wanted to prevent a competing restaurant from opening in the location. Word soon spread to other franchises not to open in Coney Island.

A Coney Island street gang called the Homicides took up residence on the Bowery, between West Fifteenth and West Sixteenth Streets, and made it their home turf. Ron Guerrero's Music Express was the headquarters for the gang's open-air disco, also known as the Zoo. The Homicides felt that the movie *The Warriors* was based on them, and when it opened at the Oceana Theater in Brighton Beach, the gang packed the theater and went wild, breaking down all barriers between art and reality. The male gang members were known for their black hats, which were stolen from Hasidic Jews, crushed, and wrapped with bandanas signifying the gang's colors. The Homicides became a fixture on the Bowery for over a decade, adding their colorful presence to the Coney of the 1970s.

Despite the decline, Coney remained popular. Wary tourists still visited, old-timers still packed the Boardwalk, and the remaining rides were still in operation. As with the rest of New York City, the infrastructure collapsed. In spite of it all, the amusement area survived. What did not survive the 1970s was Coney Island's West End, the neighborhood where I lived.

**The cave, 1975**
The Stillwell Avenue Subway Terminal was as dark and scary as a spook ride. The chamber of commerce did its best to welcome visitors as they made their way toward the Surf Avenue entrance.

THE 1970s: A DECADE OF REVOLUTION  151

**Last ride**
The Bobsled, billed as the "sensation of the 1939–40 New York World's Fair," was brought to Coney Island by Joe Bonsignore when the fair closed and installed on the site of the old Stauch's Dance Hall at the Bowery and Stillwell Avenue. Hy Singer acquired the property, then demolished the ride in 1975.

### Fall of the West End

New York City Mayor John Lindsay's administration was willing to do anything necessary to avoid the race riots that devastated many large cities across the country in the 1960s. Lindsay's walk through Harlem following the assassination of Martin Luther King Jr. helped keep violence to a minimum, and his administration sought to maintain that calm at any cost. In 1969, however, his New York City Housing Authority made policy concessions that destroyed Coney Island's West End and inadvertently led to two decades of racial turmoil at New York's best-known amusement area.

Before the 1960s, racial problems were minimal in Coney Island. The amusement area had always been a melting pot: diverse, integrated, and popular with people of all races and nationalities. When business lagged in the 1950s, the Coney Island Chamber of Commerce actively sought minority patronage by placing ads in black and Spanish-language newspapers aimed at blue-collar and lower-middle-class families and also provided minority churches and social organizations with books of discount tickets. "We catered to black people," realtor Charlie Tesoro told me. "We encouraged them to come, and they spent lots of money. Church groups used to come, and it was wonderful. We'd have two hundred buses in here on weekends during the 1950s and early 1960s. They'd drive all night from Virginia and South Carolina, get here early in morning, then leave late at night. Everybody in Coney made money."

Incidents of violent crime began to rise

**Amusement bazaar**
The Tornado was built on a narrow lot and had concession space below the tracks. Carousels, dark rides, food stands, fortune tellers, tattoo parlors, and bathhouses occupied the booths.

throughout New York in the early 1960s, particularly in Coney Island and especially in the West End. There had always been rough sections of Coney. As a child, I remember seeing drunken street brawls and knife fights, but such violent incidents were rare and usually between people who knew one another. The new trend of random violence began around 1962, when the practice of blockbusting hit Coney Island.

In early 1961, developer Fred Trump gained control of the southern half of a redevelopment site in a central Coney Island neighborhood once known as the Gut. Trump began relocating the residents so he could build his Trump Village high-rises. A stretch of the Gut near Ocean Parkway had been occupied by poor blacks since the 1890s, when workers from the stables at the Brighton Beach Race Track had been housed in shacks along the railroad tracks. The rest of the neighborhood was blue-collar Irish and Italian. It was a poor neighborhood, but many longtime residents, both black and white, were reluctant to leave their homes when Trump began evicting them.

THE 1970s: A DECADE OF REVOLUTION  153

**Playground**
On West Thirty-first Street, across from my apartment at O'Dwyer Gardens, these children set up a makeshift playground and took turns jumping from a rooftop onto mattresses.

White property owners at the site received financial compensation and were given an opportunity to relocate to Trump Village. Minority families, most of whom were on welfare, were unable to afford the apartments, so Trump had to find a way to remove them. His solution was to relocate them, with the city's assistance, to the empty summer bungalows in the West End. The bungalow colonies scattered along nearly every block throughout the middle-class neighborhood soon became "poverty pockets" of substandard housing.

I remember the effect as being immediate and devastating. The crime rate shot up, and many long-term residents of the West End fled to the safety of the new Trump Village and Warbasse high-rises. The sudden exodus created a glut of vacancies in the neighborhood apartment houses, which were soon filled by the city's most poor and desperate people. In September 1962, two New York City police officers, Nicholas Panico and Robert Byrnes, were shot to death on the Boardwalk near Coney Island Houses by a deranged gunman who was then chased down and killed by the police in a shootout near Washington Baths. The murderer, who had also killed his landlady and wounded a boy from Sea Gate, lived in a bungalow on West Thirty-second Street, a block away from my apartment. I had a morbid fascination about the murder and walked over to see where the man lived after finding his address in a newspaper story. A lot of Coney Island addresses began appearing in the papers in connection with sensational crimes.

I recall a bungalow colony across the street from my family's apartment building called Sea Breeze Court. It was composed of eight tiny bungalows facing a central courtyard, with a picket fence entrance on Surf Avenue. After standing vacant for years, it was soon crammed with dozens of families moved there from the Trump site. Coney Island Houses, where we lived, was integrated and had experienced little racial strife. But the kids from the bungalows were a wild bunch and began hanging out in the park at Coney Island Houses. The fights that broke out involved not only children from the bungalows and the projects, but also their parents. Black parents had fistfights with white parents. Tensions ended quickly when the bungalows were leveled following a conflagration caused by a faulty heater. The relocations and fires became a pattern. When three children burned to death in a bungalow fire on West Twenty-fifth Street, no one seemed to care. The city kept placing families in the bungalows anyway.

Lou Powsner, a Coney Island businessman and neighborhood activist, remembers what happened during this period. "When

Fred Trump got the approval for Trump Village," Powsner told me, "his firm was paid by the city for each family that they relocated. I heard of Trump coming to property owners on the side streets who owned the wooden summer bungalows. He'd say, 'You've got those empty bungalows sitting there and nobody in them. What are you getting for your bungalow in the summertime?' The owner would say $600, and Trump would say, 'Look, I can get you $200 a month for a year-round tenant.' The owner would say, 'But we don't have any heat in these bungalows.' Trump would tell them, 'You can put in a space heater and they can heat their own water. The city of New York will pay for it.'"

Powsner later confronted Trump at a New York City Board of Estimate hearing. "I said to Trump, 'Why didn't you relocate these people to Trump Village and give them first priority?' He said, 'Do you think they could pay the rent?' I said, 'Well if they're subsidized in these shacks in Coney Island, why can't they be subsidized in Trump Village?' All he said was 'That's ridiculous!' He said that right in front of the press at a news conference in front of the board of estimate."

Slumlords took advantage of white flight as an opportunity to cash in. Local speculators knew there was big money to be made in blockbusting. They bought up apartment houses cheaply, stopped maintaining them, and rented the apartments to welfare tenants until the buildings could be sold to the city at a profit after they were condemned for urban renewal. Powsner remembers how the scheme operated: "Slumlords came to our community council meetings and looked at the list of houses being taken for the next urban renewal projects. They sat in the back of the room with pencils and paper as if they were playing bingo. When another block was condemned, their eyes would light up, and they would take out their scorecard and check off another victory. The city was buying up their slum buildings at fair market value, and they were getting rich."

One of the local slumlords was a well-known butcher on Mermaid Avenue, a survivor of the concentration camps. He listened to Jewish homeowners complaining about the neighborhood and then offered to buy their houses. The price was always below market value, and the homeowners

**Activist**
Lou Powsner held a sign asking Fred Trump to clean up a lot that the developer owned.

**Dance land**
On summer nights, a wild open-air disco came together on the Bowery in front of Ron Guerrero's Polar Express ride and the Thunderbolt roller coaster.

**Capitulation**
Many blame Mayor John V. Lindsay for Coney's decline in the 1960s. Seeking the minority vote, he promised to build more low-income housing in Coney Island. He delivered, but in 1969, six months before I took this portrait, he ceded control of the tenancy in Coney's housing projects to local community groups. Lindsay, a Republican, had charmed the mostly Democratic audience when he spoke at the Tilyou Theater in 1965 during his campaign. By the end of the decade, however, his housing policies caused him to be reviled by a large segment of Coney Island.

would refuse. But after becoming victims of crime, they were desperate to sell. The butcher then halved his offer, and the owners took whatever they could get. The cycle continued until the buildings were bought by the city for urban renewal. Some owners were unable to sell their buildings and abandoned them. Unscrupulous owners purchased other houses and then torched them to collect fire insurance.

In November 1965, the well-publicized murder of an eighty-year-old woman in her home on West Twenty-fourth Street caused panic among the elderly. Senior citizens felt imprisoned in their own homes. The businesses along Mermaid Avenue began to fail, and the Coney Island Board of Trade started a shuttle bus that picked up elderly customers by appointment and took them shopping. People were afraid to go out at night, and the streets became deserted. Even the once-crowded Boardwalk in the West End became empty at night and was dubbed the Ghostwalk.

Coney Island's racial problems made news in 1965, when a weeklong disturbance hit my school, Mark Twain Junior High. A minor fight on Neptune Avenue between a black student and a white student escalated into a confrontation between gangs from Coney Island and from Bath Beach. More than thirty students were arrested. For several days, the police surrounded the school grounds, and we were kept home from school. The incident was overplayed in the media as the "Coney Rumble," but it scared many white parents into leaving the area. As bad as this seemed, things were about to get much worse.

In 1966, visionary Parks Commissioner Thomas Hoving appointed a commission to revive Coney Island's beach and Boardwalk. Architecture critic Allan Temko was a member of the commision. "I had the idea that the Boardwalk could be a much more interesting structure." Temko said. "It could be multi-level and project fingers across the sand. We thought that nothing could be solved unless the structure united the Boardwalk with the community adjacent to it. But that land didn't belong to the Parks Department. It had mostly summer cottages occupied by poor people. When Lindsay had campaigned there, he promised to build rather massive, low-cost public housing as soon as he took office as mayor. He wanted the votes, and I guess he got some. Our commmission talked about trying to revive Coney Island through some kind of citizens action committee. We wanted to coordinate various city agencies and get a strong person to manage the joint effort. But after Lindsay made that campaign promise, the will wasn't there anymore. I haven't been back since."

In 1967, Lindsay fulfilled his campaign promise. The entire West End of Coney was declared a poverty zone, the "Coney Island West Urban Renewal Program," and was slated for condemnation. Although decent housing stock in the area could have been rehabilitated, the city's redevelopment policy at that time was to demolish all existing structures and build high-rises. The big question became, "What kind of high rises?"

That year, a battle broke out between the Coney Island Community Council and the newly formed Coney Island Coordinating Committee. The council, representing fifty-six existing neighborhood and religious organizations, wanted a majority of the projects planned for the renewal area to be for middle-income residents. The committee was a newly formed militant group that advocated low-income housing. It was no secret that the low-income housing projects run by the New York City Housing Authority had become breeding grounds for crime, and local business interests rightly predicted that low-income housing would erode the neighborhood. Many in the community suspected that Mayor Lindsay had already written off Coney Island by awarding the redevelopment area to the low-income advocates. As one local resident put it, "The mayor's policy toward the city's poor was to put 'em on an island. Coney Island."

The community council demanded that

**Senseless destruction**
Many of the buildings pictured were serviceable, and there was no reason to demolish them. Tearing down the bungalows opened up new routes between blocks, and every day I took a different path to school.

the city develop a comprehensive plan to "save Coney Island." The members wanted to coordinate the various projects proposed for the Coney Island West program into a plan that would preserve the existing neighborhood and halt the middle-class exodus. When the council and the coordinating committee convened at the New York City Council to discuss the issue, the atmosphere became so hostile that Council President Sanford Garelik brought in forty helmeted riot police and asked for a thirty-day postponement to allow the two neighborhood groups to work out their differences.

In 1968, after years of contentious community meetings, the groups hashed out a controversial checkerboard plan of mixed low-income and middle-income housing projects that extended from Sea Gate to West Twenty-first Street. It was a faulty compromise that would cause problems lasting to this day.

## Old Projects to New

The new plan was implemented just as my family was moving from Coney's oldest housing project into its newest, O'Dwyer Gardens. O'Dwyer was located across the street from Coney Island Houses, and many of our neighbors had also applied for apartments there. The new apartments were spacious, with three bedrooms, two baths, terraces, modern kitchens, and ocean views. In December 1969, thirteen years after we had moved into Coney Island Houses, we left for a new life at O'Dwyer Gardens.

It would not be a peaceful transition. Just before O'Dwyer Gardens opened in 1969, a militant group called the Freedom and Peace Tenants Council of Coney Island organized a demonstration against the Coney Island offices of the New York City Housing Authority with the goal of changing the regulations concerning a tenant's eligibility for public housing. Flyers were circulated all over the neighborhood announcing a mass demonstration and march beginning at Nineteenth Street and Mermaid Avenue and ending at O'Dwyer Gardens. The flyer was in English and Spanish and stated the following: "United we stand. Divided we fall!!! We poor people will have to fight for our right to live decently. Together we shall win. The cockroaches are taking over—we have to live too! Coney Island should be made for people to live in, not roaches. Join our demonstration against the Coney Island Project Administration."

Seeking to avoid a confrontation, the housing authority set up a meeting between the Freedom and Peace Tenants Council and Albert A. Walsh, chairman of the New York City Housing Authority. At the March 7 meeting, the militant group outlined its demands for eligibility in Coney Island's housing projects. Among the demands: "First priority in public housing being built or to be built in Coney Island will be given to former site occupants of the public housing projects. Second priority will be given to other

**Future housing**
Site 5 at Surf Avenue and West Twenty-eighth Street was one of the projects of the state's Urban Development Corporation and the city's Housing and Development Administration. The mixed-income high-rises were an unfortunate compromise hammered out by the Coney Island Community Advisory Committee.

THE 1970s: A DECADE OF REVOLUTION 157

**Winter morning**
Snowy view taken at dawn from my bedroom at O'Dwyer Gardens, 1971. The complex was named for William O'Dwyer, the corrupt New York City mayor who resigned in 1951 and fled to Mexico. Early in his career, he was a magistrate at the Coney Island Court on West Eighth Street. In 1941, he was the Brooklyn district attorney responsible for protecting mob witness Abe Reles. Reles died by falling out a window while in protective custody at Coney's Half Moon Hotel.

relocatees from Coney Island West and the Coney Island Vest Pocket Sites and emergency vacantees. Third priority will be given to other Coney Island residents living in extremely sub-standard or extremely deteriorated housing, which we understand to be primarily in the target poverty area. With the permission of the applicant involved, we will consult with a representative of the Freedom and Peace Tenants Council concerning any applicant deemed to be ineligible."

Walsh gave in and signed the agreement the same day and the housing authority thereby ceded control over who lived in the projects. Before this agreement, eligibility requirements had been strict: potential tenants were screened for criminal backgrounds, convicted felons could not be tenants, and troublesome tenants could be evicted. The regulations kept the projects relatively safe, but there were rumblings that the rules were discriminatory and restrictive. As a result of the political maelstrom of the 1960s, the housing authority policies were changed, and the public housing projects would never be the same.

Operation Open House, an advocacy group located on Mermaid Avenue, was chosen to review tenant applications. The group issued a proclamation outlining the new rules and stated, "If this 'reservation approach' is adopted in the Coney Island area, it would go a long way towards removing the suspicion and mistrust which presently surrounds the operations of the New York City Housing Authority local renting office." The streamlined application review meant that once the tenant was accepted, the decision was nearly impossible to reverse.

The city welfare department's policy of placing clients in dilapidated, substandard housing in Coney Island would now cause big problems for the housing authority. The new rules called for "emergency evacuees" to be given priority housing. Almost overnight, it seemed that every building in the redevelopment area burned. The tenants of the burned-out building were the first to be relocated into the new housing projects.

Leroy F. Aarons best summed up the tensions of the time in an article that appeared in the *Washington Post* on January 20, 1969. "This Coney Island is an urban laboratory, a

microcosm of all the strains growing out of the emergence of black pride, pitted against the status quo. It is a fascinating mix, one of the few places left in the city which is even partly integrated, where the cultures abut and even mingle. This Coney Island consists of a poverty pocket, some 25 blocks long and five blocks wide, bounded at either end by almost lily-white enclaves of middle class people. . . . Here is a mixture of 50,000 people, about one-third each of white, black and Puerto Rican. The black leadership in general is in an angry mood, yet exultant with its new-found muscle. The white leadership is still recovering from the shock of its own impotency and fearful of the consequences."

The Lindsay administration's experiment of mixing middle- and low-income residents was a miserable failure. The middle-income tenants fled, and the ones who couldn't, mostly the elderly, became prisoners in their own homes. Arson fires burned night and day in Coney Island for the next five years. By 1972, the first wave of new middle-income tenants at O'Dwyer Gardens realized that they'd made a mistake and left Coney Island. The remaining tenants took a stand and organized tenant patrols. We sat at card tables in the lobby to protect people returning home from work in the evening. The crime problem stabilized in the mid-1970s, but after the first two murders in our building—both elderly tenants killed in their own apartments—the tenant patrols gave up. It was just too dangerous.

My mother was one of those who stayed on and became an advocate for the elderly tenants, lobbying for bus shelters and police escorts. She appeared before television cameras after the first killing in our building and described our murdered neighbor. "She was a little old lady who used to have a garden at her old house and enjoyed tending the little garden in front of our building. She was always cheerful and smiling," my mother said, "until they climbed in her window and beat her to death."

Because of the city's budget cutbacks, housing police were scarce and crime increased. It wasn't so much an issue of race; people of all backgrounds were victimized by the criminal element that occupied the projects. O'Dwyer Gardens became an island

**Colorful couple** Elderly residents on Surf Avenue return home from a shopping trip. Crime was so prevalent that the city began a shuttle service to take seniors on shopping trips to Brighton Beach.

within an island at the start of the 1970s. A recession slowed the housing authority's building plans, and President Richard Nixon cut federal funding for future developments. For the next six years, Coney Island's devastated urban renewal zone remained a dangerous backdrop for the amusement area.

### A Neighborhood Saved

Some good did come out of the construction delays. Longtime residents began fighting the city to save their homes from condemnation. A group of homeowners who were about to be evicted became militant and refused to accept the city's eviction orders.

One of the blocks that fought back was a tight-knit group of mostly Irish residents on West Thirty-third Street near Neptune Avenue. They lost the battle and their homes but inspired others. The New York City Housing Authority's "scorched earth" policy of urban renewal, whereby only synagogues and churches were left standing, came under attack on many fronts. On June 24, 1970, a housing authority office on West Thirty-third Street was occupied and twelve employees were taken hostage by Coney Island residents facing eviction. The incident was settled when two of the workers were relocated from Coney Island and the protesters were promised similar replacement housing.

The biggest victory was achieved by a neighborhood group led by Ralph Perfetto. Perfetto was the driving force behind Astella (Associated Tenants and Landlords), the organization that stopped the urban renewal juggernaut and saved the predominantly Italian section of Coney Island. Perfetto was born in Coney Island in 1934 and raised on West Sixteenth Street near Neptune Avenue in one of three houses owned by his grandfather. He attended school at Our Lady of Solace, and his father had been the painting contractor on the Parachute Jump. I asked Perfetto how he was able to stop the destruction of his neighborhood at a time when so many others were losing their homes and livelihoods to urban renewal.

"We first got organized back when Fred Trump started to build Trump Village," he said. "He put these big cement hoppers on Coney Island Creek, and cement dust was getting in our homes. You couldn't even open your windows. It was causing a quality-of-life problem. A group of people got together and called themselves the Associated Tenants and Landlords, and we fought Trump and won. But by the time we won, the Trump Village project was already over."

Astella soon realized that ill-conceived urban renewal was imminent and threatened their cohesive, mostly Italian neighborhood. "The city's mentality at that time," Perfetto said, "was to take an entire area, map it out, and literally draw a rectangle from Mermaid Avenue to Neptune Avenue and say, 'We're going to take out everything in this area.' The planning commissioner never talked to the neighborhood. I remember going to a 1969 hearing. The planning commissioner was Donald Elliot, and he called it the 'Master Plan.' I got up and said, 'How appropriate that you would call it the master plan. It's perfect for people who are acting like the master race.' At that time, they were taking the houses on West Twenty-first Street, and there were a lot of elderly Jewish people living there who worked hard to put their sons and daughters through school and college. The kids got married and moved out and left these old-timers back there. So now, in their twilight years, when they could finally relax and could say they were successful and could now enjoy a walk to the beach or the Boardwalk, the city was coming in to bulldoze them."

By the time Astella began fighting the city, the West End had been condemned from Sea Gate to West Twenty-first Street. The city had plans to build high-rises on the remaining five blocks east to Stillwell Avenue in the heart of the amusement area. The residents had other ideas.

"Borough President Abe Stark was at a city board of estimate hearing," Perfetto said. "I stood up at the hearing and said, 'These people came from Russia and Germany and Poland, all of Eastern Europe, and they worked for hours upon hours in sweatshops to send their children off to school and now you want to take their houses and uproot them? You remind me of another group that took people that were in their way and removed them and put them in freight cars.' Abe Stark jumped up, shaking, and said to me, 'Young man, don't say that, don't say that.' I said, 'You're pointing at these people and saying who shall stay and who shall go.' I hit them right between the eyes. So they backed off and the new planning commissioner was told to be sensitive to these people because there was a 'wild army' out there that would come out and say whatever they had to say to get the media involved."

I asked Perfetto what kind of media coverage he received. "Channel 13 came out and did a documentary on 'Coney's Italian Neighborhood,' he said, "and I walked around with my two younger sons, pointing out the good housing stock. We showed a different kind of community to the public. We were successful and started winning a lot of battles in different areas around Coney Island. The planning commissioner, John Zucotti, came down and saw that the area could be saved, so it was eliminated from the urban renewal project. Then we thought about putting in some housing, and the first project was Saltair Gardens on the site of the former P.S. 80. It was a federally funded home ownership program. Then we realized that this thing was big, and since we were working during the day and meeting at night, we couldn't handle it, so we formed the Astella Development Corporation in 1975." Astella went on to restore much of the neighborhood by building affordable

**Playground**
Children playing in a vest-pocket park on West Twenty-fifth Street, 1971.

THE 1970s: A DECADE OF REVOLUTION

**Urban renewal alternative**
Astella began building low-rise attached homes on city property that had been slated for high-rise projects.

low-rise housing on vacant city land, essentially replacing what the city had destroyed. No more high-rise slums would be built in Coney Island after 1975.

## Casino Gambling in Coney Island

Just about the time that Astella stopped the city's urban renewal plans, something happened that changed everyone's attitude toward Coney Island. In 1976, casino gambling was legalized in Atlantic City, and for the next four years, casino fever gripped Coney Island. It seemed that we would be next.

I remember the first rumors and then seeing a big billboard that the Coney Island Chamber of Commerce had placed at the Cropsey Avenue Bridge over Coney Island Creek. The sign read, "Welcome To Coney Island, The Perfect Resort for Casino Gambling." It was painted on canvas with little starbursts and crude lettering. Yellow bumper stickers also began appearing. They read, "CASINOS FOR CONEY." I became worried. Coney Island had enough problems, and I felt that if gambling came in, the amusement area would be wiped out, and the neighborhood wouldn't benefit at all. Gambling would just bring more traffic and crime.

Coney Island and Atlantic City have a rivalry that dates back to the 1870s, when each competed for the title of preeminent East Coast resort. A hundred years after the competition began, both resorts had been surpassed by modern destinations like Miami Beach and Las Vegas. When the first Atlantic City casinos opened in 1978, speculators started snatching up Atlantic City beachfront property. In August 1979, the New York State Legislature formed the Casino Gambling Study Panel to investigate the feasibility of casino gambling. The panel issued a positive report that proposed a maximum of forty casinos in five locations: Coney Island, Buffalo, the Catskills, Long Beach, and Rockaway. Annual gross revenues from the casinos were projected at $3 billion. Lobbying efforts were launched to place the required amendment to the state constitution on the ballot in 1979 or 1980.

Coney Island property owners were delirious when Mayor Ed Koch predicted that Coney Island would pull in $120 million in annual revenues from table games and slot machines. Local businesses put their differences aside and banded together to fight for a common cause. The Casinos for Coney Committee was formed, and speculators began eyeing real estate in the area. For a brief period during 1979, the asking price for property on the Boardwalk rose from $3 to $100 per square foot. Ironically, the only person to profit from the proposed gambling was real estate speculator Oscar Porcelli, who bought the Washington Baths property from owner Fred Warmers and sold it to Horace Bullard for a substantial profit.

The Casinos for Coney Committee wasn't aware that powerful forces were against them from the start. Donald Trump, son of developer Fred Trump, had casino interests in Atlantic City and wanted to protect them. Fred Trump did everything within his power to lobby the New York State Legislature into killing the referendum before it reached the voters. By the 1980s, any chance of gambling in New York State was dead. But for a few years, Coney could once again dream of competing with Atlantic City as the top East Coast resort.

Judging from what happened in Atlantic City, gambling would not have helped the local neighborhood but would have enriched some of the property owners. The old amusement area would have disappeared, and what kind of development would have replaced it is difficult to imagine. I interviewed most of the main players behind the Casinos for Coney coalition and asked them what it was like during the years of casino fever.

Charlie Tesoro, owner of Walter E. Burgess Inc., is the island's biggest realtor, and his office became the first stop for the speculators who swarmed Coney Island. "It was crazy," Tesoro said. "Limousines would pull up with guys coming up to the office from Las Vegas, in silk suits, saying, 'Sell to us now, get us some property, we wanna get in!' It was like a crazy house, like the gold rush. Steve Wynn pulled up in a limo and sent guys up to my office wearing flashy silk suits and solid-gold cuff links. Every other day you'd see limousines driving up and down Surf Avenue. It was wonderful. They'd sit at my desk and say, 'Waddaya got? We want options on everything you got. Everything!'

"They wanted options because if gambling didn't go though, they're out. But if gambling went through, they'd pay triple the asking price for the property. They're not so much gamblers when it comes to their money. They want you to be a gambler. I hadda laugh at 'em. People were even buying houses! A custodian came in from Manhattan and put every penny he had on three houses in Coney Island just because his cousin was a lobbyist and heard that gambling was gonna pass. Little guys were forming consortiums. They didn't just want to buy in the amusement zone. They wanted the residential areas, Mermaid Avenue, West Fifteenth Street."

Businessman Horace Bullard owned the

Shore Theater building, considered a prime location for a casino. Bullard tried to sell his vision of a Coney Island gambling mecca to other landowners. His plan involved combining a new amusement park with the casinos. "At the time we started," Bullard told me, "we knew that gambling had to be controlled. What we didn't want was an Atlantic City. I was trying to convince people that they shouldn't allow gambling to come to Coney Island unless it's done right. I felt that you should have one casino and one hotel, and the revenue from them would pay to rebuild the entire amusement area. I came up with a plan for Coney Island and began lobbying the whole community. I formed what's called an LDC—Local Development Company—and called a meeting. I wanted the board members that sat around the table at this meeting to be representative of Coney Island: the housing interests, Gargiulo's restaurant, the Aquarium, Our Lady of Solace Church, the landowners, Astroland, Sea Gate. On the table would be a map of Coney Island with gambling being the primary issue. We could all fight for our different interests and come up with a solution, and by voting for what the board would pass, we'd have a direction that Coney Island could go with."

**Casino site**
When gambling seemed a sure thing, Horace Bullard's Shore Theater was said to be a prime location. According to rumors, Frank Sinatra was interested in the site.

**Wishful thinking**
The Casinos for Coney Committee erected this sign at the Cropsey Avenue Bridge.

Bullard held his meeting in a Manhattan hotel and unveiled an ambitious plan. It involved pooling together all of the property in Coney Island's amusement zone, approximately eight square blocks, and building a large gambling/amusement complex. The entire facility would be above a massive parking garage at ground level. The property owners would sell their land to a newly formed corporation that would build the complex, and the landowners would be assigned an interest in the complex based on the percentage of land they had sold to the corporation. Bullard made an impressive presentation, but the landowners rejected it because they couldn't agree on the percentages or the placement of the casino. They chose to go it alone and take their chances on obtaining options from the casino builders.

Jerry Albert, the owner of Astroland Park, told me that he felt Bullard was scheming to be the only one chosen to build a casino. "I don't think that anyone was sure Bullard's idea would have worked," Albert told me. "When gambling was a hot item, everyone was talking continuously. But the feelings among the amusement ride operators weren't friendly. They were competitive as to where gambling would go. If gambling was approved for Coney Island, it was going to be on only one or two sites, and everybody else would be out of luck. They'd have to do something else. The closer it came to having gambling in Coney Island, the more jealous people got. Bullard suggested that Astroland put in amusements, and they'd build us a parking lot underneath the amusement park. But Astroland already had the amusements. Horace had an architect and was putting out renderings and drawings, and he held meetings to explain his concept of how things should be laid out. But it was always with the idea that Horace would be the one to get the gambling.

"Every day, there were rumors that options were being sold on land in Coney Island. We were in negotiations with one of the largest casino owners. The Golden Nugget was negotiating for an option on the Astroland property. I did not get the option for one reason. It was Labor Day weekend. The biggest casino owner in the United States was flying up in a Lear jet to sign the option agreement for $12 million. My lawyer said, 'It's Labor Day weekend, Jerry. Why must we go through with this meeting? Everyone is busy on Labor Day weekend. If you wait until after the weekend, I can get you $17 million.' And I said, 'The hell with it. I'm satisfied with $12 million.' I got into an argument with him, so we put off the signing till the following weekend. Guess what happened? Governor Hugh Carey held a news conference on television and said, 'As long as I'm governor of New York, there will never be gambling, because gambling is basically bad for the state.' After he made that speech, that was the end of gambling."

The merchants of Mermaid Avenue were big supporters of the casino plans. Coney Island businessman Lou Powsner had just given a speech at a governor's hearing at the World Trade Center in 1978 when he received a call from a representative of the gaming industry who wanted to discuss Powsner's analysis of casinos in Coney Island. "I asked him where he was from," Powsner said, "and he said he could not divulge that information. We later found out he was from Caesar's World. I told him that downstate, Coney Island with its tremendous Boardwalk was ripe for development. I also pointed out

**Brushed aside**
While a major luxury casino and hotel were being planned for Coney Island in the 1970s, the amusement area's six welfare hotels deteriorated. The Surf Hotel was in the Henderson Building.

**Stauch's casino**
Stauch's Baths was one of the sites considered for a casino. For years, the old bathhouse was decorated with graffiti left from the filming of *The Warriors,* a teen gang movie.

that we had an abundant labor market nearby crying for jobs, a sea of unemployment.

"We formed a local group and convened five times. Our slogan was 'Casinos Mean Jobs,' and they did. I was up to Albany five times. I went with Charlie Tesoro and with Hy Singer, who had hoped to turn Stauch's into a casino. The Russo family, owners of Gargiulo's restaurant, was also in the coalition. I met Bullard a couple of years later, when he held a meeting in a high-rise castle in Manhattan and we went over his plans, which featured an amusement park. It was a tremendous proposal."

The gambling resolution had a good chance of passing, but just before the state legislature was getting ready to vote, New York State Attorney General Robert Abrams held a press conference and said that he wouldn't want to see happen to New York what had happened to New Jersey, with crime and prostitution. The vote never made it to the floor.

"Abrams was a stooge for developers who didn't want gambling," Powsner said. "At that time, Donald Trump was a virtual unknown. On one of the trips that we made to Albany, Jerry Albert had a magazine called *Gaming*. In a sidebar, it said Donald Trump, the son of a New York developer, had underwater land in Atlantic City and was hoping to get the funds to build a major casino hotel. He got the funds and put up Harrah's Trump Plaza. We went down to defeat because Donald Trump had devised our defeat. His last move was to get together with one of the Tisch brothers and Sam Schubert, the theater owner who said that the casinos would destroy New York's theater district. And State Assembly Speaker Stanley Fink wouldn't let the bill come to the floor. It was Trump who killed it. It was all political, and it destroyed New York's opportunity to be the gambling capital."

Charlie Tesoro told me that he agrees with the theory that the Trumps fought

**Abandoned**
After the dream of gambling died, some owners of prime parcels in the amusement area abandoned their land. The Tilyou and McCullough families let their Boardwalk lot on West Fifteenth Street go to the city for back taxes. The ruins of the Wild Mouse roller coaster (right) remained on the lot.

the casino resolution. "We had everybody convinced that gambling was coming. We went to all the congressmen and senators, and they were all for it. Then Fred Trump comes in and says to them, 'You want the Mafia? You want prostitution?' We had no idea he was already in Atlantic City. And little junior there, Donald Trump, was heavily against gambling in New York. His old man didn't like the way it was gonna be handled. We did not have enough money, and the big money was against us. We had a slush fund of $50,000 to support it, and Atlantic City had $500,000 to fight it. We had busloads of supporters, we had signatures on petitions, and the trade groups on Mermaid Avenue were for it. Gambling was the only thing that would have developed the area. It would've brought in hotels and millions of dollars in investment money. I couldn't believe that New York State said it couldn't be controlled. Meade Esposito, Democratic leader of Brooklyn, told the legislature, 'Don't vote for it.' They were dupes of Trump and Atlantic City. Nobody knew that at the time. You didn't know your enemies."

In the end, gambling proved to be a bad idea. By the time it reached the legislature, New York law enforcement could see the damage in Atlantic City and the inability to keep out organized crime. When a Coney Island landlord on West Fifteenth Street assaulted a tenant and tried to evict him, the incident was played up as an example of "gambling fever." Everyone was saying that the landlord wanted to evict the tenants so that he could sell the building to speculators.

Even before the casino resolution came up for a vote, corrupt politicians were asking for bribes. Charlie Tesoro recalls several incidents. "There were a bunch of congressmen and a couple of wise guys who all wanted 6 percent. 'You want the gambling?' they'd say. 'Sign these contracts saying that such-and-such law firm will handle the case.' You wouldn't believe the corruption! These guys would come in and say, 'If you don't sign this, it'll never even pass the first session.' Nobody wanted to pay, but we didn't get gambling anyway."

Jerry Albert has no regrets and feels that Coney was better off without casinos. In 1999, I asked him if he thought the casino idea would ever be revived. "Gambling will never come back," he told me. "Every once in a while, it rears its ugly head, but definitely it will never happen, because Atlantic City is too powerful, and Coney Island, as far as I'm concerned, has become better every year, and I've been in Coney Island for forty years.

"The end of the 1960s was the low point. The trouble is that a lot of people who are in business in Coney Island have never invested any money and have let their property deteriorate. They were living with thoughts of gambling coming to Coney Island, and it was like gold fever. All the competitors basically had a shortsighted view of the situation. They were convinced that gambling was going to happen."

Horace Bullard seems to agree with Albert. "I don't believe that Trump stopped gambling," Bullard said. "I believe greed stopped Coney Island from getting gambling. Landowners' greed."

CHAPTER 19

# Images of the 1970s

I BEGAN PHOTOGRAPHING my neighborhood and the amusement area when I was a teenager so that I would have a record of what was lost during urban renewal. Coney Island had not seen much development since the building boom of the 1920s, and fifty years later, it was deconstructed piece by piece. The neighborhood did not die with dignity. Block after block lay in ruins, victims of an urban renewal policy run amok. I documented the process of decay nearly every day for a decade. Having taught myself photography and set up a small darkroom in our apartment at O'Dwyer Gardens, I captured nearly every building in Coney Island before it was razed. After a while, it seemed as if my camera became invisible, as if it were part of me. Over the years, I took nearly five thousand photographs of a community that exists only in the memories of those who were forced to leave.

**Documenting a decade**
Ticket taker at the Super Skooter on the Bowery (above); Jimmy McCullough Jr.'s Round-up on West Twelfth Street (left); photo studio on West Fifteenth Street (below).

# Coney's Bathhouses

BATHHOUSES were the first businesses in Coney Island. Even before Coney's first hotel was built in 1829, crude bathhouse shacks were set among the dunes. Bathhouses began as rickety wooden sheds in which people could change their clothes before going swimming, and grew in scale and quality during late 1800s, when more than a hundred different establishments lined the shore from Manhattan Beach to Sea Gate. Parkway, Silvers, and Manhattan Beach Baths were the most luxurious. Washington Baths and Ravenhall were billed as health resorts. Many had overnight accommodations, restaurants, and swimming pools, and offered massages and the ever-popular nude sunbathing. Prior to the 1920s, the shore could not be accessed without passing through one of the establishments.

An entire culture grew up around the bathhouses, and each establishment had a following. When I lived in Coney in the 1950s and 1960s, we patronized Ravenhall, which had opened in the 1860s. After it burned down in 1963, we switched to Washington Baths, which had the best pool in Coney Island. By the end of the 1970s, the bathhouses were gone.

**Bushman's Fire**
Bushman and Claret Baths (top) in 1969; after the 1973 fire (middle); Stauch's 1974 (bottom).

# Silvers Baths

Silvers Baths, which opened in the 1920s, was operated in the 1960s by John Bonsignore, whose father owned the L. A. Thompson ride, Stauch's Baths, and the Bobsled. Silvers was the largest and most famous of the West End bathhouses.

The sprawling complex looked like a movie theater, and my friends and I were initially confused by the enormous marquee. We wondered why the same Russian movie was always playing there.

A billboard on the side of the massive, buff-brick building advertised the baths as a cure for rheumatism, arthritis, and sciatica. The baths had a block-long rooftop "vita glass solarium" that resembled a giant greenhouse.

Bonsignore bought the baths in 1962, and in 1968, the city forced him to close down. The Board of Health wanted him to install a filter for the bath's saltwater intake one-quarter mile out in the ocean. Until then, business had been good, drawing clients throughout the New York area.

"I enjoyed Silvers, but the pressure was there," John Bonsignore told me. "It was a twenty-four-hour-a-day operation. We had the Russians giving oak branch massages. We had dormitories, a restaurant, a barber shop, a podiatrist, masseurs and masseuses, steam rooms, and two indoor plunge tanks for swimming. I had everything. The lobby had marble counters, the benches were thick marble slabs, and all the walls were glazed tile. But the city closed us down. How can you filter salt water? After you filter the salt out, what's left? The belief in salt water is that it's a natural curative. If you take all the benefits out, what good is it?"

**Lost bathhouses** Silvers Baths (top) was torn down in the 1970s. Washington Baths Annex (above left) at the Boardwalk and West Twenty-second Street closed in 1968 and suffered a series of fires in the early 1970s. Claret Baths (above right) burned in 1973.

**Cook's Baths** Thomas Cox opened his bathhouse in 1907 and expanded it several times. Cox entered politics and became a state senator, a municipal assemblyman, and president of the Coney Island Chamber of Commerce. Ruby Jacobs took over the establishment in the 1960s, and it became the winter headquarters of the Polar Bear Club. The Boardwalk entrance (above left) and lockers (above right) in 1974.

**Amusement area bathhouses**
After the Boardwalk was completed, forty-eight major bathhouse facilities and nine large saltwater swimming pools were located between West Eighth Street and West Thirty-Seventh Street. By 1970, the pools had closed, and only four bathhouses remained in the amusement area.

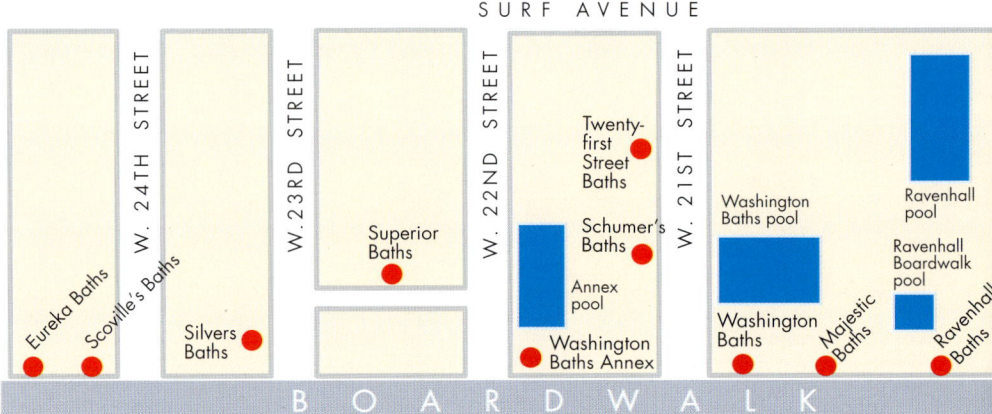

170    DECLINE AND COMEBACK

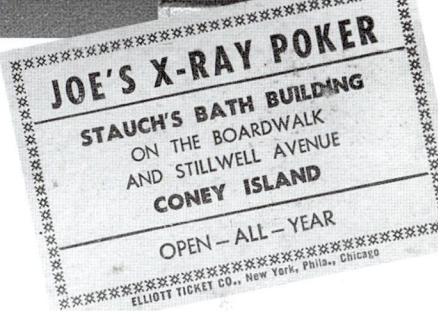

**Stauch's Baths**
Joe Bonsignore bought Stauch's Baths and Dance Hall after it went bankrupt in 1941. Ruby and Phil Jacobs took over the bathhouse operation in the 1960s and ran it until it closed. The building was torn down in 1992. The entrance (above) in 1970; Stauch's arcade (left) in 1973.

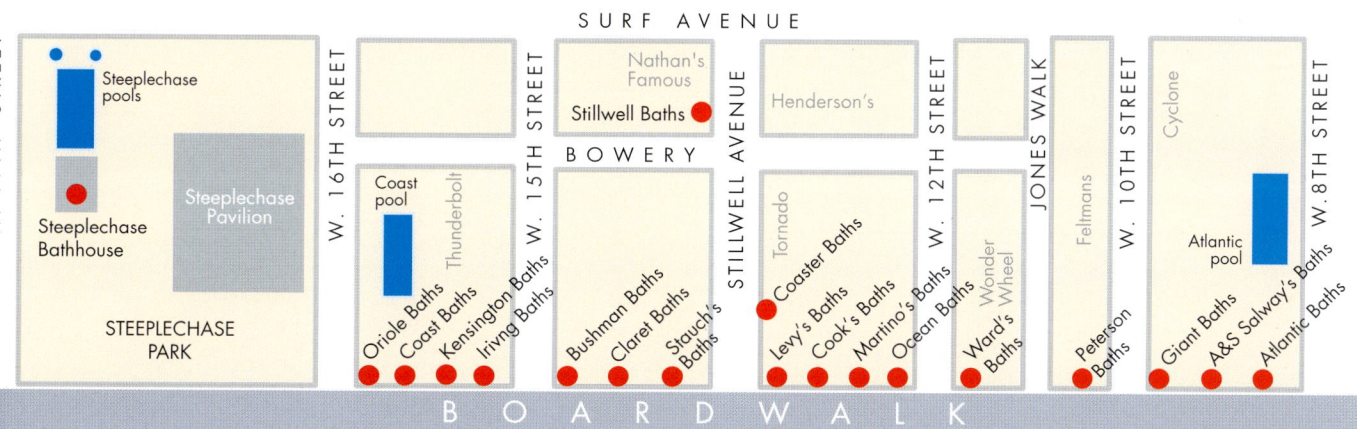

IMAGES OF THE 1970s 171

**The Mighty Atom, 1969**

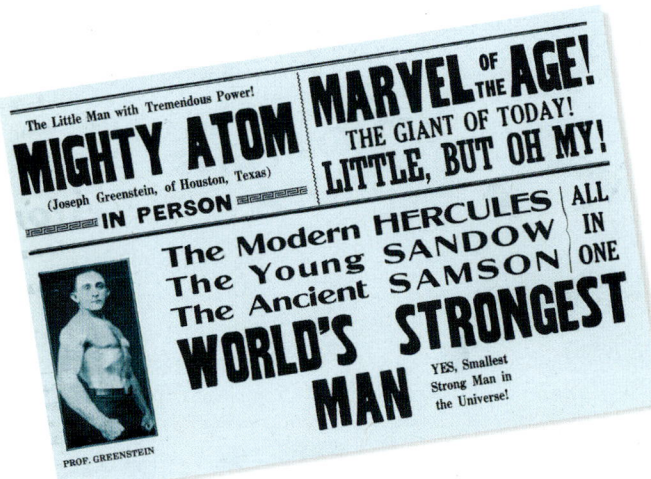

## JOSEPH GREENSTEIN
# THE LAST CONEY STRONGMAN

JOSEPH GREENSTEIN, the Mighty Atom, was a man with great physical and spiritual gifts. He held six world records for feats of strength and continued to perform well into his early eighties. A small man, only five feet, four inches tall, he twisted horseshoes with his bare hands, broke heavy chains by expanding his chest, bent iron bars on the bridge of his nose, and drove spikes into timbers with the palm of his hand. Joe and his wife, Leah, traveled the country in a beat-up truck selling patent medicines, ointments and liniments, bath oils, and laxatives. In the fall, he set up his show in the Washington Baths Annex building on the Boardwalk at West Twentieth Street and gave lectures on mind over matter and the virtues of drinking copious amounts of water. A health fanatic who recommended a low-salt, low-fat, low-sugar diet of mostly raw fruits and vegetables, he was ahead of his time. The Mighty Atom did his last strongman show at Madison Square Garden in 1976 at the age of eighty-two. He died the following year.

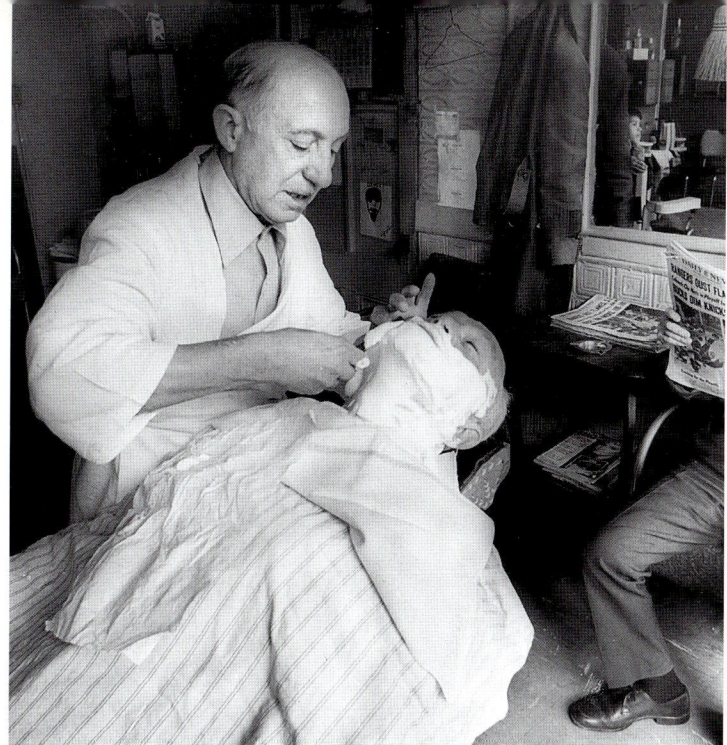

**Steeplechase barber shop** Dan's Barber Shop, a small building filled with Steeplechase memorabilia, was on West Sixteenth Street on property owned by the Tilyou family. Dan Cafarelli ran it until he died in 1964, and his assistant, Joey Giordano (left), took over until it closed in 1976.

**Penny arcade, 1973** David Bernstein's arcade just outside the Stillwell Avenue Subway Terminal was filled with museum-quality antique arcade machines. Today, the building houses a furniture store.

# Mermaid Avenue

THE MAIN SHOPPING district of Coney Island, Mermaid Avenue consisted mainly of mom-and-pop stores with apartments above them. The street was also the one-time home of Woody Guthrie and Barbra Streisand. There were luncheonettes, delis, hardware stores, butcher shops, doctor and dentist offices, cleaners, pet shops, banks, and a movie theater. Most of the storefronts were in three-story buildings constructed in the 1920s by William Avitable, who sold them to store owners, who in turn rented out apartments above the shops. During the 1970s, the "Avenue" underwent a radical transformation as the neighborhood and the clientele of the businesses changed. Rather than renovate or preserve the old buildings, the city began demolishing them, starting at the western end of the avenue. Luckily, the city went broke in the 1970s, and demolition ended, but not before most of the business district was gone. I photographed the area in 1974 and 1975.

**Mermaid's decline** This orthodox synagogue (above) lost its congregation as the neighborhood changed. During the 1970s, Mermaid Avenue followed the amusement area downhill as stores closed (below, opposite).

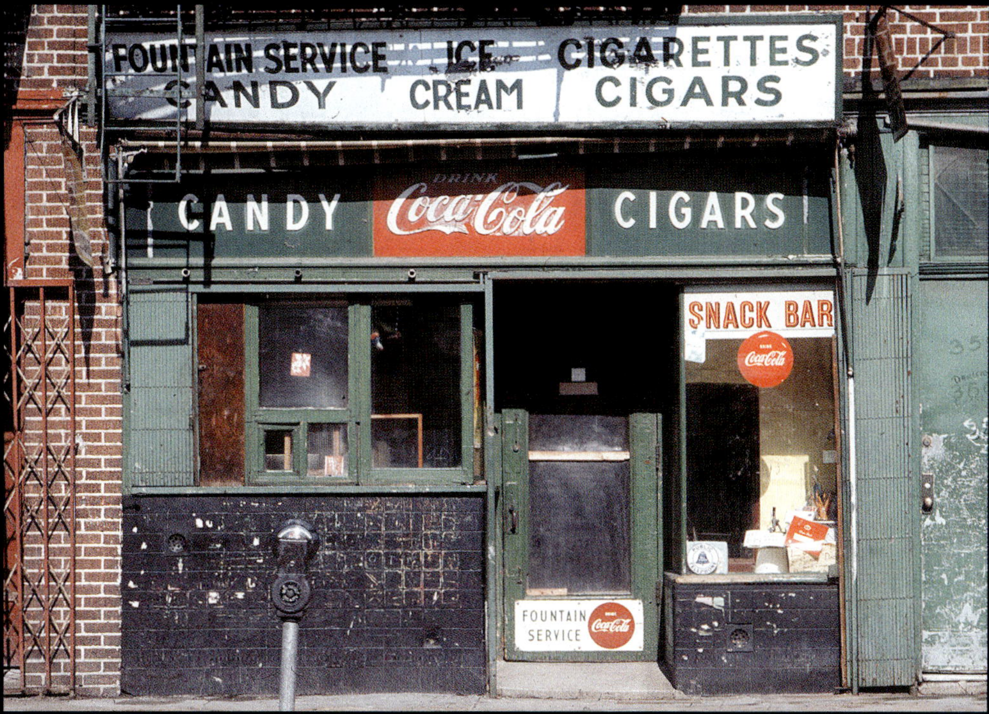
FOUNTAIN SERVICE
ICE CREAM
CIGARETTES
CANDY
CIGARS
CANDY
Coca-Cola
CIGARS
SNACK BAR
FOUNTAIN SERVICE

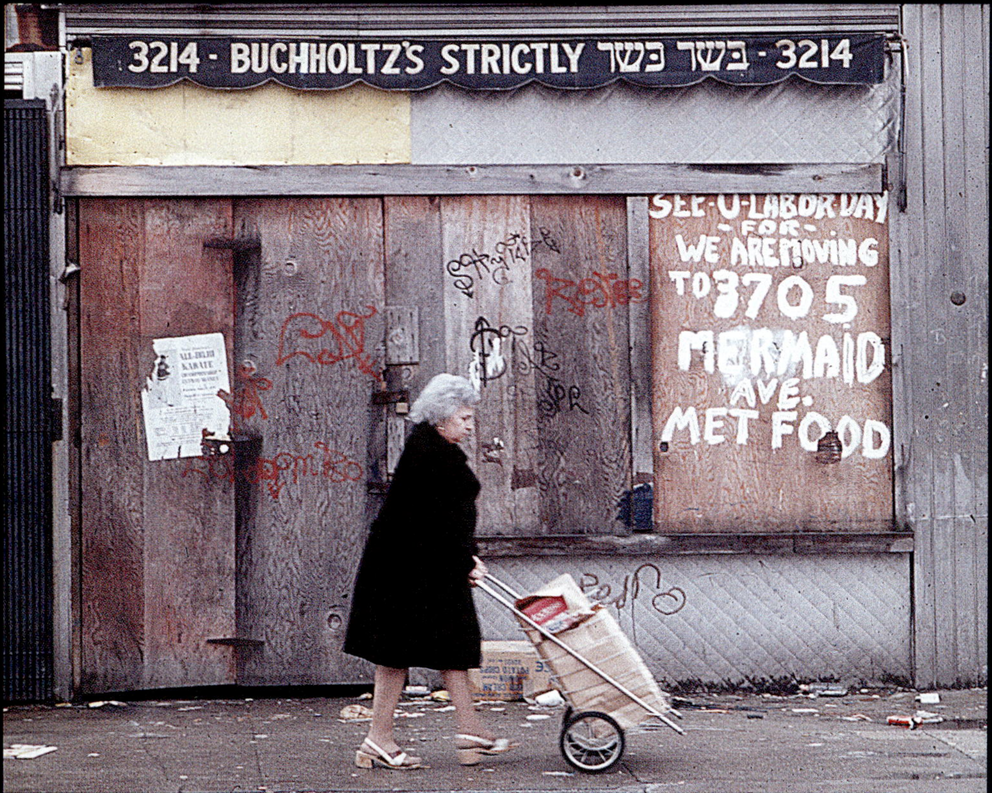
3214 - BUCHHOLTZ'S STRICTLY בשר כשר - 3214
SEE-U-LABOR DAY
-FOR-
WE ARE MOVING
TO 3705
MERMAID
AVE.
MET FOOD

**Mermaid remnants, 1975** Clockwise from top left: one of many boarded-up storefronts; Glorious Church of God in Christ; Phoenix House drug treatment center; colorful community center; graffiti on a storefront; CBS Social Club.

**Woody Guthrie's Coney Island Home** Folksinger/composer Woody Guthrie and his family lived in an apartment at 3520 Mermaid Avenue (circled) during the 1940s and early 1950s. According to his daughter, Nora Guthrie, it was his first real home, a happy and lively place visited by musicians such as Leadbelly, Ramblin' Jack Elliot, Sonny Terry, and Pete Seeger. Guthrie's children, Arlo, Nora, and Joady Ben, were born while Woody and his wife, Marjorie, lived here. When Woody died in October 1967, his family scattered his ashes in the ocean, a block away from this home that he loved.

**Huba-Huba** My favorite Mermaid Avenue luncheonette.

**Former deli** The United Kosher Deli closed in 1975.

**The Atlantis, 1971** Even in the off-season, the Atlantis was an impressive sight.

# The Atlantis: Coney's Last Nightclub

THE ATLANTIS NIGHTCLUB opened in the late 1940s in a Boardwalk building formerly occupied by Levi's Baths. During the 1950s, when the lounge was owned by Mousey Powell and Hy Schuman, top jazz combos and entertainers performed at the club. Every summer the *Brooklyn Eagle* held the Miss Brooklyn Pageant at the Atlantis. Below the bar, at street level, was Ringside Johnny's, a restaurant owned by ex-boxer Johnny Katalis.

Coney had a dozen nightclubs until the 1950s, and eighty-year-old clarinetist Sol Yaged played them all. "I worked every place where they had music in Coney Island," Yaged told me. "On the Boardwalk was the Atlantis, which was the best and had the biggest crowds. I also played the Riptide on Surf at Stillwell, the Bluebird Casino, the Eagle, the Jinx Club, the Pink Poodle in Brighton, and the old Stauch's in 1940, just before it was torn down.

"There was a nightclub near Sea Gate on the Boardwalk near Thirty-fifth Street, a very famous jazz club called Indian Village. Beginning in 1939, I played the Indian Village for four or five years. I remember they used to have miniature tom-toms on the table with mallets, and when the band would play, everyone would join in and hit the tom-toms. My first job was playing in a swing band at Gargiulo's restaurant on West Fifteenth Street, and I'll never forget it, because I never got paid. They paid me with meatballs and spaghetti."

Gerry Menditto, manager of the Cyclone roller coaster, remembers

**Classic neon**
The Atlantis sign, a landmark for fifty years, got a touch-up in 1975.

Coney's cowboy craze of the 1950s. "There was a lot of country-western music in Coney in the '50s. You had the cowboy singing at the Atlantis Bar. I remember him up on stage. It was a horseshoe-shaped bar and he was in the middle. He wore a big hat and a vest with tassels. We'd be in bed trying to go to sleep, and you could hear his voice across Neptune Avenue. The Eagle Bar, a western type bar, also had a guy singing. Every kid in the '50s wanted to be a cowboy. It was like John Wayne. It was big."

The last performer at the Atlantis was Westy Fesco, the Coney Island Cowboy. Fesco wasn't a real cowboy but sang his heart out onstage at the Atlantis until 1970. I photographed him playing for a sparse crowd at the horseshoe-shaped bar.

In the 1990s, Johnny Lambros leased the Atlantis from owner Hy Singer and opened Club Atlantis, a Boardwalk Latin dance club. It was popular but was forced to close when a concrete ramp that served as an emergency exit collapsed and was never replaced. The club, minus its famous sign, now houses Nathan's Boardwalk restaurant.

**Wild West**
Cowpokes (left) at Ward's Kiddie Park, 1971. The Eagle Bar (above) pictured shortly after it closed in 1970, had a western theme in the 1950s. Westy Fesco, the Coney Island Cowboy (below), performed at the Atlantis Bar in 1970.

# The Kister Building

**Kister's restaurant, circa 1910**

**The Kister Building** Top to bottom: 1908; 1968; 1979.

**George Kister**

For nearly a hundred years, the Kister Building served as Coney's "clubhouse." In 1895, Fred Kister bought a small lot on the north side of Surf Avenue in front of the Sea Beach Palace and opened a carousel shed. The following year, he expanded and added a three-story building next door to the carousel. Kister's restaurant occupied the two lower floors of the frame structure, and the third floor became apartments. In 1903, when Thompson and Dundy opened Luna Park, the pair put the main entrance alongside the Kister Building, making it one of the best-known locations in Coney Island. Behind his Surf Avenue building, Kister opened one of Coney's first movie theaters and a hotel. Fred's son, George, inherited the building and went into the amusement business in the 1920s, operating several whip rides. After George served two terms as president of the Coney Island Chamber of Commerce, he formed a partnership with Chris Feucht, owner of the Bowery's Drop the Dip roller coaster, and the two bought the Cyclone roller coaster in 1937. Kister and Feucht operated the Cyclone until they sold it to the Pinto brothers in 1954.

Kister divided the Kister Building into two properties and sold it to restaurant owner Louis Gargiulo and Maize Gordon, an eccentric Manhattan theater owner profiled by *New Yorker* writer Joseph Mitchell. Gordon, who resembled Mae West, spent summers in the building's third-floor apartment and was well known for her bizarre dress as she strolled the amusement area. In the 1930s, the building became the home of the Coney Island Chamber of Commerce and Walter E. Burgess Inc. and was bought by Jimmy Tesoriero. It survived dozens of fires over the years, many started by sparks from the elevated trains that ran behind it. The last fire was in 1979, and the building was demolished shortly afterward.

**Classic Coney studio**
For forty years, Herb Gaskowitz ran an old-fashioned photo studio (above) in the Kister Building on Surf Avenue. He used a massive wooden view camera and had numerous props, including a 1950s Chevrolet and large painted cutouts. The studio closed in 1971. Jimmy Tesoriero (left) sat down with photographer Gaskowitz (right) at the studio's bar.

IMAGES OF THE 1970s

## The Dragon's Cave

**Cave man**
Murray "Sporty" Kaufman (above) operated the family's Dragon's Cave ride, shown here in 1971 (top). Two versions of the ride's famous smoke-breathing dragon (above right).

The Dragon's Cave was located on the Bowery at Schweickert's Walk, next door to the Bobsled. The ride, originally called Fun in the Dark, was opened in 1941 by Joe Kaufman. Kaufman and partners Messmore and Damon had operated another ride at the location called Axis Atrocities. When Joe Kaufman died, his sons Norman and Sporty took over the cave. The signature was the smoke-spouting dragon's head that swiveled menacingly over the Bowery, red eyes glowing. The head was designed by artist and engineer Hank Banks.

"I told Hank to change the frontage of the Fun in the Dark ride," Norman Kaufman said, "and he made it look like a cave. We built the dragon head out of plaster of paris, but the steam melted it, so Sporty and I rebuilt it with resin. We also built a talking parrot in a tree, and it talked to the people waiting to go on the ride, which was cute."

The Dragon's Cave was sold to Ken Handwerker in 1983 and was operated by the Coney Island Hysterical Society for one year before it closed in 1986.

# Spookarama

**B**ILLED AS the world's only indoor-outdoor dark ride and the "longest, largest ride in Coney Island," Spookarama was the brainchild of Fred Garms, a true Coney eccentric. The 1950s-era ride was designed as a take-off on the horror film genre of the decade and the blood-red cars still make the rounds today in a shortened version of the ride. The most delightful part of the ride was the handpainted signs reflecting Garms's humor: "Coney's Largest Guillotine," "See and Hear the Invisible Man," "See Dracula's Screaming Head Chopped Off!" The animated, bright yellow Cyclops with its lighted, blinking eye was a Bowery landmark for decades.

Garms was known as a drinker, which helped him come up with the horror themes. During the 1973 Watergate investigations, he put a sign over the ride's bloody waterfall that read "Ride the Watergate." A friend described Garms: "Freddie Garms built Spookarama in 1955. He was always hitting the Chivas. For a while he had a grind tape that played outside the ride: 'See the three-breasted woman looking for a man with three hands.' He bought $1,500 worth of junked mannequins and covered them with fiberglass. His horror show was all in his head. His idea of scary was to tape a 78-rpm record at 33 rpm."

**It's spooky**
The Jones Walk cyclops (top); the Bowery cyclops (above).

**Bowery colonnade** This classic concession arcade and rooming house on the Bowery at Jones Walk was erected in the 1890s. A fire later reduced it to one story.

**Hat store** A souvenir stand in the Boston Hotel, 1970.

### Eateries

The Sodamat had a beautiful art deco facade and a wall of five-cent, built-in soda machines that mixed dozens of exotic flavors, such as champagne, loganberry, and lemon-lime, into paper cups while customers watched. The sodas were five cents until 1970. Max Cohen ran a stand, Maxie's Waffles, that served Belgian waffles with ice cream. Jimmy's Health Bar, next door, offered up frankfurters and potato chips as well as fruit drinks.

**Attention to detail** The Wonder Wheel (left), viewed from the side on West Twelfth Street. Mike Curran's Satellite Jet (foreground) had a whirling neon globe and an incongruous white picket fence. The 1903 Geneas building (top) was a former theater with an ornate facade covered with medallions, cornices, and columns. The Tornado roller coaster is behind it. Both were lost to fires. A vintage Mangels shooting gallery on the Bowery (above) had cast-iron paratrooper, tank, and soldier targets.

**Tomb of rides** This dark ride was located on the Bowery near West Fifteenth Street. It was operated by the Moran/Klein family and closed when Freddie Moran died in 1982. The ride had become the final resting place for many of the figures from Coney's other dark

**Horrors in Wax** In 1970, Lillie Santangelo's World in Wax Musee had a Bowery entrance (right) as well as an entrance on Stillwell Avenue. The museum opened in 1926 and was the oldest tenant in the Henderson Theater building. Most of the exhibits were tableaus, each in a small, dimly lit room fenced off with chicken wire. Many exhibits were of grisly dismemberments, executions, and gang murders. A lifelike victim is strangled (below); Richard Speck assaults a nurse (bottom center). President John F. Kennedy and other luminaries were also on display (bottom right).

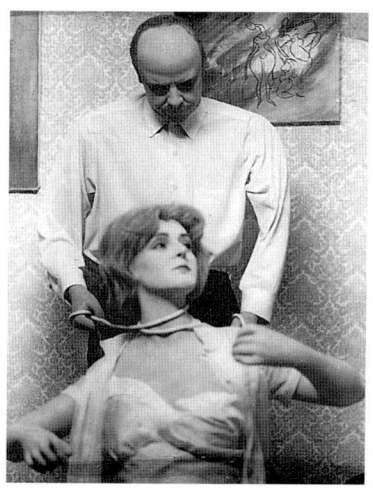

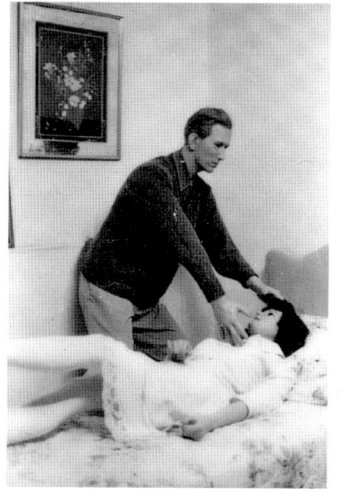

IMAGES OF THE 1970s

# Coney Island Burning

**C**ONEY ISLAND began burning in 1965, and the fires continued for the next decade. Most were arson. Fires became so commonplace that children no longer stopped what they were doing to watch. During the early 1970s, I can't recall a day going by when I didn't witness a major fire. Fires were burning when I left for school and when I returned home. I took the photographs here between 1969 and 1974. In 1970, some local kids found a way to climb into the attic of the Boardwalk pavilion at West Twenty-ninth Street. They wanted to show me the clubhouse they'd built. I climbed through a trapdoor and found the space illuminated by dozens of candles. It looked like a church altar. I told them it didn't look safe, and they laughed. A few days later the old pavilion was gone.

**Exhaustion** A firefighter takes a breather after battling a Mermaid Avenue fire, 1974.

**Red room** A bungalow fire on West Thirty-third Street, 1973 (left). Smoke pours from the Liberal Party headquarters on Surf Avenue at Twenty-ninth Street, 1969 (opposite).

**Coney fires**
Various house fires, 1969–1970 (top two rows). Coney's last Boardwalk pavilion (above) at West Twenty-ninth Street was burned by children in 1970 (right).

**Amusements**
Two views of Sister Theresa's fortune-telling stand on Henderson Walk at the Boardwalk, in 1974 (left) and 1981 (below).

**Amusing sign**
Many found this crude advertisement for Mama Bertha's to be one of the funniest things in Coney Island. In the last panel, a woman pointed to her breast and said, "The happy Steeplechase crowd still eat HERE." Over the years, people added obscene graffiti that changed the sign's meaning.

IMAGES OF THE 1970s   191

**Parachute Go Karts**
After Steeplechase was torn down in 1966, the Parachute Jump base was leased to Frank Garto, who operated a short-track go-cart ride around the base. The carts were stored in the Parachute Jump's motor room. The ride opened in 1967 and closed in the early 1970s.

**Last remnants** Steeplechase Park's Boardwalk buildings were not demolished when the park was razed. The concessions and rides continued in business after the park closed but eventually burned in arson fires in the 1970s. The art deco Steeplechase Shooting Gallery (above) had a colorful sign on the side advertising the park.

**Building a dream** Jerry Bianco leaves the shed where his submarine was under construction.

**Going down** In 1970, I stood inside the unfinished submarine (above). Bianco's sketch for the sub (left) and the sub on Coney Island Creek (below).

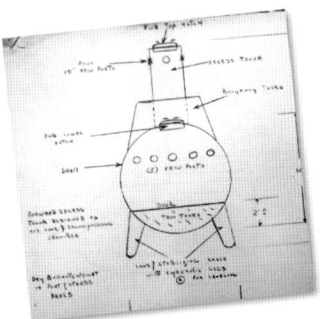

# Coney Island's Yellow Submarine

I FIRST MET Jerry Bianco in 1969, while I was snooping around the old Burns Brothers coal silos on Coney Island Creek. I noticed a strange structure of plastic sheeting stretched over a framework of wooden lattice, a sort of crude greenhouse. A small sign on the chain-link fence said "Deep Sea Technologies." I walked inside and asked Bianco what he was working on. Pointing at an object that looked like a boiler, he replied, "A submarine." Over the next year, I spent a lot of time around the old coal yards watching Bianco build his dream.

Bianco grew up around Coney Island Creek and spent his boyhood playing on its banks. He planned to use his submarine to raise the *Andrea Doria*, the ocean liner that sank off Nantucket, Massachusetts, in 1956. He had no training in submarine building and no background in raising capital. His only experience with ships was repairing and dismantling them. He had a grade-school education and had never piloted a submarine.

What Bianco did have going for him was practical knowledge of how things worked and a belief in himself and his abilities. And there were others who believed in him. He formed a corporation, took it public, and raised capital by selling shares of stock to Coney Island investors.

The submarine, completed in 1971, was a beautiful craft named *Quester I*. It was painted yellow, the cheapest anti-corrosion paint Bianco could find. But a quirk of fate led to a public relations disaster. An enormous crowd turned out the day of the launch, and the New York media latched on to the story. Bianco's dream had gone big time.

That day, a floating crane raised the sub off the dock and began lowering it into the creek. Bianco had removed the ballast from the sub to enable the crane to lift it and warned the crane operator not to lower the sub all the way into the water until the ballast was replaced. But the operator failed to listen and lowered it all the way. The *Quester I* rolled over on its side.

Bianco quickly corrected the problem, but the damage was done. The "sinking sub" became the butt of jokes in newspapers and on TV. The crane operator's mistake killed Bianco's dream. Although the fiasco deterred new investors, it did not stop Bianco. He made fifteen successful test dives in Gravesend Bay. The sub remained moored in Coney Island Creek until a 1975 storm broke it loose from its moorings and washed it ashore. Its rusting, seaweed-covered yellow hull can still be seen in the muddy creek across from West Twenty-first Street, waiting to be salvaged.

# Boardwalk Portraits

DURING THE 1970s, the old-timers, the elderly practitioners of seaside health culture, still flocked to the beach in the winter, as they had for generations. They were Coney's bathhouse patrons, introduced to the baths by their parents when they were children. Most believed that ocean air and sunshine were therapeutic and life affirming. All year long, summer and winter, these people gathered on the Boardwalk with their friends to soak up the sun and breathe salt air. Some traveled by subway from Manhattan, and others came from as far away as New Jersey. Many had season tickets to the various bathhouses, and others just enjoyed the Boardwalk camaraderie. They were a tight-knit group of all ethnicities.

Throughout the decade, as the baths folded or burned, informal gathering places sprang up to replace them. Impromptu solariums of corrugated tin painted silver were built on vacant lots. The most popular Boardwalk gathering places in winter were in front of the Child's building, the nearby sidewalk solarium on West Twenty-second Street, the west side of Stauch's on Schweickert's Walk, and in front of the Busy Bee at West Fifteenth Street. What these locations had in common were reflective surfaces that provided warmth. They also created ideal lighting for photography.

I knew many of the locals on the following pages and began taking their portraits. I developed the film in a darkroom at home and returned the next day to surprise the subjects with eight-by-ten prints. Soon, everyone began asking me to photograph them, and I obliged.

**Impromptu winter solariums** Bushman Baths (above) and the Busy Bee (below) were perfect locations for Boardwalk socializing.

194  DECLINE AND COMEBACK

IMAGES OF THE 1970s

IMAGES OF THE 1970s 197

IMAGES OF THE 1970s

# Coney Island Street Theater

THE CONCEPT of public street theater was born in Coney Island in 1966 when the Everyman Theater Company was founded as an offshoot of the Brooklyn Arts and Culture Association. Among the group's founders were Brooklyn activist Charlene Victor and actress Geraldine Fitzgerald. The company's first production was an updated version of the old morality play *Everyman*, transformed by the cast into a contemporary rock opera called *Everyman and Roach*.

Chuck Riechenthal, later district manager of Community Board 13, was Everyman's program director. "Street theater was hot for ten or fifteen years, and it started in Coney Island," Riechenthal told me. "The neighborhood was perfect for putting together a mixed group of young people. Nobody was turned away. It was a multiethnic, multiracial, multieconomic production, which was the purpose. Our rehearsals were held on the Boardwalk, in the parks, on the beach, and upstairs in the Tilyou Theater. Actor Lou Gossett, who lived in Coney Island Houses, worked with us, and Lou's mother, Helen, a beloved community leader, was one of the guiding spirits. Sam and Estelle Horwitz, who ran the Tilyou Theater, were avid supporters, and Sam even acted in the play. At the end of the show, God had to make a decree as to whether Everyman would live or die, and Sam played the role of God."

Murray Handwerker, president of Nathan's Famous, was a supporter of the arts and in 1969 tried to form a Coney Island Cultural Center. He offered the Everyman Theater Company a permanent home in the old Boston Theater, an abandoned 1907 vaudeville venue located inside a building at Surf Avenue and West Twelfth Street owned by Nathan's Famous. Riechenthal remembered the first time he saw the theater: "Lou Gossett and I walked in and knew that it couldn't be used. It would have cost millions of dollars to fix it up. Everyone else was walking around saying, 'Isn't this wonderful?'" Nevertheless, using Everyman as the nucleus, Gossett and Riechenthal formed an offshoot organization, the Boardwalk Arts and Culture Association, and held art shows at the theater for a short time before abandoning the location.

Coney Island's Everyman troupe became a phenomenon, performing throughout Brooklyn before moving to a more prestigious venue in Manhattan. After seeing the company perform in the parking lot at the Brooklyn Museum, a representative from Lincoln Center invited it to Manhattan. "At that point, nobody had ever performed outdoors at Lincoln Center," said Riechenthal, "and they said, 'Let's try it at the center's fountain.' That was the birth of the Lincoln Center Outdoors series, which continues to this day. It all started with Everyman."

After Everyman left the Boston Theater, Handwerker found a replacement troupe: the Bread and Puppet Theater. The political performance group moved into the old vaudeville house for a two-year run. The theater became a hangout for curious young people who stopped in to see the avant-garde productions. A children's workshop on bread and puppet making was held on weekends. I remember spending wild nights in the musty old theater, and the group's presence was reassuring at a time when nothing positive was happening in Coney Island.

**Puppet show**
The Bread and Puppet Theater built this giant puppet head over the entrance to its show. The puppet remained in place long after the performance group left Coney Island.

Before each weekend performance, the puppeteers used to "bally" on the streets of Coney Island. Oddly dressed performers beating drums marched down Surf Avenue with giant dancing marionettes, attracting a crowd that followed them to the theater. Bally was a traditional Coney art form that hadn't been used since the days of the sideshows in the 1950s, and no one knew what to make of it.

I asked Handwerker how he had convinced Bread and Puppet to come to Coney Island. "I made contact with the Bread and Puppet Theater at a time when they were traveling all over Europe and the world," he said. "I thought they did a fine job, and they were good for children. They were a very imaginative, progressive group, and their performances covered environmental and political matters. I read in the paper they were looking for a spot, and I told them to come down and look at the Boston Theater. I offered

**The Boston Hotel** In the 1970s, most people knew it as the fleabag Lido Hotel, but over the years, the 1907 building had housed a famous vaudeville theater, a movie house, and a sideshow.

**Paul Zaloom**
The artist returned to Coney Island in 1981.

them the building for free, just to draw people down to Coney Island. They fixed up the theater themselves. I was willing to renovate it for them if they would make a commitment, but they didn't want to do that, and I don't blame them. They performed there for two seasons, but they didn't want to stay in Coney Island. It was too provincial for them, and they moved to Manhattan."

Paul Zaloom, the Obie award–winning performance artist and host of the CBS children's television show Beakman's World, began his career with Bread and Puppet in 1971 and did a stint in Coney Island. "I was at Bread and Puppet in the summer of 1971," he said. "We were living in Vermont and we had rotating crews that were schlepping down to Coney Island. We did *Revenge of the Law*. The previous crew did a show called the *Difficult Life of Uncle Fatso* and another called *Mississippi*. I recall that next door there were some gypsy fortune tellers who had a Rolls-Royce with Florida plates. I was very impressed with the fact that they read fortunes and had a Rolls-Royce. Coney in those days was pretty much as down-and-out as Coney got, and it was a little scary. I remember hearing gunshots at night."

*Revenge of the Law* was about the 1970 uprising at the state prison in Attica, New York, and the subsequent police riot and slaying of prisoners. It was performed with giant marionettes, one of which represented Governor Nelson Rockefeller. For *Mississippi*, Bread and Puppet Theater took on the killing of students at the University of Mississippi, which occurred at the same time as the deaths at Kent State but was less publicized because the students were black. "*Mississippi* was sort of like a street show in that it didn't have a set," Zaloom said. "It was more flexible and could travel around. We did the show as a prologue in the lobby or in front of the marionette stage.

"In Coney Island, there were no elite crowds," Zaloom remembered. "We were trying to reach an audience that was different than the audience we usually played for, and I don't know if we were entirely successful. The shows weren't completely inaccessible, but they weren't lighthearted entertainment, either. In *Mississippi*, a guy got shot by the cops, and his mother held the dead body, and *Revenge of the Law* was about the slaughter of prisoners by prison guards. It was very political theater, like agit-prop or street theater, and that was always the objective of the shows."

The departure of the Bread and Puppet Theater in 1972 signaled the end of a creative era for Coney Island. The Boston Theater became a storage warehouse for Nathan's, and the giant papier-mâché puppet over the theater's entrance mystified Coney visitors for years. The building was demolished in the early 1980s.

## SAM HORWITZ
# POLITICAL SHOWMAN

**Horwitz in front of the Tilyou Theater**

Sam Horwitz played a major role in Coney Island for more than forty years. Although he served as city councilman for the area from 1973 to 1993, his real legacy was show biz. He provided magic for a generation of Coney's children. Anyone who grew up in the area during the 1950s and early 1960s remembers him best for the Saturday matinees at his Mermaid Theater. I spent many magical Saturday afternoons at the 550-seat theater, where admission was a quarter. It was a family operation, run by Horwitz and his wife, Estelle. Their daughter, Susan, a good friend, was in my class through grade school. I worked for Sam delivering advertising flyers for the Tilyou Theater, which he also operated. The pay wasn't much, but I got loads of free passes. "Movies and politics are seven-day-a-week jobs," Horwitz told me. "Never a boring day. The only problem was no days off."

I remember the Mermaid's kiddie matinee being a very special event, a kids' paradise and always a full house. I asked Horwitz what his secret was. "Mothers could drop their kids off just when the theater was opening, at 11:30," he said, "and leave them for four hours or more while they went shopping, and the kids were safe. We had cartoons and races—a bike race or a boat race—and we used to give out prizes. The cashier knew the winning number and made sure that a couple of underprivileged kids—black kids, handicapped kids—would get the prize, the kind of kid you'd like to see win. It was fixed, but in a way that the kids who never won would win something, too."

I asked him about how he put his programs together. "We didn't give the kids one cartoon—we gave them two or three, and serials with a different chapter every week, then the races and a double feature, say, Abbott and Costello or a Western. I was very selective about what I showed. Matrons took care of the kids, and the candy stand did very well. We used to break up candy bars and sell them for two cents and get a little extra revenue. We had hot dogs and popcorn. We made sure that the kids had no money left when they went home."

I told Horwitz that I remember how my friends and I used to harass the Mermaid's flashlight-wielding matrons. "Sometimes theaters got guys who wanted to molest children, and we watched very closely for that," he said. "There was a law that said a children's section had to be labeled with a sign and have a matron on both aisles so no adult could sit near a child. The matrons were licensed by the board of health and wore white uniforms, like a nurse's outfit, and they knew how to take care of a problem or call a child's mother. The matrons loved their work."

The Mermaid also had live performances. "We had some of the last of the great Yiddish performers on our stage," Horwitz said, "and Sol Yaged, the clarinetist, lived around the corner and used to play onstage with his band. There were lots of Jewish people in Coney Island at that time, and the Mermaid was always jumping. My wife and I took care of everything. Not that I'm bragging, but we really knew how to run a theater. Everyone in Coney Island liked to go there because it had a giant screen the width of the building, and we played double features five times a week and changed the programs. We made money at the Mermaid with minimum operation expense. The Mermaid bought us a new car and a house in Sea Gate."

Horwitz sold the Mermaid in 1962, after taking over the Tuxedo Theater in 1961. The Tuxedo was much larger, and he and his wife couldn't run both theaters at the same time. After the Horwitzes sold the Mermaid, it went downhill. "The fellow who bought it did not do a good job," Horwitz said. "It was a case of absentee management. He just had it as an investment and didn't want to operate it himself. When my wife and I ran it, we were there from morning till night and made sure it was clean. The new owner was a big gambler, and whatever money came in he gambled away."

★

The Tuxedo was on Ocean Parkway at Brighton Beach Avenue, where the Trump Village parking lot is now located. I remember it well, because that's where

202 DECLINE AND COMEBACK

**Sol Yaged (right) and Steve Allen**

I first saw *West Side Story*. Fred Trump had bought the theater to demolish it as part of the vast urban renewal project for Trump Village. Horwitz came to operate the Tuxedo almost by accident. The theater's projectionist called Horwitz to tell him that the theater was closing, and Horwitz approached Trump to buy the fixtures for the Mermaid Theater. Instead, he wound up operating the theater for three years, from 1961 to 1963.

It was a classy theater. On Saturdays, Horwitz wore a black tuxedo as he greeted customers in the lobby. "The Tuxedo was a blockbuster," he said. "It was a stadium-type theater with very comfortable seats. Trump had closed the theater, and the owners got a settlement. I went to him and asked to buy the seats and fixtures but instead worked out a deal to lease and operate the theater." The big problem was the air-conditioning. It had broken down, and the previous owners could not afford to have it fixed. Horwitz brought his maintenance man from the Mermaid and was able to make the repairs for $90. That was his only initial expense. "I didn't have to put any money in," he said. "I just paid rent and a percentage of the profits to Trump. I did well and he did well."

Two things made the Tuxedo an instant success. Horwitz bid on the exclusive rights in Brooklyn to screen *West Side Story*, and he had the largest theater parking lot in the country. Everything for blocks around had been demolished, and he hired four or five kids to park cars on four of the blocks. The Tuxedo was a beautiful theater with a great location and was very successful under his operation. But the site was slated for a parking lot, and the Tuxedo fell under the wrecker's ball in 1963.

★

In 1964, Horwitz took over the 2,750-seat Tilyou Theater on Surf Avenue and West Seventeenth Street, across from Steeplechase Park. He leased the theater from Marie Tilyou, taking over the theater on Labor Day 1964, a few weeks before the park closed for good. The neighborhood was deteriorating, and the Tilyou was a hard sell. Horwitz tried to bring in people by operating a jitney. "I made arrangements with a fellow who had a small bus," he said, "and advertised that we would pick up people and take them to the movies. People took advantage of it because they were afraid to go out at night. Business was lousy, and we were losing money even though we had a free parking lot next to the theater."

Horwitz's deal with Marie Tilyou was to pay rent and all the taxes on the building. "We made a mistake right from the start," he said, "because the expenses were more than the income. So we went back to Marie Tilyou. She didn't want to see me go out, so she eliminated the taxes and paid them herself." Six months later, Horwitz went back to Tilyou and got a big rent cut, but even that didn't help. Eventually, Tilyou let him operate the theater rent free. "That's how nice she was. She was just trying to keep the theater open. It was expensive to operate. It had a

**The Horwitz family at the Tuxedo**

**A good trade**
When I distributed movie circulars, Horwitz paid me with movie passes.

coal furnace and a man who shoveled coal all day. The air-conditioning was expensive, too. If it wasn't for the candy stand, we couldn't have kept our heads above water."

After Horwitz got into politics, he left the Tilyou. "When the Tilyou closed, I called Marie and said that we should take out the valuables, like the statues and the pictures. Marie said, 'Just lock up the building and give Onorato the key.' The Tilyou was a treasure trove of memorabilia. Soon after, vandals broke in and destroyed the interior. All of the Steeplechase stuff was stolen, and what they could not steal, they destroyed."

CHAPTER 20

# The Trials of Norman Kaufman

NORMAN KAUFMAN was the first to try his hand at resurrecting Steeplechase Park. In 1967, just after developer Fred Trump's bulldozers finished leveling the historic park, Kaufman leased half of the vacant site for $20,000 a year to build a parking lot. Trump didn't realize, however, that Kaufman was a dreamer with ambitious plans. Kaufman began adding rides and concessions to his parking lot until he had pieced together an odd little amusement park, which—much to the chagrin of Coney Island purists—he named Steeplechase Park.

"I was a little stupid or naive," Kaufman told me in 1999. "I thought that I could build up the new Steeplechase into a powerhouse that the city couldn't take away. I was thinking that I could stop whatever plans the city had for the Steeplechase site. Rather than have them come up with something, I figured I could build this amusement park into something that the city would be proud of and leave intact."

Norman Kaufman is a large man, now in his early seventies, with a gray goatee, a sunburned face, twinkling eyes, and a large belly. Local artist Richard Eagan described him as the "Buddha of the Midway." His office is located in a tiny metal shed on the Bowery next to the Jumbo Jet, go-cart rides, and batting range that he runs with his son Kenny. Kaufman grew up in a Coney Island family that owned a photo studio and souvenir stand on Surf Avenue in the 1930s. "I began working in a darkroom at the age of eleven," Kaufman said, "developing photos for twenty cents an hour before automatic

**The dreamer**
Norman Kaufman in the ticket booth of the Dragon's Cave, a ride his family owned on the Bowery, 1960. Over the years, Kaufman added a number of rides. In 1973 (opposite), the midway had a monorail and a kiddie park.

picture machines were invented." During the early 1940s, his father operated the infamous "atrocity" show on the Bowery in partnership with Messmore and Damon, the company that manufactured the show's animated figures. The attraction was also known as the Torture Chamber. "The show had medieval atrocities and modern atrocities that the Japanese were doing during World War II," Kaufman said. "The figures would be screaming and wiggling as they were tied down and tortured. It didn't do well during the war, because people didn't want to see that kind of stuff."

Kaufman's father eventually got into an argument with his partner and threw the entire show into the street. Norman later reclaimed some of the show's figures and used them in the family's Bowery spook house, the Dragon's Cave. Before his Steeplechase adventure, Kaufman worked all over Coney

Island; he managed the Water Flume ride in Astroland Park and later opened a slot-car race on Surf Avenue.

Kaufman and his partner, Irving Vichinsky, had trouble with landlord Fred Trump right from the start. The Steeplechase site was below grade and had to be leveled for parking. Trump's lease required Kaufman to spread ash on the parking lot surface, and Kaufman found a way to get the ash for free. Dewey Junior High School was under construction on a site near the Coney Island transit yards that had once been used as a dumping ground for ash from steam locomotives. The builders needed a place to dispose of the excavated material, and Kaufman provided one for free: Steeplechase Park. "Trump thought that we made a fortune by letting them dump the ash on his property," Kaufman remembers. "He counted the trucks coming in and thought we were putting something over on him. But I never made a dime from it." Trump accused Kaufman of taking advantage of him, threatened to terminate the Steeplechase lease, and placed a sign over the park's entrance that read, "closed by order of the landlord."

Trump then came to the site with a pail and a shovel and began taking samples of the ash. "He put it in his car," Kaufman recalled, "and said to me, 'I'm gonna have this tested, Kaufman. You don't have ash here.' It was a pressure play. At times, Trump would park his Cadillac in front of my entrance, so I said, 'You're blocking me off, Trump.' He'd say, 'I know what's going on here, Kaufman. You got no lease. You have to get out now. He was shoveling and yelling, 'You got no lease.' Whether you were big or small, that's the way he did business. It was always at your own level."

The harassment escalated when Kaufman began to install rides in the parking lot. "Trump didn't like the idea that I was bringing in rides rather than parking. He was getting a percentage and thought we'd make more money with parking than by taking up space with amusement equipment." Kaufman came in one morning to find his big parking sign knocked down, so he put it back up. The next day, he discovered a mound of debris blocking the entrance, so he called a builder friend to clear it away. A few days later, a heavy chain appeared across the entrance, but Kaufman had it cut down. "Trump came back," Kaufman told me, "and said, 'Hey Kaufman, you got my chain. Give me back my chain.' He wanted us out."

Kaufman took out a restraining order against Trump and also went to the Sixtieth Precinct to file an enforcement complaint against the developer. Fred Trump couldn't understand why Kaufman wasn't intimidated by him and seemed to enjoy the confrontations. "He couldn't figure out how I operated," Kaufman said. "He thought I was connected to Meade Esposito, the Democratic leader, but I wasn't connected to anybody. Trump wanted to put the pressure on us to get an increase in rent. He was a tough guy, but we figured out a way to get to him. He had a tremendous memory and would remember everything that ever took place from the time you started with him. He would rattle it right through, and he would just keep going and never stop talking. You never had a chance to get a word in. What

**Old and new**
Jumbo Jet ride on the Steeplechase site in 1974. The Steeplechase horses (circled) had just been returned from Florida to their original home.

**Kaufman's Steeplechase**
This view was taken from the Parachute Jump. The Jumbo Jet is at center left.

Irving and I did was distract him, and then I could tell him my thoughts. As one of us distracted him, the other would jab away with our point. It worked."

★

The first ride that Kaufman installed on the Steeplechase site was a German roller coaster called the Jumbo Jet, a ride he still owns today. The coaster became his centerpiece and his nemesis. Over the years, the Jumbo Jet has had some accidents and has been closed down on numerous occasions. The park had few permanent structures and was laid out more like a carnival or fairground than a formal amusement park. The main entrance was at the western end of the Bowery. By drawing people down the Bowery past Sixteenth Street, just as the original Steeplechase Park had done, the park kept the west end of Coney Island's amusement area alive.

Kaufman ran a legitimate park, but during its first year of operation, he leased out space to freak shows and road workers, which hurt his reputation. What I liked best were the sleazy traveling illusion shows: the ape girls, headless girls, spider girls. These attractions were housed in trailers, and the park sometimes seemed like a low-life "cracker show" in the Deep South. Most of these crooked carnies were just passing through, which was lucky for them, because the Coney crowds sometimes became hostile. The Homicide street gang even kept a headquarters on part of the Steeplechase site in an abandoned shipping container used as a clubhouse.

Most people dismissed Kaufman's park, because they compared it with the original Steeplechase Park. The unfair comparisons bothered him: "We had fourteen kiddie rides and twenty-six majors and spectaculars. A major is a standard ride. A spectacular is something that's unusual. There were quite a number of spectaculars, like the Jumbo Jet, the Italian Skooter rides, and a German swing ride. We were the first ones to have this new equipment, and it was better than average. These were newer rides that Coney Island didn't have for many, many years."

As the park began to grow, Kaufman needed financial backing to expand it into a permanent amusement park, so he found an investor, a local doctor. The man turned out to be an embezzler and then wound up in jail for murdering his wife. By 1968, the park was attracting large crowds. Fred Trump was now happy, because he was getting a percentage of the park's gate, so he extended Kaufman's lease. Then, much to Kaufman's surprise, Trump offered him a job. "He liked that I got ahead and won," Kaufman said.

**Remnants**
The barren Boardwalk side of the Steeplechase site in 1973. The track for Frank Tilyou's antique car ride snaked along the Boardwalk. It was the last new ride installed at Steeplechase in 1962. In the distance to the left can be seen the Thunderbolt, Tornado, and Cyclone roller coasters.

"Trump don't like anybody winning but him. But I knew he was just being cute with his offer."

In 1969, after failing to obtain a zoning change to build high-rise housing, Trump sold the Steeplechase site to the city for $4 million, clearing a $1.5 million profit. The city was legally required to continue Kaufman's lease for $20,000 a year, the same deal he had with Trump. When Mayor John Lindsay's administration applied for federal funds to convert the site into a public park, Kaufman was asked to leave. But he wouldn't budge, because he knew the wheels of government turn slowly.

Nineteen seventy-two turned out to be an eventful year for Kaufman. He learned that the Steeplechase race course, the namesake ride that the Tilyous had sold to Pirate's World, an amusement park in Dania, Florida, was up for sale. Pirate's World had gone out of business. Kaufman bought the ride and sent twelve workers to Florida to number the tracks, horses, and various other pieces, and then he trucked them back to Coney Island for reassembly on the original site. He stored the ride in containers while he made plans to rebuild it. It was an exciting idea that, according to Kaufman, did

not sit well with some of his competitors on the island.

Soon after Kaufman purchased the horse ride, the city started legal proceedings to evict him from the site. He suspected that Coney Island's other ride operators were leaning on the city to get rid of him. The main issue seemed to be that Kaufman's "temporary" park was not required to meet the same expensive code requirements as the permanent rides, enabling him to operate at an advantage. When I asked Kaufman about his problems during those years, he said, "The landlords around here were putting pressure on the city, saying that I was paying less for rent than they were paying in taxes and I had twice as much property. Some of them were politically connected and started going after me. They were saying, 'Norman is a gangster.' They all thought I was influential. All my life I'm not connected with anybody." I asked him about his political connections at the time. "I made a $25 donation to the Democratic Shamrock Club," he said. "That was it."

In 1973, the U.S. Department of Housing and Urban Development offered the city $2 million, half the funds needed to build a public park on the Steeplechase site, as part

of the federal open space program. A city task force working in conjunction with the Coney Island Neighborhood Improvement Organization was formed to analyze Coney Island, and the resulting report included a recommendation that the city condemn and take title to the west end of the amusement area, starting with Steeplechase Park.

The pressure to evict Kaufman's park intensified in 1974 when the city tried to raise Kaufman's yearly rent from $20,000 to $158,446, the amount that an appraiser said the lease was worth. The city then filed a civil suit against Kaufman. Kaufman's lawyers claimed that the city was harassing him, because the judge had ruled that Kaufman could stay through 1975 with a slight increase in rent to $30,000 a year. Kaufman complained, claiming that he was losing $150,000 a year. New York Economic Development Administrator Ken Patton disagreed and asserted that Kaufman was "making ten times his rent, or $200,000 a year, by subleasing concessions on the site."

The situation got uglier later that summer when an employee was killed on the Jumbo Jet while trying to retrieve a patron's hat. During the investigation into the mishap, it was discovered that the rides in Steeplechase Park were operating without a license. The New York City Department of Consumer Affairs filed suit and tried, unsuccessfully, to have the park shut down. The case was dismissed, but the resulting publicity was bad for Coney Island.

In January 1975, the city launched an inquest, headed by Investigations Commissioner Nicholas Scopetta, to examine charges of corruption among city officials concerning the leases on two city-owned sites in Coney Island: the Cyclone roller coaster and Steeplechase Park. The dispute spilled over into the papers. Dewey Albert of Astroland said in a January 18, 1975, *New York Times* story that the decision to let Kaufman stay had been "determined by politics." Coney Island landlord Hy Singer was quoted in the same story: "The city hasn't put their best effort behind the case because there's collusion between the Department of Real Estate and the City Planning Commission and Norman Kaufman."

Kaufman countered the allegations by suing Singer for slander. "I was angry and hurt," Kaufman said. "I was going to pursue it because that article really stung me." His lawyer, Hyman Bravin, told the *Times*, in the same story, that the eviction suit and licensing problems were the result of "harassment" by Kaufman's competitors. When Singer denied making the statement, Kaufman filed a lawsuit against the *New York Times*. "Next thing you know, the *Times* ran a full-page story about me, implying that I was connected with wise guys and that I was politically connected," Kaufman said. It was during this dark period that Fred Trump began calling to offer his support. "He called me up and said, 'Listen, Kaufman, it's good to be in the papers. Don't worry about it. It's good that they know ya.'"

Late in 1975, the Department of Consumer Affairs pulled the park's license and ordered the park closed down. Kaufman responded by taking his case to the New York State Supreme Court, where a judge ordered the city to reinstate the license. No sooner had he reopened than a city inspector found 137 electrical violations at the park. "I lost the season," Kaufman told me.

Despite these setbacks, Kaufman continued his plans for expanding the amusement

**Crespi's last stand**
Steve "The Count" Crespi (below) was the last concessioner from the old Steeplechase. He ran the gift Shop on the Boardwalk at West Nineteenth Street (above) until 1973, when it was torched by members of the Homicides street gang.

park. When the city put the Cyclone roller coaster up for bid in 1975, he saw an opportunity. "I wrote Mayor Lindsay and told him that rather than have the Cyclone torn down, I would move it to Steeplechase at no cost to the city of New York. I thought that once I moved the Cyclone and permanently put it into that location, I'm good for life. Whatever investment I made, I could make back in one year." The city refused the offer.

Next Kaufman offered to restore the Parachute Jump. When the city turned down his plan, he tried to buy the Bobsled ride, which was about to be torn down by owner Hy Singer. Singer declined the offer and demolished the historic ride. The year ended badly when Kaufman was robbed of his car and $14,000 in cash outside his home in Manhattan Beach. "It was a set-up job," Kaufman said. Two years later, in April 1977, Justice Carmine A. Ventiera ordered Kaufman to appear at a hearing because of his refusal to take out the $1 million insurance policy required by the city's Department of Real Estate. The judge ruled in Kaufman's favor and refused to close the park's rides as the city had requested.

Two more years passed, and as the 1979 season opened, city officials renewed their attack on the Steeplechase lease arrangement, calling it a "giveaway" and recommending that Kaufman be evicted from the site so that a public park could be established. The Coney Island Landowners Association joined the fight against Kaufman, asking the city to pursue the long-delayed Housing and Urban Development grant for open space.

Kaufman finally realized that his plans were hopeless and closed his Steeplechase Park in 1981, when the city paid him $750,000 to leave the site. In 1983, Steeplechase was developed into public open space. A year later, the site became a city park, the first "special events" park in the city's history. The Parks Department announced ambitious plans to sponsor concerts, festivals, and other events that would serve as a magnet for the redevelopment of Coney Island. The first Mermaid Parade would be launched there in 1983, and the annual Irish Fair was held at the park. But mostly the park sat fenced off and idle for the next two decades.

Norman Kaufman's park was never a great one, but it served a purpose. Its entrance on the Bowery anchored the west side of Coney Island and kept the amusement area connected. Soon after the park closed, the crowds stopped coming down the Bowery, and the rides and concessions along the last block of the Bowery began to shut down. The Thunderbolt closed, the Magic Carpet ride rolled up, and the Tunnel of Laffs went dark.

**Closed again**
Ticket booths and other relics from Kaufman's park littered the Steeplechase site until the Parks Department cleared it in 1982.

CHAPTER 21

# The Steeplechase Battleground

**Master plan**
In 1989, Horace Bullard showed the plans for his new Steeplechase Park.

HORACE BULLARD, the wealthy, Harlem-born owner of the Kansas Fried Chicken chain, was unhappy with the attitude of Coney Island's landowners. He didn't think the landowners realized that what they owned was special. "Sometimes, when you've been in a place for generations," he told me, "you can't see you're sitting on a gold mine." In 1985, Bullard cast himself in the role of savior and set off on a grandiose mission to rebuild Steeplechase Park, the one-time heart and soul of the island. He didn't just want to rebuild the park. He wanted to create a bigger and better amusement park than even George C. Tilyou, founder of Steeplechase Park, could have imagined.

In 1985, Bullard contacted Charlie Tesoro of Walter E. Burgess Inc. and began buying up Coney Island property to develop a Disney-type amusement park that would revitalize the area and return Coney to its past glory. His plan was to purchase all the available properties in the amusement zone and combine them into one large parcel with the Steeplechase site at its center.

Bullard's plan required secrecy. He didn't want to alert the Coney Island landowners, so he formed Wantanabe Realty, a dummy corporation with a Japanese-sounding name.

211

**Nostalgic plan**
In December 1989, Horace Bullard hired Battaglia Inc., a renowned Southern California amusement park design firm, to design the new Steeplechase. The Battaglia plan, an impressive three-level park located between West Fifteenth and West Twenty-first Streets, paid homage to Coney's past. It incorporated the Parachute Jump and revived past attractions from Luna Park, Dreamland, and the original Steeplechase.

Charlie Tesoro would be his straw man. His first acquisition was the derelict Thunderbolt roller coaster property next to Steeplechase, which he bought from the Moran/Klein estate. He proceeded to purchase other parcels in the area and then took options on city-owned property. Tesoro was in the midst of negotiating for the Stauch's and Handwerker properties between Nathan's Famous and the Boardwalk when Bullard's identity was revealed to the sellers and his plans were foiled. The deals collapsed, and the resulting litigation left him with a patchwork of disconnected parcels. Bullard had become a controversial figure during his attempt to unify the landowners in the 1970s when casino gambling had been proposed for Coney Island. Many remained suspicious of his intentions. Bullard wound up as Coney Island's largest landowner, but his Steeplechase dreams dragged on, unrealized, for nearly two decades.

In 1998, I began interviewing Bullard and Tesoro about the quixotic attempt to develop the Steeplechase site. "I was interested in the development of Coney Island," Bullard told me. "When I saw that I couldn't get the landowners together, I decided to do it on my own. I told Charlie Tesoro that I wanted to buy the Thunderbolt, and that's how it started. Then the Parks Department came to me about the city-owned Steeplechase site, because they knew that I had tried to put together the landowners, and they wanted to know if I could save the Parachute Jump. This was in 1984, and then I decided to get involved. The city put out an RFP [Request for Proposal] for the site, and I was the only bidder. The rest is history."

Bullard obtained a lease on the Steeplechase property but felt that the site wasn't big enough for a major amusement park. He then crafted a deal with the city to combine all of his parcels and deed them back to the city when his ninety-nine-year lease on the Steeplechase site expired. This unusual "give-back" arrangement was part of a compromise enabling him to use public parkland for a private development.

Tesoro remembers Bullard approaching him with his plan: "I met Horace back in the 1970s when he was trying to put together property for a casino. I knew he had this plan of assembling the property and presenting it to investors as a package. I told him that we could get hold of Steeplechase and then buy half of Coney Island. Horace said, 'Do you think you could do that?' I said, 'Yeah. I could do that.' And I did. All except the Handwerker property behind Nathan's."

Although they were working together, Bullard and Tesoro had different visions of how the park should be developed. Bullard wanted to raise $500 million to build a huge park and restore the Parachute Jump and the Steeplechase pier, which had been damaged in a storm. Tesoro thought that Bullard should start small and expand later: "I told Horace, 'Don't go 500 mill. We could open up for 90 mill, maybe less. Build a midway and get road shows, big-big carnival type things, the Big Apple Circus. Put rides in, one or two at a time.'"

Coney landowner Jack Ward also remembers giving Bullard similar advice on how to get things done in Coney Island. "When Horace Bullard first came to Coney Island," Ward told me, "Dewey Albert and I told him that, in our opinion, what he should do was slowly develop the parcel and add a new piece every two years, or just reconstruct the Thunderbolt, which could have been easily done. He could have refurbished it, like Astroland did with the Cyclone. Horace had literally four times the land as Astroland. His response to us, and I'll never forget it, was: 'It's not a big enough impact.'" Bullard wanted his park to be "Disneysized," to draw investors with big capital.

Tesoro also cited Astroland as a model. Astroland's founder, Dewey Albert, had started small in the early 1960s and slowly built up a successful operation by leasing space in the park to tenants. Tesoro told me that he devised a similar plan, one that could be carried out for $75–80 million: "I said to Bullard, 'Let's get started by getting outsiders to come in and rent for a nominal fee to pay the property taxes, and when you're ready to build, you throw 'em out.' I had plans for a midway, parking, sewers, portable bathrooms. I made a sketch for a big midway stretching from the Bowery across the Steeplechase property, branching off to Surf Avenue. I told him that we could blacktop the whole property and add rides, go a little at a time. But Bullard said, 'No, no, no, I'm not doing it your way.'"

Tesoro felt strongly that Bullard should wait until he had the financing in hand before he revealed the plans for his project to the press. The problem, as Tesoro saw it, was politics—the political connections of the Coney Island competition. "You gotta have a slush fund, a political fund for donations," Tesoro explained to me. I asked Tesoro if racism toward Bullard, who is black, could have been a factor. "It's not racial," he said. "David Dinkins was mayor when this was going on—you just gotta answer to the party, because if you cross the organization, you ain't going nowhere."

By the time Bullard's plans became public in 1985, he had acquired several major properties near Steeplechase Park: the Thunderbolt parcel, between Surf Avenue and the Boardwalk; the Washington Baths parcel, a full city block at West Twentieth Street; the Shore Theater building; and a Surf Avenue parcel adjacent to the Stillwell Avenue Subway Terminal. But his attempt to purchase Herman Singer's Stauch's Baths and the Henderson properties on Stillwell Avenue failed. Singer had signed an agreement to sell Stauch's and was in contract with Tesoro when he discovered that Wantanabe Realty was a front for Horace Bullard.

Singer had believed that Wantanabe was owned by Japanese investors and had even told Tesoro that he thought he'd seen the Japanese buyers taking photographs of his

**Coney boosters**
Charlie Tesoro (left) and Matt Kennedy, ninety-one year-old executive secretary of the Coney Island Chamber of Commerce, 1995.

**Site plan**
Level one of the proposed park included carousels, a Sam Gumpertz sideshow, Henderson's Theater, the Steeplechase race course, Thompson and Dundy's Flying Contraption ride, Paul Boyton's Shoot-the-Chutes, and a new Pavilion of Fun.

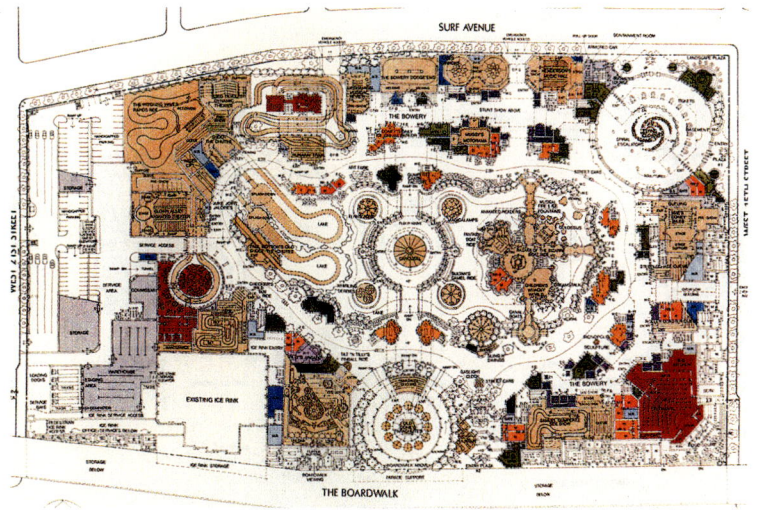

property. He proceeded to pull his property off the market before the deal closed. Bullard was disappointed: "I was in contract on Stauch's," he said. "I sued Singer, because he broke the contract. When Singer thought he had nothing, he was happy to sell it. When he found out that Wantanabe was me, he pulled out." Singer eventually settled with Bullard for a reported $250,000. Murray Handwerker, CEO of Nathan's, was also angry about Bullard's ruse. "Murray was mad," Tesoro said. "But he had no right. We had three or four covers. How does he think Donald Trump assembles property?"

If the Singer deal had gone though, Bullard would have owned or had options on two-thirds of the Coney Island amusement area—thirty acres between West Twenty-first Street and Henderson Walk—and could have combined his holdings into one giant parcel for his amusement park.

There were other repercussions from the failed deal. Singer filed a lawsuit against Charlie Tesoro: "The charges were trumped up," Tesoro said. "He accused me of forgery, fraud, and chicanery when he found out Wantanabe was really Bullard. What's the difference who's buying if the price is right? But I had to answer the suit or lose by default." Singer's case against Tesoro was eventually dismissed.

Although Bullard was missing a few pieces of his real estate puzzle, he continued with his plans for a park. He was unfazed by Coney's rough reputation, but Tesoro realized early on that the housing projects surrounding the amusement area might be detrimental to raising financial backing. "We had interested parties, Japanese and Israeli investors," Tesoro said, "but as soon as they saw the housing projects, they backed out." Bullard spent the next fifteen years trying to raise the cash to build his dream. By his own estimate, he invested nearly $16 million of his own money in planning his amusement park. He raised the hopes of people not just in Coney Island, but all over the country, as his monumental plans and their rising cost gained national attention.

> Chicken King Lays Golden Egg
> on Coney Island
> —*New York Post*, October 22, 1985

In June 1985, Bullard signed a tentative license agreement with the city of New York to build and operate a $55 million amusement park. All that was needed was the state legislature's approval. On June 18, Bullard told the *Seattle Times* that he had traveled as far as Austria to find the best new rides, and he outlined ambitious plans for a giant corkscrew coaster, water rides, and a children's zoo on the Steeplechase site.

A year later, on June 20, 1986, New York City Council's State Legislation Committee finally approved a bill allowing Bullard to lease the Steeplechase site. This approval was necessary; public parkland could not otherwise be leased to private developers. Bullard told *Newsday* on June 30, 1986, that he wanted to restore Coney Island to its golden era. "Everybody's in favor of this project," he said. "It's a dream come true for millions." Coney Island gained international attention when Bullard traveled to Europe to consult with amusement park experts at

**Reality**
Investors were wary of the city housing projects in close proximity to the Steeplechase site.

West Germany's Europia Park and Vienna's Prater Park. He optimistically predicted that the park would open by July 4, 1987.

> Poor Boy from East Harlem Rekindles Coney Island's Spirit
> —*Toronto Star,* November 11, 1986

By November 1986, Bullard had expanded his vision into an ambitious two-tiered park with a six-thousand-car garage, forty rides, three roller coasters, forty thousand square feet of concessions, a monorail, and a $3 million restoration of the Parachute Jump. The price had risen to $70 million, and the opening was extended to 1988. "It will bring a tidal wave of new business into the area," Bullard told the *Toronto Star.* "When it's finished, not only will it bring back the families, but it will also bring back all the memories to millions of people who remember what Coney Island used to be."

> Coney Island of today is a junkyard of faded glory on the sump end of Brooklyn, a place that is pinning its hopes for a rebirth on the plans of a New York fried chicken king.
>
> —*Dallas Morning News,* December 14, 1986

In the winter of 1986, Bullard announced he was going to demolish the Thunderbolt roller coaster and asked Mae Timpano to leave her home in the old Kensington Hotel beneath the landmark so development could begin. Timpano had occupied the house for thirty-six years with her boyfriend, Thunderbolt owner Freddie Moran. When Moran died in 1982, she had inherited a third of the property and sold it to Bullard, who, she told me, treated her "right." "Construction of the park will start by mid-1987," Bullard told the *Dallas Morning News.* "Sometime next summer the Thunderbolt will be gone, a victim of space limitations in the new plan." He also noted that "pieces of the roller coaster may be formed into a sculpture."

**Fantasy**
Battaglia Inc. modeled the new park's entrance on the winged angel that flanked the Creation exhibit in Dreamland Park.

By 1987, the price of Bullard's dream had risen to $100 million, but the actual plans were still going nowhere. Bullard blamed the delays on the city and told me that his redevelopment schemes had become "mired in bureaucracy." October brought more bad news: the stock market crash dried up any chance of obtaining $100 million in financing. Bullard had already spent more than $6 million of his own money on planning, land acquisition, lawyers, and a complex Environmental Impact Report that had finally been completed and submitted to the New York City Planning Commission. But he remained optimistic, telling *Newsday* on December 27, 1987: "They keep telling me it's pie in the sky. Well the pie is about to get baked."

Bullard was predicting that the park would open in 1990 or 1991, but he soon confronted a new hurdle. The first mention of a sports complex on the Steeplechase property surfaced just after Christmas 1987, when Democratic State Senator Thomas Bartosiewicz of Brooklyn attempted to block the renewal of the city's right to lease the Steeplechase site to Bullard. Bartosiewicz

**Love story** Fred Moran fell in love with Mae Timpano, and the two shared a home under the Thunderbolt roller coaster.

**Mae Timpano** Her home under the coaster had an ocean view and a rose garden. Woody Allen used it as his boyhood home in the movie *Annie Hall*.

## MAE TIMPANO
# THE ROLLER COASTER LADY

**The Moran/Klein family** Fred Moran (second from left) and his uncle Artie Klein (far right) with friends in front of the family's Bowery Skooter ride in the early 1920s.

For more than forty years, Mae Timpano lived in the house under the Thunderbolt roller coaster. She met Freddie Moran, the coaster's owner, in 1946, and their romance lasted until he died in January 1982. Moran's father, George, had built the coaster over the Kensington Hotel in 1925. Freddie grew up in the old house and lived there with his mother after his father died. Moran met Timpano when she was a waitress at a Surf Avenue restaurant. "He was such a nice man, and everybody in Coney respected him," Timpano said. "I had a real crush on him. One night he said, 'You want to come over to my house and listen to records?' I said, 'Where do you live?' He said, 'Under the roller coaster.' I said, 'Are you kidding?' I liked his personality. He was funny, and he was good to me. Whenever he put his arms around me, I felt that nobody could hurt me. We used to swim out to the end of the Steeplechase pier every day. Freddie was a good swimmer and was once a lifeguard."

Timpano moved into the house under the coaster and lived with Moran and his mother, Mollie. I asked Timpano what it was like to live there. "In the winter, it was like living in the country," she said. "I had no neighbors, and it was quiet and peaceful. The only thing you heard was the ocean rolling in. We had three bedrooms, a great big living room, a dining room, and three baths. When Gabe Pressman came to do an interview, he told me it looked like a house in Cape Cod. When strangers visited the house and heard the roller coaster go over, they'd say, 'What was that, thunder?' That's what the coaster sounded like. Over the years,

**Buffing up the Thunderbolt** The Thunderbolt was always a family operation. Fred Moran's Uncle Artie painted the supports before the season opening, circa 1950.

was part of a group called the Brooklyn Sports Foundation that wanted to build a Coney Island Sportsplex, a twelve-thousand-seat amateur sports arena and stadium, and felt that Bullard was tying up the site with his dubious amusement park plans.

In response, Bullard claimed he had foreign investors lined up and announced even more elaborate plans for his park, including an elevator ride to the top of the Parachute Jump and the rebuilding of the historic Steeplechase race course. His park would provide, he predicted, seasonal employment of fifteen hundred to two thousand workers and would serve an estimated twenty thousand daily visitors, each paying a ticket price of $19. "The park will offer family discounts, and entry point metal detectors to ensure safety," he told Newsday on December 27, "and construction will start by fall of 1988."

> The Roller Coaster Lady Will Ride
> Out of Coney Island
> —Newsday, August 3, 1988

In the summer of 1988, the stadium idea was put on hold after Bullard lined up the support of Mayor Ed Koch, Brooklyn Borough President Howard Golden, and Republican District Leader Joseph Neglia, who convinced the state legislature to grant a one-year extension on his Steeplechase lease. But Bullard made enemies among other amusement operators who questioned his intentions. Local businesspeople told me that they believed at the time that Bullard was merely a speculator with no intention of building the amusement park, and they feared that he would abandon his plans and sell the land he was accumulating for a profit.

In August 1988, Mae Timpano finally left her home in the old hotel beneath the Thunderbolt. "She's Miss Coney Island," Bullard told Newsday. "When you get close to her, you get sort of a feeling of what Coney Island used to be like." Bullard's property manager, Andy Badalamenti, moved into

a few things broke. My perfume tray fell once, and my pictures would get a little slanty."

Few people realized that anyone lived there, and Timpano liked it that way. "Some people were filming a movie on the Boardwalk and wanted to paint the house, and I wouldn't let them. I told them I didn't want it to stand out, and I didn't want anyone to know I was living there. Once someone at work found out that I lived in Coney Island and asked me if I knew who lived in that 'shack.' I said, 'What shack?' She said, 'The one under the roller coaster.' I said, 'I live there, and I love it.' She couldn't believe it."

Timpano stayed in the house alone after Moran became ill and passed away in 1982. Ron Guerrero leased the Thunderbolt and operated the ride for one more season before it closed down. "Ronnie didn't run it right," Timpano said. "He let kids run it." I asked Timpano if her children (from a previous marriage) were worried about her living alone under an abandoned coaster. "They used to complain," she said. "I went through hell with them. They'd say, 'I can't bring a date here. I can't open the Bowery gate.' Or, 'Somebody's going to come in and murder you. Get the hell out.' So I had it and I moved. But I didn't like moving. I'd rather have stayed there. I loved it."

**Relic**
The Steeplechase chimney, the last holdover from the 1897 park, was declared a hazard and demolished before Bullard obtained the site.

Timpano's house, and the demolition was delayed. Bullard's lack of construction financing kept the hotel and coaster in a state of deferred maintenance and turned the landmark into a poignant symbol of Coney's decline.

Steeplechase Plans on Track:
Hearings Set Today on Amusement Park
—*Newsday,* January 4, 1989

In 1989, Bullard finally secured financing—and a new advocate—for his park. When Security Pacific Bank's amusement division signed an agreement to finance most of Bullard's $220 million project, Sam Horwitz, the city councilman from Coney Island, jumped aboard the Bullard bandwagon, providing much-needed local political support. With financing guaranteed, all that was required prior to groundbreaking was a public hearing by the project's new cosponsor, the city's Public Development Corporation, and a vote by the New York City Board of Estimate.

Bullard was so confident of approval that he expanded his plans once again, stepping on some toes in the process. His lawyer, former New York Park Commissioner Gordon Davis, asked Deputy Mayor Robert Esnard to allow Bullard to incorporate the adjacent Abe Stark Rink and its parking lot into his project. This request did not sit well with the Parks Department or with Pat Auletta, the politically connected operator of the rink's skating concession. Auletta lashed out, telling *Newsday* that "Coney Island has been standing still while we wait to see if Horace Bullard is ever going to put a shovel in the ground."

Bullard also miscalculated when he asked the city to close West Sixteenth and Nineteenth Streets so he could combine the skating rink, Steeplechase, and Thunderbolt properties. The request angered Dewey Albert of Astroland, who'd been denied permission to close West Tenth Street, the thoroughfare that separated his park from the Cyclone, a ride he leased from the city. The Public Development Corporation (PDC) rebuffed Albert's accusations of a landgrab by pointing out that Bullard intended to cede the land he already owned to the city and lease back the combined properties. The PDC declared that if Bullard's plans fell through, the city would keep his land.

The city's planning commission, followed by the board of estimate, approved the amusement park plans in March 1989 and gave Bullard a ninety-nine-year lease. On June 17, Bullard told a reporter from Amusement Business magazine, "Coney Island is at the brink of being restored back to its heyday setting. It's a fantastic situation." To design the new Steeplechase, Bullard hired Battaglia Inc., the renowned California amusement park design firm. Construction was set to begin in 1990, with an opening date sometime in 1992. An attendance of 2.5 million was predicted for the first year of operation. The new price tag was $250 million. Bullard told Amusement Business, "Coney Island will become a tourist haven within less than 10 years."

Down by the Sea: Dreams of
Coney Island Revival Fading Away
—*Newsday,* May 19, 1991

But in 1991, Bullard was crushed when Security Pacific Bank folded its amusement park division and canceled the financing for the park. The following weeks brought more setbacks: a fire broke out in the house under the Thunderbolt, killing several guard dogs, and city engineers disclosed that the Parachute Jump, centerpiece of the new park, was in imminent danger of toppling.

Bullard became depressed. "I'm not sure that I'm going to be in a position to cover it for another year mentally," he told *Newsday*. "It's a very bad market, and I don't know when this market is going to change. We have given ourselves until the end of this year to do it. I'm not optimistic." The recession had dried up any potential financing, and Bullard's company, Coney Island Resorts, had to pay the city $2,000 a month in development rights fees to hold the site during the one-year extension granted in early 1991.

For the first time, Bullard contemplated building a scaled-down park on the land he already owned. The city had to decide whether to demolish or repair the Parachute Jump, and Bullard and the city began arguing over who would pay the $800,000 tab for structural repairs. The argument ended when an extensive examination of the Parachute Jump revealed that it was not about to collapse. Bullard agreed to share the cost of renovation with the city.

In the meantime, the Brooklyn Sports Foundation sensed Bullard's vulnerability and asked the city for permission to build the Sportsplex and stadium on the Steeplechase site. Bullard accused the Sportsplex developers of trying to sabotage his plans for the Steeplechase site. "We have a beautiful, historic park and we're trying to get it off the ground," he told *Newsday* on August 25, 1991. "It's a good project, the dollars are secondary." Robert Zeig, executive director of the nonprofit foundation, issued a blunt denial to the allegations: "If Bullard can't build it, then the site would be an ideal location for the Sportsplex."

On November 22, 1991, two days before his lease with the city was due to expire, Bullard arrived at the city hall office of Deputy Mayor Sally Hernandez-Pinero with a new partner, Steve Shalom, an Israeli investor who was ready to put $5 million into the project. The two men startled city officials by rolling in a huge model of the park and announcing that Triple 5, a Canadian shopping center developer with assets of $8 billion, had agreed to manage the park. The presentation worked. Hernandez-Pinero granted Bullard a six-month grace period to get what she called his "fantasy park" off the ground before the city withdrew its backing. The project's revised price tag was $350 million.

**Virtual Mae**
The most bizarre attraction in Bullard's proposed park was Mae's Coney Tales Storyteller Theater, in which an animated Mae Timpano "tells rousing stories of old Coney Island."

In January 1994, Rudolph Giuliani took office as mayor, and in March, Bullard received a termination notice from the city, canceling his lease on the Steeplechase site. "Giuliani did it without calling us in, without evaluation," Bullard told me. "Why would anybody in his right mind do that? He had nothing else to go there. He just sends me a letter and says, 'You're out!' I said to myself, 'He made a mistake. He's a prosecutor, Mr. G., the guy who put the mob in jail. He's not going to do anything funny.' So I brought a lawsuit." The suit forced the city to back down. Bullard was told, unofficially, that a mistake had been made and that his project would be put back on the drawing board if he raised the needed funds.

As Bullard struggled to hold on to Steeplechase, others began to show an interest in the site. In late 1998, representatives from the Disney Corporation began sniffing around Coney Island, and the landowners reacted the same way they had when casino gambling had been proposed twenty years earlier: "The big money has arrived!"

The Disney representatives—actually ABC executives looking for a Nickelodeon location—did what Charlie Tesoro says was the worst thing possible: they walked right

THE STEEPLECHASE BATTLEGROUND 219

**Contested territory**
The Steeplechase site (top) became a public park in 1983 but was fenced off and used only for special events such as the Irish Fair. The trees at left once lined Steeplechase Park's central walk. A 1950s postcard with the Pavilion of Fun (inset).

into the chamber of commerce office and said, "Disney might want to come into Coney Island. What's available?" Tesoro remembers what happened when Al O'Hagan, the chamber's executive secretary, announced that Disney was interested. "As soon as the landowners found out, everybody in Coney Island showed up, the people who never want to sell 'cause they're so independent. We had forty people up here looking to sell, people you never saw in your life, everybody except Bullard, because he was mad at everybody. They were like hungry dogs. The place was loaded! I figured the one logical place for Disney to go was Bullard's property, the Shore Theater. So I arranged a private meeting with the two ABC executives, Bullard and his wife, and an architect. We met in my office that night and gave a slide presentation of Bullard's plans. But Bullard's price for the Shore building kept going up, up, up, so they pulled out."

Bullard remembers the meeting differently. "They loved the concept, loved the idea," he told me, "but it was too small for them. We never got into a bidding war. It never even got to that point."

The Bullard fantasy park was rapidly turning into a fantasy itself. He owed the city $1.6 million in back taxes on the Thunderbolt property, and the city was threatening foreclosure. As Bullard faded from the picture, the Sportsplex plan gained momentum. Supporters of the facility had secured $67 million in financing from the state, the city, and the borough of Brooklyn, and had the strong backing of Brooklyn Borough President Howard Golden.

In May 1998, Mayor Giuliani earmarked $40 million for two new minor league ballparks and began eyeing the Steeplechase site as a location for a Mets farm team. At the same time, Bruce Ratner, owner of Forest City Development Company, was negotiating with the Brooklyn Sports Foundation and offering to build the Sportsplex at cost if he could have the rights to develop an entertainment and retail complex on an adjoining site that included Bullard's Thunderbolt property. The model being used for Coney's redevelopment was Times Square, which many had once believed beyond redemption. Ratner, a major contributor to Mayor Giuliani, had been heavily involved with the Times Square revival and seemed a good choice to help revitalize Coney Island.

In September 1998, Mayor Giuliani's office drew up a map of the Steeplechase site that showed a ballpark—but no Sportsplex or entertainment complex. The Brooklyn Sports Foundation felt that its amateur athletic arena was being pushed aside by the mayor, and its suspicions proved correct. Brooklyn Borough President Golden and other Sportsplex boosters suspected that the mayor had killed the Sportsplex because he felt it would slow the ballpark's "fast-track" construction. When Golden decided to fight the ballpark, Giuliani cut him out of the negotiations completely by making a compromise deal with leading members of the city council. The mayor quietly aligned himself with Herb Berman, head of the Brooklyn council delegation, and Council Speaker Peter Vallone. The mayor promised to support the Sportsplex at a later date in exchange for their immediate support of the ballpark. They agreed. In November 1998, Bruce Ratner withdrew his offer to build the Sportsplex and retail complex. Bullard told me that Ratner was forced out of Coney Island because the mayor strong-armed him, threatening to pull the permits on Ratner's other projects around the city unless he withdrew.

In November 1998, Giuliani assumed control of the Steeplechase site and awarded sole negotiation rights to the site to the New York Mets. A year later, the mayor announced ambitious plans to build a six-thousand-seat, $31 million baseball stadium that would provide a catalyst for the redevelopment of Coney Island. All that was needed was the approval of the city council. The mayor began twisting arms to make sure approval would be unanimous.

★

After trying for fifteen years to get financing for his project, Bullard was out. Steeplechase was taken away from him, and his dream was over. In February 2000, he filed a lawsuit against the city, seeking damages for the loss of the site. I asked him why he thought Giuliani had forced him out. "When he came into office, he could have offered help. He could have asked, 'How can we help you? We want to get this project off the ground.' But he didn't do that. In 1999, we were 120 days away from finalizing a $450 million investment package, but the mayor said, 'No, that's not good enough, you're out.'"

I asked Bullard if he thought the Steeplechase site was jinxed. "The Steeplechase property is not jinxed, but has a way of attracting these strange, eccentric characters and entrepreneurs that have evolved around it, like John McKane and George Tilyou, and Robert Moses, who wanted it destroyed. And then you have this crazy chicken-man who comes along and goes through all of these obstacles, and he keeps going, and he keeps at it, and throws money and caution to the wind. And then you got a guy like Giuliani who says that this is his childhood playground.

"It's a shame the public didn't get the revival that I proposed. I didn't get into this to make money. I came in because I saw a golden opportunity to do something artistic and significant, historical and decent, and still make money. That was my intent. I got into this for what it would do for New York and what it would have meant for millions of people across the world that have the memory of Coney Island. I wanted to restore it to its rightful place as the playground of the world."

CHAPTER 22

# Artists' Renaissance of the 1980s

**Sideshow banner**
Valerie Haller painted this sideshow banner of Michael Wilson for Sideshows by the Seashore in 1992.

**I**N THE EARLY 1980s, after the fantasy of casino riches died, Coney Island was suffering an identity crisis. What Coney needed was an image that would capture visitors' interest: a talented impresario like George C. Tilyou, or a personality like Walt Disney, or even a decent logo like the old Steeplechase funny face. It was a crisis of imagination. Creative old-timers—people like Freddie Garms, creator of the kitschy Spookarama, and Lillie Santangelo, owner of the bizarre World in Wax—were growing old, with no one in the wings to replace them.

Into this creative vacuum stumbled an odd assortment of passionate young artists drawn to Coney Island for a variety of reasons. These artists were different from the ubiquitous photography students who appeared every weekend to capture moody black-and-white images of urban ruins. What the newcomers had in common was a desire to be part of the community, to live or work here and preserve traditional Coney Island art forms. Their lives became performance art on Coney's stage.

Coney Island has always been the subject matter and inspiration for serious artists: Reginald Marsh and Joseph Stella painted it, Walker Evans and Weegee photographed it, Norman Rosten and Maxim Gorky wrote about it, and Art Young and David Levine sketched it. They portrayed and interpreted Coney, but at the end of the day, they went home. The newcomers of the 1980s came to Coney to stay.

The new arrivals weren't burdened by the cynicism and defeatist preconceptions of the business community. They were idealistic and brought with them a certain naïveté. And their timing was perfect. Milton Berger, longtime Coney Island publicist, knew Coney Island but didn't have any new ideas. He had grown old and bitter and some would say mean-spirited, not the best personality traits for a publicist. Berger did know a lot about art. When he was the publicist for Steeplechase Park, he had talked the Tilyous into sponsoring a show of Reginald Marsh's work in 1953. Berger had a favorite saying, which was a challenge to the nostalgists: "The great days of Coney Island are in the future." Events were soon to prove him right.

I was doubtful about the early efforts of these artists and didn't think they would last. I thought they were slumming. I remembered the fanciful street-theater performances of the Everyman Theater Company and the Bread and Puppet Theater in the 1960s and the 1970s, and then the long

**Clean sweep**
Richard Eagan (opposite left) and Dick Zigun (right) spruce up the Spookarama cyclops for a publicity event, 1984.

223

**Beach bunnies**
Richard Eagan and Dick Zigun's promotional organization, Coney Island Events, brought swimsuit contests back to Coney in 1984.

creative drought that followed. Coney's newest amusements were trailer rides, European creations typical of state fairs. No one was building permanent installations from scratch anymore. The William F. Mangels Carousell Company on West Eighth Street, for eighty years the premier manufacturer of outdoor amusement devices, had closed down in the late 1960s. Mangels had started an amusement museum in 1929 that had long since closed. Coney Island needed someone who could revive his dream for recognition. It needed a movement that would change its image and preserve its heritage.

### The Mayor and the Boss

The 1980s artistic renaissance was spearheaded by two very different personalities who, in their own ways, provided a new identity for Coney Island. Dick Zigun, wearing a bowler hat and a 1920s swimsuit, became the "Mayor of Coney Island," and Richard Eagan, with his straw hat, vest, and pitchman's banter, became the "Boss of the Boardwalk."

Initially, the media set its hook into Eagan because of his group's name: the Coney Island Hysterical Society. The press found it amusing but often confused the society with the slightly more serious Ivy League group known as Coney Island USA (CIUSA). But Dick Zigun and his drama degree from Yale University soon got the most ink. Reporters treated his sheepskin as an oddity, the same way they would a two-headed baby or an albino python. Zigun's academic credential usually appeared in the lead paragraph as if to reassure readers about the organization's freak show.

Eagan and Zigun arrived at the beach at roughly the same time, through different

**Coney-inspired art**
Artist Philomena Marano's cut paper artwork, *Bumper/Scrambler*, 1993.

**Waxy buildup**
Dick Zigun performed *Secrets of the Wax Museum* at Lillie Santangelo's World in Wax Musee on Halloween night, 1981.

routes. Zigun came to Coney Island in late 1979 and fell in love with it. Among the things that attracted him was the fact that the amusement area was a neighborhood full of elderly businesspeople who were as "loony and out-of-their-minds as can be." "I thought to myself," Zigun told me, "when I'm eighty years old, I want to be that healthy and out there and completely out of my mind. I would like to join this 'arts colony.' And I did."

One person was Zigun's favorite when he first arrived in Coney Island: the woman he described as "Grandma Moses on LSD," octogenarian Lillie Santangelo, owner of the wax museum, World in Wax. In his search for loft space, Zigun was referred to the Coney Island Chamber of Commerce, where he shared liverwurst-on-Wonder-Bread sandwiches with Matt Kennedy, the chamber's executive secretary. He also wound up with a ten-year lease on two floors in the old Kister Building, above the chamber's offices. Zigun planned to live in one space and use the other for a small theater, but the building burned down before he could finish renovating, so he moved to SoHo in lower Manhattan. "That was the end of my Coney dream," Zigun said. "Or so I thought."

Zigun was in Los Angeles when he received a pleading Christmas card from a

**King Neptune**
Joe Franklin, as King Neptune, and Dick Zigun celebrated the opening of the beach in 1985.

desperate Lillie Santangelo that began, "Dear Dick, I need your help, I'm in trouble." A truck had crashed into the front of her World in Wax, destroying several of the museum's displays. "She did this guilt thing with artists," Zigun said, "and I'm a sucker." Santangelo talked Zigun and his friends into

ARTISTS' RENAISSANCE OF THE 1980s

**Parachute Jump**
Cut paper by Philomena Marano.

repairing the damaged exhibits in time for the museum's 1980 Palm Sunday opening.

Zigun had returned to Los Angeles when he heard the news that John Lennon had been murdered, and he bought the musician's last album, *Double Fantasy*. He and Santangelo were surprised to find that Lennon had used a recording of Santangelo's voice on the last track of the album. Santangelo decided to install a wax figure of the murdered musician in the museum and talked Zigun into asking Yoko Ono for some of Lennon's clothing. Ono was amused at the request but turned him down. The Lennon installation of 1981 was covered by the media, prompting Coney Island USA to hold a benefit art show on Halloween to help restore the World in Wax. It was the group's first major event.

Richard Eagan, a cabinetmaker turned artist, followed a different path to Coney. "I got involved in Coney Island because of a series of dreams," he said. "I had a grandfather who was a charismatic individual, a recovering alcoholic, a really cool guy, and he used to take me to Coney Island all the time. At the turn of the eighties, I had a series of dreams about my grandfather and Steeplechase Park. I followed those dreams and went down to Coney Island and started poking around, getting to know people and making a pain in the ass of myself. That's when I became an artist. I was running a cabinet shop and realized that Coney was very potent to me." Eagan started making Coney Island–inspired assemblage in his Brooklyn shop. He also met Philomena Marano. The two joined forces and founded the Coney Island Hysterical Society.

**Drummer boy**
Dick Zigun at an early Mermaid Parade.

Marano had been raised in Bensonhurst and visited Coney Island as a child. "I had a love/hate relationship with Coney Island because it was beautiful and magical and also repulsive," she said. "It was strange and creepy and it formed a deep impression at an early age." Marano watched the Coney Island fireworks from the roof of her house and was drawn to the place: "I felt like it was this living thing calling me, because we'd go there the next day, not just to Steeplechase but to the beach. My aunts were all members of Ravenhall Baths. But we stopped going to Coney when Steeplechase was torn down. All I heard from my family was, 'It's bad there now, the whole neighborhood changed.'"

Marano graduated from Pratt Institute in 1976 and worked with pop artist Robert Indiana. "He would always talk about how he was influenced by American culture, and he talked about Coney Island quite a bit," Marano said. "I was thinking about Coney Island a lot, so I went there with an altered vision, as an artist influenced by Robert Indiana. I was blown away, because everything was so decayed. I was crazily inspired and moved and felt obligated to pay homage to this place that was neglected and forgotten. It was almost like a calling.

"I decided to do serigraphs of the shooting gallery called Unkept Promises. This comes from that feeling I had as a child, sitting on a blanket watching the Parachute Jump with a sense of promise, that something was going to happen. But years later I walked over to the Parachute Jump and it was rusted and the base was caved in and the cables were hanging down. Now that promise seemed gone."

Pratt Institute had been involved in an urban planning study of Coney Island, and Marano called one of the architecture teachers working on the revitalization project.

**Honoring a tradition**
Philomena Marano, Lillie Santangelo, and Richard Eagan (left to right) in front of the World in Wax, 1982.

The teacher put her in touch with Richard Eagan, who, coincidentally, had also called Pratt about the study. They talked by phone, and Eagan told her of his dream to rebuild Steeplechase Park.

Zigun, Eagan, and Marano finally met at a 1981 art show in Coney Island. A group called Pan Arts, which sponsored outdoor art exhibits, was having a show on West Tenth Street, next to the Cyclone roller coaster. Marano had found out about the show from a street flyer that asked artists to bring something "large" to display. "I was inspired," she said, "and decided to build a Parachute Jump, an eleven-foot jump of corner beading and wood with parachutes. I called it *Flowers from an Unkept Garden*. I was dragging my Parachute Jump out of the van and I looked down the street and there's a guy wrestling with a huge cabinet." It was Richard Eagan with his *Barrel of Fun*, a huge back-lit cabinet on wheels with a rolling barrel and images of Steeplechase Park. "That's when we introduced ourselves," Marano said. "And then, walking down the street, came Dick Zigun, handing out flyers for an exhibit he was putting together called *Tricks & Treats at the Wax Musee*. He was helping Lillie Santangelo with a fund-raiser because a truck went though her window."

Zigun's World in Wax benefit combined the weird world of Coney folk art with downtown hipster performance art. It was a groundbreaking event. Lillie Santangelo had opened the museum with her husband in 1926 and run it alone since his death. Probably the oldest and most unusual wax museum in the world, it was filled with decaying figures of long-dead politicians, bizarre murderers, athletes, celebrities, and freaks of nature. The World in Wax put images in my head that I've never been able to erase. As a kid, I loved watching the moth-eaten mechanical monkeys in the front window of the show's Bowery entrance. The monkeys played cards on a wooden barrel and cheated by holding aces with their tails. This was a mild come-on, as the figures inside the museum were particularly hideous. The dismembered-child-in-a-bathtub was especially creepy. The musty museum had a mural of Dante's Inferno and dimly lit wax tableaus filled with mayhem and dismemberment: teenaged killers, mass-murderer Richard Speck, a five-year-old

**Special events**
The logo for Coney Island Events, 1983.

ARTISTS' RENAISSANCE OF THE 1980s 227

**Mermaid Parade**
King Neptune and Queen Mermaid on the beach at the first Mermaid Parade, 1983.

mother, Nazi Adolph Eichmann, and Elvis Presley. It was Coney Island culture at its best. Santangelo knew her audience and, for $1 admission, gave them what they wanted, with signs in Spanish and English.

On Halloween night 1981, Coney Island USA presented *Tricks & Treats at the Wax Musee*. The eight-hour show had pieces by more than forty artists, including films, installations, performances, dance, music, and lectures. It opened with two artists who would later become Obie winners: Paul Zaloom, who had performed ten years earlier in Coney Island with the Bread and Puppet Theater, and Charles Ludlam.

Zaloom gave a simulated tour of New York using small found objects to represent famous landmarks and a jar of fake eyeballs to represent the tourists. Charles Ludlam performed *Escape from a Regulation Straitjacket as Used on the Murderous Insane*. Ludlam took the role of a lunatic in a straitjacket, and Everett Quinton played his nurse. Given a choice between the jacket and the snake pit, Ludlam chose the jacket and then escaped like Houdini. Ludlam also showed *Museum of Wax*, a film produced by his Theater of the Ridiculous, shot on location at the museum and starring himself as an escaped prisoner hiding among the exhibits. At the conclusion of Ludlam's performance, members of Coney Island's Polar Bear Club donned swimsuits and stood around in an ice-filled metal tub, rubbing ice on themselves while posing for pictures and lecturing on the benefits of cold-water bathing.

Dick Zigun performed *Secrets of the Wax Museum* and showed an assortment of fifty wax heads found in the museum's storage room. Zigun's "grand finale" was *A Table Top Theater,* in which a tiny paper house was set ablaze with a lit cigarette and extinguished by miniature toy firefighters manipulated by Zigun's assistant, Asa Watkins, who also squirted the audience with seltzer while dousing the fire.

Richard Eagan created an installation called *The Destruction of Steeplechase Park*, and Philomena Marano offered a piece called *Revolver*, related to John Lennon. The show was a huge success. Not only did it help Santangelo, but it also garnered positive reviews from the *New York Times*, the *New York Daily News*, and the *Drama Review*, all of which gave the Coney Island event extensive coverage.

Eagan and Marano kept in touch after the show. "We were hysterical because Coney was declining so rapidly," Marano said, "so we decided to name ourselves the Coney Island Hysterical Society." Eagan truly believed that he could get Steeplechase Park rebuilt and sought support from the public. He and Marano started a newsletter to get their message directly to the public and handed it out on Brooklyn street corners, using *Parachute on Wheels* and *Barrel of Fun* from the Tenth Street art show to call attention to their cause. Soon the pair had more than five hundred members in their organization. The newsletter asked members to share their thoughts on Coney's future and what role the society should play in the revitalization. The project also led to a traveling Coney Island/Steeplechase multimedia arts show that toured Brooklyn during 1982.

**Taking a break**
Coney Island Events sponsored a break dance contest in 1984. The Hysterical Society's mural is in the background.

Dick Zigun took a more serious approach. As a graduate of the Yale School of Drama, he wanted to set up a nonprofit arts center and museum in a permanent location, so with fellow Yalies Costa Mantis and Jane Savitt, he founded Coney Island USA. Both arts groups experienced a breakthrough in 1983. Zigun's big event was the revival of the Coney Island Mardi Gras, which he renamed the Mermaid Parade. It was a judged, costumed event held on the summer solstice, with floats, marching bands, mummers, and flags and banners. The first parade assembled in Steeplechase Park and marched down Surf Avenue. It started out small, with more marchers than observers, and within a few years, it replaced the Fourth of July weekend as Coney Island's main event. It attracted a new audience: young, white, hipster types from Manhattan. The media took notice.

The Hysterical Society's main event in 1983 was raising $7,000 to paint a twenty-five-hundred-square-foot mural on the side of the Dragon's Cave building on the Bowery. Marano and Eagan were awarded a grant from Nathan's Famous and given paints from a city arts program. The mural's location at the neglected west end of the Bowery was chosen to provide the area with a much-needed "vibrant sign of life." The mural was based on a 1915 Steeplechase advertisement with whimsical figures and the slogan, "Oh Boy! Oh Joy! Where do we go from here?" "The mural was supposed to provide sympathetic magic," Marano said. "We hoped that it would bring Steeplechase Park back. A year after that, we met entrepreneur Horace Bullard, who had the same idea, and we thought our dreams might come true."

Marano began working in Coney Island. "I was spending so much time there that I needed to make money, so I painted signs for the ride operators." She teamed up with Eagan, and both became sign painters, painting hot buttered corn signs for food stands and Pac Man images for arcades. They even painted Jack Mer's kiddie carousel on Fifteenth Street. "Richard and I painted Mer's horses," Marano recalled, "but he was so cheap that we wound up getting only $1.29 a horse."

The summer of 1983 was a turning point for Coney Island, and the proof was that the once-suspicious business community began taking notice of the arts groups. Even landlord Hy Singer tried to rent out "artist lofts" in the upper floors of the Stauch's building as if it were in trendy SoHo. As one observer put it: "We didn't get the gambling, so there were new dollar signs: the arts."

After the success of the Mermaid Parade, the chamber of commerce approached Eagan and Zigun in the fall of 1983 and asked them to submit a plan to handle Coney Island publicity and promotion for the 1984 season. The two artists had finally been accepted. Richard Eagan remembered: "We had developed these characters, and the Coney Island Chamber of Commerce decided they wanted to have somebody do events and publicity for them. I think it was Charlie Tesoro who came around with his sly smile and said, 'Youse guys, Eeeegan and Zeeegun, what a pair!' Kenny Handwerker from Nathan's backed us and let us work out of one of those old vintage 1940s offices on the second floor above Nathan's on Schweickert's Walk. It was authentic Coney Island."

Ken Handwerker—like his father Murray, the CEO of Nathan's who revived the Mardi Gras during the 1950s and sponsored the Bread and Puppet Theater in the 1970s—believed the arts could help Coney Island. According to Richard Eagan, Handwerker had a program for a "Coney Island renaissance" and ideas for promoting events and festivals. "He had a sort of utopian 'bring back Coney Island' thing, but he never got it off the ground until Dick and I came along," Eagan said. "It struck me that Dick and I were hired by the chamber to put the muscle on Milton Berger. We were seen as these starry-eyed kids, and they were sort of amused by us. Yet we actually did some really interesting

**Kid Twist**
Mark Kehoe's poster for Len Jenkin's 1987 play, starring Richard Eagan and directed by Dick Zigun. Kid Twist was the nickname of Abe Reles, the gangster thrown out a window of the Half Moon Hotel.

**Struttin' the boards**
A Boardwalk dance performance in front of Sideshows by the Seashore.

things that year, and we got a lot of press. We sponsored the first all New York City hip-hop festival and brought back the antique bathing suit contests."

The joint project of Coney Island USA and the Coney Island Hysterical Society was called "Coney Island Events." Eagan spelled out their mission in the 1984 Hysterical Society newsletter: "Dick and I now have the delicate task of juggling several hats at once without dropping any: An artist's hat, an organizational hat, and a press hat—1940s rumpled felt with press card in the band."

I asked Eagan how the two groups with different philosophies were able to work together. "We had two different arts organizations, and we talked about merging," he said. "But the closest we got was that Dick had a white phone on his desk, and I had a black one, and we screwed the pieces together into black-and-white phones." Zigun seemed more focused and methodical about his dream of a Coney Island Arts Center, and Eagan was more free-form in his approach.

After their year-long publicity stint ended, both groups became more ambitious and, in 1985, found permanent homes in Coney Island. The year began on a sad note, when Lillie Santangelo's World in Wax, the venue that had served as the first joint effort of the arts groups, closed its doors and auctioned off the wax figures. Then Freddie Garms, owner of the Wonder Wheel and Spookarama, died. Coney lost its two most eccentric characters, and Zigun and Eagan inherited their roles.

Dick Zigun signed a ten-year lease on the old Playland storefront on the Boardwalk and opened CIUSA's Sideshows by the Seashore. Zigun used the five-thousand-square-foot space to produce serious theater and dance performances and start a museum. The Hysterical Society moved to the Bowery and took over Sporty Kaufman's landmark dark ride, the Dragon's Cave, transforming the ride into an art project called the Coney Island Spookhouse.

The Spookhouse was a work in progress. Eagan came up with the idea of operating the ride when he heard that Sporty Kaufman, the ride's longtime owner, was about to close it down. "We were desperate," Marano said, "and kept saying, 'No, Sporty, we don't want this ride to go away.'" Eagan convinced Ken Handwerker, who already owned the ride's building, to buy the ride and have the Hysterical Society fix it up. "We wanted to make it into a ride-through art gallery in the dark," Marano said, "so we invited ten artists to paint the cars in different styles and asked other artists to refurbish some of the old spooks and put in new installations." The new installations included Cindy Lauper on the Parachute Jump, the Wild Boy of Coney Island, and string spiderwebs made by Dick Zigun. Eagan operated the ride, and Marano was the art director. Mark Kehoe painted a mural of Coney Island on the building's side.

While Marano was working at NBC, she ran into her childhood friend Harvey Fierstein, who was there to appear on David Letterman's show. "I told him what we were doing in Coney Island, and he was flabbergasted. He said, 'You're not going to believe this, but I have a play called *Spookhouse* based on the Dragon's Cave ride that you're working on.'" He introduced Marano to Bill Stabile, who had built the set for the play, which had closed after two days. Fierstein donated the props and sets—a giant walk-through dragon's head, a devil head, and skulls—and they were installed in the Spookhouse.

The Spookhouse was a popular attraction that enlivened the west end of the Bowery. Eagan, in his full carny getup, did the ballyhoo: "The Spookhouse! More fun than the public library. Come on in, it's spooky!" But insurance companies were spooked by a fatal fire in a New Jersey amusement park, and the ensuing insurance crisis forced the closure of the Spookhouse before the 1986 season began. It never reopened. Marano returned to her artwork and still uses Coney Island themes. Richard Eagan stayed on for one more season, working the bally on Stillwell Avenue for the Florida Shark Show and feeding the sharks with his bare hands. The Coney Island Hysterical Society folded in 1987.

## Sideshows by the Seashore

A friendly rivalry always existed between the Hysterical Society and Coney Island USA. Zigun's group took itself more seriously and considered the other groups to be "weekenders." With the Hysterical Society out of the picture, Coney Island USA became the dominant arts group and organized as a nonprofit "multi-arts center offering museum and theater programming." Its stated purpose was to "defend the honor of American popular art forms through innovative exhibitions and performances." Zigun was soon producing serious theatrical events on the Boardwalk: *Kid Twist*, starring Richard Eagan; Maxim Gorky's *Boredom*; Tom Eyen's *Why Hanna's Skirt Won't Stay Down*; and three plays by Zigun: *His Master's Voice*, *Red Letter Days*, and *The Misadventures of Alice E. Neuman*. There were poetry readings by John Giorno, Taylor Mead, Bob Holman, and Pedro Juan Pietri; avant-garde musical events including *John Cage Meets Sun Ra*, jazz, hip-hop, folk music, and alternative rock performances by Dee Dee Ramone, the members of Sonic Youth, Tuli Kupferberg of the Fugs, and the Sun City Girls. Annual events ranging from motorcycle shows to tattoo festivals were held every summer.

Coney Island USA opened the Coney Island Museum, the first since William Mangels's short-lived establishment on Surf Avenue closed in the 1940s. The organization received National Endowment for the Arts grants, as well as grants from the borough, state, and city. But even with the funding and good press, Zigun wasn't taking in enough money to pay the bills. Culture was a hard sell to Coney visitors, so Zigun tried reviving a traditional Coney art form: the sideshow.

Performance artist Paul Zaloom, a veteran of Bread and Puppet's 1971 Coney Island theater, remembers visiting Zigun in 1985,

**Taste for nostalgia**
The Coney Island Hysterical Society adopted a 1920s Steeplechase advertisement as their logo.

**Step right up**
John Bradshaw (right) with snake charmer, Serpentina, created Coney Island USA's sideshow in 1985.

ARTISTS' RENAISSANCE OF THE 1980s   231

## VALERIE HALLER
## SIDESHOW ART

**Lemon girl**
Valerie Haller (above) serves lemonade at the sideshow's snackbar, which she designed (right). Haller painted a variety of signs for Coney Island USA's museum and sideshow events.

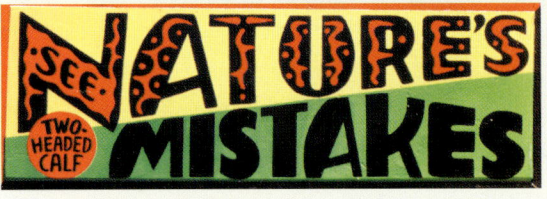

VALERIE HALLER defined the appearance of Sideshows by the Seashore in the early 1990s with her signs and design work based on a traditional Coney Island style made famous in Steeplechase Park.

"I developed a style that was classical and not too flashy, a bit art deco. It was orderly and well researched and thought out. That's my nature.

"The goal of anybody in the amusement business is not to make signage look pretty and retro, but to make it sell. What I was selling was nostalgic experience. I needed to make the colors and shapes look as pulled together as the colors and shapes on the old signs. That was my ideal. I built signs out of wood, not out of tin, which was the Coney Island style of the 1970s and 1980s: throw up a piece of tin and hire a cheap sign painter to put some paint on it.

"I looked back to the days when Steeplechase had full-time painters. I examined old postcards of the park with a magnifying glass, thinking, 'How can I use that information?' I didn't want people to think about what they were seeing, but wanted them to feel it through the integrity of the details. I felt as if I was channeling the ghosts of Steeplechase sign painters, going for a real craftsmanlike approach that was very satisfying.

"The sideshow building had some great architectural details to work with. There was a wonderful tin ceiling, wood floors, and the original rolling wooden doors from when the building housed an arcade. They could be rolled back into side wall pockets to create any configuration of opening across the front. Dick had also rescued a wooden railing that enclosed the exhibits at the Wax Musee and installed it around the sideshow stage. Everything combined to create the perfect ambience.

"We had music playing outdoors through a speaker. People would round the corner or come down the Boardwalk, and the old-timey music was playing, and the sideshow was shining like this jewel, with all these beautiful colors and banners. The press described the banners as being like Lifesavers. These candy colors were actually the ones I chose for the interior: green, orange, yellow, blue, the real amusement park colors. The sideshow was sort of a bubble compared to what existed around it.

"It wasn't artifice but an accumulation of details that came out of the same impulses that a mom-and-pop establishment would have. Dick and I actually referred to our association as a mom-and-pop one. We were there day in, day out, with other remnants of the community. We were strangely proud that we had one of the few places that stayed open off-season. Through the dead of winter we would open the museum and café on weekends without fail. We provided the odd tourist with some historical perspective and hot cocoa, and ourselves with a way to hang on until summer."

during his first season, and offering advice. "I went up to see Dick on the Boardwalk, and he had this space with big windows. He was trying to do performance art, and all the windows were open and uncovered, and he was charging a buck to get in. He told me, 'I can't get people in here.' So I said, 'Dick, you're not getting people in there for two reasons: they can see into the room and what they see is a bunch of chairs and a dingy space and a stage.' I said, 'Black out the windows so they can't see inside, and they'll give you a buck just to walk in the room to see what's in there. That's the carny thing to do.'

"I also told him that nobody out here gives a shit about performance art. I said to him, 'Put some carny acts in there, some guy who hammers a nail up his nose or eats cigarettes or walks on glass or whatever. That's what belongs in Coney. It's not like there's a bunch of highfalutin' season-ticket-holders schleppin' up and down the Boardwalk. It's people who are broke.' So Dick went and put all those knuckleheads in there."

Zigun remembers the encounter differently: "I asked Zaloom how he got people into the Bread and Puppet Theater, and he essentially told me he did bally. He didn't specifically recommend bringing in a sideshow. That came later. I had the 1985 season booked for music and performance art and poetry slams, and people weren't coming in. Based on Zaloom's advice, I started going out in front of the place and beckoning people in and became the 'pointer guy.' Being the pointer guy was a way of not being a barker but putting the focus on the sideshow."

Zigun's sideshow was started by John Bradshaw, who made his living running freak shows at carnivals. Steve Zeitlen, a member of the CIUSA's board of directors, had worked with Bradshaw a year or two earlier at the Smithsonian Folklife Festival. "We booked Bradshaw for Labor Day weekend in 1985 as 'The One Man Sideshow,'" Zigun said. "Bradshaw told me to hire an actress who wasn't afraid of snakes, and he would provide the snake. We got Louisa Jatoba, who became our first snake charmer. Suddenly the place that couldn't get anybody inside had a nonstop line at the door for four days. So I borrowed more money to keep us going into the 1986 season." Bradshaw was booked for the 1986 season and created Bradshaw's Circus of World Curiosities, a traditional "10-and-1" circus sideshow that had ten acts and one thrown in for free.

Zigun had his theater and an artistic vision for Coney Island, and soon he had a new look, one that brought back the whimsical yet classic visual style of Steeplechase Park. The person behind that look was his new design director, Valerie Haller, who joined CIUSA in 1988. Haller designed and produced all the sideshow's banners, signs, and theatrical sets and created the sublime ambience that attracted customers to Sideshows by the Seashore.

Haller first visited Coney Island as a child with her grandmother and returned in 1976 when she was a student at the School of Visual Arts. Coney Island was part of her

**Coney Museum**
Valerie Haller's sign (above). The museum at Coney Island USA has relics from long-lost amusements, including a horse from the Steeplechase ride (left) and fun house mirrors.

ARTISTS' RENAISSANCE OF THE 1980s    233

**New location**
The bally stage at Sideshows by the Seashore West Twelfth Street theater.

**The water's fine**
The traditional opening of the beach on the summer solstice, circa 1986.

family history. Her grandmother, a young maid working for a family in New Jersey, took a day off to visit Coney with a girlfriend. While there, she met her future husband. "I knew I had to go to the Boardwalk, where my grandparents met," Haller said. "I kept hanging out at Coney, and I didn't have a boyfriend. One of my coworkers saw a profile and picture of Dick Zigun and slapped it down on my desk and said, 'You should go out with this guy. I think you're perfect for each other.' So I went out to the sideshow and batted my eyelashes and said, 'I'm an artist and I can help you.' We didn't really connect until I came back that fall for the *Kid Twist* play."

Haller began building stage sets for CIUSA's next production: Tom Eyen's *Why Hanna's Skirt Won't Stay Down*. "It was the first stage set that I built, and I threw myself into it," Haller said. "The play takes place in a broken-down funhouse, and my set was this fractured cabinet of Dr. Caligari. I also did the sets for four other productions and worked on sprucing up the museum."

John Bradshaw left the sideshow in 1991 after his young daughter was shot in the leg by a stray bullet near their home in Far Rockaway, and he took his sideshow banners with him. Haller had to come up with new ones. "That's when I figured out how to paint banners. I did some research, and since I had painted figuratively in college, I knew I could do it. Japan colors were the paints of choice, a commercial oil paint. The canvases used to be primed with white lead, but I just used gesso. I had to find someone to make the canvases for me, because they had to be stitched by a commercial awning company and then I had to find the rings used for securing them. It was quite a production, but it was rewarding because it was our own show and it got popular."

Zigun had his own sideshow and continued producing plays in the off-season. The audiences who visited Coney in the winter were adventurous souls who read about the performances in the *Village Voice* and came down to the deserted Boardwalk for a different type of theatrical experience. "The weekend plays were great," Haller said. "People had to be intrepid to get out to Coney Island, but once they did, they were enchanted. Enchanted but frightened because it was after dark in the winter. The less intrepid ones came for the afternoon show, but it didn't matter, because Coney on a winter afternoon was beautiful. You could go to Nathan's, stroll the beach, and then see a play in this strange little place. Dick directed most of the plays. They weren't masterpieces, but they were charming and original. The atmosphere took the play a long way."

Haller received a National Endowment for the Arts fellowship and moved her studio to the sideshow, where she and Zigun lived. I asked Haller what it was like to live on the Boardwalk. "When I first started living there, it was rough, drafty, and really cold. We didn't have a heater in the living space, and it was so cold that it would wake me up. I liked the off-season better, because in the summer, when we were working, it was nonstop carny life. The brain-numbing noise went from noon until after midnight. We faced the Himalaya and Hellhole rides, so we would hear pounding music all night long. The mosquitoes would come in though the rotten ceiling. We were very aware that we were at the beach."

Haller left the sideshow in 1994. It was still in the red, and in 1995, the landlord, Ralph Ricci, began eviction proceedings against Zigun for back rent of $51,000. CIUSA's ten-year lease was up, and Ricci wanted the sideshow out. When it was revealed that a McDonald's restaurant was planning to take the sideshow's Boardwalk space, the eviction became a media event. ABC's *Nightline* gave Zigun an entire thirty-minute show, and the *New York Times* ran several articles. Zigun characterized it as a battle between "McCulture and Americano Bizarro." The Vourderis family, owners of the Wonder Wheel, and the Alberts, owners of Astroland Park, offered to pay Ricci the back rent if Zigun could get a new five-year lease. The landlord refused the offer.

It wouldn't be the last time that the community would offer to bail him out. Zigun's reputation as a poor businessman was well known, and some in the amusement community resented his nonprofit status. Radical lawyer Ron Kuby represented Coney Island USA pro bono, and the cast of the freak show staged a demonstration outside the civil court in Brooklyn, with a show of sword swallowing and fire eating, but to no avail. Coney Island USA lost its Boardwalk headquarters in September 1995 and was forced to move to a new location.

CIUSA's new venue, the Child's building

on Surf Avenue, a block away, had a completely different feel. The space was bigger but darker, and Zigun lost his sunny "front yard" on the ocean and beach. "We lost the affluent carriage trade," Zigun said. "On Surf Avenue, we have a rowdier nighttime crowd. For some, the move meant the destruction of the artistic environment created by Valerie Haller. Some people miss that artistic environment."

But the sideshow continued, with a larger museum, music events, and the freak show. Zigun introduced several new programs, including an *Ask the Experts* history series, an *Exotic-Erotic* burlesque show

**Summer fun**
The annual Mermaid Parade (above) has replaced the Fourth of July as Coney's biggest draw. Ruby's Bar (left) is a popular post-parade destination. The Great Fredini hosts the *Exotic-Erotic* burlesque show (top) at Sideshows by the Seashore.

## MARIE ROBERTS
# THE PROFESSOR

IN 1996, Dick Zigun found a new artist-in-residence for Coney Island USA: Marie Roberts, who comes from a Coney background. Her father, Kenneth Cornelius, was named for Kenneth Sutherland, Coney's nineteenth-century political boss. Dreamland plays a large part in the Roberts family saga. Two of Marie's uncles were electricians who worked in the park on the night it burned in 1911, and her grandfather, a Coney Island firefighter, battled the blaze. Her father and her uncle Lester Roberts watched the magnificent park burn.

It was Uncle Lester who became the family's true carny. After the Dreamland fire, the park's freak show was reorganized by Dreamland's manager, Sam Gumpertz, into the Dreamland Circus Sideshow. Lester Roberts was hired as the "talker." His golden voice lured customers throughout the sideshow's heyday during the 1920s. In his later years, Roberts anointed himself "Professor Roberts" and used his gift to sell patent medicine, pressure cookers, and marriage manuals.

Lester's friends were sideshow freaks who spent time at the Roberts family home in Gravesend, where Marie still lives today. Visitors included the world's smallest man, Baron Pauci, and the armless and legless

wonder, Violetta, who stayed in the room Marie now uses as her studio. Lester and Marie were close, and she didn't realize how unusual her uncle was. With these credentials, it's not surprising that Coney Island has influenced her artwork.

Marie Roberts leads a double life as an academic and a carny. She's a professor of art at Fairleigh Dickinson University in New Jersey and also paints banners for CIUSA's Sideshows by the Seashore. The irony of Roberts being a professor would not be lost on her Uncle Lester, the family's first Professor Roberts.

I asked Roberts how she became involved with the sideshow. "When Uncle

**Artist-in-residence**
Marie Roberts poses with a vintage dark ride car at the Coney Island USA Museum, 2000 (above). Roberts's painting (left) of Sideshows by the Seashore.

**The professor** Marie Roberts's uncle, Lester Roberts, in the ticket booth of the Dreamland Circus Sideshow (right). Roberts's drawing of the bally at Sideshows by the Seashore (above).

Lester died in 1989, I got all his sideshow stuff because nobody wanted it," she said. "Later, I opened the *New York Times* and saw an article about this guy who does freak shows. That's when I met Dick Zigun." It was the first time that Roberts encountered someone who understood both halves of her life, the academic and the carny. She began drawing and painting the sideshow performers and convinced Zigun to teach at her university, where he directed the school play and taught screenwriting and alternative art. Roberts and her students began painting new banners for the sideshow.

Roberts's art-world friends couldn't figure out what she was doing. "A lot of people decided I had gone off the deep end," she said. "But it feels right. At my age, I can do what I want. When my mother died in 1995, I got really upset. I had lost Lester and my father. I wasn't going to hear the Coney Island history anymore, the patter. I wouldn't have anybody to speak carny with. Dick and I started working together, and it's as if the sideshow is my family. I feel safe there. I can hear the patter. I just sit there and listen. It's funny, but I don't feel safe anywhere else."

ARTISTS' RENAISSANCE OF THE 1980s   237

**Banner days**
Marie Roberts's stage banner for Sideshows by the Seashore (right) depicts a fire-eater, snake-charmer, sword-swallower, elastic lady, bed-of-nails, and Koko the Killer Klown.

**Family tradition**
Bally at the Dreamland Circus Sideshow (below), 1920s. The show was located at Surf Avenue and West Eighth Street. Lester Roberts stands at center with arms folded.

based on the *Tirza's Wine Baths* show of the 1950s, a *Cycle Slut* motorcycle show, and the Coney Island Film Festival. Zigun also continued serving as the unofficial spokesperson for Coney Island.

As it turned out, Zigun became the impresario that Coney Island needed at the end of the twentieth century. He remains the most visible of all the Coney Island personalities and the only artist from the early 1980s who stayed on. He still lives above his establishment like the impresarios of an earlier age. Although he is seen by some in the business community as a prima donna and has endured jokes about "Dick Zigun USA," he helped craft a new legacy for Coney Island after the disastrous decade of the 1970s. "I created an image of honky-tonk chic. A hipster in Coney Island," Zigun said. "When you're in the media's eye, you need to make a visual impact in one second that conveys a message. That's why I play the character of the Mayor of Coney Island and wear the hats and cool glasses. I don't have to say anything. It's visual communication. That's what old-timers like Milton Berger never understood."

Zigun sees no other life for himself beyond Coney. I asked him what he'd like to be doing when he's seventy years old. "I'll be semiretired, a member of the board emeritus, and still have my home in the Child's building. The young folks will be doing the balance of the work at the sideshow while I go back to being a playwright. I'll probably be doing exactly the same thing I'm doing now, chasing Koko the Klown down the street, cleaning the toilets, and doing the bookkeeping."

**Bally, 2000**
The bally at Sideshows by the Seashore (above left). Mermaid Bambi (above) performs at the *Exotic-Erotic* burlesque show. Dick Zigun (left) has become a Coney Island icon.

ARTISTS' RENAISSANCE OF THE 1980s   239

CHAPTER 23

# The 1990s: Survivors

CHANGE IS constant in Coney Island. The forces of nature, fires, and urban renewal and the fickle tastes of the public have all taken their toll on Coney's historic structures. Like stage sets, Coney's buildings were expected to change every season. Yet, despite all odds, many relics of Coney's golden era still exist. Some can be found by looking behind renovated facades; others are in plain sight but have just been moved or refurbished. In the early 1990s, as a millennial project, I began a search for Coney's survivors, the island's oldest buildings, the ones that had survived many uses over more than a century. I called the survivors Coney Island vernacular architecture. These are the buildings I hoped to see landmarked.

A small problem arose, however. Most of the buildings I chose to document did not remain standing into the twenty-first century. Landmarks like the Half Moon Hotel (1927) and Engine 44 firehouse (1895) were demolished before the end of the 1990s. Therefore, I expanded the project to show Coney's changing landscape by shooting "after" pictures from the same point of view as the vintage photographs.

There are also many true believers who remained in Coney Island when things got bad and who always thought Coney would be restored to its former glory. These stalwarts are said to have "sand in their shoes." Of the many true believers, I chose six from different walks of life to profile. Three of them died in the 1990s before the current Coney revival began.

**Centurian**
The Coney Island lighthouse, which was erected in 1890 at the end of Sea Gate, is the country's last manned lighthouse. Frank Schubert, the keeper for forty years, still lives in the keeper's house. The new light and its windmill appeared in *Scientific America* (right) in 1890. The structure in 1995 (far right).

**Venerable profile**

Dating from the late 1880s, the Grashorn building, at Surf Avenue and Jones Walk, is the oldest building in the amusement area. Henry Grashorn operated a hardware store (above) that, for more than sixty years, met the unusual needs of Coney Island's ride owners. The clapboard facade, dormers, cast-iron cresting, chimneys, and fish-scale shingles were removed when the building was renovated in the 1980s, but the mansard roof retains its shape (left).

THE 1990s: SURVIVORS 241

# Saving Coney's Last Boardwalk Palace

**Terra-cotta delight**
The Childs building (above) is the last of the grand 1920s Boardwalk structures still standing. A steamboat (right) docks at the Steeplechase pier, seen from the Childs roof garden in the 1940s. A terra-cotta medallion adorns the facade (far right).

The CHILDS Boardwalk restaurant, on the Boardwalk at West Twenty-first Street, was built in 1923 in Spanish Colonial Revival style by the firm of Dennison and Hirons. The stucco and terra-cotta palace has marble columns and a facade decorated with polychrome, nautical-themed medallions by the Atlantic Terra-Cotta Company. A story in the September 1924 issue of *The American Architect and Architectural Review* described the building: "The carnival spirit of Coney Island demands color; it permits almost anything. Childs Restaurant strikes a new note of beauty in surroundings that are naturally festive. . . . The Childs Building shows that beauty and permanence have a place in Coney Island, where gaudy makeshifts have been the rule." The restaurant closed in the 1950s and became a candy factory. In 2001, the building was put up for sale, sparking an all-out effort to have it declared a landmark and prevent its demolition.

242   DECLINE AND COMEBACK

**Childs on Surf** The 1917 Italian Renaissance–style Childs restaurant building is located at the corner of Surf Avenue and West Twelfth Street (top). When the Boardwalk was constructed and West Twelfth Street was carved through to the beach in 1921, the building had to be jacked up and moved thirty feet to the west. Today, its main tenant is Coney Island USA (above); the Coney Island Museum is on the second floor. The barrel-tile roof and paired corbel brackets beneath the projecting eaves have survived years of renovations, but the archways did not.

**Lost landmark**
The Half Moon Hotel in a 1930s postcard (far left). The ornate Moorish-style hotel became a navy hospital after World War II and a nursing home in 1950. The structure fell to the wrecker's ball in 1995 (left) and was replaced by a modern nursing home.

**Engine 44**
The firehouse on West Fifteenth Street was one of the most beautiful buildings in Coney Island. It was constructed in 1895 to battle Coney's plague of fires. The owners, the Russo family of Gargiulo's restaurant, celebrated the building's hundredth birthday by demolishing it in late 1995 before it could be landmarked.

**Bowery's demise**
In 1998–2000, all of the historic structures on the stretch of the Bowery between Stillwell Avenue and West Fifteenth Street were demolished. The Dragon's Cave building is at lower right. The circled building dates from 1903 and over the years housed every kind of ride and game offered on the Bowery.

244　DECLINE AND COMEBACK

# Playland

SILVER'S PENNY ARCADE, between Surf Avenue and the Bowery near Fifteenth Street, was built in 1930. Alex Elowitz began working at Silver's as a change boy in 1939 and bought the business, then called Playland, in 1957. Elowitz's brother, Stan Fox, became Playland's manager. The brothers kept the arcade open year-round. "In the 1960s," Fox said, "the Loews and Tilyou movie theaters were open and people would go to Playland before the movies. We stayed open Thanksgiving and Christmas week. Sometimes we got a nice New Year's Day when there would be thousands of people on the Boardwalk and we made good money."

When Steeplechase Park closed in 1964, business fell off. The family finally sold the arcade in 1977. It closed in 1981, and the building, now owned by developer Horace Bullard, has stood empty since.

**Arcade men** Alex Elowitz (top left, third from right) at Silver's in the 1940s; Stanley Fox (left) at the empty arcade, 2000. The interior of Playland is decorated with Larry Milliard's humorous 1950s murals depicting Coney Island scenes (above).

**The north side, 1920** The north side of Surf Avenue (looking west from West Eighth Street) once bustled with amusements. From right: the L. A. Thompson Scenic Railway building, the Kister carousel, the Kister restaurant, and the towering entrance to Luna Park.

**The north side, 1999** The only amusement left on the north side of Surf Avenue is the B&B Carousell. A flea market and furniture stores have taken the place of the fantasy buildings that once lined the street. The Luna Park high-rises stand on the site of the amusement park.

**Brighton carousel** The carousel building (left), opened in 1879, is shown on the grounds of the Brighton Amusement Park in 1900.

**Up the creek** Coney Island Creek and the Stillwell Avenue Bridge in 1969 (top) and the new bridge in 1999 (above). One of the most polluted and neglected waterways in New York, the creek is undergoing a $114 million cleanup. Environmental groups and government agencies are studying the creek in hopes of restoring it to its natural state.

**Saved** In 1999, the landmark carousel building was disassembled and moved from the site of Brighton Beach Baths to Coney's Aquarium, where it will eventually be used as an exhibit hall.

**Henderson Walk, circa 1920** The narrow walk was one of the thoroughfares that connected Surf Avenue to the beach.

**Henderson Walk, 1999** The alleyway has changed little in eighty years. The Shore Hotel (1903) and Henderson's Theater (1899) still line the walk.

**End of Bowery**
Bowery entrance to Steeplechase Park circa 1903 (above). In 2001 the Bowery leads to a brick wall at the new KeySpan Park (left).

**Nature preserve**
The Thunderbolt roller coaster, shown at right in 1974, closed in 1983. As Virginia creeper and morning glories covered the structure, it became a popular nesting site for birds. The coaster was one of the most photographed Coney landmarks and made numerous appearances in Hollywood films, the last being the appropriately titled *Requiem for a Dream*, released in October 2000. The Thunderbolt in 1999 (below), a year before the landmark was demolished by the city.

# A Tragic Loss

THE KENSINGTON HOTEL, located beneath the Thunderbolt roller coaster, was known to New Yorkers as Woody Allen's boyhood home in the 1977 movie *Annie Hall*.

The hotel was built in 1895 on Coney Island's original shoreline, which at that time was farther inland than it is now and was lined with hundreds of wood-frame bathhouses, restaurants, concert halls, dance halls, and hotels. Over the last century, fire and urban renewal resulted in the loss of all of these buildings with one exception: the Kensington Hotel, the last remaining original waterfront structure in Coney Island.

The old hotel has had many close calls. It miraculously withstood the disastrous Bowery fire of 1903 and the Steeplechase fire of 1907, which burned every building on both sides of the Kensington.

During the 1920s, the hotel was transformed into a home by George Moran, who owned several amusements on the Bowery. When the Boardwalk was built and the beach extended in 1923, the Kensington Hotel was hidden away behind the new buildings lining the Boardwalk. When Moran decided to erect the Thunderbolt roller coaster on the property in 1925, he saved the hotel by running the steel supports for the coaster right through the building. "You don't tear down buildings in Coney Island if you can help it," he said at the time.

The hotel was once again revealed in the 1970s when the buildings lining the Boardwalk were demolished. The Kensington was leveled by the New York City Buildings Department on November 17, 2000.

**Coaster house** The Kensington in 1900 (top) and in 2000 (above). The structure was caught between an owner who neglected it and the city, which considered it an eyesore. There were no winners. Some saw it as a symbol of Coney's decline, but to most, it was a monument to survival.

**Impresario**
Fred Henderson hooked up with John McKane's crony Anson Stratton in 1895, and the two opened a bathhouse. Henderson later built a theater and restaurant.

**Henderson program**
The theater presented the best in vaudeville.

**The Henderson building.** Impresario Fred Henderson's first vaudeville theater on Surf Avenue burned in 1899, and he replaced it with a fireproof brick structure that housed a restaurant and music hall (top). It was gutted in the 1903 Bowery fire, but the outer walls were saved, and the interior was restored (above). In 1923, when Stratton's Walk was widened into Stillwell Avenue, the Henderson building was cut in half, and the music hall's stage was demolished. A new facade was added, and the building is still standing today.

**B&B Carousell** Named for original owners Bischoff and Brienstein, the carousel is the last remaining ride on the north side of Surf Avenue. The magnificent 1919 ride was built a block away, at the factory of William Mangels. The horses and chariots were carved by the great craftsmen of the golden age of carousels: Marcus Illions, Charles loof, and Charles Carmel. At the center of the ride is a brightly painted Gebruder organ that plays classic carousel tunes, and to the side is a brass ring holder. The B&B is owned by Tilyou descendant Jimmy McCullough (at right with granddaughter Jamie Meluso) and stays open year-round. At left is the king horse, an armored Illions with a portrait of Abraham Lincoln painted on its side.

THE 1990s: SURVIVORS

**Reversal of misfortune**
By 1981, the Parachute Jump was a rusting, vandalized hulk, destined for demolition or collapse (right). When the ride was given landmark status, in 1988, the event marked a turnaround in the decay of Coney Island. In 1993, the tower underwent a restoration and was repainted in its original colors (below).

### Before the Boardwalk

In 1918 (above), various restaurants, summer homes, bungalows, bathhouses, and boat-rental concessions lined the shore. Most structures were built on pilings right over the beach. When the city reclaimed the shoreline and began construction of the boardwalk in the early 1920s, most of the buildings were demolished. Some were moved by teams of horses to the beaches at Gravesend Bay, three blocks to the north.

### After the Boardwalk

Upon completion of the Boardwalk, the area between the new promenade and the surviving bungalows was filled in with bathhouses. Some were still standing in the 1970s (right top). Sea Gate Villa is at left. Villa Ferro is the brick building at center, and Lincoln Baths is behind it. The 1923 Villa Ferro is the last existing building in the West End with Boardwalk frontage. Alongside it are the ruins of Coney Island's last surviving bungalow colony (right bottom).

## JIMMY TESORIERO
## CONEY LOYALIST

In the 1980s, real estate agent Vincent "Jimmy" Tesoriero was asked by his son John why he stayed in Coney Island. "You could have a nice office in Long Island. You don't need this," his son told him. Tesoriero, then in his seventies, was well-off, and his office in the Kister Building on Surf Avenue had burned four times over the years. Angered by his son's question, he said, "I own the building, and I own the land next door and the building next door to that. I can't move out of Coney Island. It's my life." He loved Coney and never thought about leaving.

Tesoriero specialized in amusement insurance and had handled the insurance and real estate needs of nearly every ride and amusement in Coney Island, from Steeplechase Park to Nathan Handwerker's real estate portfolio. If you wanted to buy a ride, lease concession space, or get the right permits to operate in Coney Island, he was the man to see.

Tesoriero was a master at the biggest game in Coney Island and had worked in local real estate since 1929. His first job was office boy for the Surf Avenue company Bailey and Berrara. Tesoriero made his initial business contacts when Berrara, a devout Catholic, asked him to drive the pastor of Our Lady of Solace around Coney in the company car to make sick calls and give communion to locals in their homes.

Ten years later, Tesoriero went to work for Walter E. Burgess in the Kister Building next to the entrance to Luna Park. Because he spoke both Neapolitan and Sicilian dialects, he was able to translate for Italian clients. He met his wife, Rose Dimino, when she was working in another realty office on West Twenty-fifth Street. Her family, which had started out as fishmongers in the Italian section on West Fifteenth Street, owned buildings all over the island. Rose and Jimmy were married in 1935 in Our Lady of Solace, had the reception at Casa de Amour on Mermaid Avenue, and spent their honeymoon at the Half Moon Hotel. Their first home was an apartment on Mermaid Avenue in a building owned by Rose's uncle.

The young couple soon had three children, John,

**Family man** Jimmy Tesoriero with his secretary, left, and his wife Rose, 1966 (above). The Tesorieros at the 1948 Coney Island Chamber of Commerce annual dinner at the Half Moon Hotel (circled below).

Marie, and Charles. Needing to earn more money, Tesoriero left Burgess to go out on his own, working three jobs, seven days a week, until two in the morning. He managed the Dragon's Gorge ride at Luna Park, sold Coney Island real estate, and worked for draft board 144 in the Loews Theater building. At one point he was offered a partnership in Luna Park, but as the park's bookkeeper, he knew that Luna was going bankrupt. He returned to Burgess.

When Walter Burgess died in 1944, his widow, Dorothy, offered Tesoriero a partnership. In 1961, Tesoriero bought the business and kept Dorothy as his bookkeeper. After his sons John and Charlie graduated college, they went to work for their father. Rose also joined the company, making it a family business as well as Coney's preeminent real estate company. Tesoriero served two terms as president of the Coney Island Chamber of Commerce and helped guide the organization through its tough years.

In 1979, the historic Kister Building burned for the last time and had to be demolished. The family moved the business to an office on Surf Avenue at West Fifteenth Street. Despite the declining revenues, Tesoriero surprised everyone by deciding to rebuild. The 1980s were one of Coney's darkest periods, and during construction, materials were stolen and the site was vandalized. When the building opened, it was repeatedly burglarized. The police refused to help and, much to the family's surprise, told them they should move. They stayed anyway. When Tesoriero retired in 1990, his son Charlie took over the business and kept it open, running it with his father's guidance. Now run by Charlie and his wife, Claire, the business is still a major force in Coney Island and the first stop for anyone interested in Coney real estate.

## RUBY JACOBS
# KEEPING THE FAITH

**Ruby Jacobs, 2000**
The "conscience of Coney" at his popular Boardwalk restaurant.

Ruby Jacobs, who died in 2000, operated Coney Island's Boardwalk bathhouses for two decades: Stauch's, Clarets, Cook's, and Bushman, four landmarks with a rich history. The Coney Island native was born on May 22, 1922, at his family's home at Twenty-third Street and Railroad Avenue. He got his start in local business as a teenager selling Fudgie-Wudgie bars along the beach. After serving in World War II, Jacobs opened the Mastercraft camera shop in lower Manhattan. On weekends, he spent time in Coney beachcombing. He struck up a friendship with Henny Stephens, who owned Clarets Baths. In 1959, Stephens was ready to retire and regarded Jacobs as the son he never had. He told Jacobs that, of all the people he knew who loved Coney Island, no one loved it as much as Jacobs. Stephens gave Jacobs the bathhouse and for a while helped him run it.

Operating the bathhouse became a family affair: Ruby ran it on weekends and in the evening after working at the camera store. His wife, Sylvia, and his brother, Phil, took over on weekdays. Soon Ruby was running Bushman, Cook's, and Stauch's as well. "We rented out bathing suits, towels, umbrellas, and beach chairs," Ruby told me. "The baths had hot and cold showers, wet and dry steam, and solariums for nude bathing. Customers came early and stayed until we closed. They wanted sun and fresh air. They weren't afraid of Coney Island and would not think twice about taking the subway at ten at night." Holders of season passes had their own locker rooms, which they decorated with linoleum, carpet remnants, plants, mirrors, and furniture. Many customers had originally come with their parents and later, as adults, continued to return to the baths every season.

Ruby's daughter Cindy described the clientele. "They were whole families from different ethnic groups. They brought little grills to cook their food—pierogi, knishes, macaroni dishes—and would share what they made. There were school principals, doctors, lawyers, actors, people from every walk of life. What they did never mattered—what they shared was a love of the beach. Everyone was safe and happy. It was a different time, and the bathhouses represented a way of life."

In the winter, the bathhouses became a hangout for Ruby and his beachcomber friends. They sat around an old potbelly stove roasting potatoes and chestnuts and talking about what they'd found on the beach. "Ruby was the king of the beachcombers," Cindy said. "He had the first metal detector ever used on Coney and was an expert on gold and diamonds. He weighed what others found and gave them advice on what was valuable. These people needed the money, and he wanted to be sure they weren't cheated by pawnshops. He was called 'eagle eye.' People were impressed with his ability to find objects and said he could see through the sand. He even began to snorkel in the surf to find treasure."

Jacobs was generally known for his kindness. "Anyone who needed to borrow money went to Ruby," Cindy recalled. "If the person paid it back, that was fine, and if not, Ruby would say, 'It's his problem, not mine.' He knew what it was like to be poor because he had grown up that way."

In the 1980s, the bathhouses closed due to declining patronage. But Jacobs did not give up on Coney Island. "When everyone said Coney had become a dump, Ruby still saw it as a great resort," Cindy said. "It represented his youth." In 1985, he opened Ruby's Old Thyme Bar and Restaurant on the Boardwalk. Like the bathhouses, it became a meeting place for all sorts of people, from the onetime patrons of the bathhouses to the young newcomers.

Ruby's Bar is a boxy storefront, about forty feet wide, open to the beach and Boardwalk. The simple bar of black marbled formica runs the length of one wall. The walls, painted Mediterranean blue, are covered with more than six hundred photos, enlarged postcards of Coney's golden age mixed with photos of Ruby and his friends. An island in the center of the space holds a clam bar, deep fryers, a popcorn maker, hot dog cookers, a soft ice-cream machine, and cotton candy spinners. Signs advertise Jamaica beef, slush puppies, and giant lollipops. The jukebox is always playing full blast: Elvis, Latin beat, Frank Sinatra.

Jacobs had a standard answer when asked to point out the best item on the menu. "Look out there at the ocean," he'd say. "Smell the air and look at the whole tapestry of people. That's the best item on the menu." He saw the ocean and beach as the "elixir of life." Jacobs was sure that Coney Island would rise again, and his affection for the place never wavered.

**Meeting place**
Phil and Ruby Jacobs ran Stauch's like a social club.

## JIM PRINCE
# PRINCE OF MERMAID AVENUE

**Mardi Gras float** Willie Palumbo (above), was Major's original owner and taught Prince the business.

**M**AJOR PRIME MEATS butcher shop has been in the same location on Mermaid Avenue since 1934, and Jimmy Prince, who now owns the store, has worked there since 1949. The shop is an unusual landmark, the oldest survivor on a street that has undergone dramatic change over the decades. It has an outdoor loudspeaker that plays old-time music: the Inkspots, the Mills Brothers, Bing Crosby, Ella Fitzgerald, Frank Sinatra. Prince placed three park benches out front, and in good weather, locals sit there and enjoy the music. In a neighborhood where shopkeepers have been burglarized, looted, and even murdered, Major Meats has thrived. Two of the reasons for Prince's success are his affection for Coney Island and his approach to running the business.

"When I first came, I knew that Coney Island was an amusement area, but I didn't know that people lived here," Prince told me. "I was young and raising a family, and I loved the place. My boss, Willie Palumbo, instilled in me a love for the business. It's an old-fashioned store with sawdust on the floor. We have only the best quality and we stand by our reputation. I give my customers the best of everything. I go out of my way to freezer-wrap for them and give them cooking instructions, and call a cab when they have too many bundles. When kids come in, I give them a slice of bologna or a piece of candy. You make a little fuss over people, and you have compassion—it's not all about dollars and cents. I treat customers as if the store's on Fifth Avenue, and they love it. That's why when I go home at night, I don't have big locked roll-down gates. Instead, my windows are all lit up and gaily decorated.

"You had to have a love for Coney Island to stay through all those years of hardships and tough times. There were once several butcher shops within a one-block area of us, but when the neighborhood started to change, they closed. I like to see something that's special taken care of in a special way, and Coney Island is very special. Respect is the number one thing. In our neighborhood, it's even more important than other neighborhoods, because people here are not used to it, and when it's given to them, they're exuberant. I roll out the red carpet, and customers come in with a completely different attitude. I'm taking out of the community, and it's up to me to put something back.

"I think about how people enjoy going back to their old neighborhoods and seeing familiar sights. They dream about the things they grew up with, the butcher, the candy store. When those things are taken away, people are heartbroken. So many people were born and raised in Coney Island, and when they go down Mermaid Avenue, they are devastated because there's nothing familiar. Everything's gone. It's like their childhood has been taken away.

"Most of the people who lived here and enjoyed Coney Island have moved away or died. The only place that survived was Sea Gate. Then the city came in and put up the projects. The drug dealers did anything they wanted in the projects, and the tenants lived in fear. Many were old people, and some were young and had children. The drug dealers had no fear. After a while the police wouldn't even go in the projects. But what about the nice people living there? They became prisoners.

"Over the years, many people have come back into the store and said, 'Oh gee, Mr. Major, how are you? It's good to see you. I'm so glad you're still here. I remember coming in as a kid, and I remember the sawdust.' I hear this from people time and time again. They come back into the community and see my store, and in their minds they become children again. They remember the sawdust and the slice of bologna, and they appreciate that there's something they can associate with their childhood."

**Community pride** Jimmy Prince (above left). The Major Little League team (below), circa 1950s.

## MATT KENNEDY
# TAKE ME TO DREAMLAND

**Coney power brokers**
Clockwise from lower left: Matt Kennedy (circled), Assemblyman Howard Lasher, N.Y.C. Police Chief Robert Johnson, Jack Ward, Charlie Tesoro, City Councilman Sam Horwitz, Brooklyn Borough President Howard Golden.

Matt Kennedy took over as executive secretary of the Coney Island Chamber of Commerce after Bill Nicholson died in 1968 and held the position until he retired in 1996 at age ninety-two. Kennedy was ninety-seven when I last interviewed him. Both sides of his family have roots in the earliest days of Coney Island's development. His grandfather, James Sangunitto, was a light keeper at Norton's Point ferry pier in the 1870s. His father, police lieutenant Matthew Kennedy, was in charge of the Coney Island precinct the night of May 27, 1911, when Dreamland burned. Lieutenant Kennedy, a much-decorated veteran of Coney's numerous fires, directed the harrowing rescue efforts.

**Family studio**
Matt Kennedy spent his boyhood at his grandmother's photo gallery (circled) next door to Dreamland.

Kennedy was born in 1904 in a house near Coney Island Creek, about four blocks from Dreamland. "I was young, but I remember Dreamland very well," he said. "My grandmother had a photo gallery next to the park, called Sangunitto's, on Sheridan Walk at Fifth Street. My mother had six boys and used to farm us out. She took me to stay at the photo studio. I remember that the Dreamland towers were mostly red and white, and there were so many lights. At the park, I saw the house of flames and the midget village with the lilliputians. I remember Bostock's wild animals and Bonavita, the animal trainer with one arm. He was a thrill for kids."

Kennedy knew gangster Frankie Yale, who controlled the local bootlegging, and has vivid memories of life in the 1920s during Prohibition. "Frankie Yale worked out of the Harvard Inn cabaret on the Bowery," Kennedy told me. "He used to bring the liquor in from Gravesend Bay and up Coney Island Creek to Wheeler's shipyard and unload it near the Cropsey Avenue Bridge. Yale had a boat on the creek named the *Cigarette* that nothing could catch. The restaurants served liquor in teacups. For a while, Gargiulo's restaurant even sold homemade wine by the jug. Railroad cars filled with grapes were brought in behind Mangels's ride factory on West Eighth Street. Everyone on West Fifteenth Street would go down and get grappa grapes and make wine in their cellars."

Kennedy also remembers one of Coney's infamous speakeasies. "Indian Village was an open-air saloon with a long bar, a big, open rathskeller type of place. I used to go there during Prohibition and get gin or beer. It was supposed to be near beer, but it was spiked with ether or something. It's a wonder we're still around after drinking that stuff."

Kennedy and Bill Nicholson grew up together. "Bill and I used to play on Coney Island Creek. Before it was filled in, it used to run across Ocean Parkway, behind Coney Island hospital. We had rowboats and a few canoes, and we'd improvise by building rafts. We swam in the creek back then, but it had a muddy bottom, and the tide wasn't strong enough to keep it clean. The creek was neglected, really.

"Bill and I were in a club called the White Arrows, a rinky-dink baseball and football team with kids from the neighborhood. The team played in Seaside Park. I remember when Theodore Roosevelt came to the park bandstand in 1912 to give a speech when he was running for office. The teachers made all of us kids from the school line up in front of him to greet him."

Kennedy lived in an area north of the Gut that was condemned in 1959 for the construction of Warbasse Houses. He doesn't believe that the area should have been demolished for housing projects. "It was a residential neighborhood of families, with mom-and-pop stores on Neptune Avenue. My parents owned the house, and my brother lived there until it was condemned. The city didn't pay fair market value. My parents got a pittance for it after living there sixty years."

After Kennedy replaced Bill Nicholson at the chamber of commerce, the organization faced a number of challenges. "The problem with the Coney Island landowners is that they lack unity. The landowners don't give a damn. If they were unified, they'd be a very potent factor. Each one was on his own, in a kind of shell, and that's why the city passed them by. But Rudy Giuliani pulled it off and built the stadium, and now Coney is finally getting good press. The publicity is great."

## AL MORGENSTERN
# LUNA PARK ROMANCE

Alfred Morgenstern never wanted to leave Coney Island. He had worked there for nearly forty years, until 1961, when developer Fred Trump bought his home on West Second Street and had it demolished. Morgenstern then moved his family to Brighton Beach and watched Coney deteriorate. He always believed that Coney would make a comeback. The comeback had just begun, spurred by the new ballpark, when I interviewed the former resident.

Born in 1905, Morgenstern came to Coney Island from Canada with his two sisters in 1923. They had immigrated to Saskatchewan from Austria, but when his sisters were unable to find Jewish husbands, they moved to Brooklyn and settled on West Third Street in the Coney Island neighborhood known as the Gut.

For seven years while in school, Morgenstern worked summers at Luna Park, first as a ticket taker, then as a barker selling tickets to the Mile Sky Chaser roller coaster. Luna Park, opened in 1903, was in its heyday in the 1920s. "General admission was twenty-five cents," Morgenstern said. "I was paid thirty-five dollars a week and worked seven days a week, from noon to midnight. We had to work every day of the week. Steeplechase Park was more for kids, but Luna was for adults. Luna had a million good attractions. It had a ballroom, a railroad, a carousel, a shoot-the-chutes, and a show of Alaskan huskies. Someone had to buy ice for the dogs to sit on. There was also a thrilling attraction known as Carver's Diving Horses. Those horses dove from a height of 150 feet into a tank full of water. A colorful Czechoslovakian marching band used to ballyhoo all along the park and out the gate. People would admire their colorful costumes, and for a while the musicians rode on horseback.

The area outside the park was just as lively, with freak shows on Surf Avenue. "The freak shows in Coney Island—oh my god, they had a lot of them," Morgenstern recalled. "They had the fat lady, midgets, and the Georgia peaches: two youngsters

**True love**
Alfred Morgenstern and wife, Lee, at the entrance to Luna's Mile Sky Chaser, 1932.

**Taking a dive**
Carver's Diving Horses in Luna Park, 1937.

with little heads. They weren't intelligent but they conversed. I used to go see the show, and one time the guy running it said to me, 'Would you marry one of these girls?' It was very funny.

"The park had two trained elephants, both females. No one could train the males—they just didn't listen—but the females were great. A lot of people used to leave hats and other stuff in my ticket booth when they went on the coaster, and these elephants would come out and pay me a visit. I always had candy, and each elephant knew I had something and would put her trunk in the booth and scoop up the hats and wear them. When the customers saw the elephants wearing their hats, they'd start laughing.

"I married a girl I met while working in Luna Park. She saw me working the booth in 1931. She was a stunning creature, just stunning. I enjoyed life until my wife died. Now I'm in a retirement home, and I'm going to be ninety-six years old."

## PAT AULETTA
# FIELD OF DREAMS

The Auletta family lived in Coney Island Houses in the 1950s, the same time I did. In 1994, the city honored Pat Auletta by naming the Steeplechase pier for him. His two sons, Ken Auletta, a writer for *The New Yorker,* and Dick Auletta, who handles public relations for the Brooklyn Cyclones baseball team, were at the dedication. Pat Auletta always believed that baseball would come to Coney Island, but people thought he was crazy. He passed away in 1991, never seeing the new stadium.

For years, Pat Auletta ran a well-known sporting goods store on Stillwell Avenue and sponsored local Little League teams, among them teams that included young Sandy Koufax and Gil Hodges. In his later years, Auletta became a force in Coney Island politics. He also ran concessions for the Parks Department. His last concession was renting skates at the Abe Stark Rink.

I asked Pat Auletta's sons what their father would have thought of the Brooklyn Cyclones. "My dad was always a promoter of a stadium in Coney Island," Ken Auletta said. "I thought it was a pipe dream. Dad had the concession for Manhattan Beach umbrella rentals and then won the skating rink concession. He had the sporting goods store. He was working late at night, closing up all alone. Anyone who stayed in Coney Island was either someone who couldn't escape or a hopeless optimist. I put Dad in the optimist category.

"Coney Island was the place where he grew up as a kid and the place where he would die. He always believed it would reclaim its former glory. He'd say, 'The beaches are going to come back, the people are going to come back, we're going to get a major league baseball team here, and it's going to restore Coney Island.' At some point I realized that it's not my job to disabuse my dad of his dreams. He was in his seventies, and I let him have his dreams. I didn't share his dreams but I hoped he was right. It was almost a religion. Coney was his faith, and you can't disabuse someone of his faith. He just wanted to believe."

Pat Auletta grew up on Seventeenth Street between Neptune and Mermaid Avenues, where his father had a barbershop near Tennenbaum's candy store. "My parents met on Mermaid Avenue and went to high school together," Dick Auletta told me. "My mother's father owned Tennenbaum's. My mother was Jewish, and in the 1930s it was unheard of for an Italian Catholic to marry a Jewish girl. Then her sisters married Italians, all from Coney Island, all friends. That's what the community was about. It was a melting pot.

"After my mother died, he would put up a huge Christmas tree on the Steeplechase site in her memory. And there's a little vest-pocket park on West Twenty-fifth Street named after her. When Parks Commissioner Henry Stern dedicated the Steeplechase pier for my father, he commented that the only other husband-and-wife team that each has something named after both of them in New York is John and Jackie Kennedy. It was a nice thing for him to say. My folks gave so much to the area. My father, wherever he is, is clicking his heels. This stadium was a dream of his. He fought for it."

**Celebrity opening** Brooklyn Dodger Gil Hodges, Dick Auletta, Pat Auletta, Ken Auletta, and Dodgers pitcher Rex Barney (left to right) at the opening of Pat's Coney Island sporting goods store on Stillwell Avenue, 1949.

**Business lunch** Nathan Handwerker, founder of Nathan's Famous; Irving Rudd, public relations director of the Brooklyn Dodgers; and Pat Auletta (left to right), 1949.

CHAPTER 24

# Jones Walk

**J**ONES WALK is Coney Island in microcosm. The walk is a narrow, block-long alley connecting Surf Avenue to the Boardwalk, the last of eleven walks that ran to the ocean before the city streets were carved through in the 1920s. Jones Walk divides two oceanfront properties that were developed in the 1870s by Coney Island pioneers John Ward and Charles Feltman. Astroland Park now occupies the Feltman property, but John Ward's descendants still own the Ward property, making them the last of Coney's original families to own property in the amusement area.

Beginning at Surf Avenue, Jones Walk crosses the Bowery and disappears beneath the Wonder Wheel, where it connects to the Boardwalk via a tunnel and ramp underneath a concrete platform that once supported Ward's Baths. While strolling the walk, it's possible to experience what Coney Island was like before 1920, when the beach was private property and visitors navigated tiny, private alleyways to get to the beach and bathhouses.

The Ward Realty Corporation owns Jones Walk from the Bowery to Surf Avenue, but in recent years, the family has sold off a patchwork of its holdings, including the land under the Wonder Wheel and several parcels along West Twelfth Street. The Wards also own the Boardwalk kiddie park property leased by the Vourderis family. John Ward first leased the three-hundred-foot-wide lot in 1873 from the town of Gravesend for the sum of $230 a year and constructed a bathhouse and private boardwalk along the beach. In 1884, he bought the property from the town for $10,000 and sold off the small lots between the Bowery and Surf Avenue, keeping only the walk and the valuable beachfront property.

The origin of the name *Jones* is a mystery, even to the Ward family. During a search of historic property maps, I noticed that the name first appears on an 1889 land map as the owner of a small parcel just off Surf Avenue. After examining the property records, I discovered that Catherine Jonas bought the parcel in October 1884. The name Jonas was probably transformed at some point into Jones. Around 1910, the city began mapping streets to the ocean, and Jones Walk was destined to become West Eleventh Street. The

**Jones Walk**
An early-morning view of the Wonder Wheel, pony ride, high-striker, and Assembly Restaurant on the flag-decorated walk, circa 1932.

thoroughfare was supposed to start at the ocean and cut through the center of Luna Park to Neptune Avenue. But by 1920, the cost of condemning the private property was too high, and the city abandoned the idea.

Jones Walk is anchored at both ends by historic structures: at the Surf Avenue end is the Henry Grashorn building, a wood-frame structure that was erected in the late 1880s and is the oldest building in the amusement area; at the other end is the landmarked Wonder Wheel, constructed in 1920. A row of concession stalls flanks the east side of the walk along a brick building that is the only remnant of the nineteenth-century Feltman's restaurant, which burned in 1976. The Ward family rents the stalls to independent concessions.

Versions of every type of Coney Island amusement can be found here, with new and old technologies side by side: a gypsy astrologer, shooting galleries, photo booths, a tattoo parlor, the Spookarama dark ride, a high-striker, hot dog stands, a skin-the-cat game, a basket toss, a water race, Skee Ball, souvenir stands, a test-your-strength game, a penny arcade, and a computerized photo-on-a-T-shirt booth. After sundown, the walk comes ablaze with lights and is filled with deafening music and the shouts of "hot-wired" barkers.

I met with Jack Ward at the office he shares with the Coney Island Chamber of Commerce and Charlie Tesoro. Ward is an attorney who gave up a Manhattan practice to return to his roots in Coney Island. He is a tall and imposing man of fifty-eight, with a ruddy complexion and white hair. Ward is the only person I know who can walk around Coney Island in a suit and tie, even in summer, and still look right at home. It's remarkable, I told him, that he's come back and works out of an office in the heart of Coney Island. After practicing law in Manhattan for twenty-five years, he explained, his lease was up, and the attorneys he worked

**Jones Walk, 2001**
Deno's Wonder Wheel Park occupies the southern portion of the walk. The High Flyer and Wonder Wheel rides are shown.

**Coney aristocrat**
Ward's family has owned property on Jones Walk since the 1870s.

with moved to the World Trade Center. "I just didn't want to go in there," he said. "Charlie had this office here, and I came back to the source."

I asked Ward about his family's title to Jones Walk. "It was never clear if the property owners actually owned the walks," he said, "or if they just had easements. My father was the one who settled the issue. When my grandfather purchased the block, it was an open walkway from Surf Avenue to the beach, and it remained that way through Coney's heyday and through the 1940s. At that time, the Bowery went from Steeplechase Park, all the way through Feltman's Beer Garden to the Cyclone. It had been determined from the outset that the Bowery was private property.

"One day, my dad was drinking with Charlie Feltman, and they had a discussion about the Bowery. At that time, Feltman had a little passenger train that ran right across the Bowery and into the rear of Feltman's Beer Garden. It had a little crossing gate and stoplight at Jones Walk, and when the train went by, Charlie Feltman said to my dad something to the effect that he didn't think that Feltman's was getting enough traffic from the Bowery, and he wanted to expand the Bowery entrance. My father said, 'What do you mean not enough traffic? That's our property, and we're trying to attract people up to the Wonder Wheel and our amusements.'

"Well, they got into a fight, and my father said to Feltman, 'I'm going to close the Bowery entrance to Feltman's.' Charlie said, 'You can't do that. It's public property, and there's an easement.' They'd been friends since they were kids, but you never could tell my father that he couldn't do something. He was normally a nice guy, but once he was told he couldn't do it, he closed off the Bowery and put up the concession stands as you see them today along the walk.

"Feltman sued my dad, and the case went all the way up to the court of appeals, which ruled in favor of my dad. The courts decided that Jones Walk was private property, and based on that, my dad closed the southern end of Jones Walk and extended a concrete platform to cover the walk from the Wonder Wheel to the beach, where the Spookarama was built. Before the court of appeals decision, we owned the property, but everyone assumed that the public had an easement over it for egress. But my father said no."

Jack Ward's grandfather, William Ward, leased some of the property to Alfred Garms, who built the Wonder Wheel in 1920. I asked about the strange, circuitous property lines on some of the parcels, and he explained that a twisting boat ride once ran along West Twelfth Street, and the property lines were drawn along the boat ride. The Wards have since sold off the boat ride and the Bowery parcel where the Virginia Reel coaster ride was located. During the 1940s, nearly all of the remaining concession space on the walk was leased by the Frleta family.

Nowadays, the northern end of the walk is the territory of two old-timers: seventy-one-year-old Wally Roberts and eighty-four-year-old Phil Frleta, who between them have put in more than a century on Jones Walk. Frleta is a smooth talker with an ongoing beef against Roberts: a disagreement over the use of microphones, the high-tech headset mikes that talkers use to blast their pitch to customers.

Frleta, who has worked in Coney Island for seventy-one years, once operated fourteen stalls along Jones Walk. "The changes I've seen around here are out of this world,"

**Next generation**
Dennis (left) and Steve Vourderis (right) own Deno's Wonder Wheel Park, at the heart of the amusement area.

he told me in his gravelly voice. "In the old days, at every stand, I'd have thirty or forty people at this hour. You wouldn't even be able to walk here."

Frleta came to Coney in 1939 when he was twelve years old. He worked for his Aunt Dora at the high-striker behind Nathan's and lived in a rooming house at Jones Walk and the Bowery for fifteen years. Today, Frleta has just one stand: a basket toss, a simple game of skill that involves tossing a softball into a wooden bushel basket. He's had this basket stand for ten years and says he works it as a hobby "just to stay in the game."

"I didn't allow any microphones on the walk," Frleta said. "I had fourteen games on Jones Walk and nobody used mikes. Wally Roberts brought the mikes to Jones Walk, and now there's so much noise that you have to call the customers in. It used to be that just a wave of your hand would bring 'em in." He then demonstrated his technique, using a hypnotic, three-fingered wave. "When the mikes first came in, I had a gun game, shooting cigarettes off a shelf, and you couldn't hear anything. You couldn't talk to a person, the mikes were so loud. The gun game was a walk-in, but when it came time to talk to people, they couldn't hear you."

Across the walk, an intense, muscular man wearing a tank top stood behind the counter of the water race game. The man is Wally Roberts's son-in-law, Pete, who was wearing a headset with a microphone. "I didn't talk to Pete for a long time," Frleta said, pointing to his nemesis. "Pete used to blast on the mike all the way from the Bowery. He thought he owned the walk. Wally's people are young. They're aggressive, and I no longer care. I only run this stand for one reason, to stay healthy. I work a hundred days a year, and that's all. If I make money, that's fine, but if I don't feel like opening up, I just stay closed."

I watched as one of Frleta's workers used the old trick of "accidentally" rolling a ball into the path of a girl coming down the walk. "Could you get that for me?" he asked.

**"It's a hobby"** Phil Frleta, the grand old man of Jones Walk, started working in Coney when he was twelve years old.

When she picked it up, he had her. Once the ball was in her hand, she was playing the game. "This is the only game I work, and it's completely legitimate," Frleta said. "I could work it illegitimate, but I won't. I refuse. I could get these guys off the road where I could make triple the money. My policy is very simple: I'd rather take in two dollars, give out a dollar, and have 'em leave happy. And next time, they'll play the game again. If they play these games with road guys, the guys beat 'em for a lot of money. Then we get a bad reputation, and they'll never play the game again."

Frleta was referring to crooked carnival workers, also known as "grifters," who cheat the "marks," or customers. The basket game he runs is sometimes called an "alibi store." The game's not rigged—it's just difficult to play, and the operator will try to explain how to win as you lose more money trying to learn the technique.

"Road workers rob everybody," Frleta said. "If you have no conscience, it's all right, but I can't afford a heart attack. If I have one beef with a customer per season, that's a lot. I had one road guy work for me two or three years ago, and every second customer was a beef. I says, 'Look, I'm here all season, and I don't get a beef, so the next time you have a beef, you're through.' The next customer, he has a beef! I says, 'Get the hell out of here. You're through.' He must have thought I was kidding."

Frleta rose slowly from his chair, carefully scanning the passing crowd. His weathered features, square jaw, and billboard cap made him look more like a midwestern farmer than a carny. "Yesterday was a blank, but today I'm gonna make a coupla bucks."

He's a pro, and I watched him work a "collection" routine, where a carny keeps a tab for the customer. "No charge, no money, no prize," he said, as he lured a young couple over with a wave of his hand to let them try the game for free. The young man threw the ball, and it bounced out of the bushel basket. "No," Frleta said in a sincere, grandfatherly voice. "Throw it straight. There, that's close! Try to take the big one." He took a $20 bill from the man. It cost $1 to play, but he didn't give the man his change. He just held on to it.

Frleta demonstrated the game by effortlessly tossing two balls into the basket. He was all gestures, always pointing to the prize. "Two in for two dollars, and I'll give you the jumbo up there," he said, pointing to the "plush," a big pink teddy bear. The young man tossed the balls into the bushel basket, and they bounced out. "I owe you eighteen dollars," Frleta said. "That's it, try it again. Two in for two dollars. I owe you sixteen dollars." Frleta kept the man's change and handed over two balls instead. The man tossed the balls again and missed. "Whoa. Easy. One more, that's the way! Two in like that you got it. Here's ten, I owe you four." The man put one ball in, and the other bounced out. "Easy, easy, look, that's the way, with two in like that you got it, try again, try again, I owe you two dollars. . . ."

★

Walter "Wally" Roberts is a relative newcomer to Jones Walk, having opened in 1955 after leaving the military. He has several stalls on Jones Walk, and all of them are wired for sound. Roberts's end of Jones Walk is a family operation: his wife, daughter, and son-in-law all work the games. And they're all wired except Ben, the "wizard" of the walk. Ben is Wally's brother-in-law, a soft-spoken philosopher-sage and mechanical genius. He's the last of a breed of operators who build their own games and equipment, a throwback to Coney Island's inventive ride builder William Mangels.

Wally Roberts has a difference of opinion with Phil Frleta concerning the microphones: "You can't run a group game, any kind of a group game, whether it's a water game or a roll-down group game, without a microphone. It's utterly impossible. You don't work to the individual in these games. You've got to have a minimum of two people, because it's a race, a race between two to twelve people. I've been in the business almost all my life, and I've never seen a group game being run without a microphone. I never told Phil not to use a microphone. He's the king. The king of the beefs, and he's really got some moves. I could tell you stories, but I won't."

In 1955, Roberts opened the Gold Mine souvenir stand at the corner of Surf Avenue and Jones Walk next door to Charcoal Dan's $1.19 Steaks in the Feltman's building. "I changed the name of the stand from Brown's Souvenirs to the Gold Mine because it was catchy," Robert's said. "We sold costume jewelry and did engraving."

Roberts was soon joined by his longtime partner, Doc, and the two obtained exclusive rights to the Shoot-Out-the-Star gallery game and soon opened eight locations throughout Coney Island. "When they came out with the Shoot-Out-the-Star, we had a deal with Feltman, who made the guns, for the exclusive use in all of Coney Island, because no one else wanted to try it."

Roberts was successful and bought the historic Grashorn building from the Bass family. He remodeled it by covering the beautiful clapboard facade with asbestos shingles, then opened a penny arcade below and created summer apartments above for his family. Roberts now has so much terri-

**Gold mine**
Wally Roberts and his family work a penny arcade, water races, and a greyhound race on Jones Walk and the Bowery.

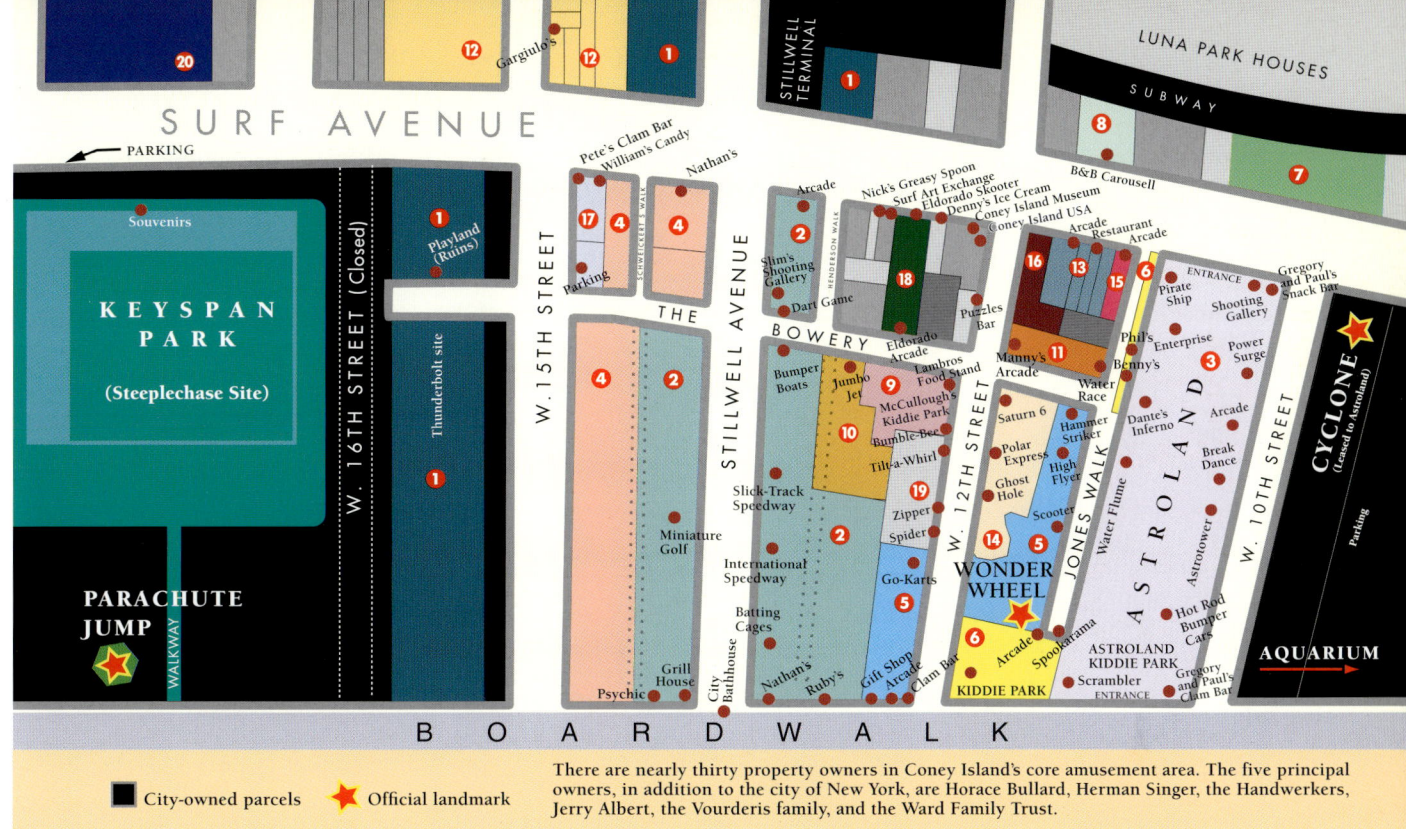

There are nearly thirty property owners in Coney Island's core amusement area. The five principal owners, in addition to the city of New York, are Horace Bullard, Herman Singer, the Handwerkers, Jerry Albert, the Vourderis family, and the Ward Family Trust.

tory that he's taken Frleta's place as "King of the Walk."

At the north end of Jones Walk is Deno's Wonder Wheel Park. The park, with the landmarked Wonder Wheel as its centerpiece, has been cobbled together over the last two decades by the Vourderis family. Denos Vourderis bought the Wonder Wheel and the adjacent Spookarama dark ride in 1983 from Freddie Garms, whose father had built the wheel. Vourderis started out as a hot dog vendor on the Boardwalk. The story goes that he promised to buy the wheel for his girlfriend if she married him. She married him, and years later, he acquired the wheel.

The idea for a park came from his two sons, Dennis and Steve, who now run the park. When a mysterious fire destroyed Mike Curran's skooter ride, adjacent to the Wonder Wheel, in 1986, the property became available and was added to the park. Wonder Wheel Park and the adjacent Astroland Park now make up the core of Coney Island's traditional amusement center. Every kind of ride can be found here. Freddie Garms's Spookarama has been reduced from its original size and lovingly restored. The most bizarre element of the Wonder Wheel Park is a McDonald's restaurant that leases space in the Vourderis Boardwalk kiddie park. The fast-food chain seems oddly out of place among the independent operators of Coney Island, but it could have been much worse. Coney Island could have had the "McWheel." Vourderis had planned to install huge golden neon arches on the 150-foot Wonder Wheel, but the New York City Landmarks Preservation Commission rejected them in 1993.

Jones Walk divides the interests of two aggressive and competitive Coney Island families. The Alberts of Astroland and the Vourderis family were once rivals but now work together for the good of Coney Island by sponsoring fireworks displays and music festivals. The combination of large, family-run parks and small, independent operators along Jones Walk is true Coney Island. As Frleta told me, the motto of Jones Walk is "come as you are, and bring the green."

**Who Owns Coney Island?**
(as of July 2000)
❶ Horace Bullard (also owns a full city block not shown on map)
❷ Herman Singer
❸ Jerry Albert (Astroland park is the only property that has not been subdivided.)
❹ Handwerker family (Nathan's Famous)
❺ Vourderis family (Wonder Wheel Park)
❻ Ward Family Trust
❼ Charles Tesoro
❽ James McCullough
❾ George Tilyou
❿ Geaneas family
⓫ Persily family
⓬ Russo family (owners of Gargiulo's restaurant)
⓭ Lambrianakos Realty
⓮ Ron Guerrero
⓯ Walter Roberts
⓰ Mike Weiss
⓱ Scavullo family
⓲ Eldorado Properties
⓳ Mugalli Saleh
⓴ Fred Trump estate

JONES WALK

### CHAPTER 25

# Coney 2000

**Beach days**
Deno's Wonder Wheel against a backdrop of Luna Park Houses, Warbasse Houses, and Trump Village high-rises (opposite); sunbathers (above).

UNTIL THE bulldozers began churning up the mud of Steeplechase Park in April 2000, few believed that the new Coney Island ballpark would ever be built. It was almost as if a curse had been placed on the site by developer Fred Trump, who had demolished the historic park in 1966. For more than thirty years, the grandiose proposals made by ambitious dreamers had failed to materialize, and the site seemed doomed to lay fallow and vacant forever.

But something finally happened. It may have been coincidental, but shortly after Trump died in June 1999, Mayor Rudolph Giuliani proposed the new ballpark. The Steeplechase curse was finally broken. The mayor's scheme to revive Coney Island was approved by the city council in the spring of 2000, and a year later, Coney Island had a new stadium, a minor league baseball team, national recognition, and funding for much-needed improvements. The two years between the mayor's proposal and the stadium's completion were a time of excitement and apprehension for local residents, businesspeople, landowners, and preservationists. The city had betrayed them before. No major plans for development had been proposed for Coney Island since the disastrous urban renewal schemes of the 1970s. It remained to be seen whether the results would have long-term benefits.

As a Coney Island native with friends and family who still live and worked in the area, I was curious about how the sudden attention would affect my old neighborhood and what the final outcome would be.

Before the 2000 season opened, Coney Island would lose two of its most passionate believers. In January, Vincent "Jimmy" Tesoriero of Walter E. Burgess Inc., Coney's long-standing real estate office, died at the age of eighty-nine, and in April, seventy-seven-year-old Rubin "Ruby" Jacobs, owner of Ruby's Old Thyme Bar and Restaurant, died after a long illness. It was sad and ironic that Ruby and Jimmy, men with an unwavering belief in the future of Coney Island, would not live to see the coming resurrection.

The year had begun on a traditional note with the Coney Island Polar Bear Club's swim in the frigid waters of the Atlantic. There was a small problem with the weather: it was warm. The first day of the new millennium began with the temperature reaching a balmy forty-five degrees—a harbinger of the freakish weather to come. The 2000 season would be one of the wettest on record, with a succession of rained-out weekends. Weather is the main topic of conversation in Coney Island. Like farmers, Coney's concessioners and amusement operators are at the mercy of the weather, with their livelihood depending on it.

The warm weather brought an early start to the season. The first promotional stunt of the year took place on April 8, when Astroland promoter Dick Zigun, wearing an explorer's pith helmet, unearthed a time capsule that had been buried beneath the Astroland tower since 1964. The steel capsule was opened to reveal a shriveled Nathan's hot dog, a petrified knish, a lady's watch, and some Bonomo's Turkish Taffy, as well as memorabilia and clippings from the early 1960s. The rumor was that Zigun and his assistant, Sarah Rusczyk, were unable to find the real capsule, so they had hidden a new one several days before. It was a corny idea, but the newspapers picked up the story and ran with it.

The following day, a late snowstorm caused all the rides and amusements to stay shuttered. It was during this chill that Zigun was unceremoniously fired from his position as publicist for Astroland park, a job that had helped him subsidize his nonprofit organization, Coney Island USA. It was an inauspicious opening to the season.

Several days later, on April 12, the unbelievable happened. After weeks of backroom maneuvering, the New York City Council, led by speaker Peter Vallone and councilman Herb Berman, unanimously approved construction of the new Coney Island baseball park. The projected opening date was June 2001, just over a year away. Not only was the ballpark approved, but an additional $61 million was promised for Coney Island improvements, including renovation of the Boardwalk and Parachute Jump, new restroom facilities, a new bathhouse, and retail stores along Surf Avenue.

After hearing the news, I called Coney Island real estate man Charlie Tesoro to get his opinion on the ballpark. "Charlie boy," he said to me, "stop dreaming. It's never gonna happen." I told him that it was happening, that the stadium had just been approved, but he couldn't believe it. "I'll call you back," he said. I realized how close to the vest Giuliani had played it; even the business community hadn't heard the news yet.

The biggest surprise of all was that construction of the ballpark started the next morning, which is unheard of in a city mired in red tape. A blitz of heavy machinery attacked the Steeplechase site. Something was finally happening in Coney Island, and all it took was just what it has always taken: the will of a politician wielding absolute power.

★

A month into the season, I decided to check out the progress of construction and find out what effect the new ballpark was having on the amusement area. It was May 14, 2000, Mother's Day. The temperature was ninety-three degrees; a premature heat wave was bringing early crowds. I took the F train from Brooklyn Heights, the old Culver Line, the only line in New York that still uses the name of its founder, Andrew Culver. From the elevated structure, I could trace the history of Coney Island. As the train rolled through the old center of what used to be the town of Gravesend, I looked down on the seventeenth-century home of Gravesend's founder, Deborah Moody, and the old Gravesend Cemetery. The train passed over Shell Road and Coney Island Creek and by the site of the original Coney Island Toll House. I then saw the imposing ugliness of Trump Village, the towering development located opposite the old Mangels amusement factory on West Eighth Street, which now houses the motor vehicle bureau.

The train came to a stop at the Stillwell Avenue Subway Terminal, for years the spookiest ride in Coney Island. Crowds rolled down the ramps, pulled by gravity through the cavernous concrete structure. The ramps resemble cattle chutes or a bad walk-through dark ride. The structure always smells like a urinal, even in winter. I walked past the oldest token booth in the entire transit system under high ceilings with peeling black paint. Limestone leached out of the concrete girders, forming dripping stalactites; massive insulated steam pipes and dim bare bulbs dangled from above, giving the feel of a dark basement.

I walked out the fare gates and through the terminal's concession arcade, a tunnel that ends in the blinding daylight of Surf Avenue. Only three businesses were still open in the arcade. One was the Islander Eating Place, also known as "Nick's Greasy Spoon," where the spoons really are greasy.

**Sweet tooth**
John Dorman's Philips sweet shop had stayed open for business twenty-four hours a day in the Stillwell Avenue Subway Terminal since 1930. Construction of a new terminal forced the shop to close in 2000.

Nick's was open twenty-four hours a day to feed countless transit workers and night owls. This was its last week in the terminal arcade before it would move out of the shadows to a new location across Surf Avenue. Alongside Nick's was a concession stand bursting with bright inflatable beach toys: yellow, orange, and purple crayons; generic Japanese cartoon characters; balloons; balls; animals; and an inflatable cigar inscribed with "Big Spender." The toys glowed eerily in the dark.

At the entrance to the terminal was John Dorman's Philips candy store, flanked by the boarded-up ruins of two bars that had closed years ago. I stopped at Philips for a cup of coffee and the traditional complimentary chocolate cookie. Dorman had operated the stand for fifty-five years, but this was his final season. The Stillwell terminal was about to be demolished and replaced with a $250 million high-tech terminal-retail complex. Dorman told me he hadn't found a new location, but the New York City Transit Authority would let him stay for a little while longer.

As my eyes adjusted to the sunshine, I made my way down Surf Avenue to see the ballpark site for myself. The once-neat lawn was a sea of mud. Bulldozers had just crushed a row of old plane trees, the last remnant of the central garden of the old Steeplechase Park. Massive concrete footings from the Steeplechase pavilion had been unearthed and piled on mountains of sand. The excavations for the ballpark's foundation were finished, and workers were leveling the wooden forms. It was an amazing spectacle. No city project had ever moved so fast.

Alongside the site, the police were lining up on West Sixteenth Street for the morning shakeout and getting their assignments from the brass. Sixteenth Street, known in the 1890s as Tilyou's Walk, would soon be closed and covered by the ballpark. I stopped at the Clam Bar on the corner of Fifteenth Street and Surf Avenue. The woman behind the counter was laughing. "Are you looking for Mr. Big?" she asked. "He was just in here for a coffee, and then he went across the street." She pointed toward the old Loews Theater on Stillwell Avenue, and I saw a figure in blue work clothes standing on the corner.

Andy Badalamenti doesn't talk to you—he talks at you—and even if he doesn't know the question, he has the answer. He lectures, moralizes, expounds, and harangues; he thumps your chest and grabs your arm for emphasis. Badalamenti knows Coney Island inside out and has been the right-hand man for two of Coney's most controversial figures: Horace Bullard and Hy Singer. He ran the Bobsled and the Tornado roller coasters for Singer, then became the property manager for Horace Bullard's Loews Theater and the Thunderbolt roller coaster. His office was in the old Kensington Hotel underneath the Thunderbolt, the same building that was Woody Allen's boyhood home in the movie *Annie Hall*.

I asked Badalamenti what he thought about the new ballpark. "It'll never happen," he replied. "Horace is suing the city. He's gonna stop the construction." Badalamenti said he'd buttonholed Giuliani when he came to Nathan's a few weeks earlier and told the mayor about Horace's big plans for the Steeplechase site. I cringed as I thought about what Giuliani's reaction must have been. We walked over to the Thunderbolt entrance, and Badalamenti unlocked the gate. "I gotta show you something," he said, and we walked over to the Playland building. Badalamenti, who also works for the police department, uses the vacant building to feed and shelter police horses during the summer. Inside the collapsed interior, he showed me some muddy footprints next to his cat food that were as big as a human hand. "There's a raccoon living here," he said. And he was right—a very large raccoon was living in Playland, eating the cat food and wandering around the property.

We moved out into the sun to sit at "Chez Andy," a peaceful, private courtyard under the Thunderbolt that he had set up with metal tables, chairs, and a colorful patio umbrella. A mulberry tree in bloom twisted up through the front of the old coaster. Morning glories and Virginia creeper covered the structure, and rosebushes planted by former owner Freddie Moran blossomed along Kensington Walk. A downy woodpecker tapped its way up the coaster's wooden supports. Crows were roosting on the railings, and blackbirds were perched on a TV antenna mounted on the first curve. English sparrows hopped along the overgrown catwalks. The property was a peaceful and beautiful nature preserve. We talked about the future of the old unused coaster.

I left the Thunderbolt compound and headed up to Twelfth Street, where impre-

**"Bust 'em up!"** "Looch" has worked in Coney Island for forty-seven years. His dart game is in the landmark Henderson building on Stillwell Avenue.

**Last season**
The Thunderbolt roller coaster and Kensington Hotel, three months before the city demolished the historic structures.

sario Bobby Reynolds had set up the perfect Mother's Day exhibit: a two-headed baby in a jar. A grind tape of Reynolds's soothing voice crooned from a loudspeaker, warning passing women to avoid drugs and alcohol during pregnancy or face the consequences of birth defects. It was a public service message. Reynolds saw me and launched into his spiel: "Frrrrreeeeaks, wonders and curiosities, a panorama of the strange, the weird, the odd, the bizarre, the macabre, and the unusual." He pointed to the two-headed baby and became sincere: "Give up show business? Never! It's my life."

Around the corner, Dick Zigun, self-proclaimed "mayor" of Coney Island, was standing in the middle of Twelfth Street, looking slightly grizzled and concerned, directing people toward the "tip" in front of his Sideshows by the Seashore. His snake charmer, Serpentina, wasn't there, so he was doing the bally himself. Zigun stood on the platform in front of the sideshow, wearing an albino python wrapped around his shoulders, waving customers into the show. He seemed to be developing the persona of one of the "crazy old people" that had attracted him to Coney Island in the first place.

I took a seat at the sideshow's Freak Bar and greeted doe-eyed Sarah Rusczyk, who was tending bar. Antonio Torres Jr., also known as Tony but better known as Koko the Killer Klown, was at the bar bemoaning his divorce. Rusczyk told me that she was leaving the sideshow for a "real" job. Stanley Fox and Dan Pisark, two Coney Island natives, joined me at the bar, and then Bobby Reynolds drifted in to check out his competition. Zigun was a little peeved that Reynolds had opened his "pickled punk" exhibit in the same building as his sideshow, and Reynolds found it amusing. The rivalry is good publicity, and the press will play up the "battling sideshow" angle as they do every year: "Who has the real Fiji Mermaid?"

Stan Fox once managed four penny arcades in Coney Island but was now working for a Korean amusement concern that sells arcade equipment. Fox told me that he'll be running Manny Cohen's penny arcade while Cohen is on vacation, so we walked over to see Manny. The century-old arcade, owned by the Persily family, is one of the oldest surviving buildings on Coney Island's Bowery. The two-story building withstood a serious fire in the 1980s and lost its upper story. All that remained from the old building were

**Show business is my life**
Sideshow veteran Bobby Reynolds on Mother's Day, 2000.

**Room with a view**
Ruby's (above and right) is a restaurant, bar, art gallery, and social club.

the foot-thick wooden beams supporting the roof, wood so hard you can't drive a nail into it.

Fox serviced one of his computer photo booths before we headed to Ruby's Bar for a visit I'd been dreading. Ruby Jacobs had died a month earlier, and I couldn't imagine the bar without him. Cindy Allman, one of his two daughters, sat on a bench with her daughter greeting a line of people who'd come to pay their respects. A toothless man named Tommy was offering his services. "I'll sweep up or do anything that you need, Cindy, out of respect for your father. Anything." Cindy was distraught and weeping.

Visitors who knew and loved Ruby stopped to give their condolences to the Jacobs's extended family, which includes Peato and Sammy, who'd worked with Ruby for a total of eighty-nine years between them. Ruby's eighty-four-year-old brother Phil, as grumpy as ever, was tending bar.

Cindy told me how she and her sister, Melody, had come to the beach before the funeral to get some Coney Island sand to place in her father's grave. They had been alone on the deserted Boardwalk except for a staggering homeless man who approached them. The women were frightened until the man said, "You're Ruby's girls, aren't you?" He told them how Ruby had helped him out on numerous occasions. The man offered to escort them to their car "out of respect" to their father. All day long, people came by, sharing stories and offering help. Ruby's family had decided to keep the bar open and run it with his children and grandchildren working the counters. A fourth generation would keep the family's Boardwalk tradition alive.

I stopped at the B&B Carousell to see Mike Saltzstein. The B&B is surrounded by the "thieves' market," a string of thrift shops and junk stores. The carousel is the only ride left on the north side of Surf Avenue, and Saltzstein, the co-owner and manager, keeps it open all year long. Dressed in a white T-shirt and blue work pants, Saltzstein stood with his hands in his pockets and greeted me with a sly smile and a nod of his head. This was his version of a warm hello.

As I pointed at the stadium construction, Saltzstein waved his hand in disgust. "That stadium's not gonna help me. I'm on the wrong side of the street." I told him, "Maybe it's not your location that's the problem, Mike. Maybe it's your bad attitude." That started our usual banter. "Am I really the meanest guy in Coney Island?" he asked, feigning concern. "Yeah, Mike, you're the meanest," I answered. "Do people really think that?" he asked. "Yeah, Mike, they say you're a real bastard." He broke into a big self-satisfied grin and laughed. He liked to play the hard guy, but as everyone knew, he was really a sweetheart.

"How many times do you think I've heard that music?" he asked me over the sound of the B&B's organ. "Too many times," he said, answering his own question. Blanca, his young assistant, laughed behind the chicken wire covering her ticket booth and shook her head. "She's heard this before," Saltzstein grumbled. "I'm getting rid of her. We can't get along anymore." Then they both laughed like an old married couple.

★

The following day, I visited the Surf Avenue real estate office of my old friend Charlie Tesoro. He and his wife, Claire, were telling me about the new stadium's effect on Coney Island real estate prices. "When the stadium was approved, I got sixty or seventy calls a day, as opposed to the usual three or four," Charlie said. "They think there are bargains in 'rundown' Coney Island."

The speculators who besieged his office looking for cheap investment property did not realize that there are no bargains in Coney Island. None of them knew how tightly the owners hold on to their land. As if to prove this point, the front door intercom interrupted us, and Tesoro buzzed in a bearded man in a gray sports coat. The man was fortyish and spoke with a Russian accent. "I'm interested in commercial property," he said. Tesoro told him that everything available was in the million-dollar range. "Not a problem," the man said. After a short discussion, Tesoro took the man's phone number and gave him a business card. "They're all looking for bargains," he said with a wink.

A month into the 2000 season, Coney Island had settled into a recognizable form. What the press and much of the public had yet to realize was that Coney had never died. Coney's true believers were often accused of wallowing in nostalgia, but the media was the worst offender, endlessly looking for the nostalgic hook and pining for the "good old days." Coney's anchor businesses had been stable for at least a decade: Astroland park and the Cyclone roller coaster, Wonder Wheel Park, Nathan's Famous, the New York Aquarium, the Kaufman family's attractions,

**Bally boys**
Koko the Killer Klown (left) and Dick Zigun, with his albino python (right), warm up the crowd at Sideshows by the Seashore.

**Open 24 hours**
Nathan's Famous has been a Coney Island tradition since 1916.

**Classic neon**
The Wonder Wheel sign, with its rotating cars, is a work of art.

**Heart of Coney**
The center of the amusement area at dusk (left to right): Cyclone roller coaster, Astroland, Jones Walk, Deno's Wonder Wheel Park, and West Twelfth Street.

the B&B Carousell, McCullough's kiddie park, Gregory and Paul's restaurants, Ruby's Bar, the Eldorado Skooter, Sideshows by the Seashore, Gargiulo's restaurant, and a supporting cast of food stands, penny arcades, and concessions. Even the sleazy "bust-out joints," the crooked trailer games parked on the vacant lots along Stillwell Avenue, were a Coney Island tradition.

### The Coney Island Czar

On Memorial Day, I was again on the F train, reading the paper and heading back to Coney Island. Two stories about Coney Island were in the news: The first was about the FBI's search beneath the concrete floor of an auto body shop on Stillwell Avenue for the remains of a Brooklyn man who had disappeared in 1994. The article said that "cadaver-sniffing dogs, backhoes and jackhammers" were being used to search the shop, which was owned by a Columbo family Mafia soldier. The second story was about Brooklyn Borough President Howard Golden's demand that the city keep its promise to appoint a "Coney Island Czar" to oversee the beach and Boardwalk. The title gave me chills and brought back memories of Robert Moses, the "dictator" who had cut a destructive path through the island in the 1940s. Golden still didn't realize that Coney already had a czar, and his name was Giuliani.

The weather was gloomy, with a threat of rain. The concessioners were in a bad mood, because the second installment of their rent was due right after Memorial Day and they needed a good crowd. All over the island, the talk was about the new ballpark. I met with Kenny Kaufman, Norman Kaufman's son and third-generation Coney Islander who runs the batting cages on Stillwell Avenue, which were voted the best in the city. He was helping his father set up a new boat ride at Stillwell and the Bowery and told me he was excited about the ballpark because of the "crossover" potential for his batting cages. The new ride being installed was a water ride, yellow boats with water cannons that putter around a big tank blasting each other. The Kaufmans' park (a batting range and Go-Kart City) was coming together nicely. Kenny Kaufman had given up his welding career to join his father in the amusement business and had big plans for their stretch of Stillwell Avenue, which includes the Jumbo

**Little Odessa**
The increasing Russian presence in the amusement area is best exemplified by Alexander Gerson (left), who bought the historic Herman Popper Building on Surf Avenue in 1998, renovated it, and opened an art gallery.

Jet roller coaster. The family had finally assembled the little amusement park that Norman Kaufman always wanted.

Late in the afternoon, I hooked up with an unrelated Kaufman, Coney Island historian Seth Kaufman, to check out the Steeplechase site. This Kaufman has a degree in civil engineering and worked on a structural analysis of the Parachute Jump for his senior thesis at Cooper Union. We strolled onto the site as if we belonged there and began sifting through piles of debris looking for artifacts. We managed to find pieces of pottery and glass and bits of unidentifiable metal. Neither one of us could express what it was we were really looking for. The foundation of the ballpark was being poured right alongside the concrete footings of the original park. I fantasized about finding a "King Tut's tomb," a forgotten tunnel entrance leading to the Steeplechase Park of my childhood. My reverie was shattered when a security guard in an SUV pulled up and asked us to leave.

★

All summer, the stadium construction moved along as the cost rose another $9 million. Mayor Giuliani ignored any criticism and pushed the project toward its June 2001 opening. In July, an obscure connection was revealed between Mayor Giuliani and Coney Island. Soon after the mayor's battle with prostate cancer forced him out of the U.S. Senate race against Hillary Clinton came the revelation that his father, Harold, had been a small-time criminal who once served sixteen months in Sing Sing state prison for the armed robbery of a milkman. Even more surprising was the revelation that in 1962 the mayor's father had been involved in a wild shootout in the Brighton Beach section of Coney Island while trying to settle a loan-sharking dispute with mobster Mickey "Scans." Investigative reporter Wayne Barrett had discovered the stories about Giuliani's father and had written about them in his book *Rudy! An Investigative Biography*. The mayor made no attempt to deny the stories and would only say, "My father died nineteen years ago, and the details of his life died with him as far as I am concerned."

This glimpse into Rudy Giuliani's past helped explain what drives him. In a July 31, 2000, *New Yorker* piece titled "The Sins of the Father," the mayor was quoted as saying of his father's disreputable past: "I am not going to discuss that. It has no relevance to me and to what I do as mayor of New York City or to my life." But his father's past did seem relevant. I wondered if Rudy Giuliani was trying to reach back to his childhood

**The next generation**
Kenny Kaufman, Norman Kaufman's son, is the third generation of his family to work in Coney Island. His batting cages on Stillwell Avenue were voted the city's best.

and return to happier days at the Steeplechase Park of his youth. Or perhaps he was trying to erase the hidden shame he felt about his father's criminal activities.

Regardless of the mayor's motive, Steeplechase had become a common theme for Giuliani. He reminisced about the park in his State of the City addresses two years in a row. It came up again in August of 2000 when he showed up for the groundbreaking of the park. After the event, the mayor took a leisurely stroll on the Boardwalk and stopped to shake hands with patrons at Ruby's Bar and then ate a hot dog at Nathan's. It was one of several visits he made that summer. In the past, politicians had only come to Coney during campaigns, but Giuliani began making it a habit. As the mayor's comparisons between Disney parks and Coney Island also became more frequent, I began wondering about the new image that the city was seeking for Coney Island.

The season's last performance for Coney Island USA was the Biker Slut Festival held at Sideshows by the Seashore on the evening of September 8. The annual event starred biker/artist Indian Larry and his wife, Mermaid Bambi. The custom choppers were lined up along Surf Avenue and Twelfth Street, chrome and custom paint gleaming like jewels. Indian Larry's bike was displayed on a pedestal at the entrance to the sideshow alongside an ice sculpture bust of the biker. Arcade owner Manny Cohen, himself a biker, went down the line of bikes expounding on the virtues of each machine.

Late that night, as I walked to the subway, I glanced over at the B&B Carousell, a brightly lit outpost on the darkened north side of Surf Avenue. The organ was playing, the carousel was spinning, and several leather-clad figures wearing Hells Angels colors were riding the horses, grabbing for the brass ring. It was my last image of Coney Island's 2000 season.

### Death of the Thunderbolt

But stranger events were yet to come. On September 16, First Lady Hillary Clinton visited Coney Island, accompanied by vice presidential candidate Joseph Lieberman. Instead of eating a Nathan's hot dog or riding the Cyclone, Clinton visited Mark Twain Junior High School for a staged photo op with a group of handpicked honor students. Three weeks later, Monica Lewinsky arrived. The twenty-seven-year-old knew how to

**Demolition day**
A postcard of the Thunderbolt roller coaster circa 1930 (above). On November 17, 2000, the city tore down the Thunderbolt roller coaster before it could gain landmark status (right).

have a good time: she took a ride on the Cyclone as part of an "Americana" segment for a British television station.

Then came the death of the Thunderbolt. I had been expecting something dramatic since the first discussions about "Disnifying" Coney Island had begun in 1998 when Giuliani compared the potential revitalization of Coney Island to the revival of Times Square. He claimed that the Mets would do for Coney what Disney had done for Forty-second Street. Shortly after the stadium groundbreaking, the city ordered the hit on the dilapidated Coney landmark.

There were many reasons for saving the Thunderbolt. The classic coaster and the hundred-year-old Kensington Hotel below it were the best surviving examples of what I call Coney Island vernacular architecture, buildings that had been transformed over time for multiple uses. The Kensington had been not only a hotel, but also a brothel, a bathhouse, and a private home; it had withstood fires, storms, and urban renewal. It was the last original shoreline building in existence. Many people saw the building as a symbol of Coney's decline, but it actually was Coney's monument to survival.

On November 16, 2000, representatives of the New York City Department of Housing Preservation and Development arrived in Coney Island to make a visual inspection of the Thunderbolt. They talked to the preservationists and other locals, including Dick Zigun and caretaker Andy Badalamenti. The representatives seemed reasonable and open to suggestions and made no mention of the impending demolition.

But the next morning, HPD launched a sneak attack. Dick Zigun phoned me at 6 A.M. to tell me the coaster was coming down. Horace Bullard arrived at the scene and told reporters that Giuliani was a "dictator" who "doesn't like that black people want to create major developments." Mae Timpano, who had lived in the hotel for forty years, showed up and cried as she reminisced about her life under the coaster. Zigun called

**Street naming**
The Vourderis family, owners of the Wonder Wheel, gather on the Boardwalk for a ceremony to rename West Twelfth Street after Denos Vourderis, who bought the ride in 1983.

the demolition "an assassination of a piece of history." The coaster's cars and signs were removed from the rubble by the wreckers and placed near the Playland building. It took several days for the structures to die. The coaster did not come down easily.

Giuliani returned to Coney Island a week after the demolition for a ceremony at the ballpark site to announce the team's new name: the Brooklyn Cyclones. The name had been chosen in a contest won by a Suffolk County police detective named John Diffley. The mayor held a press conference with Mets owner Fred Wilpon and denied ordering the demolition of the Thunderbolt, brushing off further questions about it. Then he changed the subject and said that he wanted to have a parade when the ballpark opened. "We should have a parade right down Surf Avenue," he said. "A good, old-fashioned parade."

Jack Ward, a local landowner from a longtime Coney Island family, later told me that "Giuliani put $39 million into that stadium, and he wasn't going to have people looking out at a dilapidated piece of garbage that was falling down." Ward also made an optimistic prediction that the city would eventually condemn the vacant land between the stadium and Stillwell Avenue, pay

**Sweet deal**
According to the real estate magazine *Grid,* Giuliani gave the Wilpons, owners of the Mets and Cyclones, the city-sponsored ballpark along with 50 percent of the signage fees, naming rights up to $250,000, and a twenty-year lease linked to ticket sales. Maximum rent is $510,000; if fewer than 120,000 seats are sold, the Wilpons pay nothing. They also get 100 percent of the profits from concessions and parking fees.

off the absentee landlords, and lease the land to developers to restore the amusement area.

Giuliani left, but the roller coaster's cars remained on the site. Colleen Whyte, of the American Coaster Enthusiasts, contacted the Philadelphia Toboggan Company, which offered to take the cars and restore them for the company's Roller Coaster Museum. Whyte arranged for a truck to transport the cars and called Dennis Vourderis, owner of the Wonder Wheel, who offered to use his forklift to move the cars to a safe space on his property. But Horace Bullard refused to permit him on the property, and neither would the city. It was a stalemate. By the end of the year, the vandalized and burned remains of the cars disappeared beneath the winter snow.

### 2001: A Coney Island Odyssey

Less than two hours into the new year, the first New York City murder of 2001 was committed in Brighton Beach, when a seventeen-year-old stabbing victim died in Coney Island Hospital. The ensuing publicity overshadowed the fact that Coney Island's crime rate had dropped 50 percent since 1993. A few weeks later, Coney's image suffered further indignities when a Hollywood film crew arrived to use the amusement area as a sordid backdrop for a scene involving a methadone clinic. A few blocks away from the film crew's dirty artificial snow, construction of the baseball stadium had been continuing at a furious pace all winter to meet the opening day in June, an impossibly close deadline.

Support and hype for the Brooklyn Cyclones began building slowly. In the spring, the stadium was given the name KeySpan Park, with naming rights sold to the energy company that had once been Brooklyn Union Gas Company. Disappointed locals had hoped it would be named Coney Island Stadium or Steeplechase Park, but KeySpan paid the fee. The ballpark slowly came to be embraced as a symbol for the resurrection of landmarks past, a nostalgic combination of the Brooklyn Dodgers and Steeplechase

Park, two fabled institutions lost nearly a half century ago. Much to the surprise of everyone involved, tickets for the games began to sell out once the schedule was announced. Excitement was building for a minor league team that had been seen just a year before as an embarrassment for Brooklyn natives, who had wanted their major league franchise back.

In March, the Coney Island Chamber of Commerce, feeling bypassed by the stadium planning process, issued a resolution stating the chamber's deep concern "for the preservation of Brooklyn's historic playland" and resolved that "any future development, scheduled for the south side of Surf Avenue, east of the baseball stadium be restricted to amusement rides and games." The chamber also went on record as opposing the "proposed construction of a little league field on prime waterfront property. The area located between the Boardwalk and the baseball stadium should be reserved for amusement equipment and games. We do support a little league field at another location."

The resolution was penned by Al O'Hagan, chamber secretary, who had been hospitalized with a heart ailment when Community Board 13 had approved a decision to build a little league baseball field on valuable commercial land along the Boardwalk. It was too late, however, to change the decision.

On May 26, the city launched a preemptive attack on Coney's grit. A special team of police officers, directed by the mayor's office, made a sweep of the flea market vendors and furniture stores along Surf Avenue, issued summonses, and arrested vendors for selling stolen merchandise. The ostensible issue was zoning. The city had decided to crack down on vendors who were operating nonamusement businesses in the area zoned only for amusements. Until the crackdown, the vendors, most of whom ran their seedy, open-air bazaars out of storefronts and metal shipping containers, were the only businesses willing to operate in the area.

**Final season**
Mike Saltzstein, co-owner of the B&B Carousell, shortly before his untimely death on July 4, 2001.

The stores had filled a need for low-income residents and were now being told to close up and get out. Baseball was not good news for them.

The first time I saw the completed stadium was from the train platform at the Stillwell terminal about a month before opening day. It seemed big. John Ingram of the Manhattan firm Jack L. Gordon Architects had designed KeySpan Park. It was an oversized, colorful jumble of textured cinder block that was hard to absorb visually from the outside. The light towers were topped with thirty-foot-wide multicolored, neon hoops designed to flash when a player hit a home run. From Fifteenth Street, the stadium looked like a space station, a landing pad for flying saucers guided by the circular light towers and the freshly painted Parachute Jump. The black monolith from the movie *2001* would be right at home on the pitcher's mound. KeySpan's vacant storefronts on Surf Avenue had all the charm of a suburban shopping mall. The stadium provided a perfect bookend for the Aquarium, which, like KeySpan, was set apart from the amusement area. The ballpark seemed to use the amusement area as backdrop. Parking lots formed a buffer zone separating the park from the rest of the neighborhood. The only connection to

**Lost soul on a vacant lot**
Andy Badalamenti still parks his car on the site of the Thunderbolt roller coaster (top). The crumpled Thunderbolt cars sat in front of the abandoned Playland building for a year after the demolition (inset).

Coney Island was an elevated walkway to the Boardwalk.

On the sandy wasteland of the Thunderbolt site, the ride's cars were sitting in a heap, crushed and contorted, tufts of horsehair stuffing poking out of the torn leather seats. Mae Timpano's rosebushes had miraculously survived the bulldozers and were blooming, stunted and pink. Scattered about in the weeds were tattered pieces of paper, check receipts from Freddie Moran's Kensington Corporation, and old oyster shells from a long-forgotten restaurant. I ran into Andy Badalamenti, the Thunderbolt's caretaker, who continued to park his car on the site. I asked him how he was holding up. "How do you think I feel?" he snapped. He stopped and looked me in the eye and said, "I feel like a lost soul on a vacant lot." As I walked back toward Stillwell Avenue, an excited young Giuliani supporter handed me a flyer announcing the mayor's opening day parade.

★

On Monday, June 25, 2001, the early-morning air was heavy and humid as teams of city workers in fluorescent orange vests furiously cleaned the Boardwalk, removed trash, and cleared brush from the vacant lots surrounding the ballpark. The streets were cleaned and then cleaned again by an army of sanitation workers. Graffiti on the Stillwell Avenue Subway Terminal was painted over by transit crews. The forbidden flea markets were closed up tight, and the *New York Times* had installed shiny blue news racks on every corner of Surf Avenue to provide newspapers for the upscale crowds expected to descend on Coney Island for opening day. KeySpan Park's sound system was being tested and echoed eerily across the amusement area—"Testing. 1-2-3-4"— counting down the hours until the gates opened for the first time.

All the amenities that Coney Island had lacked for so long miraculously materialized: trash cans, fresh paint, clean streets. A media army took up positions on Surf Avenue. Police barricades were in place along the street, and parked cars were towed from the parade route. A procession of street sweepers circled for hours. West Seventeenth Street and Stillwell Avenue were closed to traffic. Crowds of baseball fans began arriving early, and from some of the conversations, it was obvious that many had never visited Coney Island before. Some wandered aimlessly, taking in the sights. Reporters ambushed older fans and asked them to reminisce about the Brooklyn Dodgers or Steeplechase Park.

Late in the afternoon, the mayor's parade began marching down Surf Avenue from West Fifth Street. Mayor Giuliani and his paramour, Judy Nathan, led the parade while

**Triumphant march**
Mayor Rudolph Giuliani threw a parade for the opening of KeySpan Park (left). He marched from West Fifth Street to the new ballpark with his girlfriend, Judy Nathan. Not everyone was happy about the ballpark (above).

mounted police, little leaguers, fire trucks, and a police department marching band brought up the rear. A smattering of cheers and boos greeted Giuliani, but the biggest cheers were reserved for Gerry Menditto, manager of the Cyclone roller coaster, who rode in the back seat of a green Cadillac convertible. A cry rose from the crowd of locals—"Gerr-y! Gerr-eee!"—as the mayor's procession made its triumphant entrance into KeySpan Park.

Once inside the park, an excited Giuliani held a press conference at home plate before the official opening ceremony. "I used to kid around when I was running for mayor. I would say to people in Brooklyn, 'What can I promise you that would get you to vote for me?' And they'd say [imitating a Brooklyn accent], 'Bring baseball back ta' Brooklyn.' Well, somehow we did it, and it's great!"

The press dispersed, and the stadium started to fill up. As the ceremonies began, the man who would benefit most from the mayor's largesse was introduced. Fred Wilpon, owner of the Mets, stepped up to the mike: "Good evening fellow Brooklynites. We are thrilled to play ball in this beautiful park, and none of this would have happened without Mayor Giuliani. This is particularly nostalgic for me, because I grew up in Bensonhurst and lived five minutes from here." Fred Wilpon's son Jeff, general

**Thank you**
Giuliani (above left) presses the flesh at the opening day ceremonies at KeySpan Park, while Senator Charles Schumer (right) talks on a cell phone.

**You're welcome**
Fred Wilpon (right) thanks the mayor for giving his organization the Steeplechase site.

manager of the Cyclones, introduced the mayor: "At one time, this was only a dream, but for the past eight years, this city has been blessed with a mayor who is the greatest baseball fan ever to hold office. Ladies and gentlemen, Rudolph Giuliani!"

The mayor, wearing a Cyclones cap, stepped to the microphone: "Congratulations. It's great to have baseball back in Brooklyn where it belongs, and it's even better to have it at this beautiful ballpark in what used to be the most famous amusement park in the whole world. We've been waiting a long time for this, and Coney is at the center of the universe again. Steeplechase Park! All Right!"

The setting of the stadium was breathtaking. The upper decks provided an unobstructed view of the ocean, the Parachute Jump, and the pier. I climbed the steps to the press tower. The private luxury boxes were named for Coney landmarks: Steeplechase, Dreamland, and, ironically, Thunderbolt. A sunny patio held a full open bar and a spread of seafood. I sat next to the mayor and Senator Charles Schumer, while munching on crab legs and gazing at the sunset and sailboats. I looked down Surf Avenue to the building where I had grown up and became disoriented. Where was I? I could not believe that something this promising was happening in Coney Island.

The ballpark had replaced something that had been stolen many decades ago. Instead of Fred Trump's housing project, there was a new "pavilion of fun." The curse of Walter O'Malley, who had taken the Brooklyn Dodgers away, and Fred Trump, who had destroyed Steeplechase, had finally been lifted. Once again, there was laughter and excitement on a site where a field of green meets an ocean of blue.

**Starting line-up**
The Brooklyn Cyclones (center) take the field for the first time on opening day, June 25, 2001. Their opponents were the Mahoning Valley Scrappers (left).

**Headlines**
Coney Island made national news as Mayor Giuliani gave interviews with the Parachute Jump as a backdrop.

The mayor tossed out the first ball, the Cyclones players were introduced, and the game began. Foul balls were soon peppering Surf Avenue. The Nathan's hot dogs cost almost as much as admission. Souvenirs were selling out. Any doubts I had about the stadium's atmosphere were gone. As daylight faded and the banks of colored lights came on, the atmosphere said Coney Island.

The game, played before an ecstatic crowd, came to a storybook finish, with the Brooklyn Cyclones beating Ohio's Mahoning Valley Scrappers with a three-two victory in the tenth inning. A thundering fireworks display on the beach followed the game's dramatic climax. It was a great day for Coney Island. It also underscored what had been possible yet denied for so long. In the weeks following the afterglow of this summer evening, anything seemed possible as New York rediscovered Coney Island.

By all standards, the Cyclones' first season was a resounding success. A thousand seats were quickly added to the ballpark, bringing the capacity to seventy-five hundred. At $6 to $10, tickets were affordable for families, and all but two games sold out. Brooklyn fans put aside their major league ambitions and embraced a Mets farm team from the Class A New York–Penn League. The old interborough rivalry between the Brooklyn Dodgers and the New York Yankees was replaced with new Class A rivalry between the Cyclones and the Staten Island Yankees. Cyclones management reached out to new fans by offering a variety of special promotions: Russian Night, Jewish Night, Old Dodgers Night, and Boy Scout Night, when Scouts were allowed to sleep overnight on the grass.

The publicity surrounding the team was a boon for Coney Island, and the media

**Beach ball**
The Brooklyn Cyclones won their home opener. From that point on, nearly all the season's games were sold out.

**Mission accomplished**
Mayor Giuliani, smiling like a kid at his first baseball game, leaves KeySpan Park on opening night.

had a field day. The fans and the ballpark didn't increase the amusement area's small-business revenues much, but the exposure did. Coney once again had national attention. *The New Yorker*, *Time* magazine, *Islands* magazine, *Metropolis*, and *U.S. News and World Report* all did pieces on Coney Island's "renaissance."

All summer long, new proposals for Coney unfolded. Some, like a new hotel and baseball hall of fame, seemed like pipe dreams, but others were more realistic and long overdue. Construction of a new $250 million Stillwell Avenue Subway Terminal was begun, a summer of weekly fireworks displays was announced, professional boxing returned for the first time in fifty years, and ferries docked at the Steeplechase pier for the first time since the 1940s. *New York* magazine declared that the shorefronts of Coney and Brighton Beach were hip places to live and featured the Cyclones baseball cap in its style section. The Labor Day crowds that swarmed to the amusement area were the largest in a half century. Local real estate prices started to rise as a flood of Russian immigrants began buying up property all over Coney Island.

In the fall, construction started on two new beach pavilions with showers and bathrooms, facilities that Coney had been lacking for years. A grassroots, nonprofit organization called Friends of the Boardwalk was formed to coordinate, improve, and encourage the revitalization of the neighborhood. And Coney received a big boost when Marty Markowitz replaced Howard Golden as Brooklyn borough president. Markowitz demonstrated his affection for Coney Island by immediately agreeing to play the role of King Neptune in the 2002 Mermaid Parade. Coney Island was once again in transition.

# Amusement Milestones

**C**ONEY ISLAND in the early twentieth century was the center of the amusement-manufacturing industry. The island served as a laboratory, testing ground, and national showroom for mechanical amusements, a fact that set it apart from the trolley parks and theme parks of the world. The roller coaster was invented in Coney Island, as were such rides as the Whip and the Tickler.

On one block of West Eighth Street, between Surf and Neptune Avenues, were the William F. Mangels Carousell Company, Marcus Illions Carousel Works, Pinto Brothers ride manufacturers, L. A. Thompson Company, and Feltman Shooting Gallery Company, as well as numerous electrical shops, metal fabrication plants, machinists, and carpenters, and a rail yard to bring in freight and supplies.

Mangels was the most famous ride manufacturer. William F. Mangels founded his company in the 1880s, moved to Coney Island, and set up shop at West Eighth Street and Tickler Lane. The company specialized in galloping horse "carousells" (the spelling he preferred) with overhead transmissions that made a galloping rather than a rocking motion. Mangels could provide any carousel animal, from large birds to mythical figures.

Mangels also designed a dozen Coney Island roller coasters, or pleasure railways, as he called them. Among them were the Ziz for Feltmans, the Roosevelt Rough Riders, the Red Devil, the Ben Hur Race, the Rocky Road to Dublin, and the Giant Racer on Surf Avenue. The company made shooting gallery backgrounds and targets, boat races, Roman chariot ticket booths, organs and orchestrians, high-strikers, steam engines, and electric engines. All of the company's products were spectacular works of art.

The Pinto Brothers opened on West Eighth Street in the 1920s and began manufacturing Ford merry-go-rounds—small carousels mounted on the backs of Model T pickup trucks—and later branched out into all kinds of amusements.

L. A. Thompson, whose founder, LaMarcus Thompson, invented the roller coaster, manufactured scenic railways and carousels. Legend has it that Thompson filled special orders for Arab shieks who wanted the number of carousel horses to match the number of wives in their harems so they could all ride at once.

Among other amusement manufacturers were Morris Goldberg's Skee Ball factory on Neptune Avenue and the Feltman Shooting Star Company, operated by Harry Miench in a nondescript building on West Twenty-second Street and Surf Avenue. Feltmans was the island's last amusement manufacturer. The company moved to New Jersey in the late 1970s, ending the Coney Island ride-manufacturing tradition.

| | | | |
|---|---|---|---|
| **1823** ◆ Shell Road opens | West Brighton Hotel | Surf Theater | ◆ L.A. Thompson Oriental Scenic Railway |
| **1829** ◆ First hotel, Coney Island House | **1877** ◆ Ulysses S. Grant gives opening address at Manhattan Beach Hotel | **1884** ◆ Elephant Hotel ◆ Switchback Railway, world's first roller coaster | **1902** ◆ Galveston Flood Building |
| **1845** ◆ Pavilion and steamboat pier at Coney Island Point | | | **1903** ◆ Luna Park ◆ First Mardi Gras |
| **1863** ◆ Peter Ravenhall's Ravenhall Hotel | ◆ Sea Beach Palace moves to Coney Island | **1891** ◆ Razzle Dazzle | ◆ Leapfrog Railway on Dreamland pier |
| **1865** ◆ Peter Tilyou's Surf House | ◆ Iron Tower moves to Coney Island | **1892** ◆ Coney Island Athletic Club ◆ New Brighton Theater | **1904** ◆ Ziz coaster ◆ Dreamland |
| **1868** ◆ William Engeman's hotel, Ocean House | **1878** ◆ Hotel Brighton ◆ Iron Pier ◆ Aquarium at Seaside Park ◆ The Concourse | **1894** ◆ Atlantic Yacht Club | **1906** ◆ Drop the Dip coaster ◆ Roosevelt Rough Riders coaster |
| **1872** ◆ Charles Feltman's Ocean Pavilion | | **1895** ◆ Paul Boyton's Sea Lion Park, world's first enclosed amusement park | ◆ L. A. Thompson Scenic Railway |
| **1875** ◆ Culver Plaza ◆ Coney's first carousel, built by Charles Looff, at Vanderveers Hotel | **1879** ◆ Brighton Beach Race Track | **1897** ◆ Steeplechase Park | ◆ Brighton Beach Amusement Park |
| | **1880** ◆ Surf Avenue ◆ New Iron Pier | **1898** ◆ Jackman's Shooting the Rapids | |
| **1876** ◆ Paul Bauer's | **1882** ◆ George C. Tilyou's | **1901** ◆ Loop-the-Loop coaster | **1907** ◆ Rocky Road to Dublin coaster |

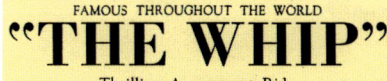

- Whirl Fly coaster
- 1908 ◆ Steeplechase pavilion
- Ben Hur coaster
- 1911 ◆ Municipal Baths
- Giant Racer coaster
- Dreamland Circus Sideshow
- 1916 ◆ Eden Musee
- Nathan's Famous
- 1920 ◆ Wonder Wheel
- 1923 ◆ Boardwalk completed
- New Stauch's Baths
- Childs Restaurant
- 1924 ◆ Coney Island Chamber of Commerce
- 1925 ◆ Thunderbolt coaster
- Gold Mine dark ride
- Loews Theater
- 1926 ◆ Tornado coaster
- 1927 ◆ Cyclone coaster
- Half Moon Hotel
- 1929 ◆ Mangels's American Museum of Public Recreation
- 1930 ◆ Comet coaster
- 1941 ◆ Parachute Jump and Bobsled coaster move to Coney Island
- 1955 ◆ Spookarama
- 1957 ◆ New York Aquarium
- 1963 ◆ Astroland Park
- 1983 ◆ Mermaid Parade
- 1985 ◆ Sideshows by the Seashore
- 2001 ◆ KeySpan Park

AMUSEMENT MILESTONES 287

# Selected Bibliography

Barrett, Wayne, with Adam Fifield. *Rudy! An Investigative Biography of Rudolph Giuliani.* New York: Basic Books, 2000.

Blair, Gwenda. *The Trumps: Three Generatons That Built an Empire.* New York: Simon and Shuster, 2000.

Brand, Stewart. *How Buildings Learn: What Happens After They're Built.* New York: Penguin Books, 1994.

Burns, Ric, and James Sanders, with Lisa Ades. *New York: An Illustrated History.* New York: Alfred A. Knopf, 1999.

Burrows, Edwin G., and Mike Wallace. *Gotham: A History of New York City to 1898.* New York: Oxford University Press, 1999.

Caro, Robert A. *The Power Broker: Robert Moses and the Fall of New York.* New York: Alfred A. Knopf, 1974.

"The Coast-line." *Shore and Beach* 63, no. 4 (October 1995): 3–10.

Cohen, Paul E., and Robert T. Augustyn. *Manhattan in Maps, 1527–1995.* New York: Rizzoli, 1997.

"Coney Island." *Atlantic Monthly* 34, no. 203 (September 1874): 306–12.

Coney Island Chamber of Commerce. *Annual Report.* Brooklyn: 1951, 1952, 1954, 1958, 1960, 1961, 1964.

*Coney Island: An Illustrated Guide to the Sea.* Brooklyn: Truax and Co., 1883.

"Coney Island: Its Architecture Is the Stuff that People's Dreams Are Made Of." *Architectural Forum* 87, no. 2 (August 1947): 83–87.

*Coney Island Souvenir and Traveller's Guide: Season of 1882.* Brooklyn: Lain and Co., 1882.

"Coney Island: To Heaven by Subway." *Fortune* 68, no. 2 (August 1938): 61–68, 102–4, 106.

Department of Parks. *The Improvement of Coney Island, Rockaway, and South Beaches.* New York: 1937.

Dolkart, Andrew S., and Susan Tunick. *George and Edward Blum: Texture and Design in New York Apartment House Architecture.* New York: Friends of Terra Cotta Press, 1993.

Dore, Arthur G., ed. *The Boardwalk.* New York: Coney Island Boardwalk Opening Celebration Committee, May 1923.

Ford, James L. *Hot Corn Ike.* New York: E. P. Dutton, 1923.

Friedman, Robert I. *Red Mafiya: How the Russian Mob Has Invaded America.* Boston: Little, Brown, 2000.

Frommer, Myrna Katz, and Harvey Frommer. *It Happened in Brooklyn: An Oral History of Growing Up in the Borough in the 1940s, '50s, and '60s.* New York: Harcourt Brace, 1993.

Groth, Paul. *Living Downtown: The History of Residential Hotels in the United States.* Berkeley: University of California Press, 1994.

Jacobs, Jane. *The Death and Life of Great American Cities.* New York: Modern Library, 1993.

Kolbert, Elizabeth. "The Sins of the Father." *The New Yorker* 76, no. 31 (July 31, 2000): 80–81.

Koolhaas, Rem. *Delirious New York.* New York: Oxford University Press, 1978.

Kostof, Spiro. *The City Shaped: Urban Patterns and Meanings through History.* London: Thames and Hudson, 1991.

"The Land of Mechanical Fun." *Boardwalk Illustrated* no. 1 (1923).

Levi, Vicki Gold, and Lee Eisenberg. *Atlantic City: 125 Years of Ocean Madness.* New York: Clarkson N. Potter, 1979.

Lindner, Marc, and Lawrence S. Zacharias. *Of Cabbages and Kings County: Agriculture and the Formation of Modern Brooklyn.* Iowa City: Iowa University Press, 1999.

Manley, Seon. *Long Island Discovery: An Adventure into the History, Manners, and Mores of America's Front Porch.* Garden City, N.Y.: Doubleday, 1966.

McCullough, Edo. *Good Old Coney Island: A Sentimental Journey into the Past.* New York: Charles Scribner's Sons, 1957.

Miller, Benjamin. *Fat of the Land: Garbage in New York, The Last Two Hundred Years.* New York: Four Walls Eight Windows, 2000.

Miller, Rita Seiden, ed. *Brooklyn USA: The Fourth Largest City in America.* New York: Brooklyn College Press, 1979.

Mitchell, Joseph. *Up in the Old Hotel.* New York: Vintage Books, 1993.

Mittelbach, Margaret, and Crewdson, Michael. *Wild New York: A Guide to the Wildlife, Wild Places, and Natural Phenomena of New York City.* New York: Crown Publishers, 1997.

"New Half Moon Hotel Completed." *Coney Island Times*, April 30, 1927.

Onorato, Michael P., ed. *Life without Steeplechase Park: The Diary and Papers of James J. Onorato, 1967–1971.* Bellingham, Wash.: Pacific Rim Books, 2000.

———*Steeplechase Park: Demolition of the Pavilion of Fun, 1966.* Bellingham, Wash.: Pacific Rim Books, 2000.

———*Steeplechase Park: The Diary of James J. Onorato, 1928–1964.* Vol. 2, 1940–1949. Bellingham, Wash.: Pacific Rim Books, 2000.

———*Steeplechase Park Sale and Closure, 1965–1966, Diary and Papers of James J. Onorato.* Bellingham, Wash.: Pacific Rim Books, 1998.

Percy, Townsend. *Percy's Pocket Dictionary of Coney Island.* New York: E. Leypoldt, 1880.

Pilat, Oliver, and Jo Ranson. *Sodom by the Sea: An Affectionate History of Coney Island.* Garden City, N.Y.: Garden City Publishing, 1943.

*Prospect Park & Coney Island Railroad Company, Dreamland, Catherine A. Balmer, and Charles L. Feltman and Alfred Feltman v James E. Morey, Nina Hayes, Elizabeth B. Pine, William Lott, Henry Lott, Cynthia M. Hyatt and Hattie Keith.* Summons and Complaint, Supreme Court, County of Kings, New York, August 8, 1912.

Ralph, Julian. "Coney Island." *Scribner's Magazine* 20, no. 1 (July 1896): 3–20.

"The Riegelmann Boardwalk: The Pride of New York." *Boardwalk Illustrated* no. 1 (1923).

Snow, Richard. *Coney Island: A Postcard Journey to the City of Fire.* New York: Brightwater Press, 1984.

Stern, Robert A. M., Thomas Mellins, and David Fishman. *New York 1960: Architecture and Urbanism between the Second World War and the Bicentennial.* New York: Monticelli, 1995.

Sullivan, Robert. *The Meadowlands: Wilderness Adventures on the Edge of the City.* New York: Doubleday, 1998.

U.S. Army Corps of Engineers. *General Design Memorandum: Atlantic Coast of New York City, Rockaway Inlet to Norton Point, Coney Island Area.* Vol. 1 and 2. New York: Department of the Army, New York District, April 1992.

Van Zandt, Roland. *Chronicles of the Hudson: Three Centuries of Travelers' Accounts.* New Brunswick, N.J.: Rutgers University Press, 1971.

Vergara, Camilo José. *The New American Ghetto.* New Brunswick, N.J.: Rutgers University Press, 1997.

Waldman, John. *Heartbeats in the Muck: A Dramatic Look at the History, Sea Life, and Environment of New York Harbor.* New York: Lyons Press, 1999.

*The WPA Guide to New York City: The Federal Writers' Project Guide to 1930s New York.* New York: New Press, 1992.

Zion, Sidney. *Loyalty and Betrayal: The Story of the American Mob.* New York: Harper Collins, 1994.

# Index

## A

Aarons, Leroy F., 158–59
Abe Stark Rink, 142, 149, 218
Abrams, Robert, 165
Adler, Florence, 74
air shows, 101
Albert, Dewey, 137, 140–42, 148, 209, 213, 218, 265
Albert, Jerry, 141, 164, 165, 166, 265
Allen, Steve, 203
Allen, Woody, 216, 249
Allman, Cindy, 255, 272
Al the Ice Cream Man, 78, 86
Ambrose Channel, 96–97
*American Yachting Annual*, 29
*Amusement Business*, 218
amusement industry
  after building of Boardwalk, 53, 55
  competition in, 150–51
  competition with, 133–34
  development of, 1, 26–39
  milestones in, 286
  ride manufacturers, 224, 251, 286
  survival of, 151, 273–74
  *See also* carousels; dark rides/attractions; roller coasters; sideshows; *specific park*; *ride*
*Annie Hall* (film), 216, 249
apartment houses, 40, 57
*Architects and Builders Magazine*, 31
Armstrong, James, 13
arts, 200–203, 223–39
Astella (Associated Tenants and Landlords), 160–62
Astroland, 137–38, 140–42, 147–48, 164, 213, 265
Atlantic City (NJ), rivalry with, 27, 162–63, 165–66
Atlantic Yacht Club, 29, 40, 91
Auletta, Dick, 259
Auletta, Ken, 259
Auletta, Pat, 218, 259
Austin, George C., 25
Avitable, William ("Willie"), 61–62, 174

## B

Badalamenti, Andy, 217–18, 270, 280
Bader, Charles, 17–20
Banks, David, 29
Barrett, Wayne, 275
Bartosiewicz, Thomas, 215–17
baseball. *See* Brooklyn Cyclones; KeySpan Park; New York Mets
bathhouses
  Bushmans, 168, 194
  Clarets, 168, 169
  Cook's, 170
  decline of, 149, 168–71
  as first resort businesses, 1, 10
  Municipal, 42–43
  Silvers, 169
  Stauch's, 150, 165, 168, 171, 255
  Washington, 105, 107, 108, 169
  in West End, 84–85, 89
bathing, recreational, 5, 16
Battaglia Inc., 212, 215, 218
Bayview, 91–92
beaches, disputes over, 41–45, 46, 49–50
Beame, Abraham, 147
Berger, Milton, 223, 229
Bergoffen, Herman, 61
Bianco, Jerry, 193
Biker Slut Festival, 276
*Boardwalk*, 53
Boardwalk Arts and Culture Association, 200
Bobsled, 150, 210
Bonsignore, Joe, 150
Bonsignore, John, 169
Bostock, Frank, 1
Bowery, 30, 31, 113, 120, 184, 210, 230–31, 244, 247, 262
Boyton, Paul, 23, 26, 29
Bradshaw, John, 231, 233, 234
Bread and Puppet Theater, 200–201, 223, 233
Brighton Beach, 11
Brighton Beach Race Track, 40, 153
Brooklyn Cyclones, 277, 278–79, 283–84
*Brooklyn Daily Eagle*, 13, 20, 46, 178
Brooklyn Flatbush and Coney Island Railroad, 11
Brooklyn Museum of Art, 108, 111
Brooklyn Rapid Transit Company, 56
Brooklyn Sports Foundation, 217, 219, 221
*Brooklyn Union*, 13
Bullard, Horace, 150, 163–64, 166, 211–21, 229, 277
bungalow colonies
  building of, 40, 41
  end of, 90, 253
  ethnic mixtures in, 145
  as low-income housing, 154–55
  in West End, 84–85, 89
Burgess, Walter E., 254
Buschman, Albert, 26
Byrnes, Robert, 154

## C

Calabro, Paul, 127
Campbell, James E., 41–42
Canarsee (tribe), 2, 3
Carfano, "Little Augie", 62
Carleton Court, 89
Caro, Robert, 73
carousels
  B&B Carousell, 251, 272–73, 276
  Brighton, 246
  Feltman's, 141
  manufacturers of, 224, 251, 286
  McCullough family's, 136
  Villa Eileen, 79
  Weber's, 55
Casinos for Coney Committee, 162–63
Childs building, 235, 242
Childs Restaurant, 107, 243
civil defense, 101–3
Clam Bar, 134, 140
Clarke, Allan, 7
Clinton, Hillary, 276
Coast Holding Company, 52–53
Coler, Byrd, 24
Commissioners of the Common Lands (Gravesend), 6, 7, 10, 16
Concourse, 51
Coney Island
  amusement milestones, 286
  artists' renaissance in, 223–39
  author's childhood experience of, 77–130
  cultural role of, 40
  current ownership of, 265
  decline of, 146–202
  division of, 4–6
  and end of Steeplechase, 136–44
  geology of, 3, 18–19
  infrastructure of, 15, 43–44, 151
  Jones Walk, as microcosm of, 260–65
  maps of, 4, 18–19, 27, 170–71, 265
  during 1920s, 56–63
  during 1930s, 64–76
  19th-century development of, 6–25
  redevelopment of, 221, 266–84
  settlement of, 2–4
  surviving historic buildings, 240–53
  true believers, 254–59
  as world-class resort, 40–56
Coney Island and Brooklyn Railroad, 7
Coney Island Athletic Club, 12, 24, 31
Coney Island Boardwalk
  author's childhood experience of, 88
  boosterism following, 52–56
  building of, 50–52
  development along, 53, 55, 60, 253
  portraits of locals, 194–99
  proposals for, 27–29, 41–42, 45, 48
  realignment of, 65–67, 72
Coney Island Chamber of Commerce
  author's visit to, 80–81
  and Cyclone controversy, 148
  and end of Steeplechase, 137, 139–40, 142–44
  founding of, 49–50, 57
  minority patronage, encouragement of, 152
  projects financed by, 60
  promotional campaigns of, 53–54, 55–56, 162, 229
Coney Island Channel, 95–96
Coney Island Community Council, 156
Coney Island Coordinating Committee, 156
Coney Island Creek, 246
Coney Island Events, 227
Coney Island Hotel Corporation, 60
Coney Island Houses, 75, 76, 82–90, 117, 154
Coney Island Hysterical Society, 224, 228, 229, 230–31
Coney Island Landowners Association, 65, 210
Coney Island Lighthouse, 95, 240

Coney Island Mardi Gras, 74, 75, 142–43, 256
 *See also* Mermaid Parade
Coney Island Museum, 231, 233, 243
Coney Island Plank Road, 7
Coney Island Point, 7, 14
 *See also* Sea Gate
Coney Island Polar Bear Club, 228, 267
Coney Island Railroad, 17
Coney Island Road and Bridge Company, 6, 14
Coney Island Sportsplex, plans for, 217, 220–21
Coney Island Taxpayers Alliance, 41–42
*Coney Island Times*, 60, 61
Coney Island USA (CIUSA), 224, 228, 230, 231–39, 243, 268
Conway, William, 147–48
Cook, Fred, 76
Coopey's Corner, 85
Corbin, Austin, 10, 12, 13, 25
Craig, Charles, 55–56
Creepy Beach, 91–92, 93
Crespi, Steve ("The Count"), 209
crime, 90
 arson, 159, 188–90
 and casino gambling, 165
 corruption, 15–16
 organized crime, 62, 274
 press coverage of, 140, 142, 143, 278
 street gangs, 151, 156
 violent crime, 152–53, 154, 156
Culver, Andrew R., 12, 14, 25, 28–29
Culver Plaza, 12, 14, 21, 24, 25, 60

**D**
*Dallas Morning News*, 215
Dankewrs, Jaspar, 5
dark rides/attractions
 Coney Island Spookhouse, 230–31
 Crazy Ghosts, 91, 92, 117
 Dragon's Cave, 182, 205, 229, 230
 House of Madness, 116
 Magic Carpet ride, 115, 210
 Spookarama, 183, 223, 265
 Torture Chamber, 117–19, 205
 Tunnel of Laffs, 186, 210
Democratic National Convention, 54
Deno's Wonder Wheel Park, 261, 262, 265

Denson, Charles
 father of, 77, 91–94, 123–24, 127–30
 grandparents of, 127
 mother of, 83, 89, 93–94, 107, 108, 127, 128
 sister of (Diana), 86, 87, 93
DeWolf, Derick, 4
Dimino, Rose, 254
Disney Corporation, 219–20
*Dissent*, 76
Dorman, John, 269
*Double Fantasy* (Lennon), 226
*Drama Review*, 228
Dreamland, 1, 12, 29–30, 38–39, 43, 44–47, 257
Dreamland Circus Sideshow, 236–38
Dudley, Dave, 94
Dundy, Elmer ("Skip"), 23, 29, 36, 180

**E**
Eagan, Richard, 205, 223, 224, 226–31
Elowitz, Alex, 245
Engeman, William, 7, 10, 11, 13, 25
Engeman, William, Jr., 11
Engineers Club of New York, 42
Everyman Theater Company, 200–201, 223

**F**
Feltman, Charles, 14, 17, 49, 260, 262
Feltman's Restaurant, 14, 47, 65, 142, 261
Ferree, Barr, 31
Ferrovechio, Larry, 145
Fesco, Westy ("Coney Island Cowboy"), 179
Fierstein, Harvey, 230–31
fires
 1903 (Bowery), 30, 40, 250
 1907 (Steeplechase Park), 32
 1911 (Dreamland), 38, 44, 257
 1932 (Boardwalk), 65
 1940s (Luna Park), 36
 1963 (Ravenhall), 113–14
 1969–1974, 188–90
 1979, 180
 protection from, 41
fireworks, 111, 142
flea markets, 279, 280
*Fortune*, 65
Fox, Stanley, 245, 271–72
Freedom and Peace Tenants Council of Coney Island, 157–58
Frleta, Phil, 262–64
Furey, Robert, 15
Futterman, Paul, 139

**G**
gambling, campaign to promote, 162–66, 212
*Gaming*, 165
Garelik, Sanford, 156
Garms, Alfred, 262
Garms, Fred, 183, 223, 230, 265
Gaskowitz, Herb, 181
Gaynor, William J., 48
Gerson, Alexander, 276
Gilbert, Joseph, 127
Gilbert, Ruth, 127
Giuliani, Rudolph, 1, 219, 220–21, 257, 267, 274–78, 280–84
Golden, Howard, 220, 221, 284
*Good Old Coney Island* (McCullough), 79
Gorky, Maxim, 30
Gossett, Lou, 89, 200
grab joints, 64, 65
Grashorn building, 20, 241, 261, 264
Gravesend, 2, 3, 4–6, 24, 47–48
Gravesend Houses, 75
Greenstein, Joseph ("Mighty Atom"), 172
Guisbert's (Gysbert's) Island, 4
Gumpertz, Samuel, 38, 41
Gut (neighborhood), 74, 76, 153
Guthrie, Woody, 174, 177

**H**
Haller, Valerie, 223, 232, 233–35
Handwerker, Ken, 229
Handwerker, Murray, 75–76, 141, 200–201, 214
Handwerker, Nathan, 64, 259
*Hartford Courier*, 5
Heller, Joseph, 86
Henderson's Theater, 149
Henderson Building, 250, 270
Henderson Walk, 246
Hernandez-Pinero, Sally, 219
Hodges, Gil, 259
Holiday, J. S., 20–21
Homicides (street gang), 151, 207, 209
horse racing, 11, 40–41, 153
Horwitz, Sam, 202–3, 218
hotels
 Boston, 66, 184, 200–201
 Brighton, 15
 early, 6–7, 12
 Elephant, 20–24
 Grand Union, 24–25
 Half Moon, 57–63, 81, 84, 87, 244
 Kensington, 106, 215, 216–17, 249, 271
 Manhattan Beach, 13
 Pavilion, 15, 28
 Surf, 164

Vandeveers, 13
 Whitney, 88
Hoving, Thomas, 156
Hudson, Henry, 60, 62
Hughes, Charles, 40

**I**
"The Improvement of Coney Island, Rockaway and South Beaches" (Moses), 65–66
Ingram, John, 279
Iron Pier, 12, 17
Iron Tower, 12
*Islands* magazine, 284
Italian community, resistance to urban renewal, 160–62

**J**
Jackass Club, 119–20
Jacobs, Jane, 82
Jacobs, Ruby, 170, 171, 255, 267, 272
Jaffee, Herman J., 3
Jatoba, Louisa, 233
Jeffries, Jim, 24
Johnson, Anthony, 2
Johnson, Barent, 5
Jones Walk, 260–65

**K**
Kaiser Park, 65
Katen, Garret, 17
Kaufman, Kenny, 274–75
Kaufman, Murray ("Sporty"), 182, 230
Kaufman, Norman, 182, 204–10
Kaufman, Seth, 275
Kehoe, Mark, 229, 230
Kennedy, Matt, 213, 225, 257
KeySpan Park, 1, 221, 247, 278–84
Kieft, Willem, 2
King, Martin Luther, Jr., assassination of, 143, 152
Kister Building, 80, 180–81, 225, 254
Kister, Fred and George, 180
Kitzmeyer, J. F., 40–41
Klink, Carlton, 150
Koch, Ed, 147
Koko the Killer Klown, 238, 271, 273
Koufax, Sandy, 259
Kowalski, William, 17
Kramer, Theodore, 26–27
Kuby, Ron, 235

**L**
Lafferty, James V., 20
La Guardia, Fiorello, 62, 64, 65
land disputes
 over beaches, 41–45, 46, 49–50

over Dreamland site, 45–47
McKane and, 8–25
Morey-Lott lawsuit, 47–49
Moses and, 64–76
during settlement years, 2–4
over Steeplechase site, 206–10, 211–21
See also specific property; urban renewal
Laux, August, 14
Lennon, John, 226, 228
Lewinsky, Monica, 276–77
Lewis, Nelson P., 42
Lichtbau's Lockers, 74
Lido Building, 106, 147
Lieberman, Joseph, 276
Lindsay, John V., 73, 147, 152, 156, 208
Loew's Theater, 61, 149, 151
"Looch" (concessionaire), 270
Ludlam, Charles, 228
Luna Park, 23, 29, 36–37, 180, 258
Luna Park Houses, 147–48, 245

# M

McCabe's Bar, 93, 94, 129, 130
McCullough, Edo, 79
McCullough, Jimmy, 251
McCullough family, 136
McDonald's restaurant, 235, 265
McKane, John Y., 1, 8–25, 42, 43, 47, 76
McLaughlin, Hugh, 14, 24
Magaw, Van Brunt, 6
Major Prime Meats, 256
Mangels, William F., 45, 251, 286
Manhattan Beach, 13, 25, 57
maps
 amusement parks, 27, 34, 36, 38, 45, 265
 bathhouses, 170–71
 Brighton Beach, 11
 Coney Island, 3, 18, 19
 divisions of Coney Island, 4
 early transportation, 17
Marano, Philomena, 224, 226, 228–29, 230–31
Markowitz, Marty, 284
Mark Twain Junior High School, 156, 276
Marlo, Michael, 107
Marsh, Reginald, 223
Massabarkem, 3
Matthewson, Douglas, 64
Mattinoh (Nyack chief), 2
Menditto, Gerry, 148, 178–79, 281
Mermaid Avenue, 174–77
Mermaid Parade, 226, 228, 235, 284

Mermaid Theater, 202
*Metropolis*, 284
monarch butterfly migration, 114–15
Moody, Deborah (Lady), 2, 4
Moran, Freddie, 215, 216–17, 270, 280
Moran, George, 249
Moran/Klein family, 216
Morey-Lott suit, 47–49
Morgenstern, Chuck, 74
Morgenstern, Alfred and Lee, 258
Moses, Robert, 1, 64–76, 274
*Municipal Life*, 43
Murray, Mike, 15

# N

Nathan, Judy, 280–81
Nathan's Famous, 65, 149, 229, 274
Native Americans, 2, 3
*Newsday*, 214, 215, 217, 218
*New York American*, 55
New York Aquarium, 67–73, 147–48, 149
New York City, 24
New York City Board of Aldermen, 41–42, 45
New York City Department of Parks, 64–65
New York City Housing Authority, 75–76, 82, 152, 156, 157–58, 160
New York City Sinking Fund Commission, 64
*New York Daily News*, 125, 126, 143, 228
*New Yorker*, 275–76, 284
New York Mets, 220, 221, 277
*New York Post*, 214
New York State Supreme Court, 49, 209
*New York Times*, 75, 76, 140, 147–48, 209, 228, 235, 237, 280
New York World's Fair, 67, 135, 136
Nicholls, Richard, 4
Nicholson, William, 80–81, 133–34, 136, 137, 139–40, 142, 144, 257
nightclubs, 178–79
*Nightline* (TV program), 235
Norton, Mike ("Thunderbolt"), 15
Norton's Point, 28
Norton's Point Trolley, 89
Nyack (tribe), 2

# O

Ocean Pier, 11
O'Dwyer, William, 158
O'Dwyer Gardens, 157, 158–60
O'Hagan, Al, 220, 279
O'Malley, Walter, 282
Ono, Yoko, 226
Onorato, Jimmy, 68, 112, 132–33, 135–36, 137, 138, 139, 140, 144
Onorato, Michael, 135, 139, 289
Op Dyck, Guisbert, 2, 4
Opelika (Alabama), 93–94, 127, 129
Operation Open House, 158
Ortiz, Carlos, 125–26

# P

Palumbo, Willie, 256
Paluso, Ralph, 148
Panico, Nicholas, 154
Parachute Jump, 67, 68–71, 122–26, 192, 210, 218, 252
parks, public, opposition to, 26
Patton, Ken, 209
The Pavilion (dance hall), 6, 7, 28
Pelican Beach, 79
Pennoyer, Robert, 2
Perfetto, Ralph, 160–62
Philips candy store, 269
Phoenix City (Alabama), 94
Pinto, Sylvio, 147–48
pirates, 79
Pisark, Dan, 145, 271
Playland, 245, 280
Point Comfort House, 15, 28
police, 15
pollution, 16, 114, 117
portrait studios, 58–59, 180
postcards, 27
*The Power Broker* (Caro), 73
Powsner, Lou, 154–55, 164–65
Pratt Institute, 226–27
Prince, Jim, 256
Prospect Park and Coney Island Railroad, 12, 47
prostitution, 16, 149
Public Development Corporation (PDC), 218
*Puck*, 16

# Q

*Quester I* (homemade submarine), 193

# R

racial unrest, 135, 142–44, 152, 156
Raphael, Murray, 148
Ratner, Bruce, 221
Ravenhall, Richard, 7, 20

real estate, as Coney's driving force, 1
 See also land disputes; *specific property*; urban renewal
Reed, Alonzo, 6, 7, 28
Reles, Abe, 81, 158, 229
*Requiem for a Dream* (film), 248
Reynolds, Bobby, 270–71, 272
Reynolds, William, 29–31, 38, 45–47
Ricci, Ralph, 235
Riechenthal, Chuck, 200
Riegelmann, Edward, 42, 44, 50–51, 55–56
Roberts, Lester, 236–38
Roberts, Marie ("The Professor"), 236–38
Roberts, Walter ("Wally"), 262, 264–65
roller coasters, 1, 56–57
 Cyclone, 147–48, 210
 Jumbo Jet, 206, 207, 209, 274–75
 Tornado, 150, 153
 See also Thunderbolt roller coaster
Rosenthal, Irving, 138–39
Ruby's Bar, 255, 272
*Rudy! An Investigative Biography* (Barrett), 275
*Rural Gazette*, 21

# S

Saltzstein, Mike, 272–73, 279
Samuels, Alexander, 24–25
Santangelo, Lillie, 223, 225–26, 227–28, 230
Schumer, Charles, 282
*Scientific American*, 23, 240
Scopetta, Nicholas, 209
Sea Beach Line, 56
Sea Beach Palace, 10, 14–15, 20
Sea Beach Railroad, 14
Sea Breeze Court, 154
Sea Gate, 28–29, 40, 101, 102–3
Sea Gate Villa, 90
Sea Lion Park, 26, 29
*Seattle Times*, 214
Security Pacific Bank, 218
Sedge Bank, 5, 10, 11
 See also Manhattan Beach
Serpentina (snake charmer), 231, 271
Shalom, Steve, 219
Sharkey, Tom, 24
Shell Road, 6, 7
Shore Theater, 163, 220
sideshows, 65, 66, 119
Sideshows by the Seashore, 223, 230, 231–39, 271, 276
Singer, Herman ("Hy"), 150, 209, 213–14, 229

Sixtieth Precinct, 114
slumlords, 155
Sluyter, Peter, 5
Smith, Alfred ("Al"), 60, 61–62
Stark, Abe, 142, 161
Stauch, Louis, 31
Steen, Leonard ("Chuck"), 68–71
Steep Club, 111
Steeplechase Park, 32–35
   author's childhood experience of, 78, 79–81, 98–100, 109–12
   and Boardwalk, 49–50
   controversies over, 1, 203–10, 211–21
   end of, 132–44
   and Giuliani, 275–76
   mechanical horse race at, 27, 32, 34, 208
   opening of, 26–27
Stephens, Henny, 255
Stern, Henry, 259
Stillwell, Nicholas, 6
Stillwell, Thomas, 5
Stillwell, William H., 9–10, 11
Stillwell Avenue Subway Terminal, 56, 57, 61, 79, 101, 143–44, 149, 151, 268–69, 284
storms, 78, 88
street games, 85–86
street theater, 200–201
Streisand, Barbra, 174
strip joints, 65
Stryker, Jaques, 17
Surf Avenue, 21, 73, 245
Surf Theater, 84, 85
Sutherland, Kenny, 40, 62

**T**

Temko Allan, 156
Terhune, John, 6
Tesoriero, John, 134
Tesoriero (Tesoro), Charlie, 81, 152, 163, 165–66, 211–14, 219–20, 229, 254, 268, 273
Tesoriero, Vincent ("Jimmy"), 80, 133, 138–39, 181, 254, 267
Thompson, Frederick, 23, 29, 36, 180
Thunderbolt roller coaster
   Bullard's plans for, 212
   closing of, 210, 248
   demolition of, 215, 271, 276–78, 280
   and Kensington Hotel, 106, 216–17, 249

Tilyou, Edward, 53–54, 55
Tilyou, George C., 1, 21–24, 26–29, 32, 40, 49, 88
Tilyou, George C., III, 135
Tilyou, Marie, 132–38, 144, 203
Tilyou, Peter, 7, 10, 21
Tilyou Theater, 112, 114, 117, 139, 202, 203
*Time* magazine, 284
"Times Square" (Stillwell and Surf), 60, 149
Timpano, Mae, 215-19, 277, 280
Title I. *See* urban renewal
Tops the elephant, 23
*Toronto Star*, 215
Torres, Antonio, Jr., 271
transportation to Coney Island
   ferries, 28, 29, 88
   railroads, 7, 9, 14–15, 56
   toll roads, 6–7
Trip to the Moon, 23
Trump, Donald, 162, 165–66
Trump, Fred
   and casino gambling, 162, 165–66
   and end of Steeplechase, 138, 139–40, 206–8, 267, 282
   and urban renewal, 74, 153–54, 203, 258
Trump Village, 7, 154, 155
Tuxedo Theater, 202–3
Tweed, William ("Boss"), 15

**U**

U.S. Department of Housing and Urban Development, 208–9
*U.S. News and World Report*, 284
Uale, Francesco, 62, 81, 257
urban planning, lack of, 1, 27
urban renewal
   and amusement industry, 135, 214
   author's childhood experience of, 104–8
   enactment of, 73–76
   mixed-income housing projects, 156–60
   neighborhoods destroyed by, 90, 153–54, 155–56
   resistance to, 160–62

**V**

Van Salee, Jansen, 2
Ventiera, Carmine A., 210
Vichinsky, Irving, 206–7
*View of Brooklyn and Staten Island from Coney Island* (Laux), 14
Villa Ferro, 145, 253
*Village Voice*, 234
*Vineyard*, mutiny aboard, 79
Vogel, Edward, 73

Voorhies, John, 25
Voorhies, Stephen, 5, 13
Vourderis family, 262, 265, 277

**W**

Walsh, Albert A., 157–58
Wantanabe Realty, 211–12, 213–14
Warbasse high-rises, 154
Ward, Charles, 42
Ward, Jack, 213, 261–62, 277–78
Ward, John, 260
Ward, William J., 60, 262
*The Warriors* (film), 150, 151, 165
*Washington Post*, 158–59
WEAF (radio station), 55–56
West End, 85
   author's photo documentation of, 147, 167–203
   construction boom in, 57
   residential development of, 61
   as resort, 88–89, 90
   urban renewal in, 76, 82, 152–56
West End Improvement League of Coney Island, 42
West End Line, 14
Western Division, 5, 10, 11
   *See also* Brighton Beach
Whitehouse, Samuel, 48
Whyte, Colleen, 278
William F. Mangels Carousel Company, 224, 251, 286
Wilpon family, 278, 281–82
Wonderland Associates, 30–31
Wonder Wheel, 57, 185, 260, 261, 265, 274, 277
World in Wax Musee, 187, 225–26, 230
*The World Rushed In* (Holiday), 20–21
*World Telegram and Sun*, 138
World War II remnants, 101–3
Wray, Albert A., 47, 48
Wyckoff, John, 7

**Y**

Yaged, Sol, 178, 202, 203
Yale, Frankie, 62, 81, 257

**Z**

Zaloom, Paul, 201, 228, 231–33
Zaret, Murray, 140
Zeig, Robert, 219
Zeitlin, Steve, 233
Ziegler, William, 29
Zigun, Dick, 223, 224–39, 267–68, 271, 273, 277
Zoo (open-air disco), 151, 155

# Acknowledgments

Of the many people I need to thank, I must begin by crediting the late Bill Nicholson and Al the Ice Cream Man for indulging and stimulating my childhood interest in Coney Island.

My loving wife, Judith Dunham, who inspired me to complete this lifelong project, endured my long trips to Coney Island, contributed her considerable editorial skills and wisdom, and never wavered in her support. I could not have done this book without her.

My family, Gwynne and Larry Wolin and Diana Denson, provided continual and much-appreciated encouragement. Adam Hochschild offered valuable feedback on my writing at a crucial stage in my endeavor. Susan Subtle helped move this book closer to publication in many ways. Seth Kaufman generously assisted with research and feedback.

Numerous people graciously allowed me to interview them and shared their stories about Coney Island's past and present. For their many contributions, I want to thank Florence Adler, Jerry Albert, Cindy Allman, Ken Auletta, Richard Auletta, Andy Badalamenti, Laura Bergen, Jerry Bianco, Gregory Bitezakis, John Bonsignore, Paul Brigandi, Horace Bullard, Steve Crespi, John Dorman, Richard Eagan, Larry Ferrovechio, Ted Florentz, Stanley Fox, Phil Frleta, Michael Gargiulo, Frank Giordano, Howard Gresh, Valerie Haller, Murray Handwerker, Don Harold, Benny Harrison, Sam Horwitz, Phil Jacobs, Ruby Jacobs, Stanley Katz, Kenny Kaufman, Murray Kaufman, Norman Kaufman, Matt Kennedy, John Lambros, Philomena Marano, James McCullough, Gerald Menditto, Gloria Montalvo, Al Morgenstern, Chuck Morgenstern, Paul "Slim" Newton, Al O'Hagan, Michael Onorato, Judy Orlando, Ralph Perfetto, Dan Pisark, Lou Powsner, Jimmy Prince, Marsha Rappaport, Rose Resk, Bobby Reynolds, Chuck Riechenthal, Gene Ritter, Marie Roberts, Walter Roberts, Larry Rosenblum, Mike Saltzstein, Melody Sarrel, Vincent Seyfried, Peter Spanakos, Leonard Steen, Allan Temko, Charlie and Claire Tesoro, John Tessoriero, Mae Timpano, Antonio Torres Jr., Steve Urbanowitz, Dennis Vourderis, Jack Ward, Colleen Whyte, Paul Zaloom, and Dick Zigun. Special thanks to Charlie Tesoro for being a wise guy and to Michael Onorato for providing me with unpublished letters written to him by his father, James J., about Coney Island and Steeplechase Park.

For their help with research, I want to thank the following individuals and organizations: Marianne LaBatto and Professor Anthony Cucchiara, Brooklyn College Library Archives and Special Collections Division; Anna Gasner, Pfizer Inc.; Sean Ashby, Brooklyn Historical Society; Professor John Manbeck, Kingsborough College; Victor Remer, Children's Aid Society; Ron Schweiger, Brooklyn Borough historian; Kenneth Cobb, City of New York Municipal Archives; Julie Moffat and Judith Walsh, Brooklyn Public Library–Brooklyn Collection; Patricia M. Splendore, Brooklyn Public Library; Dennis Bader and Kelly Tearney, New York City Council on the Environment; Daniel Marshall, St. Francis College Archives; Kings County Clerk's Office, Department of Property Records; Ron Levine, New York City Housing Authority; Sprague Library, Electric Railroaders' Association; J. V. Martin and Ralph Wikke, Termite Art Productions; Andrew Miller, U.S. Army Corps of Engineers; Jonathan Kuhn, New York City Department of Parks and Recreation; New York Historical Society; Lt. Jack Lerch, Mand Library, New York City Fire Department; Sandra Parmley, Battaglia Inc.; Susan Tunick, Friends of Terra Cotta; David Osborn, La Guardia and Wagner Archives, La Guardia College; and Museum of the City of New York.

Thanks also go to Linda Bouchard for helping out at crunch time and to Julie Bennett and Philip Wood at Ten Speed Press.

## AUTHOR PHOTO CREDITS

The location of each photograph is noted by the following abbreviations after the page number: t=top, c=center, b=bottom, l=left, r=right.

Photographs by Charles Denson: ix-t, ix-b, 77, 80, 84-br, 86-t, 87, 90-t, 90-b, 92, 93, 95, 96, 97, 101, 102, 103, 104, 105, 106, 107, 108, 109, 110-t, 110-b, 111-t, 111-b, 112, 113, 114-bl, 114-br, 115, 116, 118, 119, 120, 121, 122, 123, 124, 126-b, 129-t, 129-b, 130-t, 130-c, 130-b, 131, 144-t, 144-b, 145-t, 146, 149, 150, 151-t, 151-b, 152-t, 152-b, 153, 154, 155-b, 156, 157-t, 157-b, 158–59, 160, 161, 162, 163-t, 164, 165, 166, 167-t, 167-bl, 167-br, 168-t, 168-c, 168-b, 169-t, 169-bl, 169-br, 170-l, 170-r, 171-t, 171-b, 172, 173-tl, 173-tr, 173-b, 174-t, 174-b, 175-t, 175-b, 176, 177-t, 177-bl, 177-br, 178-t, 178-b, 179-tl, 179-tr, 179-b, 180-tl, 180-cl, 180-b, 181-t, 182-t, 182-bc, 182-br, 183-t, 183-b, 184-tl, 184-tr, 184-b, 185-l, 185-tr, 185-br, 186, 187-tl, 187-tr, 187-bl, 187-bc, 187-br, 188, 189-t, 189-b, 190-tl, 190-tr, 190-cl, 190-cr, 190-br, 191-tl, 191-tr, 191-b, 192-t, 192-b, 193-tl, 193-tr, 194-t, 194-b, 195, 196, 197, 198, 199, 200, 201-t, 204, 206, 207, 208, 210-t, 210-b, 213-t, 214, 218, 220-t, 233-b, 234-t, 235-t, 235-c, 235-b, 236-t, 239-tl, 239-tr, 239-cl, 240-br, 241-b, 242-t, 242-br, 243-b, 244-tr, 244-cl, 244-bl, 244-br, 245-cl, 245-tr, 245-br, 246-tl, 246-cl, 246-cr, 246-br, 247-b, 248-t, 248-b, 249-b, 250-br, 251-t, 251-bl, 252-t, 252-b, 253-c, 253-b, 255-t, 255-b, 261, 262-t, 262-b, 263, 264, 266, 267, 269-l, 269-r, 270, 271, 272-t, 272-bl, 272-br, 273, 274-t, 274-c, 274-b, 275-t, 275-b, 277, 278, 279, 280-t, 280-b, 281-l, 281-r, 282-tl, 282-b, 282–83-c, 283-tr, 283-b, 284-t, 284-b, 285-collage. All Charles Denson photographs copyright © 2002.

Collection of Charles Denson: 7-tr, 7b, 9, 10-t, 12-t, 12-bl, 12-br, 13-t, 13-b, 14-b, 15-tl, 15-b, 17-t, 17-b, 21-t, 21-b, 22-t, 22-b, 23-b, 25-b, 28-t, 28-b, 29-l, 32-b, 35-t, 37-t, 37-bl, 37-br, 41-b, 42, 43-t, 44-bl, 49-b, 50, 51-b, 52, 54, 55, 58-59, 61-t, 61-b, 63, 64-t, 64-b, 65, 66-bl, 67-b, 72, 73-t, 78 (photo by John Van Alst), 83, 84-t, 85, 88-b, 89-b, 89-tr, 117 (photo by Michael Greenbaum), 125, 127, 128-b, 128-t, 138-tl (photo by Mort Karman), 141-b, 142-t, 142-b, 163-b, 180-tr, 180-br, 203-cr, 209-t, 241-t, 242-bl, 243-t, 246-bl, 249-t, 250-tl, 250-bl, 250-tr, 257-b, 276-b.